bilingualism:
a social approach

Palgrave Advances in Linguistics

Consulting Editor:
Christopher N. Candlin,
Macquarie University, Australia

Titles include:

Monica Heller (*editor*)
BILINGUALISM: A SOCIAL APPROACH

Martha E. Pennington (*editor*)
PHONOLOGY IN CONTEXT

Ann Weatherall (*editor*)
LANGUAGE, DISCOURSE AND SOCIAL PSYCHOLOGY

Forthcoming:

Noel Burton-Roberts (*editor*)
PRAGMATICS

Susan Foster-Cohen (*editor*)
LANGUAGE ACQUISITION

Palgrave Advances
Series Standing Order ISBN 1–4039–3512–2 (Hardback) 1–4039–3513–0 (Paperback)
(*outside North America only*)

You can receive future titles in this series as they are published by placing a standing order.
Please contact your bookseller or, in the case of difficulty, write to us at the address below with
your name and address, the title of the series and the ISBN quoted above.

Customer Services Department, Macmillan Distribution Ltd, Houndmills, Basingstoke,
Hampshire RG21 6XS, England

bilingualism:
a social approach

edited by
monica heller
university of toronto

First published 2007 by
PALGRAVE MACMILLAN
Houndmills, Basingstoke, Hampshire RG21 6XS and
175 Fifth Avenue, New York, N.Y. 10010
Companies and representatives throughout the world

PALGRAVE MACMILLAN is the global academic imprint of the
Palgrave Macmillan division of St. Martin's Press, LLC and of
Palgrave Macmillan Ltd.
Macmillan® is a registered trademark in the United States,
United Kingdom and other countries. Palgrave is a registered
trademark in the European Union and other countries.

ISBN-13   978–1–4039–9677–0 hardback
ISBN-10   1–4039–9677–6 hardback
ISBN-13   978–1–4039–9678–7 paperback
ISBN-10   1–4039–9678–4 paperback

This book is printed on paper suitable for recycling and
made from fully managed and sustained forest sources.
Logging, pulping and manufacturing processes are expected to
conform to the environmental regulations of the country of origin.

A catalogue record for this book is available from the British Library.

Library of Congress Cataloging-in-Publication Data
Bilingualism : a social approach / edited by Monica Heller
    p. cm.
Includes bibliographical references and index.
ISBN-13:   978–1–4039–9677–0
ISBN-10:   1–4039–9677–6
ISBN-13:   978–1–4039–9678–7 (pbk.)
ISBN-10:   1–4039–9678–4 (pbk.)
    1. Bilingualism. I. Heller, Monica.

P115.B54279 2007
306.44'6—dc22

                                          2006052852

10   9   8   7   6   5   4   3   2   1
16   15   14   13   12   11   10   09   08   07

Printed and bound in Great Britain by
Antony Rowe Ltd, Chippenham and Eastbourne

contents

series preface

christopher n. candlin

This new *Advances in Linguistics Series* is part of an overall publishing programme by Palgrave Macmillan aimed at producing collections of original, commissioned articles under the invited editorship of distinguished scholars.

The books in the Series are not intended as an overall guide to the topic or to provide an exhaustive coverage of its various sub-fields. Rather, they are carefully planned to offer the informed readership a conspectus of perspectives on key themes, authored by major scholars whose work is at the boundaries of current research. What we plan the Series will do, then, is to focus on salience and influence, move fields forward, and help to chart future research development.

The Series is designed for postgraduate and research students, including advanced level undergraduates seeking to pursue research work in Linguistics, or careers engaged with language and communication study more generally, as well as for more experienced researchers and tutors seeking an awareness of what is current and in prospect in adjacent research fields to their own. We hope that some of the intellectual excitement posed by the challenges of Linguistics as a pluralistic discipline will shine through the books!

Editors of books in the Series have been particularly asked to put their own distinctive stamp on their collection, to give it a personal dimension, and to map the territory, as it were, seen through the eyes of their own research experience.

Liminality, boundary-crossing and the dis-solidarity of so-called community, whether in terms of the state, the workplace, the institution, the profession or the neighbourhood, compel a parallel dynamic in our description, interpretation, and above all explanation, of modes of communication. Such a dynamic, centred as it would have to be on interaction and on the practices of the site, sits oddly now with a structural and system-focused, and frequently a-social and a-historical view of language. Where language boundaries are themselves increasingly fluid, whether through in-country or cross-country migration or as a consequence of communication technology, constructs like bilingualism in turn demand a new focus and a new emphasis. More than this, they need a reinterpretation. What Monica Heller's inspiring and original book does is to tell us to start from a fresh place. Focus on the site, focus on the resource, integrate the practices, and above all, focus on the speakers and the capillary process of language use and language meaning, and not chiefly on the system and the structure. Such a starting point refreshes how we place bilingualism as a disciplinary inquiry within Linguistics. Rather than a site principally for a study of form, it becomes a means of investigation into the social, and, increasingly as Heller's distinguished authors point out, a means of redefining the *polis* and the state. As such bilingualism – or rather becoming and being bilingual – inevitably imbricates the historical, lending weight to the now quite general argument in the analysis of discourse, that the micro-interactional has to be set within an understanding of the ideological. Thus, bilingualism is not just a window on diversity, but a display of evidence of social action and social position, where, as Heller brilliantly argues, language as complex and significant performance is central.

Christopher N. Candlin
Senior Research Professor
Department of Linguistics
Macquarie University, Sydney

acknowledgements

I first have to thank Chris Candlin, the editor of this series. He opened a door and asked me to walk through it, and since then has provided me with tremendous support in my various articulations of slightly off-beat ideas. Huamei Han was an editor's dream assistant, engaging with every aspect of the book, from its intellectual foundations to punctuation, with an eye at once critical and committed. The book is what it is because of the deep engagement of all the contributors; my conversations with them have had a profound impact on my own thinking and laid the foundations for the collective position we have taken. I am particularly grateful to a few individuals who gave more than their fair share of time and energy to exchanges about the ideas behind this book: Emanuel da Silva, Alexandre Duchêne, Huamei Han, Mireille McLaughlin, Melissa Moyer, Jeremy Paltiel, Joan Pujolar, Mary Richards, Andrée Tabouret-Keller, Kit Woolard, and the students in my course on Language, Nationalism and Post-nationalism. I am also grateful for the research support of the Social Sciences and Humanities Research Council of Canada.

notes on contributors

Jannis Androutsopoulos is Junior Professor on Mediated Communication at Hannover University (Germany). A native of Athens, Greece, he holds a PhD in Germanic linguistics from the University of Heidelberg. From 2000 to 2003 he was a research fellow at the Institute for the German Language in Mannheim. Jannis has published extensively in the fields of sociolinguistics, text analysis and media discourse in German, English and Greek. His current research focuses on language variation in media discourse, the sociolinguistics of computer-mediated communication, language and adolescence, and language use in popular culture. Recent publications include the volume *Discourse Constructions of Youth Identities* (ed. with A. Georgakopoulou, 2003) and a Theme Issue of the *Journal of Sociolinguistics* on *Sociolinguistics and computer-mediated communication* (guest ed. 10(4), 2006).

Peter Auer received his academic training at the universities of Cologne, Manchester and Constance, where he also worked as an assistant professor of General Linguistics. From 1992 to 1998 he was professor of German linguistics at the University of Hamburg. Since 1998, he has held a chair of German linguistics at the University of Freiburg (Germany). He has done extensive research on bilingualism, social dialectology, prosody (particularly on rhythm and intonation), verbal interaction, and syntax from a conversational point of view. Book publications include *Bilingual Conversation* (1984), *Phonologie der Alltagssprache* (1990), *Language in Time* (1999, with E. Couper-Kuhlen and F. Müller) and *Türkisch aus dem Munde der Anderen* (2004, with I. Dirim).

Benjamin Bailey received his PhD in Linguistic Anthropology from UCLA. He is currently Associate Professor in the Department of Communication at the University of Massachusetts-Amherst. His work focuses on the negotiations of ethnic and racial identities in face-to-face interaction. He is interested in linking details of the work that social actors do in face-to-face interaction to the cultural and sociohistorical forces that permeate specific contexts of interaction, particularly in urban, immigrant America. Publications addressing bilingualism include *Language, Race, and Negotiation of Identity: A Study of Dominican Americans* (2002) as well as articles in *Pragmatics, Language in Society* and the *Journal of Linguistic Anthropology*.

Emanuel da Silva is a PhD candidate in the Department of French at the University of Toronto. His research focuses on language ideologies, transnationalism, diasporic communities and the discursive (re)constructions of identity as seen through a critical, sociolinguistic and ethnographic framework. His thesis involves a qualitative examination of the Portuguese-Canadian community of Toronto and how some of its young people negotiate their languages and identities. He is also currently working on a research project directed by Monica Heller, entitled 'La francité transnationale: pour une sociolinguistique de la mouvance'.

Alexandre Duchêne is Lecturer in Sociolinguistics in the Department of Language and Communication, University of Basel (Switzerland), and co-investigator with Ingrid Piller of a research project funded by the Swiss National Research Foundation on 'Language, Identities and Tourism'. He completed his PhD on the United Nations' discourse on linguistic minorities. His major research interests include discourse in international organizations, bilingualism and social inequality, and language ideologies in expert discourse. His recent publications include a co-edited book (with Monica Heller), *Discourses of Endangerment* (2007), and a forthcoming monograph, 'Language, Ideologies and International Organizations'.

Paul B. Garrett is Assistant Professor in the Department of Anthropology at Temple University (Philadelphia, USA). He is a linguistic anthropologist whose research and teaching interests include language contact phenomena, language socialization, political economy of language, ideologies of language, and the creole languages and cultures of the Caribbean region – particularly the island of St Lucia, where he has conducted long-term ethnographic fieldwork. His recent publications include: 'Language Socialization: Reproduction and Continuity, Transformation and Change' (with P. Baquedano-López) in *Annual Review of Anthropology* 31 (2002); 'An "English Creole" That Isn't: On the Sociohistorical Origins and Linguistic Classification of the Vernacular English of St Lucia' in *Contact Englishes of the Eastern Caribbean* (eds M. Aceto and J. Williams, 2003); 'Language Contact and Contact Languages' in *A Companion to Linguistic Anthropology* (ed. A. Duranti, 2004); and 'What a Language is Good for: Language Socialization, Language Shift, and the Persistence of Code-Specific Genres in St Lucia' in *Language in Society* (2005).

Monica Heller is Professor at the Ontario Institute for Studies in Education of the University of Toronto. Her work in the area of bilingualism has focused on its social, economic and political aspects; her fieldwork has focused on its relation to social change, and in particular to social difference, social inequality and ideologies of community, nation and the state in francophone Canada. Her major publications in the field of bilingualism include: *Codeswitching: Anthropological and Sociolinguistic Perspectives* (ed., 1988); *Voices of Authority: Education and Linguistic Difference* (ed. with M. Martin-Jones, 2001); *Elements d'une sociolinguistique critique* (2002); *Linguistic Minorities and Modernity: A Sociolinguistic Ethnography* (2nd edition, 2006); and *Discourses of Endangerment: Ideology and Interest in the Defense of Languages* (ed. with A. Duchêne, 2007).

Alexandra Jaffe is Professor of Linguistics at California State University, Long Beach. Since 1988, she has done research on the French island of Corsica, where she has examined both bilingual practice and discourses about bilingual practice and identity in the context of minority language shift and revitalization. Her interests lie in the relationship of these practices and discourses to wider ideologies and political economies of language. These themes are taken up in her book *Identities in Action: Language Politics on Corsica* (1999). Since 2000, she has been doing research on Corsican bilingual schools, and how they create and define the bilingual person. Publications on this work include: 'Misrecognition Unmasked? "Polynomic" Language, Expert Statuses and Orthographic Practices in Corsican Schools' in *Pragmatics* 13:3/4 (2003); '"Imagined Competence": Classroom Evaluation, Collective Identity and Linguistic Authenticity in a Corsican Bilingual Classroom' in *Linguistic Anthropology of Education* (eds S. Wortham and B. Rymes, 2003); and 'Talk Around Text: Literacy Practices, Cultural Identity and Authority in a Corsican Bilingual Classroom' in *International Journal of Bilingual Education and Bilingualism* 6:2–3 (2003).

Marilyn Martin-Jones is Professor of Languages in Education at the University of Birmingham, UK. Her main areas of interest are: bilingualism, bilingual literacy, discourses about bilingual education and interactional practices in classrooms in bilingual settings. Most of the research that she has conducted over the last 25 years has been of a sociolinguistic and ethnographic nature. This empirical work has been written up in journals such as the *International Journal of the Sociology of Language*, the *International Journal of Bilingualism and Bilingual Education*, *Applied Linguistics*, *Language and Education* and *Linguistics and Education*. Two recent publications include: *Multilingual Literacies: Reading and Writing Different Worlds* (ed. with K. Jones, 2000) and *Voices of Authority: Education and Linguistic Difference* (ed. with Monica Heller, 2001).

Luisa Martín Rojo is Associate Professor of Linguistics at the Universidad Autónoma de Madrid. Her work generally applies sociolinguistic and pragmatic perspectives to research on the languages of minorities in Spain. Her contribution in this volume is part of a larger piece of research into the discursive dimension of social exclusion (sexism, racism), and the relationship between language policies and immigrants' integration. She is currently a member of the editorial boards of *Discourse & Society*, the *Journal of Multicultural Discourses*, the *Journal of Language and Politics* and *Spanish in Context*. Her publications include: *Hablar y dejar hablar(sobre racismo y xenofobia)* (ed. with collaborators, 1994); *Poder-Decir o el poder de los discursos* (ed. with R. Whitaker, 1998); *Asimilar o integrar? Dilemas ante el multilingüismo en las aulas* (with collaborators, 2002); and articles in the *Journal of Pragmatics*, *Discurso y Sociedad*, *Folia Linguistica* and the *Handbook of Pragmatics*.

Mireille McLaughlin is a PhD candidate in Sociology and Equity Studies at the Ontario Institute for Studies in Education of the University of Toronto. Her studies focus on the impact of the new economy on linguistic minorities in Canada and abroad. For her thesis, she is applying a critical sociolinguistic approach to the restructuration of the Acadian artistic market when challenged by global processes. She is currently working on a research project titled 'La francité transnationale: for a sociolinguistic of mobility' which is directed by Monica Heller.

Lorenza Mondada is Professor of Linguistics at the University of Lyon2 and director of the research laboratory ICAR (CNRS). Her research deals with the organization of talk in interaction in various everyday, conversational, institutional and professional settings and addresses the issues of grammar in interaction, categorization practices, the constitution of institutional and interactional order, and multimodality. She is the author of: *Verbalisation de l'espace et fabrication du savoir: Approche linguistique de la construction des objets du discours* (1994); *Décrire la ville: La construction des savoirs urbains dans l'interaction et dans le texte* (2000), and *Interactions et acquisitions en contexte* (with L. Gajo, 2000). Her work has also appeared in such journals as *Discourse Studies*, *Sociolinguistica*, *Langages*, *Intellectica*, *Cahiers de praxématique* and the *Revue Française de Linguistique Appliquée*.

Melissa G. Moyer is Associate Professor in the Department of Filologia Anglesa at the Universitat Autònoma de Barcelona (Spain). Her current research deals with language and immigration in institutional contexts in the city of Barcelona. Her publications include *The Blackwell Guide to Research Methods in Bilingualism* together with Li Wei (2007), *La Cárcel de la Palabra* in collaboration with Jesús M. de Miguel (1988), as well as numerous articles and book chapters on the sociolinguistics of Spanish–English bilingualism in Gibraltar.

Shaylih Muehlmann is a doctoral student in Linguistic Anthropology at the University of Toronto. She studies language, environmental discourses, political ecology and language endangerment. Her research is focused on the ways environmental and linguistic processes intersect in the construction of social inequalities.

Donna Patrick is Associate Professor in the Department of Sociology and Anthropology and the School of Canadian Studies at Carleton University, Ottawa, Ontario. Her research centres on the political, social and cultural aspects of language use in the Inuit communities of Northern Quebec – in particular, minority language rights and policy and the interrelations between language and political economy, ideology, and globalization. Recent publications include *Language Rights and Language Survival* (ed. with J. Freeland, 2004) and *Language, Politics, and Social Interaction in an Inuit Community* (2003).

Joan Pujolar is Professor in the Department of Languages and Culture of the Universitat Oberta de Catalunya (Spain). He investigates how language use in multilingual contexts plays a role in the processes of reproduction of – or resistance against – social inequalities. In his fieldwork in bilingual Catalonia, he has researched in different contexts how the use of various linguistic varieties and languages can serve to construct social identities and divisions in terms of ethnicity, gender, age and class. His major publications in the field include: *Neue Herausforderungen für die katalanische Soziolinguistik* (ed., thematic issue of *Grenzgänge: Beitrage zu einer modernen Romanistik*, no.14, Leipziger Universitätsverlag, 2000) and *Gender, Heteroglossia and Power: A Sociolinguistic Study of Youth Culture* (2001).

Mary Richards is a PhD candidate in the Department of Sociology and Equity Studies at the Ontario Institute for Studies in Education of the University of Toronto. Her research interests include minority language education and immigration. Her PhD thesis research focuses on processes of inclusion and exclusion within a French-language high school in Toronto, by examining the trajectories and experiences of immigrant and refugee youth and their families. She is currently engaged as a research assistant on a research project entitled 'La francité transnationale: pour une sociolinguistique de la mouvance' (lead researcher, Monica Heller).

Christopher Stroud is Professor of Linguistics at the Department of Linguistics, University of the Western Cape and a Professor of Bilingualism at Stockholm University, Centre for Research of Bilingualism. His research has focused on multilingualism in relation to sociopolitical and cultural change and reproduction, and has comprised studies in multilingual education and socialization, the politics of language, ethnographic approaches to literacy, language contact, particularly the sociolinguistic development of new (Portuguese) varieties and the sociopragmatics of code-switching, and language ideological debates. He has worked extensively with such issues in Mozambique, Papua New Guinea and Sweden, Singapore and South Africa, where he is currently working on developing the notion of linguistic citizenship to the politics of South African multilingualism.

Andrée Tabouret-Keller est à Strasbourg (France) professeur émérite de l'Université Louis Pasteur et membre du Groupe d'étude sur le plurilinguisme en Europe à l'Université Marc Bloch. Ses recherches ont porté sur les situations linguistiques et culturelles complexes, principalement en Europe de l'Ouest et au Bélize, en s'attachent à l'analyse des processus de contact, à leurs causes et leurs effets tant dans la vie des personnes et dans les réseaux sociaux, ceci en tenant compte des institutions, de l'histoire, de ses déterminants économiques et idéologiques. Ses principales publications dans ce domaine incluent: *Acts of Identity: Creole-based Approaches to Language and Ethnicity* (R.B. Le Page et A.T.K. eds; 1ère édition 1985, 2ème édition 2006); *Vernacular Literacy: A Re-evaluation* (A.T.K. ed., 1997); *Le nom des langues. I: Les enjeux de la nomination des langues* (A.T.K. ed., 1997); *Le discours sur la langue sous les régimes autoritaires* (P. Sériot et A.T.K. eds, *Cahiers de l'ILSL*, no.17, Univ. de Lausanne, 2004).

Lukas D. Tsitsipis is Professor of Anthropology and Linguistics at the Department of French, Aristotle University of Thessaloniki (Greece). He received his PhD in Anthropology from the University of Wisconsin. His work on bilingualism has concentrated on aspects of language shift among Albanian speakers of modern Greece who are bilingual in a local Albanian variety and Greek. His main theoretical interests focus on language praxis and linguistic ideology, perspectives on power relations, the political economy of language, narrative performance, and the relations between micro- and macro-parameters in the dynamics of linguistic change and hegemony. He has authored three books: *An Introduction to the Anthropology of Language* (1995, in Greek); *A Linguistic Anthropology of Praxis and Language Shift: Arvanitika (Albanian) and Greek in Contact* (1998), and *From Language as Object to Language as Praxis* (2005, in Greek). He has published articles in such journals as *Word, Semiotica, Journal of Pragmatics, Language in Society*, the *International Journal of the Sociology of Language, Anthropological Linguistics* and the *Journal of Sociolinguistics*.

1
bilingualism as ideology and practice[1]

monica heller

why bilingualism?

Bilingualism is today as much a topic of academic research and public debate as it has ever been in the period since the end of World War II, as globalization and the new economy, migration and the expanded and rapid circulation of information, keep the question at the forefront of economic, political, social and educational concerns. The purpose of this book is to explore one particular set of approaches to the topic which seems particularly useful for understanding what bilingualism might mean today, in this context of social change, and how new understandings of it, as ideology and practice, also contribute to linguistic and social theory. In particular, the book aims to move the field of bilingualism studies away from a 'common-sense', but in fact highly ideologized, view of bilingualism as the coexistence of two linguistic systems, and to develop a critical perspective which allows for a better grasp on the ways in which language practices are socially and politically embedded. The aim is to move discussions of bilingualism away from a focus on the whole bounded units of code and community, and towards a more processual and materialist approach which privileges language as social practice, speakers as social actors and boundaries as products of social action.

On the one hand, then, the book argues against the notion that languages are objectively speaking whole, bounded, systems, and for the notion that speakers draw on linguistic resources which are organized in ways that make sense under specific social conditions (or, to use a Foucauldian approach, within specific discursive regimes). If we understand, organize, and draw on those resources as belonging to whole, bounded systems we call 'languages', it is because that notion makes sense in the context of the ways language has been bound up in ideologies of nation and state since the nineteenth century (Hobsbawm 1990). As long as we are able to maintain that discourse, as long as conditions sustain the relations of power that are embedded in it, we will work in many ways, from spontaneous talk to institutional structures, to

1

reproduce it, both by reiterating it and by neutralizing or erasing challenges to it (Irvine and Gal 2000; see also Moyer and Martín Rojo, this volume). Now that conditions are changing, it is possible to challenge the hegemony of that view, and to offer another one better able to account for the ways speakers are drawing on their resources at a time when boundaries are often deliberately played with (see Bailey, this volume). So, on the constructive side, the book offers a view of language as a set of resources which circulate in unequal ways in social networks and discursive spaces, and whose meaning and value are socially constructed within the constraints of social organizational processes, under specific historical conditions. It argues that hierarchies are not inherently linguistic, but rather social and political; language is but one terrain for the construction of relations of social difference and social inequality. It situates the study of bilingualism in the domain of studies of ideology, social practice and social organization.

The book therefore argues against a notion of language as connected to but distinct from society and culture, and for a view of language as one form of social practice (see Tsitsipis, this volume). This view allows studies of language practice to contribute directly to social theory, by offering tools to discover how social action and social structure are linked, and how agency articulates with social organization. How do we construct our world? What are the limits on our scope of action? If we want to change things, how do we find out where to begin to act? Within these general questions, the book will focus in particular on how language practices understood by speakers to be linked to different categories (different 'languages') are tied to other forms of structuration, notably nation and ethnicity (although a similar approach could be brought to bear on other forms of social categorization, such as gender, race and class). Put differently, understanding language as a set of ideologically-defined resources and practices constructs language as a fundamentally *social* phenomenon. In this respect, it also reflexively constructs our analyses as a form of social action, and situates our disciplines (centrally, linguistics, anthropology and sociology, but also such disciplines as political science, education or history) within the modes of regulation and discursive regimes of our times.

Finally, the book focuses on what the concept of 'bilingualism', and the communicative forms and practices associated with that notion which have long been the subject of debate and analysis, can tell us not just generally about language and social process, but more specifically about the social relations, social meanings and relations of power which inform the material conditions of our lives.

The central argument of the book is that a critical social perspective on the concept of bilingualism, combining practice, ideology and political economy, allows us to examine the ways in which that idea figures in major forms of social organization and regulation. It has been centrally linked to the construction of discourses of state and nation, and is therefore tied to the regulation of citizenship (and related processes, notably colonialism, neo-colonialism and migration) and of ethnonational identity, to education, to the role of the state in the organization of economic activities, and to the construction of what it means to be a competent person on an individual level (and therefore to general ideas about competence and normalcy, in ways which link the social and the moral order; cf. Cameron 1995; Tabouret-Keller 1988). It is also tied to other central forms of social organization, notably religion, often with complicated relations to the state. Other forms of social categorization (notably race, gender and class) are also usually involved, in complex structurations of relations of power. Under current conditions of late modernity, the discourse of bilingualism is increasingly produced by non-government organizations (NGOs) and agencies of supranational bodies, such as the European Union, the United Nations or UNESCO, frequently in terms of human rights, ecology and biodiversity. Throughout this history, academics have played a major role, both as producers of legitimizing expert discourses and as activists (see Muehlmann and Duchêne, this volume).

The book argues that it is fruitful to examine these processes historically, from a political economic perspective, but that the questions it raises require linking linguistic form to linguistic ideology and practice in a number of sites and in a number of ways. It proposes a series of angles of attack, which are meant to be suggestive, rather than exhaustive, but which do attempt to cover the terrain from agency to structure, from interaction to institution, from practice to ideology and discourse. It is intended to raise questions about the origins, functioning and consequences of ideologies and practices related to what has come to be known as 'bilingualism', but which, the volume also argues, can be understood as a wide variety of sets of sociolinguistic practices connected to the construction of social difference and of social inequality under specific historical conditions.

why bilingualism now?

Bilingualism has long been a major topic of public debate, as nineteenth-century concerns about making an equivalence among language, nation and state met multiple counterexamples which constituted obstacles to the nation-building enterprise. So, to the extent that nineteenth-century nationalism, especially of the Romantic variety, posited the naturalness and desirability of the existence of nations understood as organic, and as culturally and linguistically homogeneous units (Hobsbawm 1990), bilingualism necessarily stood as a potential problem for the maintenance or reproduction of such nations, or as a threat to their boundaries. At the same time, relations among nation-states required some kind of negotiation of power, and such negotiations could be conducted through the management of linguistic differences as well as through discussions of geographical boundaries, disputes over shared resources, or other areas of mutual interest.

Of course, the language–nation-state nexus did not emerge fully-formed in nineteenth-century Europe. Woolard (2004b) points out that language ideological debates invoking ties between Spanish and Spain were circulating in the seventeenth century; more generally, she argues that the ideologies we associate principally with nineteenth-century Europe need to be situated in the context of the long process of development of discourses linking language to various forms of political authority and legitimacy, and specifically to the tensions between secular and spiritual sources thereof. Nonetheless, our current debates can probably be best understood as tied to the emergence of the modern, liberal democratic nation-state in the late eighteenth and nineteenth centuries.

Thus we have France debating at the time of the Revolution how best to construct a unified France in which all could equally benefit from the values of the Revolution, that is, through bringing the message to the people through their own language varieties (whether Breton or Gascon, Picard or Occitan) or by assuring that everyone spoke the same language (Grillo 1989; Higonnet 1980). The result of the debate, as we well know, was the promotion of monolingualism in the name of *liberté, égalité et fraternité*. This was part and parcel of a process which can be understood as a form of internal colonialism (Hechter 1975), and was institutionalized largely through education and the military. Nonetheless, decades and even centuries of work were undertaken to establish the homogeneity which was only ever partially realized on the ground (cf., e.g. Weber 1976; McDonald 1990; Jaffe 1999; Lafont 1997; Boyer 1991). Similar struggles, each with its own specificities, could be found across Western Europe around the same period; while Italy engaged in a famously similar project of 'making Italians', in many other cases (classically, that of Germany), the ideological construction of the nation preceded the use of that construct to justify the establishment of a corresponding state (Bauman and Briggs 2003; Hobsbawm 1990).

Similar issues also arose, perhaps even with greater urgency, in the polyglot empires of Central and Eastern Europe. This has been most extensively examined with respect to the Habsburg Empire, which encountered in the nineteenth and early twentieth centuries the limits of the possibility of reproducing an imperial regime, and for which the discourses of nineteenth-century Romantic nationalism proved especially difficult challenges (cf., e.g. Rindler-Schjerve 2003; Gal 1995). Attempts to balance the reproduction of central imperial power with the demands of diverse regions through policies of multilingualism (including some forms of bilingual education) seem not to have been able to withstand the difficulties of asserting such control in the face of a powerful alternative model (that is, of nation-statehood), one which had to appeal to local elites who could use nationalism as a means of asserting regional control (and Irvine and Gal 2000 point out that this was also true in the various regions of the failing Ottoman Empire, especially where Western

European-style nationalism could allow regional elites to stake a claim to membership in the charmed circle of 'advanced', 'Western' societies).

When they were not focusing on developing the standard monolingual forms and practices underpinning the nation-state; establishing temporal and spatial claims to territory and national identity; or establishing the relationship between dialect and standard (and hence dealing with the problem of bilingualism by ignoring it, or, effectively, willing it to disappear), disciplines such as folklore studies, anthropology, demography, sociology, psychology and of course, linguistics (especially historical linguistics and dialectology), were all drawn into the scientific exploration (and legitimation) of what is fundamentally a politically- and economically-informed set of converging ideologies, whether regarding the management of diversity internal to an empire or a nation-state (whether established or posited), or regarding the management of relations between such entities. Bilingualism had to be explained and evaluated. Sometimes it was integrated into the dominant model as a special case of multiple monolingualism (this is, for example, the case in Bloomfield's classic text on language; Bloomfield 1933). Sometimes it was pathologized, its consequences for the health of 'normal' individuals, groups and political entities weighed and positions taken as to what, if anything, needed to be done about it (cf. Tabouret-Keller 1988). And sometimes it was brought to bear on broader concerns about the regulation of diversity and about the nature of language, culture and society.

It is difficult here to trace in detail the extent to which the emerging disciplines of the social sciences addressed bilingualism in the nineteenth and early twentieth centuries. Demography certainly became involved in the management of bilingualism through censuses in the mid nineteenth century (Gal 1993); dialectology and historical linguistics can also be seen as ways to make homogeneity out of diversity. Linguistics and anthropology, often carried out by missionaries, were, of course, famously involved in the exportation of Western European ideologies of language and nationhood in the exercise of colonialism, first in the general national-Enlightenment project of making order in those terms, and then in the service of determining modes of colonial control: languages and groups were homogenized and bounded, and divided up along those lines among imperial powers and missions (Irvine and Gal 2000; Fabian 1986; Meeuwis 1999a, 1999b; Patrick 2003; Stroud, this volume).

Attention to the properties of the messiness of bilingualism emerged more strongly in the period following World War II, perhaps as empires crumbled, and imaginations turned to liberation. Not surprisingly, discourses of resistance to centralizing states take up the legitimizing discourse of the state for their own purposes, and so, while attention to bilingualism increased, the terms usually remained the same (see Jaffe, this volume). It is only very recently that the grounds for understanding it have begun to shift.

As I mentioned at the outset, this is a result of the ways in which our habitual areas of enquiry (communities, social networks, identities, situations) insist these days on moving and shifting faster than they did before, thus challenging our ways of asking questions about them. In a Kuhnian 'scientific revolution' mode (Kuhn 1962), we might argue that our disciplines' ability to make bilingualism as a problem disappear by ignoring, normalizing or pathologizing it has now encountered the problem of having accumulated too much detritus of unexplained phenomena, or else conditions are making it impossible to keep that strategy up; the mess we don't want to face keeps pushing itself front and centre. Tensions between the state, religious institutions, the corporate sector and the grey and black markets (Castells 2000); labour migration and populations displaced by political conflicts (Inda and Rosaldo 2002; Pries 2001; Portes 1997); rapid circulation of increasingly commodified cultural artefacts and symbolic resources (Harvey 1989; Hannerz 1996; Appadurai 1996; Kearney 2004); all contribute to the blurring of boundaries and the multiplication of social positionings (Pujolar, this volume). Tools of enquiry refined when the focus was on boundaries, stability and homogeneity require refashioning for addressing movement, diversity and multiplicity. This book primarily attempts to lay the groundwork for such a refashioning, by proposing ideology, practice and political economy as a basis for rethinking what bilingualism means for understanding language and society.

In the next sections, I will review some of the major ways in which linguistics, sociolinguistics, linguistic anthropology and the sociology of language have addressed bilingualism since the 1950s, with the aim of showing how the structural-functional approaches which were helpful for the reproduction of dominant ideologies of language as autonomous system and of society as made of homogeneous units, have been critiqued by more interpretive, political economy- , process- and practice-oriented approaches which have been the inspiration for this book.

bilingualism, ideologies of language, and linguistic theory and method[2]

Scholarly work on bilingualism is usually understood to have taken off after the 1953 publication of Uriel Weinreich's examination of bilingualism in Switzerland, *Languages in Contact: Findings and Problems* (Weinreich 1953). This highly influential study took a descriptive, almost taxonomic, approach. Drawing on empirical data from a bilingual community in Switzerland, Weinreich sought to classify types of bilingual forms, and hence types of bilingualism, with central concerns forming around to what extent one or more grammars could be said to be involved, how aspects of one grammar might influence another, and what kinds of conditions (mainly social, but also psychological) might explain why things look one way or another. In some sense, Weinreich's approach was an extension of descriptive linguistic methods to the phenomenon of bilingualism: an attempt to maintain a tradition which sought simultaneously to discern universal patterns of linguistic order, and to discover the links among language, cognition and society.[3]

Each one of these questions has led to separate, albeit interrelated, streams of research. Some of the more socially-oriented streams will be taken up in the next section. Here I want to focus on current versions of the linguistic issues. These are probably best handled by examining what has emerged as the most central areas of enquiry; while much could be said by looking at such fields as bilingual language acquisition (cf. Köppe and Meisel 1995) or bilingualism, cognition and the brain (Grosjean 1982; Grosjean 1995; Kroll and Groot 2005; Paradis 2004), I will examine here the concept of 'code-switching', which helps us focus on questions of linguistic theory because it highlights the issue of linguistic structure.

The term 'code-switching' itself is vexed, with authors varying in what they mean by it; some today, as we shall see, wish to distance themselves from it altogether. The term was largely meant to capture a form of bilingual behaviour which has been thought to allow for particularly fine-grained empirical analysis of the relationship between bilingualism and linguistic theory, that is, what the intersections of codes in bilingual performance can tell us about universals of linguistic structure. The concept of code is clearly related to that of language, insofar as both refer to autonomous and bounded linguistic systems; it has been preferred in the literature largely to make a distinction between large-scale moves from one language to another (say from one set of activities or group of speakers to the next), and the kind of close relations within utterances or conversations that analysts have wished to understand. However, the boundaries between such phenomena are usually fuzzy, and so it is no surprise that definitions of code-switching have been bountiful, and arriving at watertight taxonomies difficult.

Code-switching data have been used to test linguistic theories, largely in order to explore what kinds of global theories of language can account for such data, on the assumption that such an accounting will help develop theories which represent, in some way, the nature of an underlying universal linguistic system which is common to all linguistic form and performance (Heller and Pfaff 1996). Muysken (1995) has actively pursued the development of generative theory from this perspective.

However, the field has perhaps been most influenced by ongoing debates between Poplack and Myers-Scotton (cf., e.g. Poplack 1988; Myers-Scotton 1993a, 1993b). Both have sought universal descriptions for code-switching data, but from different angles. Poplack has sought to use the tools of variationist sociolinguistics and descriptive grammar, aiming at a grammar which embeds the notion of variability in its core, and seeking explanations purely within the realm of grammatical structure and process. Myers-Scotton has aimed at an account which presupposes relations among grammars and a means of explaining their interrelationships. She seeks explanations, moreover, which tie linguistic phenomena to cognitive and social ones. These approaches have in common that they privilege a notion of universal grammar. They have all been controversial in the details of their accounts, but the greatest controversy has concerned the relationship between linguistic and other phenomena. This problem has been addressed by analysts who question the basis of the enterprise itself, arguing for a radically different view of language as social practice (cf., notably, Meeuwis and Blommaert 1994), but that view will be treated in greater detail below. For the moment, I want to focus on a different critique, one which remains focused on linguistic performance, but worries about the relations between utterance-level grammar and other forms of linguistic structure. This critique lies at the basis of the contributions to this volume of Auer and Mondada, and informs the contributions of other authors here (notably Bailey).

Here, one central critique has long been formulated by Peter Auer (1984; 1998; this volume), who argues that much code-switching data can best be accounted for by understanding it as embedded in interaction. The argument is that the nature of code-switching is linked to (possibly also universal) dimensions of the regulation of conversation, the nature of which is best captured by some form of ethnomethodologically-inspired conversation analysis. This theoretical move is much more than an extension of linguistic theories to the level of discourse or conversation, however. What it does is to posit a radical rethinking of the grounds of linguistic theory, by placing language as performance at the centre of how we think about language generally. In a collection of articles on this theme edited by Auer (1998), Alvarez-Cáccamo pushes this line of thought to its logical outcome; he argues that if we think of language as practice, and put the speakers, not the system, at the centre of our analysis, we have then to wonder why we need a concept of autonomous linguistic system at all. Instead, Alvarez-Cáccamo suggests, what if we replaced the idea of code with the idea of linguistic resources which are socially distributed, organized certainly by speakers individually and collectively, but which do not necessarily ever have to correspond to some closed and wholly describable system? What if language were part of a set of practices which had varying manifestations (both for individuals and sets or networks of people), but which could not be firmly distinguished from other kinds of behaviour? What if grammar were the order speakers impose, more or less successfully, on their linguistic resources?

In this vein, Woolard (2004a) argues, drawing on Bakhtin (1981), that utterances can best be understood as inherently heteroglossic, that is, that what underlies variability is the multiplicity of voices (stances, perspectives, social lives) which emerge in any given stretch of social performace. Speakers, again, are understood to draw on linguistic forms which index social experience, and which circulate in meaning-saturated social worlds (see also Pujolar 2001).

From the perspective of linguistic analysis, then, we are left with a set of questions which are foundational; bilingualism has brought us to question the nature of the concept of language itself. As we will see in the next section, approaches to bilingualism which have taken a more socially- or culturally-informed angle have led to much the same set of questions.

bilingualism in culture and society: structural-functionalism

The most influential approaches to understanding bilingualism in a world where bilingualism was not supposed to exist came initially from Weinreich (1953), and scholars such as Mackey, Ferguson and Fishman (Mackey 1968; Ferguson 1964; Fishman 1968). These authors approached bilingualism from the perspective of an analysis of the ways in which different languages, or language varieties, might correspond to different social functions. Weinreich was among the first to examine bilingualism in terms of a related set of linguistic forms and social functions, in an attempt to describe structurally-different linguistic manifestations of bilingualism as they might relate to different functional distributions of linguistic varieties in a community. Mackey's work on typologies of bilingualism followed in this vein. Both were concerned with what might be termed a 'languages in contact' approach, in which the focus remained relations between or among linguistic systems, albeit in connection with their social distribution.

Ferguson's concept of *diglossia* famously pointed to the ways in which even different varieties of one language could be assigned different functions within a hierarchy of prestige and status, with the 'high' language convention-ally involving more institutionalized functions connected to the distribution and definition of valued resources, and the 'low' language connected to everyday life and relations of solidarity among marginalized segments of the population. The concept seemed applicable to situations where the linguistic varieties in question were conventionally thought of as different languages altogether.

Fishman extended this concept to broader ways of conceptualizing functional differentiation across *domains*, with an understanding that domains were primarily connected to social activities (often institutionalized: religion, work, education, the family, and so on) which might or might not be equally prestigious or otherwise connected to power and status differences. Fishman's work laid the foundations for much subsequent research concerned with the measurement, statistically or through other means, of the scope of functions associated with specific language varieties, understood as a reflection of the extent to which a language had a social basis for reproduction.

These structural-functional approaches have also, over the past forty years or so, allowed for measuring deviation from the norm as an index of assimilation, or of language loss or endangerment, whether seen from a linguistic, demographic, sociological or social psychological perspective. Many of these have also been inscribed, explicitly or implicitly, in political movements for linguistic minority autonomy (and hence we tend to have the greatest number of these emerging in areas such as Canada, Belgium, Catalunya or Corsica; cf. Jaffe 1999, this volume; Patrick 2003, this volume; Pujolar 2001), in state-organized language policy and language planning (cf., e.g. Wright 2003; Spolsky 2004) or more recently in movements for the protection of minority languages within a concept of linguistic ecology, which defends linguistic diversity as an inherently positive thing (cf. Skutnabb-Kangas 2000; and, for a critique, Blommaert 2001; Duchêne and Heller 2007).

There are more examples of such studies than I could possibly do justice to. For our purposes here, let me mention a few categories: (1) studies of the 'linguistic vitality' of minority communities, designed to measure the extent to which the community is likely to be able to reproduce itself as a bounded unit in which bilingualism is possible as long as it is kept in clear functional distribution with the minority language (cf. Landry and Allard 1996); (2) studies of assimilation based on census returns measuring shifts of numbers of minority language speakers over time (cf. Castonguay 1996); (3) survey-based studies of functional distribution of languages by domain in specific communities, where the lack of a 'full' range is understood as a deficit to be repaired (in the terms of Catalan sociolinguistics, the concept of a 'full range' of domains is associated with *normalizació* or 'normalization', that is, extending the range of uses of a minority language, in this case Catalan, to cover the full range of functions existing in Catalan society; Aracil 1982; and see Boix and Vila 1998 for a discussion of such work, especially as it applies to the Catalan case); and (4) studies of the linguistic manifestations of language contact as associated with structural analyses of the social conditions of that contact, as a means of discovering what kinds of social structures are linked to what effects on linguistic structure (cf. Poplack 1988; Mougeon and Beniak 1991; Dorian 1981; Clyne 2003).

Within this range of types of study, particular attention has been paid to a variety of what Fishman would probably have called *domains:* we have studies on the role of legal institutions in providing an infrastructure for the production or reproduction of specific visions of bilingualism and bilingual communities (cf. Woehrling 1996), and on the role of education in actually engaging in the process of production and reproduction (or suppression) of bilingualism (cf. Baker 2006; Heller and Martin-Jones 2001; Mejia 2002; Martin-Jones, this volume). Quite a lot of attention has been paid to language practices and socialization in bilingual couples or families (e.g., Philippe et al. 1998; Heller and Lévy 1994; Deprez 1994/1999; Okita 2002; Piller 2002; Varro 2003; Zentella 1997), somewhat less to bilingualism in the workplace (e.g., Heller et al. 1982; Goldstein 1997; Roy 2003) and to the link between bilingualism and income-earning (that is, to the value of bilingualism on the job market; Vaillancourt 1996; Grin 2003), and very little to institutions such as religion or health.

The structural-functional paradigm has been extremely productive, allowing in particular the development of a discourse regarding the relative advantages or disadvantages of specific forms of bilingualism for specific groups. It has, however, remained resolutely committed to a paradigm in which languages are understood as whole, bounded systems, associated, moreover, with whole, bounded communities. This set of assumptions has been increasingly challenged, in part by the very studies it inspired: so often what is found is a set of bilingual practices or ambiguous affiliations which persist over time, contrary to efforts to stamp them out, which emerge where they have in principle no business emerging, or which seem simply not amenable to structural-functional analysis and explanation (for a general critique of structural-functionalism in the sociology of language, see Williams 1992). Indeed, many of the studies cited above of domain-related bilingualism can be understood as representing the results of close ethnographic examinations of some of these domains, which have led to a more critical ethnographic perspective on the arguments and phenomena developed in the structural-functional paradigm (e.g. work by Goldstein, Martin-Jones, de Mejía, Varro, Deprez, Roy and myself; see below for a more extended discussion, as well as many chapters in this volume, for example those by Martin-Jones, Jaffe, Bailey, Garrett, Da Silva et al., and Moyer and Martín Rojo). Such approaches have also been heavily influenced by careful ethnographic community-based analyses of bilingual practices in political economic context, such as Gal's (1979) study of gendered patterns of bilingualism in a shift from agriculture to industry on the Austrian-Hungarian borderland; Woolard's (1989) study of post-Franco Barcelona; or Urciuoli's (1996) study of working class Puerto Ricans in Spanish Harlem (New York).

The constant emergence of traces of different languages in the speech of individual bilinguals goes against the expectation that languages will neatly correspond to separate domains, and stay put where they are meant to stay put. Structural-functional approaches failed to turn up solid taxonomies and classifications; while they persist in many ways, they have also been succeeded by interactionist, ethnographic, and, more recently, critical approaches. In the following section, I will examine first an interpretive approach to bilingualism anchored in a focus on bilingual practice in social interaction, the role of bilingualism in the construction of cultural meaning, and their ties and challenges to a structural-functional approach, and then outline some of the ways in which both structural-functional and interpretive approaches are giving way currently to critical analyses concerned with ideologies of bilingualism in political, economic and historical context, and their involvement in the production and reproduction of relations of social difference and social inequality.

bilingualism in social interaction

While many studies using structural-functional approaches were concerned with large-scale social patterns, interactionists have been concerned with the manifestations of bilingualism in social interaction. Now, some of this work has been functionalist in inspiration, insofar as it gave rise to a long series of studies aimed at typologies of functions of bilingual practices, notably of code-switching, in interaction (cf. Gumperz 1971, 1982; Zentella 1981; McClure 1981; Auer 1984), but, at the same time, it was also the difficulty of establishing those typologies, or even some basic distinctions, which led those researchers towards more interpretative and less structuralist approaches.

Blom and Gumperz (1972) formulated an initial, influential, distinction, between *situational* and *metaphorical code-switching*, which attempted to capture not only the ways that domain analysis could account for distribution of languages, but also the messy ways in which bilinguals imported linguistic resources across domain boundaries. The assumption was that domain-based distribution was central to the attribution of meaning to linguistic varieties, and that conventional situational or domain distribution could then serve as a meaning-making resource for bilingual speakers across domains. Cultural meaning, in terms of the substantive understanding of identities and social relations (what it means to belong to specific groups, to engage in specific language practices), is understood to flow from political economic relations.

While in the long run the distinction between situational and metaphorical code-switching proved to be inadequate as a full account (and see Maehlum 1996 for a critique of the ethnographic material on which it was based), it did introduce into the debate some essential ideas, notably those concerned with looking at bilingual speakers as social actors within social networks, engaged in the practice of making meaning, and those concerned with conversation, or discourse, itself, as a site for meaning-making. What the distinction failed to account for were forms of code-switching whose meaning could not be said to be metaphorical in the strict sense, that is, they did not refer in any way to any substantive meaning which might be linked to activities or domains with which they were putatively conventionally associated. Instead, they tended to cluster around the management of the conversation or the contextualization of content, that is, in Auer's (1984) terms, to be *participant-oriented*, or oriented towards management of the unfolding of talk, that is, of the participation of conversational partners, or *discourse-oriented*, that is, oriented towards the framing of what was being said. In many ways, the contrast between linguistic resources understood as belonging to distinct codes itself served as the relevant resource, that is, as a contextualization cue in the sense of Gumperz (1982), or as indexical (Silverstein and Urban 1996). This takes the deployment of linguistic resources a long way away from any direct relationship between a language and a domain (or, even less, a community of speakers).

Interactionist approaches to bilingualism began, then, to explore more directly the ways in which bilingual resources could be involved in the construction of social meaning, both in terms of the construction of social categories (primarily those connected to ethnolinguistic identity, but also those connected to local social roles, such as speaker and addressee; see chapters in this volume by Mondada, Auer, Bailey and Garrett), and in terms of the contextualization of talk (see for example papers in Heller 1988). Bilingual resources in interaction or performance (see, for example, an emerging body of work on multilingual rap and *rai*; e.g. Billiez 1998; Androutsopoulos, this volume) are particularly rich sources for the exploration of voicing and footing, that is, ways in which speakers signal stances and perspectives on their own utterances as well as on those of others, and are available as windows onto interactional processes of learning (especially, of course, learning language; cf. Dirim and Auer 2004). Beyond such general sociolinguistic concerns, though, such phenomena illustrate the permeability of boundaries, whether between languages or sociolinguistic domains. They also point to the impossibility of direct associations between language and identity, and rather to the complex, often ambiguous and multiple nature of all these concepts. They also raise the question of the creative use of linguistic resources for aesthetic purposes, or more broadly in the construction of cultural meanings which may lie far afield from the political economic bases of the distribution of linguistic resources (Rampton 2002; Androutsopoulos, this volume).

The question then arises of what link there might be, if any, between structural aspects of distribution of linguistic resources and the uses speakers make of them in interaction, whether in terms of the organization of interaction or in terms of cultural meaning of categories and of practices, or more simply of the making of meaning in the broadest sense. Structural accounts have to take into consideration the messiness of actual usage, and interactional accounts, in order to arrive at useful explanations, have to take into consideration the situation of speakers in space and time. The following section addresses some of the ways those links have been attempted.

critical approaches to the study of bilingualism and society: community, identity, language

Recent approaches have attempted to make linkages by appealing to four sets of concepts. The first set has to do with calling into question the nature of some of the foundational concepts in many of the disciplines interested in bilingualism, namely community, identity and language; rather than treating these concepts as natural, and bounded, phenomena, it has become more common to see them as heuristic devices which capture some elements of how we organize ourselves, but which have to be understood as social constructs (in the definition of which we as researchers participate as much as anyone else; cf. Gal 1995; Blommaert 1999; Heller 2002). Since we are discussing social constructs (that is, since that is the ontological position we take regarding the nature of the phenomenon under investigation), it becomes possible to investigate some of the fuzziness and complexity that persistently emerge in data. Social constructs by definition have to get constructed, and processes of construction can be long and complicated. People do not necessarily agree on what to construct or how to construct it, and even if they do, it can take time to find the way there. In many areas long associated with linguistic minority movements, for example, it is increasingly difficult to find consensus on who counts as a Catalan, or a Francophone, and people are increasingly loath to primarily identify with one superordinate category (say, an ethnolinguistic one) over others equally relevant to their lives (say, gender), if they are willing to participate in the game of categorization at all.

In addition (this is the second set), such a perspective requires asking questions about who is doing what, and with what resources. This entails looking at language as a set of resources which are socially distributed, but not necessarily evenly, and so speakers have to act within certain kinds of structural constraints (cf. Giddens 1984). For example, working class speakers far from the sites of definition of what counts as 'good' language, or prestigious performance, are placed at a disadvantage in situations where their linguistic performance is judged by members of classes other than their own; they have to do what they can with what they have, given the structural relations of inequality in which they find themselves (and this of course can include resistance as well as collaboration).

The third set of concepts further investigates these questions, this time by seeking to explain why people do what they do, not just in terms of what kinds of resources they can muster, but also in terms of what they do with what they can gain access to, and why they act in certain ways with them. If the uneven distribution is understood as not random, but rather the product of a history of political economic processes, then the question of the relationship between power, social organization and (material and social) ecology comes to the fore (cf. Barth 1969; also Urciuoli 1995). Further, as Gumperz (1982) pointed out, linguistic resources are understood as conventionally having certain value and as connected to certain frames of interpretation; however, it is always someone's notion of what counts, and someone's ability to control access both to resources and to the definition of their value, which ultimately make a difference to people's lives. Processes of social selection are centred around interactions and performances which are evaluated, not as indices of mastery of conventions, but as indices of other kinds of competence (intelligence, work skills, personality, and so on). So the question here is, what resources are assigned what value, by whom, how, why and with what consequences? How are these issues manifested in education, in legal institutions, in the field of health care, in the reproduction of state structures? How do speakers draw on their linguistic resources in the situations they find themselves in, to accomplish what, or with what perverse or unintended consequences?

The final set of concepts involves the ways in which people make sense of their engagement in these processes. Generally understood as a matter of *language ideology* (cf. Schieffelin et al. 1998; Blommaert 1999; Kroskrity 2000), this area of enquiry investigates the discourses in which processes of attribution of value to linguistic forms and practices are inscribed, along with the processes of construction of social difference and social inequality with which they are associated. Our ideas about language(s) are, in other words, not neutral; we believe what we believe for reasons which have to do with the many other ways in which we make sense of our world, and make our way in it. Why are so many governments in North America and Europe now concerned with 'literacy'? Why does it matter whether or not there is a policy regarding official languages, or languages of education? Why do languages get taught the way they do?

All these concepts provide a means for reorienting studies of language, community and identity, and hence of bilingualism, away from autonomous structure and towards process and practice. What emerges now is a sense of bilingualism as only one perspective on a more complex set of practices which draw on linguistic resources which have been conventionally thought of as belonging to separate linguistic systems, because of our own dominant ideologies of language, but which may more fruitfully be understood as sets of resources called into play by social actors, under social and historical conditions which both constrain and make possible the social reproduction of existing conventions and relations, as well as the production of new ones. Political economic conditions are changing: the new economy places much greater emphasis on communicative skills in general, and multilingualism in particular, than did the old (Cameron 2001; Gee et al. 1996; Heller 2003; Castells 2000); nation-states try to reposition themselves advantageously on the dynamic and increasingly globalized market (del Valle 2007, in press; Duchêne and Heller 2007); labour migration takes new, mobile and transnational shapes (Portes 1997). On the whole, critiques of the discourse of globalism as legitimization of expanding capital notwithstanding (cf. Tsing 2000), there are observably new degrees, and maybe even types, of mobility of people, discourses and resources which make it harder and harder to do the work of uniformization from which an interest in the 'problem' of bilingualism initially sprang (see Pujolar, and Da Silva et al. this volume, for further discussion).

Each contributor to the book takes up some aspects of these shifts, with variable emphasis on linguistic systems, resources, practices and ideologies; nation, state, civil society, community and identity; political economy and interaction; social institutions and the workplace. Many examine the particularities of our times, as shifting understandings of bilingualism help us better describe and explain postcolonialism, post-nationalism and the globalizing new economy. The final section of this introduction provides an overview of these contributions, as part of the overall argument of the book.

outline of the book

The book is divided into four parts. The first part, 'Bilingualism, Nation, State and Capitalism', contains five chapters, covering relations between bilingualism and ideologies of state and nation from the nineteenth century to the present day. It includes consideration of the relationship between nationalism and the expansion of market capitalism, the construction of the nation-state, colonialism and postcolonialism (Stroud), postcolonial and late modern minority language movements (Jaffe), post-national political economic changes and their effects on ideologies of language and nation-state (Pujolar), as well as more recent developments involving NGOs and supranational agencies in developing discourses of linguistic human rights, ecology and biodiversity, especially as concern postcolonial minority and indigenous movements (Muehlmann and Duchêne; Patrick).

The second part, 'The State, the Economy and their Agencies in Late Modernity', contains four chapters, moving the level of analysis to institutional discourses and practices in late modernity. The section covers the regulation of bilingualism in a variety of institutional settings (schooling, the so-called 'language industries', tourism, the mass media and the internet, health care, the workplace) as connected to new conditions of mobility and of the expanding and changing role of language in the knowledge and service economy. It examines such themes as migration and citizenship (Moyer and Martín Rojo); education (Moyer and Martín Rojo; Martin-Jones); the commodification of language and authenticity in the new economy (Da Silva et al.); and popular culture and identity in the mass media and the internet (Androutsopoulos).

The third part, 'Identity Practices', moves analysis to the construction of links between bilingualism, social position or categorization (identity) and power, in communicative practices in everyday life. Its two chapters (by Garrett and by Bailey) treat issues related to mobility and multiplicity, whether related to geographical mobility or to other forms of social movement and multiplication or blurring of categorization, participation and affiliation. This part also considers the problem of production and reproduction of categories and relations of power as connected to bilingualism from the perspective of the social practices of language socialization (Schieffelin and Ochs 1986) and of the confrontation (or convergence) of multiple social categories (Bailey 2000). Both chapters emphasize the importance of examining local practices of social agency and construction of (bilingual) subjectivity.

The final part, 'Linguistic Form and Linguistic Practice', addresses in its three chapters (by Tsitsipis, Mondada and Auer) some ways in which a practice- and discourse-oriented view of bilingualism speaks to more traditional linguistic forms of analysis, whether focused on variation, interaction or linguistic features, as well as to sociocognitive approaches and theories of action and interaction. They argue that a close examination of linguistic practice requires rethinking our ideas about language as autonomous system.

The final chapter considers new directions for research on 'bilingualism' in the light of the new ways we can think of it that have been laid out in the volume. It focuses on the relationship between ideologies of language, what counts as research on 'bilingualism', the relationship to social theory, and implications for research methods, as well as on the role of such research in public debates.

A postface by Tabouret-Keller challenges our monolingual practices in its form: we have decided to publish it in its original French, with a summary in English. Somehow, a book on innovative approaches to bilingualism, but published entirely in English, seemed like a contradiction in terms. Of course, we could have adopted a more radical approach, but the weight of institutional routine lay heavy on us, and this was as radical as it was possible to get under conditions which may not be as open to challenge as we think. Beyond form, Tabouret-Keller, who has been a major participant in most of the major debates on bilingualism from the post-war period on, challenges us to remember the historical conditions in which we are always inscribed, and the social and ideological positions from which we necessarily speak.

notes

1. My thanks to Jannis Androutsopoulos, Melissa Moyer, Joan Pujolar, Lukas Tsitsipis and Andrée Tabouret-Keller for comments and suggestions on an earlier draft.
2. The third, fourth, fifth and sixth sections draw heavily on M. Heller (2006), 'Bilingualism', in C. Jourdan and K. Tuite (eds), *Language, Culture and Society*, Cambridge: Cambridge University Press, pp. 156–67.
3. While there is no space here to develop discussion of the genealogy of this disciplinary orientation, it is worth noting the long-standing tension between disciplines embedded in Romantic (and sometimes social Darwinist) perspectives, and those embedded in rationalist Enlightenment perspectives (both of which have been associated in complicated ways with imperialist and fascist projects (Errington, 2001; Irvine and Gal 2000; Fabian 1986; Hutton 1999) and with movements of postcolonial and late modern liberation. Certainly the post-war orientation to universalism and structuralism can be understood as a reaction to the ways in which ideologies of linguistics and anthropology were taken up in fascism.

references

Alvarez-Cáccamo, Celso (1998). From 'switching code' to 'code-switching': Towards a reconceptualization of communicative codes. In Peter Auer (ed.), *Code-Switching in Conversation*, pp. 29–50. London: Routledge.
Appadurai, Arjun (1996). *Modernity at Large: Cultural Dimensions of Globalization*. Minneapolis: University of Minnesota Press.

Aracil, Lluis (1982). *Papers de sociolinguistica.* Barcelona: Edicions de la Magrana.

Auer, Peter (1984). *Bilingual Conversation.* Amsterdam: John Benjamins.

—— (ed.) (1998). *Code-switching in Conversation: Language, Interaction and Identity.* London: Routledge.

Bailey, Benjamin (2000). Language and negotiation of ethnic/racial identity among Dominican Americans. *Language in Society* 29(4): 555–82.

Baker, Colin (2006). *Foundations of Bilingual Education and Bilingualism.* Clevedon, UK: Multilingual Matters.

Bakhtin, Mikhail (1981). *The Dialogic Imagination* (trans. C. Emerson and M. Holquist). Austin: University of Texas Press.

Barth, Fredrik (ed.) (1969). *Ethnic Groups and Boundaries.* Boston: Little, Brown.

Bauman, Richard, and Charles Briggs (2003). *Voices of Modernity: Language Ideologies and the Politics of Inequality.* Cambridge: Cambridge University Press.

Billiez, Jacqueline (1998). L'alternance des langues en chantant. *LIDIL* 18: 125–40.

Blom, Jan-Petter, and John Gumperz (1972). Social meaning in linguistic structures: Code-switching in Norway. In J. Gumperz and D. Hymes (eds) *Directions in Sociolinguistics: The Ethnography of Communication,* pp. 407–34. New York: Holt, Rinehart and Winston.

Blommaert, Jan, (ed.) (1999). *Language Ideological Debates.* Berlin: Mouton de Gruyter.

—— (2001). The Asmara Declaration as a sociolinguistic problem: Reflections on scholarship and linguistic rights. *Journal of Sociolinguistics* 5(1): 131–42.

Bloomfield, Leonard (1933). *Language.* New York: Holt, Rinehart and Winston.

Boix, Emili, and F. Xavier Vila (1998). *Sociolinguistica de la llengua catalana.* Barcelona: Ariel Linguistica.

Boyer, Henri (1991). *Langues en conflit.* Paris: L'Harmattan.

Cameron, Deborah (1995). *Verbal Hygiene.* London: Routledge.

—— (2001). *Good to Talk?* London: Sage.

Castells, Manuel (2000). *The Information Age: Economy, Society and Culture* (3 volumes). Oxford: Blackwell.

Castonguay, Charles (1996). L'intérêt particulier de la démographie pour le fait français. In J. Erfurt (ed.) *De la polyphonie à la symphonie. Méthodes, théories et faits de la recherche pluridisciplinaire sur le français au Canada,* pp. 3–18. Leipzig: Leipziger Universitätsverlag.

Clyne, Michael (2003). *Dynamics of Language Contact.* Cambridge: Cambridge University Press.

del Valle, José (in press). *Spanish in Brazil: Language Policy, Business and Cultural Propaganda.* Language Policy.

—— (2007). Embracing diversity for the sake of unity: Linguistic hegemony and the pursuit of total Spanish. In A. Duchêne and M. Heller (eds), *Discourses of Endangerment: Ideology and Interest in the Defense of Languages.* London: Continuum.

Deprez, Christine (1994/1999). *Les enfants bilingues: langues et familles.* Paris: Didier.

Dirim, Inci, and Peter Auer (2004). *Türkisch sprechen nicht nur die Türken: über die Unschärfebeziehung zwischen Sprache und Ethnie in Deutschland.* Berlin: Walter de Gruyter.

Dorian, Nancy (1981). *Language Death: The Life Cycle of a Scottish Gaelic Dialect.* Philadelphia: University of Pennsylvania Press.

Duchêne, Alexandre, and Monica Heller (eds) (2007). *Discourses of Endangerment: Ideology and Interest in the Defense of Languages.* London: Continuum.

Errington, Joseph (2001). Colonial linguistics. *Annual Review of Anthropology* 30: 19–39.

Fabian, Johannes (1986). *Language and Colonial Power*. Cambridge: Cambridge University Press.

Ferguson, Charles (1964). Diglossia. In D. Hymes (ed.), *Language in Culture and Society*, pp. 429–39. New York: Harper and Row.

Fishman, Joshua (ed.) (1968). *Readings in the Sociology of Language*. The Hague: Mouton.

Gal, Susan (1979). *Language Shift: Social Determinants of Linguistic Change in Bilingual Austria*. New York: Academic Press.

—— (1993). Diversity and contestation in linguistic ideologies: German speakers in Hungary. *Language in Society* 22(3): 337–60.

—— (1995). Lost in a Slavic sea: Linguistic theories and expert knowledge in 19th century Hungary. *Pragmatics* 5(2): 155–66.

Gee, James, Glynda Hull, and Colin Lankshear (1996). *The New Work Order: Behind the Language of the New Capitalism*. Boulder, CO: Westview Press.

Giddens, Anthony (1984). *The Constitution of Society*. Berkeley, Los Angeles: University of California Press.

Goldstein, Tara (1997). *Two Languages at Work: Bilingual Life on the Production Floor*. Berlin: Mouton de Gruyter.

Grillo, Ralph (1989). *Dominant Languages*. Cambridge: Cambridge University Press.

Grin, François (2003). Language planning and economics. *Current Issues in Language Planning* 4(1): 1–66.

Grosjean, François (1982). *Life With Two Languages*. Cambridge, MA: Harvard University Press.

—— (1995). A psycholinguistic approach to code-switching: The recognition of guest words by bilinguals. In L. Milroy and P. Muysken (eds), *One Speaker, Two Languages: Cross-disciplinary Perspectives on Code-switching*, pp. 259–75. Cambridge: Cambridge University Press.

Gumperz, John (1971). *Language in Social Groups*. Stanford: Stanford University Press.

—— (1982). *Discourse Strategies*. Cambridge: Cambridge University Press.

Hannerz, Ulf (1996). *Transnational Connections: Culture, People, Places*. London: Routledge.

Harvey, David (1989). *The Condition of Postmodernity*. Oxford: Blackwell.

Hechter, Michael (1975). *Internal Colonialism: The Celtic Fringe in British National Development*. Berkeley and Los Angeles: University of California Press.

Heller, Monica (ed.) (1988). *Codeswitching: Anthroplogical and Sociolinguistic Perspectives*. Berlin: Mouton de Gruyter.

—— (2002). *Éléments d'une sociolinguistique critique*. Paris: Didier.

—— (2003). Globalization, the new economy and the commodification of language and identity. *Journal of Sociolinguistics* 7(4): 473–92.

Heller, Monica, Jean-Paul Bartholomot, Laurette Lévy and Luc Ostiguy (1982). *La francisation d'une entreprise montréalaise: une analyse sociolinguistique*. Montréal: Office de la langue française, Gouvernement du Québec.

Heller, Monica, and Laurette Lévy (1994). Les contradictions des mariages linguistiquement mixtes: les stratégies des femmes franco-ontariennes. *Langage et société* 67: 53–88.

Heller, Monica, and Marilyn Martin-Jones (eds) (2001). *Voices of Authority: Education and Linguistic Difference*. Westport, CT: Ablex.

Heller, Monica, and Carol Pfaff (1996). Code-switching and code-mixing. In P. Nelda, H. Goebl, W. Wölck and Z. Stary (eds), *Internationales Handbuch der Kontaktlinguistik*, pp. 594–610. Berlin: Walter de Gruyter.

Higonnet, Patrice (1980). The politics of linguistic terrorism and grammatical hegemony during the French Revolution. *Social Theory* 5: 41–69.

Hobsbawm, Eric (1990). *Nations and Nationalism since 1760.* Cambridge: Cambridge University Press.

Hutton, Christopher (1999). *Linguistics and the Third Reich: Mother-tongue Fascism, Race and the Science of Language.* London: Routledge.

Inda, Jonathan, and Renato Rosaldo (eds) (2002). *The Anthropology of Globalization: A Reader.* Oxford: Blackwell.

Irvine, Judith, and Susan Gal (2000). Language ideology and linguistic differentiation. In P. Kroskrity (ed.), *Regimes of Language: Ideologies, Polities and Identities*, pp. 35–81. Santa Fe, NM: School of American Research Press.

Jaffe, Alexandra (1999). *Ideologies in Action: Language Politics on Corsica.* Berlin: Mouton de Gruyter.

Kearney, Michael (2004). *Changing Fields of Anthropology: From Local to Global.* Lanham, MD: Rowman and Littlefield.

Köppe, Regina, and Jürgen Meisel (1995). Code-switching in bilingual first language acquisition. In L. Milroy and P. Muysken (eds), *One Speaker, Two Languages: Cross-disciplinary Perspectives on Code-switching*, pp. 276–301. Cambridge: Cambridge University Press.

Kroll, Judith, and Annette de Groot (eds) (2005). *Handbook of Bilingualism: Psycholinguistic Approaches.* New York: Oxford University Press.

Kroskrity, Paul (ed.) (2000). *Regimes of Language: Ideologies, Polities and Identities.* Santa Fe, NM: School of American Research.

Kuhn, Thomas (1962). *The Structure of Scientific Revolutions.* Chicago: University of Chicago Press.

Lafont, Robert (1997). *Quarante ans de sociolinguistique à la périphérie.* Paris: L'Harmattan.

Landry, Rodrigue, and Réal Allard (1996). Vitalité ethnolinguistique: une perspective dans l'étude de la francophonie canadienne. In J. Erfurt (ed.), *De la polyphonie à la symphonie. Méthodes, théories et faits de la recherche pluridisciplinaire sur le français au Canada*, pp. 61–88. Leipzig: Leipziger Universitätsverlag.

Mackey, William (1968). The description of bilingualism. In J. Fishman (ed.), *Readings in the Sociology of Language*, pp. 554–84. The Hague: Mouton.

Maehlum, Brit (1996). Codeswitching in Hemnesberget: Myth or reality? *Journal of Pragmatics* 25: 749–61.

McClure, Erica (1981). Formal and functional aspects of the code-switched discourse of bilingual children. In R. Duran (ed.), *Latino Language and Communicative Behavior.* pp. 69–94. Norwood, NJ: Ablex.

McDonald, Marion (1990). *We Are Not French.* London: Routledge.

Meeuwis, Michael (1999a). Flemish nationalism in the Belgian Congo versus Zairean anti-imperialism: Continuity and discontinuity in language ideological debates. In J. Blommaert (ed.), *Language Ideological Debates*, pp. 381–424. Berlin: Mouton de Gruyter.

—— (1999b). The White Fathers and Luganda: To the origins of French missionary linguistics in the Lake Victoria region. *Annales Aequatoria* 20: 413–43.

Meeuwis, Michael, and Jan Blommaert (1994). The 'Markedness Model' and the absence of society: Remarks on code-switching. *Multilingua* 14(4): 387–423.

Mejia, Anne-Marie de (2002). *Power, Prestige and Bilingualism: International Perspectives on Elite Bilingual Education.* Clevedon, UK: Multilingual Matters.

Mougeon, Raymond, and Edouard Beniak (1991). *Linguistic Consequences of Language Contact and Restriction: The Case of French in Ontario, Canada.* Oxford: Oxford University Press.

Muysken, Pieter (1995). Code-switching and grammatical theory. In L. Milroy and P. Muysken (eds), *One Speaker, Two Languages: Cross-disciplinary Perspectives on Codeswitching*, pp. 177–98. Cambridge: Cambridge University Press.

Myers-Scotton, Carol (1993a). *Duelling Languages: Grammatical Structure in Codeswitching.* Oxford: Oxford University Press.

—— (1993b). *Social Motivations for Code-switching: Evidence from Africa.* Oxford: Oxford University Press.

Okita, T. (2002). *Invisible Work: Bilingualism, Language Choice and Childrearing in Intermarried Families.* Amsterdam: John Benjamins.

Paradis, Michel (2004). *The Neurolinguistic Theory of Bilingualism.* Amsterdam, PA: John Benjamins.

Patrick, Donna (2003). *Language, Politics and Social Interaction in an Inuit Community.* Berlin: Mouton de Gruyter.

Philippe, C., Gabrielle Varro, and G. Neyrand (eds), (1998). *Liberté, égalité, mixité... conjugales. Une sociologie du couple mixte.* Paris: Anthropos.

Piller, Ingrid (2002). *Bilingual Couples Talk: The Discursive Construction of Hybridity.* Amsterdam, PA: John Benjamins.

Poplack, Shana (1988). Contrasting patterns of code-switching in two communities. In M. Heller (ed.), *Codeswitching: Anthropological and Sociolinguistic Perspectives.* pp. 215–44. Berlin: Mouton de Gruyter.

Portes, Alejandro (1997). Immigration theory for a new century: Some problems and opportunities. *International Migration Review* 31(4): 799–825.

Pries, Ludger (2001). The approach of transnational social spaces. In L. Pries (ed.), *New Transnatioinal Social Spaces: International Migration and International Companies in the Early Twenty-First Century*, pp. 3–33. New York: Routledge.

Pujolar, Joan (2001). *Gender, Heteroglossia and Power: A Sociolinguistic Study of Youth Culture.* Berlin: Mouton de Gruyter.

Rampton, Ben (2002). Ritual and foreign language practice at school. *Language and Society* 31(4): 491–526.

Rindler-Schjerve, Rosita (ed.) (2003). *Diglossia and Power: Language Policies and Practice in the 19th Century Habsburg Empire.* Berlin and New York: Mouton de Gruyter.

Roy, Sylvie (2003). Bilingualism and standardization in a Canadian call center: Challenges for a linguistic minority community. In R. Bayley and S. Schecter (eds), *Language Socialization in Multilingual Societies*, pp. 269–87. Clevedon, UK: Multilingual Matters.

Schieffelin, Bambi, Kathryn Woolard, and Paul Kroskrity (eds) (1998). *Language Ideologies: Practice and Theory.* Oxford: Oxford University Press.

Schieffelin, Bmbi, and Elinor Ochs (eds) (1986). *Language Socialization Across Cultures.* Cambridge: Cambridge University Press.

Silverstein, Michael, and Greg Urban (eds) (1996). *Natural Histories of Discourse.* Chicago: University of Chicago Press.

Skutnabb-Kangas, Tove (2000). *Linguistic Genocide in Education or Worldwide Diversity and Human Rights?* London: Lawrence Erlbaum.

Spolsky, Bernard (2004). *Language Policy.* Cambridge: Cambridge University Press.

22   bilingualism: a social approach

Tabouret-Keller, Andrée (1988). La nocivité mentale du bilinguisme, cent ans d'errance. In *Euskara Biltzarra*, pp. 155–69. Vitoria-Gasteiz: Eusko Jaurlaritzaren Argitalpen-Zerbitzu Nagusia.

Tsing, Anna (2000). The global situation. *Cultural Anthropology* 15(3): 327–60.

Urciuoli, Bonnie (1995). Language and borders. *Annual Review of Anthropology* 24: 525–46.

—— (1996). *Exposing Prejudice: Puerto Rican Experiences of Language, Race and Class.* Boulder, CO: Westview Press.

Vaillancourt, François (1996). Le français dans un contexte économique. In J. Erfurt (ed.), *De la polyphonie à la symphonie. Méthodes, théories et faits de la recherche pluridisciplinaire sur le français au Canada*, pp. 119–36. Leipzig: Leipziger Universitätsverlag.

Varro, Gabrielle (2003). *Sociologie de la mixité. De la mixité amoureuse aux mixités sociales et culturelles.* Paris: Belin.

Weber, Eugene (1976). *Peasants into Frenchmen.* Stanford: Stanford University Press.

Weinreich, Uriel (1953). *Languages in Contact: Findings and Problems.* London and Paris: Mouton.

Williams, Glyn (1992). *Sociolinguistics: A Sociological Critique.* London: Routledge.

Woehrling, José (1996). Le droit et la législation comme moyens d'intervention sur le français: les politiques linguistiques du Québec, des autorités fédérales et des provinces anglophones. In J. Erfurt (ed.), *De la polyphonie à la symphonie. Méthodes, théories et faits de la recherche pluridisciplinaire sur le français au Canada*, pp. 209–32. Leipzig: Leipziger Universitätsverlag.

Woolard, Kathryn (1989). *Double Talk: Bilingualism and the Politics of Ethnicity in Catalonia.* Stanford: Stanford University Press.

—— (2004a). Codeswitching. In A. Duranti (ed.), *A Companion to Linguistic Anthropology.* pp. 73–94. London: Blackwell.

—— (2004b). Is the past a foreign country? Time, language origins, and the nation in Early Modern Spain. *Journal of Linguistic Anthropology* 14(1): 57–80.

Wright, Sue (2003). *Language Policy and Language Planning: From Nationalism to Globalisation.* New York: Palgrave Macmillan.

Zentella, Ana Celia (1981). Ta bien, you could answer me in cualquier idioma: Puerto Rican codeswitching in bilingual classrooms. In R. Duran (ed.), *Latino Language and Communicative Behavior*, pp. 109–31. Norwood, NJ: Ablex.

—— (1997). *Growing Up Bilingual.* Oxford: Blackwell.

part one
bilingualism, nation, state and capitalism

2
bilingualism: colonialism and postcolonialism

christopher stroud

introduction

In this chapter, I will explore the idea of bilingualism as a social construct by arguing that shifting notions of bilingualism are at base the outcome of competition among institutions, groups and individuals around questions of citizenship, language and the state. I will suggest that this claim is best advanced by way of a historical illustration that shows how the transformation of societies from colonial to postcolonial states not only reconfigured the relationship of actors and agents to state, market and civil society, but was simultaneously regulated through practices and ideas about languages and their interrelationships, that is, bilingualism.

a note on colonialism, postcolonialism and language

Both colonialism and postcolonialism comprise complex, multifaceted and contradictory social processes and semiotics. Language (and multilingualism) is a particularly pertinent lens through which to view these processes, as it is just as vital to the reproduction and resistance of colonial orders as it is to their postcolonial transformation. At the same time, the cultural and material dynamics of colonialism and postcoloniality serve to constitute language as a historically and socioculturally specific construct.

Colonialism[1] is a rubric for a range of exploitative situations, comprising cultural, material and economic processes that have variously been understood in modernist as well as postmodernist terms (Comaroff 1998). In traditional, liberal modernist historiographies, colonialism is presented in terms of states answering their call to civilize the native, that is, as a fundamentally *political* project. This perspective on colonialism is customarily narrated in linear chronicles of 'public events and heroic actions' (ibid: 324) in ways that enhance 'the authoritative self-representation, in particular of the nation-state' (ibid). In this context, language was an important means for exercising control

25

over people and their relationships; by projecting languages onto delimited geographical areas in ways that mimicked the situation in the European nation-state, linguistic descriptions united some people into communities of speakers and divided others (Errington, 2001). This 'specific logic' of territoriality was common to both missionaries and colonialists alike, who shared an interest in organizing distinct and linguistically defined communities into identifiable administrative units. Christian colonial linguistics also provided the political project of colonialism with an ideological raison d'être for its expansionist politics, namely, the notion of Babel and Ur-Sprach (Errington 2001) and a particular stance on linguistic diversity as moral degeneration after the fall from Eden. One task the Christian linguists set themselves was to reinvent original culture in the image of a pure language (Errington 2001; Blommaert 1999).

On another wing of modernist historiography, Marxist accounts of colonialism lift forth the material and political economic truths of imperial conquest by painting a picture of colonialism as capitalist exploitation of peoples and resources. Here, colonialism appears as a massive organization for the extraction of labour and material resources, and for the transformation of subjugated peoples into wage labourers. In this account, the politics of labour comprise the main site for understanding the complexity of the social transformations that took place during and after colonialism, where emerging industrialization and urbanization of a rurally based workforce was also tied to constructions of ethnic identity, race and gender. Language once again played a significant role as part of the social and semiotic processes that constructed, organized and regulated a colonial workforce of subject peoples. Fabian (1986) remarks on how the transformation of the rural African population into wage earners was an early vision of colonialism that strongly determined colonial linguistic attitudes. In particular, linguistic descriptions created sociolinguistic hierarchies within and between languages which were projected upon categories such as class, gender, ethnicity, and which legitimized the exploitation of certain groups in labour.

More recent, postmodern, understandings of colonialism complement the political and material narratives of modernism by viewing it as fundamentally a cultural project of *governmentality*, comprising 'a broad range of disciplinary and regulatory practices' (Comaroff 1998: 322) involving 'the fabrication of an entire space-time world – and the insinuation of its logic into the mundane practices of human beings-as-citizens' (ibid: 329). Colonialism inserted itself 'into the very construction of its subjects, into their bodily routines, and the essence of their selfhood' (ibid) through numerous sites of control, institutional discourses, and modes of surveillance. The regulation and knowledge of language comprised one of the more powerful techniques available at this time. Indigenous languages were invented in forms imagined by the colonial linguist, rather than in ways that rang true to the variety of local speech practices encountered by colonial linguistics (Mühlhäusler 1996;

Makoni and Pennycook forthcoming), thus conferring linguistic authority on the colonialists. The production of dictionaries and grammars in 'local' languages constrained and enforced what meanings these languages could express (cf. Makoni and Pennycook forthcoming) as well as what could be *said* more generally. Language also served as a resource (in ways similar to sex, gender, race and class) for figuring and naturalizing inequality. Norms of metropolitan speech were jealously guarded and monitored, serving as a linguistic *panopticon*, a mode of surveillance, for would-be citizens to conform to for representation, agency and citizenship. In this way, colonial linguistics provided the Western self with knowledge of subject peoples and the means to communicate in ways that were to the advantage of the colonizers and which rendered the colonial reality comprehensible to the European modern mind (Errington 2001).

A perspective on colonialism that would appear to offer a more comprehensive framework for understanding how forms of colonialism can be understood against governmentality, Christianity and political economy is to view it in terms of competing notions of citizenship. Comaroff (1998) has suggested that the problem of colonialism (and postcolonialism) would benefit from being restated in terms of a reconceptualization of the notion of the state 'as a discourse in the interconnections of governmentality, materiality, modernity and legality' (ibid.: 340). The modern nation-state is a *performative* construction, imagined and called into authoritative existence principally through a 'culture of legality', founded on a liberal notion of *citizenship* and a conception of individual rights that recognized the equality of its citizens and regulated their relation to the state and market. However, the projection of this notion of a nation-state onto colonial territories immediately resulted in a host of contradictions, as the colonial state, in contradistinction to the metropolitan state, was not founded on the equality of its rights-bearing citizens, but 'largely on the legalities of exclusion and the politics of difference' (ibid: 343). The principal contradiction revolved around the different ways of conceptualizing subjugated peoples as subjects or citizens, as traditional or modern, and in reality, both at the same time, as 'colonial regimes sought to convert "natives" simultaneously and contradictorily into *both* rights-bearing citizens and culture-bearing ethnic subjects' (ibid: 344). This push and pull of the subaltern's relationship to the culture of 'legality' is framed against evolving discourses of *modernity* and *tradition*.

One advantage of a reconceptualization of the colonial state in terms of discourses of legality is that it highlights some important continuities between colonialism and *postcoloniality*, as the problem of citizenship has also constituted the major legacy with which these societies have had to grapple. Mamdani (1996), for example, has suggested that colonial bifurcations between urban–rural, civilized–native, citizen–subject, common law–customary law find resonance in the postcolonial society's politics of identities that seek to refine a more inclusive notion of citizenship built around the construction of commonality rather than difference. And Comaroff (1998) argues that the colonial divisions between subjects and citizens have had lasting affects on postcolonial *modernities*, leading to contemporary conflicts between rights based, civil society, with its 'individualistic' solutions to governance, on the one hand, and movements that seek collective, ethnic based and customary solutions, on the other. It is then through contesting notions of citizenship and civil society that the colonial state was resisted and eventually dismantled.

Bilingualism as a social and political construct has figured massively in the emergence of competing discourses of colonial and postcolonial citizenship, engaging with a (re)problematization of citizen and community. It has been allied with social processes that order and regiment peoples into administrative constituencies, in constructing moral images of speakers and in the semiotic framing of discourses of tradition and modernity, agency and citizenship (Irvine and Gal 2000). A notion such as *code-switching*, for example, has been variously associated with moral attributes such as laziness, and debauched and anti-social behaviour, as well as resistance to state authority, whereas speaking a 'pure' language was seen as an accomplishment of a loyal citizen; the hierarchical arrangement of languages in *orders of indexicality* (cf. Blommaert 2004) translates into similar social and political hierarchies between speakers; the notion of language *domain* encapsulates a mapping of 'pure' languages onto societal functions, thereby determining who may have linguistic access to social goods.

In this chapter, I will explore in detail the contradictory narratives of citizenship that make up colonialism and postcoloniality, their ramifications for discourses of modernity and tradition, and the role played by bilingualism in how individual and group relations to the state are figured. I shall use Mozambique as an illustration, arguing that it is an apt choice for a number of reasons. Firstly, it provides a clear example of the tight linkages between constructions of bilingualism and the political economy of labour, governmentality and Christianity. In particular, the colonial notion of *assimilado*, which comprised the colonial state's crowning attempt to form a colonial citizen from a colonial subject, rested heavily on the requirement of proficiency in Portuguese and on the exclusion of local languages.

Secondly, Mozambique illustrates well the claim of postcoloniality as a continuation of colonialism. Issues of citizenship, as well as alternative modernities and reconceptualizations of legality and the state, were particularly prominent after independence and in the ensuing 15-year-long civil war. The battle between modernity and tradition, which received its most pointed expression in one of the bloodiest wars of postcolonialism ever, also involved battles over the meaning and legitimacy of different constructions of bilingualism.[2]

In the following, I shall argue, *pace* Comaroff, that historical contradictions have produced distinct and competing ideas of citizenship and rights throughout colonialism and postcoloniality, and suggest that these contradictions have found semiotic expression in different notions of bilingualism. These have been discursively constructed in figurations of the local versus the metropolitan, the traditional versus the modern, and in regimes of governmentality.

bilingualism in colonialism: mozambique

introduction: subject versus citizen

Mozambique was always a chaotic and contested, although richly imagined, construction. Lacking the financial means to establish, exploit and develop its African dominions as independent colonies on a par with Britain and France, Portugal chose instead to integrate Mozambique into the regional and European economies as a provider of labour and goods. Up until the end of World War II, the Mozambican colony was geared to the production of primary agricultural products for consumption on the European market, and to ensuring a rich source of labour for the South African mining companies. Its ports and railway brought in essential revenue through the shipping and transport of South African and Rhodesian products. The ability of the Portuguese colony to service the economies of the richer colonial powers depended fundamentally on the availability of abundant and cheap labour that could satisfy the demands for migrant labour to the South African mines, as well as the needs of the large plantations for the growing of crops for export. In order to provide this, the Portuguese state put into place an extensive system of authoritarianism and control that was upheld through violence and repression.

At the end of World War II, a decline in the competitiveness of colonial exports, coupled to a growing sense of nationalism at home in Portugal that coincided with the establishment of the fascist state, led to a change in state policy towards Mozambique; what had been primarily a *labour* colony was gradually transformed into a *settler* colony (cf. Bowen 2000). There were also external pressures on Portugal to reform its harsh treatment of its colonies. During the course of colonial Mozambique, there was a shift in the locus of power, such that 'power was not so much to do with extractive effects on colonial bodies but governing effects on colonial conduct' (Scott 1995: 192). This was a multifaceted, complex and contested development involving a transformation from the native as subject to one of a citizen of the 'overseas Portuguese province' of Mozambique, with various ramifications for the construction of bilingualism.

imagining the colonial state

bilingualism in the material construction of the local versus the metropolitan

In order to secure the necessary abundance of cheap labour required to fill its colonial undertakings towards the regional and European economies, the

Portuguese state introduced to Mozambique a gendered system – women were exempt – of forced, contracted labour known as *shibalo*.[3] This system regulated peasant existence through migrant labour and dictated the obligations of the indigene 'subject' up until the early 1960s.[4] The principle was that Africans without independent means of production or income, or who lacked sufficient personal capital, could be recruited as labour for a specified period of six months per year and for a variety of tasks ranging from the building of roads to working the South African goldmines. Bowen (2000) details the advantages (and justification) of this system for Portugal. First of all, in exchange for taking on Mozambican labour, Portugal would grant South Africa access to Mozambican ports and railways. Furthermore, not only did Portugal levy an export tax on each labourer, but it also received deferred payment in South African currency from the mining company, from which it then paid the laborer in local currency after deducting taxes. (The deferred payment ensured that wages would be spent in Mozambique.) Bowen (2000) estimates that, in this way, more than 30 per cent of the workers' wages ended up in the coffers of the Portuguese state.

Shibalo carefully specified what types of 'work' were considered to be occupations that would exempt the African from forced recruitment (farming, for example, was not considered labour). An administrative concomitant of *shibalo* was the territorial organization of native domesticity and social reproduction into rural 'homelands' that were governed by traditional 'chiefs' through African languages and in accordance with customary law. Recruiting labour in this way was economically expedient, as the responsibility for the livelihood, health and social reproduction of the workers fell to the village (and then mainly the women).

This primarily economic organization of interrelationships between colonizer and colonized found resonance in the division of labour between languages; Portuguese was tied to public and official domains and functions, and to ideas of modernity and the *metropole*, whereas African languages were restricted to the informal, home domains and to ideas of tradition and the *local*. In fact, being able to 'identify' a language in which tribal custom could be expressed was essential to the colonial delimitation of the local, and cases abound of how tribal homelands were constituted around languages that were constructed (invented) by missionaries (cf. Makoni and Pennycook 2007). In fact, much of the ethnography of the time was concerned precisely with determining bases for the administrative organization of peoples into territorial and tribal groupings. The historian Patrick Harries notes how decisions on what constituted the Tsonga language of southern Mozambique were 'frequently based on criteria that were social and political rather than scientific' (1995: 154). Remarking on how the group later to be referred to as the Tsonga was mainly comprised of east coast immigrant communities, he notes how

The Swiss missionaries rapidly laid claim to this entire diaspora. Their claim to evangelise these people, whom they collectively referred to as 'Gwamba', was entrenched by what they saw as the bismarkism [sic] of their German neighbours. For the Berlin missionaries had already laid claim to, and excluded the Swiss from, all the autochthonous chiefdoms in the northern and eastern Transvaal. (Harries 1995: 158)

In their tribalization of the Mozambican linguistic landscape, missionary linguists couched their mapping of languages in a rhetoric of territoriality, using metaphors of space and conquest to order indigenous linguistic space along lines of colonial ideas of racial compartmentalization (cf. Fabian 1986; Irvine and Gal 2000; Errington 2001). This was the case for the Gwamba language: after numerous expeditions mapping 'dialectal variations', Henri Bertoud, one of the earliest Swiss missionary linguists in the area, came to the conclusion that the Gwamba language was made up of eight branches, each of which was given 'its own territory and particular dialect', recommending that the Swiss mission 'concentrate its energies on the area between the Knomati and Limpopo rivers' (Harries 1995: 160), so that Gwamba, later Thonga, with its eight subgroups came to delimit the field of Swiss missionary activity. Once languages were constructed as indigenous and local, it became necessary to also ask questions about who could authentically own them, and therefore how they might be legitimately acquired (Stroud 2003).

The division of populations into tribes not only facilitated management of the colonies (through the appointment of 'Chiefs'/*regulos* who could serve as colonial intermediaries), it also mirrored the nation-state. The administrative units that were delimited linguistically and in terms of custom manifested the essentialist understanding of language and identity that the colonialists brought with them.

bilingualism in christian discourses of the traditional and modern

The organization of the local population as a territorially based workforce was ideologically under-girded by a discourse of 'civilizing' Christianity – 'a rhetorically construed coherence of form and content between religious missionary thought and secular political and economic ideas' (Fabian 1986: 79). The administrative category 'native' or *indigene* was actively constructed in a hierarchical system of Christian moralism, referencing a deficient, racially inferior and idle individual, an equation that justified linking Christian concepts of moral good and self improvement to economic imperatives of work and forced labour (cf. Fabian 1986). This served to give the colonial state the moral backing it needed for transforming, what was in their view, a lazy and ignorant native into a productive and god-fearing family man.

Discourses on language specifically were situated within this more encompassing moral and economic discourse of coloniality, and was one of the foundational pillars upon which the extensive system of order and control that was imposed by the Portuguese colonial government rested. The missionary linguists overlay the linguistic construction of the dimension of the *local* versus *metropole* with a second dimension, namely the *traditional* (and morally corrupt) versus the *modern* (enlightened Christianity), where colonial metalinguistic regimes represented Portuguese and local languages according to principles of evolutionary status, Cartesian thought and hierarchical order (cf. Blommaert 1999; Fabian 1986; Harries 1995).

Portuguese was deemed essential for civilized status and seen as a bona fide 'language', whereas African languages were *dialectos*, corrupt and inadequate forms of speech that held little value, although nonetheless understood according to the same ideology of languages as distinct and homogeneous systems. Portuguese was also the language of moral and religious integrity. The pivotal role of language in the civilizing mission appears in the slippage in the way the Catholic Church equated the inability to read and write or to speak and understand proper *Portuguese*, with the designation of illiterates as immoral subjects (Marshall 1993: 77, fn 9). At the same time, missionary linguists were at work salvaging the souls of local Africans through linguistic descriptions of indigenous languages; through careful comparative Bantu linguistic work, problematic Babelian diversity was to be organized into orderly categories in attempts to reconstruct the pristine past of the innocent native. The Swiss missionary Henri Junod, for example, believed that 'the Thonga language ought to be considered as the oldest element in the life of the tribe' (quoted in Harries 1995: 163), and that, in accordance with European nationalist thought, by ridding this language of foreign elements, the original proto-Tsonga would lay bare the *ethos* of the tribe.

The tension between modernity and tradition was also at the root of conflict around the language of liturgy and religion between the Catholics and Protestants with Catholics insisting on the inappropriateness of Protestant translation of religious materials into local African languages lest religious texts be used in pagan and primitive ritual. On the other hand, Protestants saw written, *standardized* local languages as instruments of modernization, 'in contradistinction to the atavistic "dialects" and "patois" that embodied all the beliefs and superstitions of "pagan" society' (Harries 1995: 166). These linguistically construed ideologies of modernity and tradition, couched in tropes of Christianity, illustrate the fundamental *political* nature of religious linguistic discourses of the time.

Closely linked to the issue of language of liturgy and education was a contest between different notions of citizenship and subjugation. The fact that Protestants offered education in local languages meant that the languages of the indigenes were given social and symbolic value as languages of potential political agency. For the Catholics, on the other hand, Portuguese, with its ideological links to moral correctness and religious righteousness, was the only conceivable contender for such a role.

The deep political nature of this religious contest over language is further
evident from the changing fortunes of the Catholic and Protestant causes
under different political conditions.[5] The Swiss missionaries in particular
were only able to carry out their activities in local languages because they
were active in areas outside of Portuguese government control, such as the
Tsonga-speaking districts of Magude, Mandjakazi and Ricatla in the south
of the country. As the Portuguese gradually gained military hegemony over
larger parts of the country, the activities of the Protestant missions became
increasingly more constrained. Legislation followed suit: in 1907, the governor
of Mozambique, Freire de Andrade, stipulated that all religious education was
to take place solely in Portuguese. Although this was subsequently revoked
by the government of the *New Republic* in 1910 after the ousting of the
monarchy, with the weakening of state ties with the Catholic Church (1911–
26), and the trend towards decentralization of the colonial administration,
the decision to employ only Portuguese in religious education was once
again reinstated in August of 1914, with the then Governor-General, Joaquim
Machado, passing a decree which guaranteed financial subsidies to qualified
teachers who instructed the indigenes in Portuguese. This acknowledgement
of teacher professionalization effectively led to the closing of many Protestant
schools (cf. Cruz e Silva 2001). The official position on the linguistic medium
continued to vacillate; the signing of the Saint Germain-en-Laye Accord in
1919 gave some renewed protection to the use of local languages in Protestant
schools, although this was once again revoked in 1921.

In other words, bilingualism took two concurrent forms: African languages
were organized as local, indigenous, owned and authentic and Portuguese as
metropolitan; and local languages were constructed as languages of tradition
and Portuguese as the language of the modern state. Bilingualism at this
time provides for a semiotic figuration of citizenship as a multidimensional
and complexly layered ideological construction, and a representation of the
colonial state as constituted in a matrix of competing discourses.

bilingualism in governmentality

Dictates on language, together with the creation of tribal lands for Africans
managed through customary law, and the conflicts between Protestants and
Catholics on the proper linguistic organization of tradition and modernity,
all conspired to define an early bifurcation of the Mozambican population
into two types of *public* (Gal and Woolard 2001): *citizens*, on the one hand,
and *subjects* or native labourers, on the other.

An important site of governmentality lay in colonial control over *local*
languages. As Harries notes,

The compilation of bilingual dictionaries also served to assimilate the
Other, for dictionaries isolated a [Thonga] word from its social context
and imposed upon it a meaning derived from European culture. ...The

meaning of words like Gwamba or Thonga Ronga or Tswa (names for languages) were changed from expressions of exclusion to become terms of social inclusion that had never existed in the mental world of the people upon which they were imposed. (1995: 165)

The institutional mechanisms and discourses that were in place to contain citizenship contained the seeds for the growth of a resistant and transformative notion of citizenship, as colonial *governmentality* required that workers be *named* and recorded for purposes of taxation and regulation (cf. also Fabian 1986). Native labour was regulated with the *caderneta*, a pass-book containing a record of the tax and labour of the holder and details of his family, replete with stamps of authorization that regulated the workers' mobility. Over time, this meant that the anonymous and amorphous African *subject* came more to resemble the individualized and civilized *citizen*, thereby undermining the racial basis on which the separation of the *indigene* from the civilized was built. In 1917, therefore, in some measure as recognition of this dilemma, the colonial government introduced the notion of *assimilado*, which stipulated that even black Africans could aspire to citizenship if they fulfilled the conditions laid down in Article 2 of Edict 317:

Article 2: Through distinguishing himself from the norm of the black race, an individual of that race or descended from it is considered assimilated to the Europeans on showing the following characteristics:
a) has entirely abandoned the habits and customs of the black race;
b) speaks, reads and writes the Portuguese language;
c) adopts monogamy;
d) exercises a profession or craft
(quoted in Marshall 1993: 72)

Of particular interest here is that religious concerns, territoriality, moralism, political economy and governance all come together in this notion of *indigene citizenship*. The requirement that the native master Portuguese appears here in the context of Christianity, work ethics, and family values – all foundational elements of the good colony.[6] As in many colonial contexts, the notion of *assimilado* had the effect of 'transforming large portions of the rural African population into a salariat, a class of wage earners – nuclear family, a degree of literacy, a modicum of private property, good health, Christian belief, work ethic, control of physical mobility' (Fabian 1986: 42). From this moment onwards, knowledge of Portuguese was cultivated as the major discourse of colonial governmentality, playing a key part in the transformation of Mozambique from a labour colony to a settler colony; eligibility for civilized status for blacks involved demonstrating ability to read and write Portuguese.

The *Acto Colonial*, which was later incorporated into the constitution of the *Estado Novo* of 1933, introduced a more thoroughgoing constitutional definition and a more intense consolidation of empire, with the Portuguese government trying to enforce an even stricter division between civilized and 'savage', with the introduction after 1930 of state-sponsored schooling that formally distinguished between settler schools and those for indigenes. In the context of the new colonial order, the role of the Portuguese language in the colonial disciplinary and moral project became even more central, and Portuguese was taught in ways that attempted to prefigure and cater to the new indigenous citizen (cf. Marshall 1993). In 1954, legislation on speaking Portuguese was further sharpened by making it a requirement that the candidate *assimilado* speak 'proper Portuguese' – a requirement that was only abolished in 1961 (Johnstone 1989: 46; Marshall 1993: 72).

The whole notion of what constituted Portuguese at this time was intimately bound up with the colonial demarcation. Portuguese was constructed as a language of religion, modernity, work and citizenship (cf. also Makoni and Pennycook forthcoming; Fabian 1986). This was accomplished at the same time that the use of the language inserted colonial values into the bodies and lives of Mozambicans, something that is nicely illustrated with the following excerpt from Junod's conversational manual. This manual provides some contemporary texts of the time that supposedly illustrate typical forms of communication between native labourer and Portuguese master. The exchange below also shows how themes of labour, colonial morality and racial authority all contribute to structuring both the exchange itself and, as a result, relations between colonizer and colonized mediated through a language appropriate to the task, namely Portuguese.

1   Good morning.
2   Good morning, sir.
3   What are you doing?
4   I am not doing anything.
5   Would you like to work for me?
6   I should like to work...What work shall I have to do?
7   You will carry boxes.
8   Where must I carry them?
9   You will take them from the customs house and carry them to my store.
10 Let us go then!
11 Carry this box.
12 It's heavy for me.
13 Trust yourself. It is not very heavy.
14 Oh, it is heavy. I cannot.
15 You are simply lazy.
(quoted in Penvenne 1995: 45)

This extract provides the settler with a model for how to communicatively call into existence, or *interpellate* (Butler 1999), a compliant worker available for hire (lines 1–6). The dialogue is an exchange of simple questions and commands that define a social space of dominance and submission (lines 7–12), where voiced opposition is perfunctorily dismissed with a minimum of polite hedging (e.g. line 15, 'you are simply lazy'). The example shows how 'socialization (...) in(to) communities of practice may entail the negotiation of ways of being in context' (Pavlenko and Piller 2001: 22, drawing on Wenger 1998), in that the native African is not only learning how to be a worker for the white man, but is simultaneously being *positioned* (Pavlenko and Blackledge 2004) linguistically as having a particular kind of (infantile) colonial identity.

Texts such as these offer illuminating insights into the social conditions under which native Africans acquired Portuguese. Native learners had little access to extended or varied input, and few opportunities for error correction in meaningful contexts of communication. This, together with the limited range of communicative roles available to the African, and the lack of speakership rights, frame strategies of acquisition such as euphemism and censorship (Bourdieu 1991). One outcome of learning under such conditions is the development of rudimentary varieties of Portuguese, such as *Português do quintal* (backyard or kitchen Portuguese), which was learnt by domestics or others in the employ of urban whites, and which served as the city's vehicular language for some time (Penvenne 1995).

While the workers' encounters with Portuguese were determined by structures of control and humiliation, acquisition and use of African languages took place in contexts of intimacy and resistance outside of the formal, public sphere of white citizenship.[7] The indigenous worker of the time crafted powerful genres of lament, expressions of anger and resistance, specifically in the form of work songs, such as the following:

> You crazy little white man, you are seeing ghosts, little white man. We've worked for you a long time, but you don't dare trust us, little white man.
> (quoted in Penvenne 1995: 60)

These forms developed out of a sense of protest – a linguistic manifestation of Scott's 'weapons of the weak' (Scott 1985), challenging the interaction order (Goffman 1967) of the status quo.

contradictions at the end of colonialism

From the turn of the century, the nature of bilingualism as a social construct was determined by two primary competing, and even contradictory tendencies, namely the increasing advance of African languages into the spheres of the public and modern, on the one hand, and renewed and fervent attempts to protect these spheres for Portuguese, on the other. Examples of

African languages encroaching into the public, civil, sphere, can be seen in the activities of François Pillard and Pastor Muti Kikobelo: Pillard introduced alternative agricultural projects in 1909 to help the African population gain ownership of farms, and Kikobelo founded the 'Home Mission' in 1907 to promote ways of financing homes. Both these organizations were African-language speaking. The Portuguese government's attempts in the mid-1900s to address some of the equity concerns of its African citizens by building a new residential neighbourhood (Xipamanine) for middle class black Africans, meant that African languages were now officially heard in a formal, urban environment. Indirectly, this also served to semiotically constitute urban *space* as African *place*, weakening the historical link between *rural* territoriality and African languages.[8]

In a contrary strand of development, the promotion of Portuguese as the sole language of citizenship and rights gathered momentum, coupled with the insistence that local languages should remain outside of the public sphere. In 1926 and 1929, the passing of two laws, Estatuto Orgánico das Missões Católicas (diplomas 167, 168) prohibited the use of local languages in all mission work. And with the introduction of a new Colonial Act (*Acto Colonial*) in the 1930s, the relationship between the Catholic Church and the state was further strengthened, when the Constitution of 1933 granted the Catholic Church overseas protection by the state (Hedges 1982), an arrangement that was formalized with the Vatican in 1940. The *Estatuto missionario* 1941, title 68, laid down that the Catholic Church would be responsible for schooling of the indigenes and that all teaching was to be in Portuguese (Marshall 1993: 90). The prohibition against use of local languages in education from 1929 generated a great deal of discontent, which resulted in the Portuguese administration publishing a clarification to the effect that the *oral* use of local languages was acceptable, although they were not to be written. This statute reinforced the laws that had already been passed prohibiting the use of local languages in mission work (Estatuto Orgánico das Missões Católicas; diplomas 167, 168). The prohibition against the use of local languages was reinforced and made effective by the requirement that those teaching *indígenas* should have a recognized, primary teaching degree.

Civil society organizations were also active in blocking the use of local languages in the public, modern sphere. A community of literate *mulatos* and blacks, the *Grémio Africano*, originally formed to protest the privileges extended to the increasing influx of white settlers, somewhat paradoxically strongly supported the state's claims for the exclusivity of Portuguese for claims to citizenship. In their eyes, the *Portuguesification* of the indigenous population was a great leap forward on the way to the greater recruitment of the African masses into the ranks of the civilized. The association of Portuguese with literacy was likewise strengthened in this period. As early as 1919, the brothers Albasine started a journal explicitly dealing with issues of racial discrimination called *O Brado Africano* (*African Action*) and founded the *Instituto Negrófilo*, with a similar agenda to *Grémio Africano*. The periodical initially carried a section in Xironga, although this was short lived. In 1931, another African language journal, *Nyeliti ya Miso* (*The Morning Star*), originally published in Tsonga, began to publish exclusively in Portuguese, long before the censorship law of 1937 which was introduced to stifle protest against the fascist Portuguese state put an effective stop to the use of African languages in the media.

What is particularly significant here is that both the *Grémio Africano* and the *Instituto Negrófilo* predominantly comprised *mulatos*, the majority of whom were already relatively privileged *assimilados*. With time, it became clear that these organizations were not so much protesting the evils of colonialism as such as they were rallying to defend their colonial status as second-class citizens and *assimilados* in the face of a growing presence of white settlers. Realizing that their fortunes lay in a stronger association with the colonial state that had granted them 'citizenship' in the first place, the organizations increasingly came to abandon their initial common cause with black Mozambicans. In other words, the racial ambivalence of their position in Mozambican society, and reflected in their citizenship status, found expression in a symbolic ambivalence with respect to language and bilingualism; clearly, the early mobilization around use of African languages and literacy, with its claims to a specific political identity, did not authenticate the experiences of the majority of the *assimilados*. We note then how bilingualism as a social construct is embedded in contesting notions of citizenship and formulations of rights across widely divergent groups of social actors in the religious, political, labour and civil spheres. These contradictions were reproduced in postcoloniality.

bilingualism in postcolonialism

introduction: the 'black man's burden'

Postcolonial states are 'first and foremost products of colonialism' (Ahluwalia 2001: 71), with Ashcroft noting that a 'postcolonial society is a society continually responding in all its myriad ways to the experience of the colonial contact' (cited in ibid: 91). In fact, social change can be seen not so much as a 'transition from one order to another, but as transformation – rearrangement, reconfigurations, and re-combinations that yield a new interweaving of the multiple social logics that are a modern society' (Stark and Brusdzt, cited in Pitcher 2004: 7).

the strong state: the local in the image of the metropole

Postcolonial Mozambique inherited a legacy of colonial bifurcation that divided the customary, rural, traditional and local from the modern, urban and national, separating the colonial subject from the citizen of the 'overseas

Portuguese provinces'. In attending to this legacy, the governing party FRELIMO (Front for the Liberation of Mozambique) initiated an ambitious programme of reconstruction whereby Mozambique was to be transformed into a modern, socialist nation-state populated by an equally modern and socialist Mozambican citizen, the *homen novo*. In essence, the new state attempted to *insert itself* into the population – and seek legitimacy for this insertion – through the formulation of new discourses of development, modernization and identity, which denied the validity of social organization around ethnicity and tribalism, and that aimed to reconfigure traditional colonial subjects into citizens. To this end, FRELIMO initiated a number of tactical reforms that addressed issues of power, such as the construction of communal villages, and state farms, and the nationalization of industry. Most importantly, the new government attempted to revitalize traditional forms of local government around so-called 'dynamo groups', with commissioners/district managers picked from the ranks of the FRELIMO cadres replacing traditional leaders, so-called *regulos* who were seen as co-opted by Portuguese colonialists.

Language came to play an important role in this transformation, as constructions and ideologies of Portuguese and African language bilingualism were plied into the service of modernization, socialism and nationalism. The FRELIMO government saw greater access to Portuguese among the population as an important means to overcome the legacy of bifurcation. Prior to independence in 1975, the revolutionary movement had seized upon Portuguese as an ideologically important part of its struggle (cf. Stroud 1999).[9] In the years following independence, one of the foremost cultural means whereby Mozambique was to be transformed into a modern, nationalist and socialist state was the political crafting of language ideological discourses on Portuguese as a language of nation-building. Initially, the Ministry of Propaganda made much of Portuguese as a harbinger of socialism, as a language appropriated from the enemy and put to work as a tool of consensus and modernization. Forms of Portuguese spoken by the 'masses' (cf. Stroud and Gonçalves 1997) were celebrated as reflecting the revolutionary spirit of liberated Mozambique. A few years into independence, however, the pendulum swung back in favour of European Portuguese as the national norm, as modernization and nation-building now took precedence over the ideological mobilization of the masses. President Samora Machel was quoted in the magazine *Tempo* as saying that

> Mozambicans are really forcing themselves to speak a correct Portuguese and are trying to preserve in a state very close to the norm of Portuguese, because only in this way will it be possible to attain the objectives [planned for] – national unity. (Couto 1981)

With this wording, the President explicitly connected a specific norm of Portuguese – the European one – to the success of the national unification project. We witness, to cite Susan Gal, 'the happy fusion of a circumscribed and internally homogenous language with a similarly configured nation' (Gal 1992: 449), and the political shift from an emphasis on the local to a revaluation of the ex-colonial metropole refigured into discourses on different varieties of Portuguese.

The semiotics of indexicality was also at play in language political discourses at this time. Portuguese texts, embedded in revolutionary wall-paintings, exhorting citizens to *work, study* and *fight*, became the cultural semiotic of the new citizen, *homen novo*. At this time, different ways of speaking Portuguese were referenced against a whole set of moral discourses; throughout the 1980s, official FRELIMO discourse on language textually and pictorially depicted those who spoke a Portuguese riddled with ungrammatical elements and syncretisms as anti-social and contra-revolutionary, beard-stubbled, bottle-toting scoundrels. Hybridity in language became equated with contamination and ignorance, rather than a sign of revolutionary commitment, and Portuguese became increasingly associated with a rhetoric of modernity, anti-traditionalism, urbanization, and co-optation of elites.

African languages (so-called *dialectos*) continued to be entextualized in discourses of local tradition. Furthermore, through semiotic processes of *erasure* (cf. Irvine and Gal 2000) that downplayed the stylistically complex genres of authority in African languages, FRELIMO succeeded in reinforcing the notion that these languages could not be used in the management of political consensus. African languages were depicted as the antithesis to Portuguese and as paradigm cases of disorder and concreteness, associated with ethnic diversity and tribal division that needed to be tamed and disciplined in the interests of national unity.[10] In other words, the governing party took over the semiotic machinery abandoned by the colonial state and spun a new mesh of existing 'social logics' around language. Specifically, a discourse of rights and citizenship discursively carried in Portuguese in the sphere of modernity was opposed to a divisive and local sphere constituted in African languages.

challenges to the state sector: bilingualism in discourses of tradition and alternative modernities

After only a few years in power, the socialist government of Mozambique experienced a crisis of legitimacy that escalated into a violent civil war, resulting in the gradual dissolution of the strong, modern and homogeneous state envisioned at the onset of independence. At the heart of the difficulties lay 'the colonial legacy, an overly ambitious expansionist state with small resources coupled to poorly implemented policies in a planned (command) economy' (Pitcher 2004: 70). External aggression and increasing domestic violence involving the RENAMO (the National Resistance Movement of Mozambique) guerrillas also added to the resulting dismal failure of many promising and well-meaning revolutionary reforms. And FRELIMO's own forced relocations and harsh treatment of traditional authorities did little to endear it to the Mozambican people; they were, in fact, actively countered by a population that often found itself supporting the former *regulos* in the subversion and sabotage of official policies (Pitcher 2004: 98) in protest against the forced relocation of small peasants to collective state farms. At this time, a conflict between the FRELIMO state with its liberal/socialist politics of rights, citizenship and modernity through Portuguesification encountered an alternative 'movement' with roots in a perception of rights and participation as ethnic and collective, and linguistically mediated in local languages and discourses outside of, or alongside, the modern state.

West (2005) argues that much of this alternative modernity is built on traditional African ideals, ideas and principles. Referring to how 'power in Africa has long depended more on wealth in people than wealth in things, that is, more on the cultivation of social relations, and to attract and sustain subordinates through patronage and feeding of the social body', West notes how 'sorcery discourse' comprises one particular language of power among multiple languages of power able to express an 'emergent African political ethics', namely respect for the collectivity (2005). In today's Mozambique, sorcery discourse that emphasizes power subordinated to the collective good provides a powerful political critique of 'unharnessed' neoliberal democracy, which is perceived as the triumph of the insatiable individual over the collective, and equated with an evil type of sorcery.

Applied to language, this position would account for an emerging tendency to remove discourses on language from the public sphere of liberal citizenship, where the very discourse of the rational and disinterested speaker manifesting voice and agency, is replaced by language as the expression of collective voice and authority. The bipartite construction inherited from colonialism (whereby Portuguese was constituted as the language of modernity, while African languages remained local) was premised on a particular idea of governance and liberal citizenship that has increasingly come under general attack.

One expression that this has taken is the use of violence. Although often seen as an illegitimate and extraneous political tool, violence has solid customary roots in Mozambique as a (legitimate) form of political action (cf. Newitt 1995; Sko n.d.). Matters of language were also framed within discourses of violence as a political dynamics. In accordance with FRELIMO's modernist ideologies, the state and its apparatus comprised the main arena for the regulation of language; Portuguese was the legitimate language of state authority, and the language used by nurses, doctors and teachers, as well as by local authorities in their contact with the population. African languages at this time were not accorded official functions at state or government level and were discursively removed from the here-and-now as languages of tradition. Furthermore, the imagining of the nation-state was written into FRELIMO's practices and ideologies of Portuguese. The guerrilla movement RENAMO systematically attacked the state institutions and infrastructures such as schools, hospitals and roads, and murdered teachers and nurses in bursts of violence. The targets of these attacks were the representative institutions and agents of urban modernity – frequently women. As Portuguese comprised such a central metaphor for urban modernity and citizenship, it was inevitable that Portuguese and its speakers were also compromised. In traditionalist stances, bilingualism carried heavy connotations of conflict at this time, and in areas of the country controlled by RENAMO, local African languages were mandatory and there are reports claiming that RENAMO would only spare the lives of ambushed civilians if they could prove mastery of local vernaculars. With Mamdani (1996), we can interpret this as a failure of postcolonial democratization and the search for local and indigenous solutions to agency and voice.

There were, however, competing representations of African languages that saw them as both traditional and available as instruments of political modernity at the same time. Several articles in the weekly magazine *Tempo* by the author and politician Honwana argued for the importance of maintaining local languages as vibrant and viable languages of community and politics, suggesting that loss of language would involve loss of identity and rootlessness. This is an expression of the postcolonial precursor to an ecological stance on multilingualism and diversity compatible with a discourse of linguistic human rights.

retraditionalization in the modernization of mozambique: bilingualism in competing governmentalities

In the aftermath of the erosion of the socialist project, Mozambique has come to occupy a position on the periphery of the world economy; its citizens have increasingly come to rely on whatever economic, political and social mechanisms that are available to reduce economic uncertainty, such as informal markets, lineage networks and religious organizations. Processes of *re-traditionalization* have contributed to this ongoing realignment of the power of the state in relation to other social and civil forces, as have latter-day market economic reforms that have reinforced the tendency towards a 'contraction of social space occupied by State ideology' (Nugent 2005). These developments have been phrased in competing, *alternative* narratives of modernity incorporating fundamentally different ideas on the relationship between state, citizen and civil society (cf. Comaroff 1998), succinctly captured in the notion of the re-traditionalization of the African state (Chabal and Daloz 1999). Here, political power is weakly institutionalized, personalized and particularistic, organized around patronage, and linked to particular ideas of legitimacy and accountability of a patrimonial character (cf. Stroud 2002: 259). Political leaders gain their political mileage on the basis of how well they project a sense of personal wealth and importance, at the same time that they are expected to act as benevolent providers to their constituencies. A notable aspect of this alternative modernity is that customary authorities enjoy a renewed and extensive local support (Pitcher 2004: 99), which together with lineage networks, comprise the primary means through which rural people mediate their experience of the state.[11]

All these current complexities and contradictions between postcolonial state and various levels of civil society have altered the nature of 'state', 'market', 'civil society', and the 'urban–rural' divide, and affected conventional understandings of the meaning of citizenship. Practically, this can be seen in developments such as a renewed tenacity of the institution of chieftancy, and acknowledgement of 'the importance of cultural symbols, practices and the invention of tradition as mechanisms in mediation of power' (ibid: 23). Today, with assistance from the Ford Foundation and later USAID money, Mozambican authorities are actively exploring new forms of local government that build on traditional forms of authority, and in the area of education, a curriculum focus on the local and the traditional is winning in-roads in the form of experimental bilingual programmes. Where once ethnicity was anathema to the state, it now appears as one important resource for the state to engage with the rural population. Likewise, churches have become increasingly politically vocal to the extent that they offer important networks of welfare and support to their constituencies.

Not surprisingly, the changing nature of the state–citizen relationship finds expression in ideologies and practices of bilingualism. As political power has become more open to diverse voices, so have local economies of communication grown in importance. The framing of African languages as local languages of politics has become an essential semiotic for the decentralization and multi-plication of political agency throughout Mozambican society. The strong links between religion and language carried over from colonial times (cf. Cruz e Silva 2001), and reinforced through the process of retraditionalization and Mozambique's peripheral place in world economy, is also actively nurtured in today's context. Most of the church services are conducted in local languages (e.g. Methodists use Changana/Citswa; Presbyterians Ronga, although the Universal Church conducts its charismatic services in Brazilian Portuguese). Given the traditional importance of religion as a centring institution for African languages, it is not surprising that competition and conflict around language should appear most forcefully in the religious sphere. A fairly recent instance of such civil society resistance to state regulation of African languages was a violent protest by speakers of Chope against the exclusive use of Nyanja as a liturgical language.

In the realm of formal politics, the move towards decentralization, and in particular, the advent of a multiparty politics, has contributed to the increasing political importance of local African languages in official arenas. Election campaigns are now also conducted in local African languages, and linguistic virtuosity in mastering many local languages has become an important resource in political display. The use of African languages also contributes more widely to the vernacularization and popularization, that is, democratization of Mozambican politics. In the sphere of civil society, vernacular literacy programmes have been used actively by rural women to create a private and gendered space for themselves as they no long have to rely on male literacy brokers for help with their written communications (cf. Stroud 2002; Veloso 2002), and are free to broach topics that were previously taboo. Growing civil society involvement in matters of language can be observed in uses of Portuguese among different segments of the population to mobilize opinion and express political agency, often in metaphorically code-switched interactions with African languages, accomplishing rhetorical effects that are perceived as challenging conventional language meanings and values (cf. Stroud 2004). Although these uses transgress against norms of good, authoritative usage of Portuguese, it is precisely this transgression that gives high agency to those who use such strategies. This is because the *performative* (Butler 1999) construction of meaning relies upon the 'inherent indeterminacy of symbolic structures' (McNay 2000), a condition which allows individuals to reproduce, resist or transcend constraints of social in their quotidian practices as individuals are never completely determined by acts of speech (cf. Stroud 2004: 150).

In this period of competing and retraditionalizing 'modernities', the prime characteristic of bilingualism as a social construct is the manifold contestations over who shall regulate and control discourses around languages – the Church, state, NGOs (foreign as well as domestic) or grassroots organizations. The ensuing complexity of civil and political society, and a more complex figuration of citizenship in modern Mozambique, has thus given rise to a proliferation of practices and perceptions of bilingualism.

discussion

Throughout the establishment and development of colonial citizenship, Portuguese coexisted in a hierarchical relationship to Mozambican languages. This was bolstered by an ideological and religious discourse that mapped ideas of culture and civilized humanity onto essentialist notions of language, race and territoriality, and by principles of governmentality that circumscribed the limits, and linguistic requirements, of citizenship for the native African. Changes in the political economy, domestic reform and continual resistance to Portuguese rule resulted in a gradual shift in conceptions of race and citizenship, and to changing practices and perceptions of bilingualism, including shifts in ideas of significance associated with the different languages. The most important legacy of colonial development with respect to bilingualism was the crystallization of two distinct tendencies, one where Portuguese was firmly linked to citizenship and rights to the exclusion of other languages, and one where local vernaculars were increasingly being promoted in public arenas as languages of civil society and (racially inclusive) citizenship.

In ways similar to the colonial state, postcoloniality has grappled with contending discourses on the position of Portuguese and African languages vis-à-vis discourses of tradition and modernity, the local and metropole, and how rights and citizenship ought to be mediated in a nation-state. Whereas the official tendency in the transitional Marxist state was to identify Portuguese with modernity, socialism and nationalism (nation-state building), and to disengage with the local African languages as reactionary (while nevertheless attempting to raise to prominence the 'worker' and Mozambican who spoke these languages), today's Mozambique is increasingly constructing local African languages as officially valuable.

This development has gone hand in hand with the weakening of central control and a re-shuffling of civil or social forces in Mozambique in ongoing attempts to find new political forms. Among other developments, the play of ethnicities tied to language, rather than being in opposition to government, has come to define its *modus operandi*. This means that besides the two discursively imagined constructions of bilingualism in relation to citizenship, rights and public arenas that accompanied the colonial phase of Mozambican history, a third discursive construction of bilingualism has developed in postcoloniality, which positions local languages (and the ethnicities and collectivities they represent) as outside of and parallel to a civil and political society built on individual rights and a notion of liberal citizenship, in favour of the collectivity (cf. West 2005). This discourse has developed in tandem with the deconstruction of the strong state and the growing reliance on religious and 'traditional' forms of organization to provide alternative markets of support for an increasingly disempowered people.

Situating bilingualism as a social construct in this way illustrates the workings of *linguistic citizenship* (Stroud 2001, 2004), an attempt at a comprehensive *political* stance on language that suggests that attention to the various forms that the relationship between state, citizen, identity, and (civil) society is linguistically mediated and organized, as well as contested and transformed through struggles over language is central to an adequate understanding of language in society and history. Linguistic citizenship focuses attention on the historical, local and culturally contingent nature of these processes, as well as the shifting significance of language in citizenship across time and space, and across different political and economic structures (Stroud and Heugh 2004). It encourages reflection on how perceptions and practices of language position individuals in the nexus of the state, market and civil society, that is, to language as a political and economic *field* in the sense of Pierre Bourdieu (1991), where what is at stake is who gets to define the value of (a specific) language, with implications for how voice and agency are distributed over varieties and languages. Developments in the refiguration of local languages and Portuguese have thus gone hand in hand with the decentralization of the Mozambican state and the shift in the balance of forces from a strong state to a more diverse cacophony of social voices.

conclusion

In this chapter, I have argued that different ideas about languages and their linguistic relationships, both functional and formal, as manifested in contesting notions of bilingualism situate varieties/languages in (competing) hierarchical economies of value, determine what languages should/can be mastered, by whom, and for what functions and purposes, and constrain modes of access to, and acquisition of, each variety. I have also attempted to show how a perspective on bilingualism as a political and economic field reveals how the organization of citizenship in societies is mediated by a historically variable sociopolitical and cultural organization of language practices and beliefs about language and language learning.

notes

1. It would be more correct to speak of colonialisms here, rather than colonialism, in recognition of the very different manifestations that colonial exploitation took in different parts of the world and at different times.
2. This is not to deny the many differences between different colonial regimes with important consequences for subsequent postcolonial developments (cf. Nugent 2005).
3. This was in direct response to a requirement in conjunction with the internationalization of African imperialism in the 1880s that Portugal develop Mozambique as a bona fide colony in an attempt to break the power of the private companies.
4. The system of *indiginato* remained in place until 1961 when it was finally dismantled.
5. Meeuwis (2001) in particular points out how many of the linguistic battles fought between Catholics and Protestants in the Belgian Congo were manifestations of metropolitan language ideological battles raging at the centre.
6. The category of *assimilado* was abolished in 1974.
7. This did not apply to the 'languages' that missionary linguists had constructed. In fact, local resistance to local forms would be an exciting topic to study further.
8. African languages began increasingly to encode differences of socioeconomic status *within* the urban metropolis; migrant workers returning to their rural homes in provincial Gaza took with them Xironga, the main language of the colonial capital Lorenço Marques (often only heavily Xironga-accented Xichangana), as Xironga was widely perceived to be a language of great status (Feliciano Chimbutane, personal communication,).
9. The important role of Portuguese as the language of the independence movement may have been a political reconstruction of the true state of affairs to support FRELIMO's use of Portuguese in nation-building. Local languages (also Swahili) were often used in the liberation camps. However, much of the FRELIMO elite was educated in Portugal and there had existed a number of Lusophone resistance groups prior to FRELIMO emerging as the most important one.
10. As pointed out by Pitcher, 'Socialism had to compete ideologically with nationalism and modernization: alongside discourse praising "workers", there existed a parallel discourse denouncing backwardness and applauding rational man, and a nationalist discourse condemning tribalism and emphasizing unity' (Pitcher 2004:

71). This ambiguity comes across clearly with respect to language debates at this time – African heritage praised, but African languages seen as backward.
11. It is debatable exactly how 'traditional' these structures of decision-making mutual support are. Chabal and Deloz (1999) argue that many 'traditional' structures actually predate colonialism and that the effects of colonialism are often exaggerated. It is, however, indisputable, that European colonizers did introduce forms of leadership that they considered traditional, but that had little to do with the real pre-colonial situation.

references

Ahluwalia, Pal (2001). *Politics and Post-colonial Theory. African Inflections.* London and New York: Routledge.

Blommaert, Jan (ed.) (1999). *Language Ideological Debates.* Berlin and New York: Mouton de Gruyter.

——— (2004). *Discourse Analysis.* Cambridge: Cambridge University Press.

Bourdieu, Pierre (1991). *Language and Symbolic Power.* Cambridge, MA: Harvard University Press.

Bowen, M. (2000). *The State against the Peasantry: Rural Struggles in Colonial and Postcolonial Mozambique.* Charlottesville and London: University of Virginia Press.

Butler, Judith (1999). Performativity's social magic. In Richard Shusterman (ed.), *Bourdieu: A Critical Reader*, pp. 113–28. Oxford: Blackwell Publishers.

Chabal, Patrick, and J.-P. Daloz (1999). *Africa Works: Disorder as a Political Instrument.* Oxford: James Currey.

Comaroff, John L. (1998). Reflections on the colonial state in South Africa and elsewhere: Factions, fragments, facts and fictions. *Social Identities* 4(3): 321–61.

Couto, Mia (1981). Ainda problema da linguas: Submissao cultural. *Tempo*, 18 January.

Cruz e Silva, Teresa (2001). *Igrejas Protestantes e Consciência Política no Sul de Moçambique: O caso da Missão Suíça (1930–1974).* Maputo: CIEDIMA

Errington, Joseph (2001). Colonial Linguistics. *Annual Review of Anthropology* 30: 19–39.

Fabian, Johannes (1986). *Language and Colonial Power.* Berkeley and Los Angeles: University of California Press.

Gal, Susan (1992). Multiplicity and contention among ideologies: A commentary. In P. Kroskrity, B. Schieffelin and K. Woolard (eds), *Language Ideologies.* Special Issue of *Pragmatics* 2, pp. 445–50.

Gal, Susan, and Kathryn Woolard (2001). *Language and Publics: The Making of Authority.* Manchester: St Jerome Publishing.

Goffman, E. (1967). *Interaction Ritual: Essays on Face-to-Face Behaviour.* New York: Doubleday Anchor.

Harries, Patrick (1995). The historical origin of standard Tsonga in southern Africa. In Raj Mesthrie (ed.), *Language and Social History: Studies in South African Sociolinguistics*, pp. 154–75. Cape Town and Johannesburg: David Philip.

Hedges, David (1982). *Education, Missions and the Political Ideology of Assimilation 1930–1960.* Maputo: Eduardo Mondlane University.

Irvine, J., and S. Gal (2000). Language ideology and linguistic differentiation. In P. Kroskrity (ed.), *Regimes of Language: Ideologies, Politics and Identities*, pp. 35–83. Oxford: James Currey.

Johnstone, Anton (1989). *Study, Produce and Combat! Education and the Mozambican State*. Stockholm: Institute of Education. Akademi Press.

Makoni, Sinfree, and Alastair Pennycook (2007). *Disinventing and Reconstituting Languages*. Clevedon: Multilingual Matters.

Mamdani, Mahmood (1996). *Citizen and Subject: Contemporary Africa and the Legacy of Late Colonialism*. Princeton, NJ: Princeton University Press.

Marshall, Judith (1993). *Literacy, Power and Democracy in Mozambique. The Governance of Learning from Colonization to the Present*. San Francisco: Westview Press.

McNay, L. (2000). *Gender and Agency: Reconfiguring the Subject in Feminist Social Theory*. Malden, MA: Polity Press.

Meeuwis, Michael (2001). Missions and linguistic choice making. The case of the Capuchin in the Ubengi mission (Belgian Congo), 1910–1945. In *African Language and Culture in Historical Perspective* 33: 158–88.

Mühlhäusler, Peter (1996). *Linguistic Ecology: Language Change and Linguistic Imperialism in the Pacific Region*. London and New York: Routledge.

Newitt, Malyn (1995). *A History of Mozambique*. Johannesburg: Witwatersrand University Press.

Nugent, Paul (2005). *Africa since Independence*. New York: Palgrave Macmillan.

Pavlenko, Aneta, and Adrian Blackledge (eds) (2004). *Negotiation of Identities in Multilingual Contexts*. Clevedon: Multilingual Matters.

Pavlenko, Aneta, and Ingrid Piller (2001). New directions in the study of multilingualism, second language learning and gender. In A. Pavlenko, A. Blackledge, I. Piller and M. Teutsch-Dwyer (eds), *Multilingualism, Second Language Learning and Gender*, pp. 17–52. Berlin and New York: Mouton de Gruyter.

Pennvenne, Jeanne Marie (1995). *African Workers and Colonial Racism. Mozambican Strategies and Struggles in Lourenço Marques, 1877–1962*. London: James Currey.

Pitcher, Anne (2004). *Transforming Mozambique. The Politics of Privatization 1975–2000*. Cambridge: Cambridge University Press.

Scott, David (1995). Colonial governmentality. *Social Text* 13(2): 191–220.

—— (1996). The aftermaths of sovereignty. Postcolonial criticism and the claim of political modernity. *Social Text* 14(3): 1–28.

Scott, J.C. (1985). *Weapons of the Weak: Everyday Forms of Peasant Resistance*. New Haven: Yale University Press.

Sko, E. Lee (n.d.) The pragmatics of language and violence in Mozambique's postcolonial war, 1975–1992. Paper presented at the University of Chicago.

Stroud, Christopher (1999). Portuguese as ideology and politics in Mozambique: Semiotic (re)constructions of a postcolony. In Jan Blommaert (ed.), *Language Ideological Debates*, pp. 343–80. Berlin and New York: Mouton de Gruyter.

—— (2001). African mother-tongue programmes and the politics of language: Linguistic citizenship versus linguistic human rights. *Journal of Multilingual and Multicultural Development* 22(4): 359–5.

—— (2002). Framing Bourdieu socioculturally: Alternative forms of linguistic legitimacy in postcolonial Mozambique. *Multilingua* 21: 247–73.

—— (2003). Postmodernist perspectives on local languages: African mother tongue education in times of globalization. *International Journal of Bilingual Education and Bilingualism* 6(1): 17–36.

—— (2004). The performativity of codeswitching. *International Journal of Bilingualism* 8(2): 145–66.

Stroud, Christopher, and Kathleen Heugh (2004). Language rights and linguistic citizenship. In Jane Freeland and Donna Patrick (eds), *Language Rights and Language*

Survival: Sociolinguistic and Sociocultural Perspectives, pp. 191–218. Manchester, UK: St Jerome Publishing.

Stroud, Christopher, and Perpétua Gonçalves (eds) (1997). *Panorama do Português Oral de Maputo. Vol. 1. Objectivos e metodos.* Maputo: Eduardo Mondlane University Press.

Veloso, Teresa (2002). Becoming literate in Mozambique: The early stages in Sena (Cisena) and Shangaan (Xichangana). *Perspectives in Education* 20(1): 79–96.

Wenger, Étienne (1998). *Communities of Practice.* Cambridge: Cambridge University Press.

West, Harry (2005). 'Govern yourselves!' Democracy and carnage in northern Mozambique. Unpublished paper, Department of Anthropology, School of Oriental and African Studies, University of London.

3
minority language movements
alexandra jaffe

introduction

This chapter draws on data from the French island of Corsica as a springboard for the discussion of bilingual practices and language ideologies and attitudes concerning bilingualism in minority language contexts. Contexts such as the Corsican one raise interesting questions about how bilingualism is defined and experienced, both at the individual and the societal level. This is because the processes of language domination, shift and revitalization found in such contexts both disrupt and make explicit connections between code(s) and identity(ies). This approach requires a historical perspective that examines the social, cultural, political, ideological and economic forces that make and unmake bilingual speakers. Building on the previous chapter, this chapter will look at the impact of processes of language domination on minority language practice and ideology, and crucially, on the discourses and practices that arise out of minority language revitalization movements that attempt to counteract language domination and dominant language ideologies by turning dominant language ideologies against the dominant group which invented them in the first place (essentially by accepting the legitimacy of the idea that language, nation and state do indeed coincide, just not in the particular configuration the dominant state prefers).

This approach raises a number of questions about how the bilingual person or society is imagined, and how the relationship between these imagined speakers and membership, community, and citizenship are conceptualized at various levels (local, regional, national, supranational). In minority language contexts such as the Corsican one, we find that bilingualism can be a problematic category or label, because the bilingualism that characterizes the sociolinguistic landscape in these contexts is always *unbalanced*. Viewed within the framework of dominant language ideologies, such an imbalance poses problems of legitimacy and authenticity for minority language movements, since legitimate and authorized identities are typically associated either

50

with a monolingual norm or an ideal of balanced bilingualism. This issue of legitimacy has obvious implications for the understanding of bilingualism in other contexts, in particular, the extent to which bilingualism is practised or imagined as two separate monolingualisms (linked to two separate identities) vs. as a potentially uneven mixture of codes, practices and competencies distributed across different individuals and different moments and domains of social action.

At the same time, the last ten or fifteen years have witnessed a shift away from bilingualism-as-cultural-deficit towards bilingualism-as-added-value in discourses about what it means to be bilingual in a minority language context. In part, this is related to the spread of academic arguments about the general value of bilingualism. This new element of public discourse (and in some cases, educational policy) has been a resource that minority language activists have been able to use in the defence and promotion of minority language bilingualism. The shift is also related to changing political, cultural and economic conditions. On the political side, ethnic minority language movements that began in the 1960s and 1970s now have a certain maturity, and have met at least some of their goals of minority language legitimation. In some cases, these movements have secured not just recognition, but considerable political and economic resources from the state, and have successfully created significant cultural and economic markets for minority language use. Changing political and economic circumstances have also provided new frameworks that go beyond the local and the national, and that valorize multilingualism and create markets for the expression of 'authentic' minority cultural and linguistic identities. These discursive shifts, however, should not be taken as uniform or complete; in fact, what we find are complex discursive fields that show traces of both dominant discourses about language tied to the nationalist frameworks that dominated minority language movements for so long, and new discourses in which bilingualism is viewed as a cognitive and cultural benefit.

bilingualism as a deficit

the experience of language shift

In the literature on language contact and change in multilingual communities, the term 'language shift' is often used as a shorthand to describe changes in practices of language socialization and use that occur as a result of language domination that lead to progressively fewer children acquiring the minority language as their first language, in the home. It is worth pointing out that the very notion of language 'shift' (and the potential for language 'death') is linked to ideological constructs. The first is an ideology of language as a bounded, autonomous code; the term 'language shift' de-emphasizes language practice and human agency. The second is a modernist nationalist ideology of language and identity, in which individual and community identity is harnessed to a single language. The image of 'shift' is an image of a community transferring its allegiances and completely transforming its practices, whereas in fact it is clear that language domination, contact and change give rise to linguistic practices, attitudes and forms of identification that are far more mixed and complex than the term 'language shift' indicates. At the same time, in minority language contexts, experiences of linguistic change are also shaped in significant ways by the language ideologies embedded in the notion of 'shift'; these ideologies also structure the forms that minority linguistic and cultural mobilization take.

In this light, we can ask the question: how is 'bilingualism' as an ideological construct experienced and defined within the ideological framework of 'shift'? In the first phases of language shift, bilingualism is associated with, experienced as and often labelled as a deficiency and a hindrance to the development of monolingual competence in the dominant language. This is particularly true for minority language speakers whose first major exposure to the dominant language is in school, particularly when the school devalues and/or prohibits the use of the minority language. School policies and practices often treat the bilingualism of the minority language-speaking child as a 'problem', because linguistic competence in the minority language is not valued. This was certainly the case in Corsica in the first half of the twentieth century. Corsican-speaking schoolchildren were told that their job in school was to acquire French, and that it was not at all important to retain Corsican, which was typically labelled a 'patois'. Parents were advised that their use of Corsican in the home was an impediment to their children's success in learning French, which was a precondition for becoming educated and socially mobile. With varying degrees of success, a proportion of these parents tried to avoid using Corsican with their children, despite the fact that they had had no formal access to French themselves. In addition to these very explicit language hierarchies, children were evaluated with reference to school literacies – to French in its most formal and authoritative guise. This exacerbated the symbolic and political gap between French and Corsican (as an unwritten code without a literary tradition), and made it all the more impossible for children to mobilize their Corsican language competencies in the service of their school careers. Corsican in the school thus appeared in only two guises: first, as a code used in interactions in the informal, backstage and non-official spheres; and second, as 'interference' in French. Older Corsicans I interviewed reported getting back their school papers with red pencil marks around 'errors' that were glossed as 'corsicanisms'. Out in the public sphere, these language contact phenomena were routinely understood as problems of competence and were sources of linguistic insecurity. This insecurity is reflected in the ambivalence and tension associated with jokes and comedy routines which feature Corsican-influenced French. On the one hand, bilingual competence allows Corsicans to savour this kind of humour, which indexes shared practices and histories. At the same time, those histories carry the still sharp memory of stigma and insecurity.[1]

I want to suggest that these kinds of collective memories of a devalued bilingualism in the context of language domination and shift influence the discursive status of bilingualism represented in the first phases of minority language revitalization. The first influence can be seen in the relatively greater focus in early discourses aimed at reversing language shift on a lost minority language *mono*lingualism. That is, after language shift has progressed to the point where there is 'tip' in the direction of the dominant language, the kinds of bilingual practice and contact phenomena that people have direct experience with are often seen as inherently unbalanced sociolinguistic stages implicated in a progressive process of minority language attrition. This helps to explain why, in the discourse of minority language loss, authentic identity is not linked to a bilingual community of practice; it is anchored in the pre-shift society that existed before the economic, ideological and educational pressures that led to language shift.

Secondly, there is an influence on how the term bilingualism is used. It is *not* used to describe the dual language competencies of the past or present. Rather, in early sociolinguistic and political discourses it appears as a desired state of social and political parity between the two languages – as a state of *balance* that contrasts with collective experiences of ongoing language shift.

the political context of language revitalization

The kinds of experiences I have described are not, of course, the only reason that minority language movements like the Corsican one have often made monolingual minority language competence the centrepiece of their discourses about language and identity. But the monolingual norm accompanying the language hierarchies enforced in institutions like the school is a point of overlap with the political-ideological pressures brought to bear on minority language movements. That is, dominant ideological frameworks prescribe that only *one* language can be a legitimate marker of a given community. This has been most forcefully expressed in Corsican nationalist discourse, for example with a slogan 'Morta a lingua, mortu u populu' [the death of the language is the death of the people] that will be familiar to anyone who has studied or participated in other minority language movements, such as those in Brittany, Wales, Catalunya, Ireland, and elsewhere. This of course presents a dilemma for the representation of the minority language in the moment of crisis – that is, when language shift is well underway: that shift can be viewed as undermining claims to cultural identity and political autonomy. One response in nationalist discourse has been to (selectively) disconnect contemporary linguistic use/competence from cultural identity and to make claims on linguistic ownership and rights based on collective history. So, for example, in a nationalist manifesto from the early 1990s,

Corsican is represented as the sole language of Corsican cultural identity and as a 'privileged form of internal communication' (Unione di u Populu Corsu 1991: 172). In this line of argument, individual bilingualism constitutes matter out of place in the imagination of the homogeneity and unity of both dominant (external) and minority communities.

Another response in early nationalist discourse is to acknowledge the rupture of the language–culture link, but to locate the cause – and thus the responsibility – for this rupture to processes of domination coming from *outside* Corsican society: specifically, the assimilationist policies associated with 'internal colonialism'. This argument was widely promoted in France by Robert Lafont, an Occitan activist, and can be seen in one of the earliest Corsican nationalist manifestos, a document published in 1971 by the Front régionaliste corse [Corsican Regionalist Front, or FRC]. In a section entitled 'Le grand dérangement culturel'[2] [The great cultural disruption] Corsicans are described as having been alienated from their language through French cultural and linguistic policy. In this narrative of contact and domination, there is no mention of bilingualism, because bilingualism is conceived of as a *balanced* condition. Corsican subjects are described as having been led by assimilationist policies to 'n'avoir plus d'autre langue que le français' [not have any other language but French] and of having been convinced that this was good and right (FRC 1971: 55). This French, moreover, is described as the 'sous-français des colonisés, sorte de créole corse...[un] monstre philologique' [substandard French of the colonized, a sort of Corsican creole...[a] philological monster] (ibid: 54). Thus the subjects of language domination are not represented as bilingual, but as doubly disabled, *lacking* both the language of culture and the language of wider communication.

If we look at the first language legislation brought to the floor in the Assemblée de Corse (Corsican Regional Assembly), we find the emphasis on Corsican as the legitimate and authentic language of cultural identity, a recognition of its fragility, and the definition of bilingualism as a state of political parity to be achieved (at least in part) through policy. The text of the earliest motion on language policy (passed in 1983) read:

> The Assembly, having officially recognized the fundamental role of the Corsican language as the cement of culture, and of the urgency of putting into practice a concrete policy of cultural reappropriation which translates into the desire of the Assembly to give the people its language back...has decided to commit to a policy of bilingualism to be implemented in a triennial plan...from now on, the use of the Corsican language will be generalized in the names of places, villages, towns, in the context of news and audiovisual training, as well as in certain public documents. (Assemblée de Corse 1984)

To sum up, in this moment in Corsican language activism, no one labels the uses of Corsican and French circulating in society as 'bilingualism'. Bilingualism is associated exclusively with parity of status: this is represented as a desired outcome of Corsican language revitalization. The image of a monolingual Corsican world – or at least monolingual-like Corsican competence – plays a large role in the representation of the possibility of achieving a balanced bilingual condition.

shifts in the discourse of defence of corsican: language shift – and french – acknowledged as elements of identity

In the late 1980s, two documents by the Corsican Assembly's consultative Council on Education, Culture and Environment (CCECV) attempted to shift the nature of the discourse about Corsican and its defence. The first was titled 'Lingua Matria'; this was followed by a resolution brought before the Assembly on 'Coofficiality' of the two languages. The title of the first text stood in implicit opposition to the notion of the 'Lingua Materna', or 'Mother Tongue' which was often invoked in public discourse about the language. The image of the 'Mother Tongue' is clearly connected with essentialist perspectives on Corsican language and identity, and implicitly proposes native-language competence as an element of that identity. In contrast, 'matria' – the feminine version of 'patria' [Fatherland] retains some of the intimacy of the feminine, but shifts the emphasis away from the household and into the political domain. The key players are no longer family members but co-citizens; attachments are not primordial but social, collective and consensual.

The authors of the document were very explicit about the reasons for this deliberate effort to change the terms of public discourse and advocacy of Corsican, writing that 'Corsican is no longer the first language acquired...the language is neither maternal nor foreign, but a creative source of identity' (CCECV 1989: 15).

'Lingua Matria' thus acknowledged that Corsican bilingualism was unbalanced, but did not idealize either a past monolingualism or a future balanced bilingualism. Both of these documents acknowledge French not just as a language of past domination, but as a permanent part of the Corsican communicative repertoire. Bilingualism is thus represented as a contemporary condition rather than a goal of language policy. Both documents also recognize the historical and cultural importance of language as a marker of identity, but do not associate being Corsican exclusively with speaking Corsican; rather, the Corsican citizen is a bilingual one. In other words, the validation of bilingual practice in contemporary Corsican society goes hand in hand with a reworking of dominant ideologies of monolingualism and legitimate identity.

We see this in these documents with the introduction of a new, multilingual and international framework for understanding the value of bilingualism. In the 'Lingua Matria' document, this was done with the incorporation of an English-language version of the text. The textual parity of the three languages symbolically positioned Corsican as legitimate. But it also subtly disrupted the imbalance of power between Corsican and French by introducing a language dominating French on the international scene. In the Coofficiality Resolution, there is an explicit reference to the multilingual imperative of European citizenship: the implicit message is that French monolingualism is not enough.

In addition to the new framework for understanding language, power and identity provided by the European context, the discursive shifts and their language ideological implications expressed in these documents can be understood with respect to gains made by Corsican language activists during the decade of the 1980s, and their changing recognition and understanding of the implications of the advanced state of Corsican language shift for public acceptance of a language planning agenda. By the end of the 1980s, Corsican language planners could count on a greater public acceptance of the legitimacy of Corsican as a language, and as a language with a place in high-status public spheres. Secondly, there was a growing pragmatic acceptance of the fact of French language dominance as a permanent condition of Corsican society. The monolingual Corsican past was becoming further and further removed from people's experience. Language planners were also becoming aware that 'traditional' criteria of Corsican linguistic authenticity had the potential to alienate rather than mobilize younger generations of speakers because a Corsican monolingual standard devalued language contact phenomena, mixed usage and partial competencies.

the emergence of bilingualism as the 'value added' centrepiece of new educational policy

The Resolution on Coofficiality was voted down in the Assembly. Transcripts of the deliberations and the text of the final decision show that Assembly members were unable to let go of an essentialist view of language and cultural identity or acknowledge the extent of language shift. The Assembly also refused to acknowledge bilingualism as a social issue, preferring to keep the focus on individual bilingualism and its voluntary nature (for more discussion see Jaffe 1999: 184). However, the CCECV's proposals anticipated changes that were already in the making in both Corsican and French society that validated Corsican language competence as a positive benefit for French-speaking Corsicans, both as an expression of Corsican identity and as a bridge to other languages and cultures. These included academic and media partnerships with Italy.

The Corsican Assembly also made some significant strides in their negotiations with the French state over Corsican language education. Beginning in the 1990s, the Assembly was reconstituted as a 'Territorial Collectivity', charged with developing multi-year planning contracts negotiated with the French state that covered a range of issues including education. The 1994–97 contract included several important initiatives on Corsican language education. One of these exemplified the positioning of French–Corsican bilingualism as a bridge to neighbouring cultures and language, by establishing 'Mediterranean' sections in which children studied Corsican along with another Romance language (Italian or Spanish). The most dramatic development to come out of this plan was the establishment of four bilingual primary schools, and a commitment to develop bilingual education on the island. Today, just over ten years later, there is a bilingual track for each middle school (Collège) catchment area, and the Academy is working to create bilingual middle and high school tracks to serve the children coming through the bilingual programme.

Over the last ten years, new and positive discourses about bilingualism have developed both in French policy documents and in the positions articulated by bilingual teachers and the administrators responsible for Corsican bilingual education in the Corsican Academy (Académie de Corse) and by researchers and teachers training bilingual teachers at the Corsican teacher training institute. In the following section, I examine some of the key themes in these new discourses about bilingualism, selectively illustrating them with data from French Ministry of Education documents from 1995 and 2001, in the Corsican Academy's 1998 Charter for bilingual education, in Corsican Assembly language planning documents from 1997 and 2005, and in the proceedings of a conference on bilingual education organized in 2004 by A Scioliligua, a Corsican bilingual teachers' association.

The aim, in the presentation of data from this corpus, is both to provide concrete and contextually specific evidence of the shape of new discourses about minority bilingualism and to relate significant parameters of the Corsican context to those that shape other situations of minority language promotion.

key themes in the discourse of bilingual value

the old and the new:
the 'new' bilingual acknowledged but in a framework of 'balance'

In earlier political discourses of ethnic minorities, the non- or semi-speaker of the minority language undermines the community's identity claims (although of course they also legitimize claims to resources and rights on the grounds that without them the community will disappear). Over time, however, institutional gains, coupled with the acknowledgement of language shift have led to an increased attention on the linguistic individual, who has the potential to *become* bilingual by *adding* the minority language, largely through education. It is striking that in all of the documents I reviewed, there is only one indirect reference to bilingual education as a tool for creating parity of political or social status between the two languages, and this reference was in a French Ministry of Education rather than a Corsican text.

Advocating adding a minority language to the individual's repertoire does not invalidate the learner's partial competencies, but it does retain an ideal of 'balance' in the final outcome. In Corsica, this goal is articulated both by the French Ministry of Education, and by the Corsican Academy. The 2001 Ministry of Education Bulletin Officiel (BO) 33 on bilingual education in regional languages states that 'the final objective is to help the child acquire a parallel mastery of the two codes with a minimum of interferences between them'. The Corsican Academy Charter for bilingual schools asserts that its goal is to 'lead the students to a balanced bilinguality' which is defined as 'competencies in both languages that, if not completely equivalent are at least comparable, in all domains of oral and then written use' (Académie de Corse 1998: 1). Most recently, the Corsican Assembly approved a document that identifies balanced individual and societal bilingualism as a long-term objective of Corsican language education (Assemblée de Corse 2005).

This discursive emphasis on balance does several things. First of all, it represents balanced individual bilingualism as a readily attainable goal, for which the minority status of one of the languages is not a significant impediment. It is a goal, furthermore, that can be largely met through the medium of schooling. From a linguistic point of view, both of these assumptions can be challenged. From a sociolinguistic perspective, the former flies in the face of minority language communities' experiences of language shift. It is extremely difficult for the individual to have 'balanced' competencies in two languages when those languages have vastly different statuses and uses in the surrounding society. Secondly, much remains unexamined with respect to the social meanings of 'balance'. Balanced academic competencies may have currency in some social contexts and for some social actors, but 'balance' may be assessed with reference to very different language skills in other situations. There is also a more or less explicit focus on balance as measured against the formal properties of discrete linguistic systems, and in this respect, the discourse of balance implicitly endorses the monolingual norm that underlies dominant ideologies of language.

Finally, there is the question of how the balanced bilingual is best formed through education. In some contexts (such as Canada, New Zealand and Ireland) the minority language is promoted through immersion schooling. This, in effect, stakes out the school as a place where minority language monolingualism can act as a counterbalance to the dominance of English in the wider society. In this configuration, the individual has to achieve personal balance by moving between two monolingual worlds that do not formally acknowledge or enact the bilingualism that is presumably the individual's goal. In the Corsican case, French policy does not permit the immersion option, and so the bilingual individual is formed through bilingual schools. In this kind of situation, the goal of individual bilingualism is pursued within an institution that acts as a microcosmic model of societal bilingualism. In the life of individual students, however, the balance enacted within the school walls comes at a cost to balance across their daily lives, where the dominance of French is still unchallenged.

more of the old than the new: discourses of cultural specificity and the promotion of minority language bilingual education

It is clear that in a context where language shift towards the dominant language is extensive, achieving a balanced bilingualism amounts, in practical terms, to acquiring the minority language. In this respect, the discourse of bilingualism converges with earlier discourses about the essential link between the minority language and minority identity produced within a nationalist (or ethnonationalist) framework. We can see this at both the national and the regional level in French and Corsican documents I've assembled. At the national level, the 1995 French Ministry of Education Official Bulletin outlines the rationale and principles of state-endorsed bilingual education for regional languages. It justifies the bilingual format as a way of preserving regional cultural and linguistic specificity that is identified as part of a diverse national heritage. The state support is based on

the desire to exercise vigilance about the preservation of an essential element of the national heritage in its diversity, as well as the necessity of maintaining cultural identity within the national community...multi-year plans...will make it possible to better adapt pedagogical offerings to the goals expressed by families in the zones of influence of these languages. (Ministère de l'Education Nationale 1995: 1)

Here the phrase 'zones of influence' is slightly ambiguous with respect to the communicative status of those languages. However, a later reference in the document to 'activités en langue régionale dans une continuité sans heurts entre l'école et le milieu familial' [activities in the regional language that reflect a perfect continuity between the school and the family] implies that the family is regional-language-speaking. In this discourse of 'unity in diversity' we can see the continued presence of essentialist models of language and identity, as the components of the diversity of regional cultures and languages are represented as bounded and homogeneous. The French state is diverse because of the existence of homogeneous sub-groups. Diversity is not located within those sub-groups, or within individuals.

Corsican Assembly documents from 1997 and 2005 also take up the theme of a primordial language–culture connection in bounded communities. Where the Ministry of Education document casts cultural particularity within a national framework, the Corsican documents situate the value of language with reference to a more global human context. In 1997, this is expressed in a Corsican-language preamble to a document on language policy that asserts that 'a language is the expression of a community's culture, be it small or large, and is a source of wealth for all of humanity' (Assemblée de Corse 1997: 1). In July 2005, another language planning document characterizes Corsican as 'the base and the principal vehicle for the expression of our culture', and, 'like every other idiom', as 'the repository of a history and of collective values that it both expresses and reconstitutes through the unique verbal representation of the world' (Assemblée de Corse 2005: 4).

It is important to recognize the significance of the global references, which show that by the late 1990s, Corsican identity work was no longer oriented solely towards France; we will return to this below. But this shift of frame of reference does not significantly alter the terms in which difference/ diversity is conceived. Like the discourse of 'balance', this neo-Whorfian rhetoric – a cornerstone of the defence of minority languages in discourses of endangerment[3] – does not allow for internal diversity. Put another way, it makes the mixed cultural and linguistic practices and identities that are found in societies that have undergone language contact and shift 'matter out of place'. It implicitly only validates regaining what has been lost (traditional uses of the minority language) as a way of having a dual linguistic and cultural identity. Obtaining bilingual balance is thus discursively linked with the teaching and acquisition of two monolingualisms: two completely separate codes and cultures. In this framework, the focus on *form* makes it difficult for people to recognize continuities of culturally-specific communicative *practices* that may find expression in the minority language, the dominant language or in various intermediate codes. This focus also leaves minority language speakers and learners vulnerable to underspecified criteria of linguistic authenticity – the kinds of usage that might qualify or disqualify speakers as linguistically and culturally competent.

In both the French Ministry and Corsican documents I have collected, however, the Whorfian perspective diminishes over time. It is replaced with two things: (1) references to the cultural specificity of minority language education that directly acknowledge the fact of language shift, and (2) the articulation of the value of learning about specific languages and their connections with specific cultures within a pluri- or multicultural perspective. Let me take these up in turn.

acknowledging the specificity of minority language bilingualism in a context of language shift

The 2001 Official Bulletin of the Ministry of Education opens with the assertion that the interest and importance of bilingual education can be taken for granted. Bilingual education 'develops' cultural capacities; there is no reference to pre-existing linguistic or cultural knowledge. In fact, the document characterizes the mission of the minority language bilingual school as managing the 'strangeness' of French-dominant students' encounter with the minority language in the school. As a consequence, it advocates an 'active' pedagogy and a diplomatic approach to error correction that implicitly takes into consideration the potential loss of face and motivation that can come out of being held up to an unforgiving standard of minority language correctness (BO 33 2001: xix). Jean Duverger, former special attaché to the Department of the Exterior on matters of bilingualism, took up a similar position in a 2003 document he provided to the organizers of the Corsican conference on bilingualism. He placed the accent on the work of legitimation that had to be part of minority language bilingual pedagogy, writing that:

> It is necessary to be able to consecrate a lot of time to justifying and legitimizing in the eyes of the students a kind of instruction that, in most cases, is neither natural nor obvious, and does not respond to their own immediate needs...one can explain to a little Breton that it is logical for him/her to know the Breton language...But unfortunately, even in what look like favorable situations, experience shows that one has to invest extra effort to maintain students' will and motivation...towards this second language that the school proposes, that is to say, imposes. (Duverger 2004: 1)

The last line of this text makes it clear that minority language bilingual education is not a response to an *existing* bilingual society, rather it is a project for society – a top-down form of social engineering through and about language. This is also recognized implicitly in the 2001 BO, which recommends that each Academy create a pamphlet promoting the values of bilingual education.

bilingualism as participation in language revitalization

There is considerable reference in contemporary documents to bilingual education as a tool for reversing language shift. This is quite explicit in the Corsican-language preamble to the 1997 Corsican Assembly document on the Corsican language, which reads: '[The Assembly] DECLARES that the school is called upon to be cornerstone of efforts to save the Corsican language' (Assemblée de Corse 1997: 1). It is also reflected in the 2001 Ministry of Education BO's characterization of the role of the bilingual school as 'supporting' a bilingual social project by 'encouraging the practice of the regional language in the family...[and] better anchoring the practice of these languages in the daily life of the students' (BO 33 2001: i).

This is of course not new, and the Corsican investment in education-as-revitalization follows a path taken by many other minority language movements, some with a great deal of success. What does emerge in this discourse, however, are the seeds of a characterization of the minority language community in terms of collective movement towards a shared goal rather than in terms of autonomous linguistic capabilities. We see this in the 2005 Assembly language planning document, which makes this comment after citing 1999 National Institute for Statistics and Economic Studies (INSEE) results on self-reported use of Corsican:

> These results show that on the one hand, the risks of non-transmission of the language are real; on the other hand, that revitalization processes are in place and could be mobilized by strong and coherent action. (Assemblée de Corse 2005: 8)

Here we see the potential for reconciliation (as in the Lingua Matria document) of essentialist views of language-as-identity and the fact of language shift: Corsican is declared to have a significant presence in the life of the community as a result of language revitalization efforts, that is, as a result of collective action. Speaking Corsican – and becoming bilingual – is something that the society can accomplish: it is an active form of identification rather than a passive marker of identity.

The issue of agency, however, in the accomplishment of bilingualism is fairly complicated from this perspective. In earlier discourses, not speaking Corsican was problematic for the representation of Corsican cultural identity, but it could be explained by processes of language domination that were too difficult and widespread for individuals to be able to resist. In the current phase of language revitalization, Corsican schools and/or Corsican individuals are credited with greater agency, and thus stand to be held accountable if the society does not become bilingual.

The relative level and type of participation of school and community also come into question. Is bilingualism accomplished when all students go through bilingual schools and acquire academic competence? This is unlikely to be the consensus opinion, since in most minority language contexts, there are 'traditional' criteria of 'authentic' speech that contrast, and sometimes conflict with what is learned in school. If being a bilingual society requires extra-scholastic action, what should that be, and who is responsible for it? Can schools – or families – take effective action if there are few economic or social markets for minority language skills?

bilingualism and multilingual citizenship

Perhaps one of the most recent and striking shifts in Corsican discourses about bilingualism is the movement away from the learning of the minority language for the sole sake of learning about or affirming local identity. In the last several years, being bilingual has begun to be represented as an index of openness, tolerance, intercultural and multicultural competency and sensibility. For the most part, notions of 'exchange' in this discourse are social and cultural rather than economic. We see the first hints of this discourse in the 2001 BO, in which bilingual education in transborder areas is identified as a bridge to greater connections and solidarity with neighbouring regions (BO 33 2001). Bilingualism is also represented as increasing students' desire and aptitudes for learning other languages. 'Bilingualism', commented the Regional Inspector for Corsican Language and Culture, 'is only a stage on the path towards plurilingualism' (Arrighi 2004: 1). The Ministry of Education expressed similar sentiments about bilingual education in minority languages which, 'at the same time as it allows regional languages to be transmitted... supports the learning of French and primes students for the learning of other languages' (BO 33 2001: 1). The 2005 Assembly motion on language characterizes bilingualism as preparing students for 'the multilingualism that will be a necessity for every future European citizen'.

The corpus of documents from 2004 to 2005 all expand on this theme by linking bilingualism not just with language-specific knowledge, but also with values of tolerance, inclusion and cultural relativity that are the prerequisites for global, not just European citizenship. The 2005 Assembly document identifies bilingualism as a form of symbolic capital in new markets:

> The building of Europe, globalization of exchanges, tourism, shifts in population, the mixing of urban populations all lead us to shift our conceptions of language and identity from the purely local and ancestral to values of exchange and openness in all of the following: cases concerning the learning of the language by new residents, cases of contact with other language, recognition of a Mediterranean and European identity, cultural exchanges or the economic valorisation of cultural specificity (labels, 'identity' products, tourism...) (Assemblée de Corse 2005: 5).

In another document, a member of the bilingual teachers' association that organized the 2004 conference on bilingualism marries a Whorfian take on language and thought with becoming a pluricultural person, rather than with becoming more authentically Corsican:

> Each language corresponds to a vision of the world, a way of thinking of it, creating it through the verb. The child quickly acquires a relativistic perspective on the world; he/she is capable of accepting the different visions of the world that other foreign languages will present to him. This makes him a pluricultural being. (A Sciolilingua 2004b: 1)

Monolingualism emerges not as a natural or desirable state, but as a handicapped perspective, as seen in the following passage from Arrighi's closing remarks to the conference:

Monolingualism often induces a monolingual mentality and a monocultural view of the world. In the global context and throughout history, plurilingualism is overwhelmingly dominant, it is the natural state of societies. Corsicans have always used at least two languages: early Corsican and Greek, then Latin; Corsican and Italian for several centuries; Corsican and French today. (Arrighi 2004: 2)

Of some interest here is that Arrighi takes pains to characterize Corsicans as *always* having been bilingual, evoking historical periods disconnected from the recent experience of bilingual stigma in the middle and late stages of language shift.

I would like to suggest that the prominence of the global cultural, rather than the global economic marketplace in this discourse is related to several specific dimensions of the Corsican experience of language revitalization. First of all, Corsican linguistic and political activism has never succeeded (as it has in parts of Canada, for example) in creating homogeneous, equivalent spaces for the minority language. Unlike Canada, Wales, Ireland, New Zealand, Hawaii and elsewhere, there is no minority immersion education in Corsica. In these places that have created a real market for minority language skills, both in the educational sector and in the world of business and government, people have a set of experiences of that language as a commodity. This gets activated in response to changing economic circumstances: in the globalizing context, French (or being bilingual) is represented as a positive economic benefit. It is also the case that Corsican is not a language of economic power anywhere else in the world (which contrasts, for example, with the experience of French-speaking minorities). Perhaps more importantly, the linguistic connections of Corsican with Italian have, until very recently, been de-emphasized – there has never been any teaching of Italian as the 'high' version of Corsican in the same way as High German has been taught in Swiss and Alsatian schools.

In short, in places like Corsica, one of the reasons that there is far less bilingualism-as-commodity discourse may be because Corsicans have never experienced their bilingualism as a commodity (although Corsican is sometimes used to symbolically brand tourist or cultural products as authentically Corsican). Thus being bilingual is not so closely associated with having something marketable: it is more closely associated in the discourse with being a tolerant world citizen.

bilingual education, citizenship education and progressive pedagogy

For many of the teachers in the bilingual association that organized the conference, bilingual teaching was also intimately associated with cooperative education and its commitment to democratic models of citizenship. This is reflected in the following passage:

If we resituate the educational project in its proper context – that is, forming responsible citizens of the future, it seems to us that it is important to base our teaching practices on principles of education for respect, cooperation and solidarity through the use of projects that give children the chance to use one language or the other to express their own concerns, to play a role in the functioning of the school, to define as a group the projects through which they will learn. The fact of having chosen bilingualism only reinforces this motivation. (A Sciolilingua 2004a: 1)

Of note is that the bilingualism of the classroom is associated with giving the children voice, and with freedom to *choose between* codes. This implicitly legitimates code-switching, mixed language conversations and other practices that undermine the dual-monolingual view of bilingualism.

The connection between teaching bilingually and progressive pedagogies also enters into official Academy discourse: it is represented as educational 'value added' in the following comments by Arrighi:

Above and beyond its linguistic advantages, this system leads by its very nature to innovation across the board. One only has to look at the way that bilingual schools have invested in the teaching of foreign languages, in the local adaptation of national programs, in work on the environment and in citizenship education to be convinced. (Arrighi 2004: 2)

bilingualism as a cognitive benefit

Finally, the new discourse on bilingualism is permeated with references to the cognitive benefits of bilingual practice. The 1997 preamble to the Assembly document on language talks about 'intellectual development', a phrase that reappears in the 2005 Assembly document in the passage below, in which bilingualism is represented as

an advantage for our youth, offering them a unique tool for self-expression, creativity and intellectual development in the context of a bilingualism that can prepare them for the multilingualism that will be a necessity for every future European citizen. (Assemblée de Corse 2005: 4)

There are also specific references to metalinguistic competencies:

Showing children the diversity of languages and cultures makes it possible to give children the desire, a taste for learning other languages but also guarantees that they will acquire metalinguistic competencies. (Cristofari 2004: 2)

The 'metalinguistic' is affirmed as a clear educational advantage that goes beyond language learning proper. The 2001 BO makes reference to generalized 'capacités intellectuelles' [intellectual capacities]. In the 1996 document he provided for the 2004 conference on bilingualism, Duverger asserts that minority language bilingual education both has positive repercussions for the child's acquisition of literacy in the dominant language and simply creates better learners:

> learning to read and write in the first language (mother tongue) is reinforced [by bilingual education]. There is thus a benefit for the two languages... the child, put into contact early on with two languages, compares them and becomes aware of how they function and develops a metalinguistic consciousness. Moreover, at the point when they enter middle school, these children's school performance/results are significantly superior to monolingual children. (Duverger 1996: 2)

Two of the documents prepared for the same conference by members of the bilingual teachers' association emphasized bilingual children's superior qualities of abstraction and identified the movement between languages as a catalyst for the acquisition of generalized competencies and valued literacy skills in particular.

Finally, it is significant to note that the 2001 BO affirms that these metalinguistic benefits are not limited to children with balanced bilingual competence: they are an outcome of every stage in the process of learning the minority language.

> In effect, despite the differences between levels of practice in the two languages, the patterns of learning and of structuration of French and the regional language resemble each other at times, are intertwined and can form a single whole. What children learn, especially on the metalinguistic level, is transferable from one language to another. (BO 33 2001: 11).

This represents the bilingual person as an amalgam of mutually-reinforcing competencies, rather than as a place where languages as whole codes exist in balance.

conclusions: new discourses on bilingualism and implications for minority language planning

Over time, there have been some significant transformations of discourse about bilingualism within the framework of Corsican minority language activism. These changes are a result of several factors. These include changing political contexts – most notably, shifts at the national level that have both allowed and validated bilingual schooling, and devolved more authority to the Corsican Regional Assembly. There are also changes related to the development and reception of Corsican language activism and political nationalism. To the extent that they have succeeded in legitimating Corsican language and culture, these movements have been freed up from some of the restrictions of the essentializing discourses that structured how they articulated their position on language in years past. Another factor is the growing participation of Corsicans in networks of exchange that transcend national boundaries, both within the European Union and beyond. This has expanded the framework within which they conceive of linguistic and cultural identity beyond the sole reference to France and French. Finally, there has been the impact of specific educational policy. The entry of Corsican into the public schools as a medium of instruction on a par with French was both prepared by and served to promote a discourse in which minority language bilingualism has been validated in terms other than the essentialist, oppositional ones that framed the first phases of minority language activism on Corsica. Being taught bilingually – being bilingual – is now represented both as an act of specific cultural membership and as a point of access to European, Mediterranean and global forms of citizenship in which plurilingual and pluricultural competencies are valued forms of social and symbolic currency. Bilingualism becomes the cover term for acquiring minority language competence, because competence in the dominant language is actually taken for granted. Advocates of minority language bilingualism address people as (generally) monolinguals, and propose bilingualism as cultural value added. In this sense, the new discourse is evidence of historical movement away from the bilingualism-as-deficit perspective, both within the wider society and within the minority society.

These discourses have the advantage of acknowledging the lasting linguistic and cultural consequences of language domination, including the creation of multiple linguistic forms and practices and multiple identities. To return to an earlier point, they make it possible for 'shift' to be understood as an ideologically embedded concept. In this respect, they are far more in tune with the sociolinguistic reality than previous discourses and carry far fewer risks of alienating or undermining the cultural legitimacy of Corsicans who are not native speakers of the Corsican language. This discourse validates the process of learning – becoming – rather than just 'being' bilingual.

At the same time, these 'new' discourses have some 'old' discursive residue, including an unresolved tension between individual and societal bilingualism in the definition of a bilingual society. It is not clear whether each individual needs to be bilingual, or whether competence in both languages can be distributed in a variety of ways across the population.

Secondly, the new discourse of bilingualism underspecifies what will count as speaking the minority language. References to 'comparable' competencies, both formal and informal, in oral and written genres are vague about how levels of competence are to be assessed, what domains of language practice (if any) outside the school are implicated, and what registers and genres children should be assessed in. Asking these questions raises complex issues related to the ambiguous and sometimes ambivalent relationships between the minority language bilingual schools and society. The fact that the school is intended as a vector of linguistic and social change means that it sometimes stands in opposition to the sociolinguistic values, practices and priorities of that wider society. New discourses of the value of minority language bilingualism pass over in silence the conflict that can be created by having multiple sources of authority for defining 'good' or 'authentic' language in contexts of language shift and revitalization. In Corsica, and in many minority language movements, 'school language' inevitably diverges in its structure and vocabulary both from 'traditional' language from a (partially imagined) pre-shift past and with the contemporary speech of unschooled native speakers that bears the traces of dominant language contact. This complicates the question of what it means to 'speak Corsican'. At the same time, the entry of minority languages into official, public spheres and institutions prompts debates over the status of internal variation in the minority language. In Corsica, the official position in the educational system is that all regional varieties are legitimate, but there is less consensus over the legitimacy of the new hybrid forms that emerge from intra-Corsican language contact taking place between students in secondary and higher education settings. Changes in the Corsican that children and young adults are learning are taking place faster than changes in the social imaginary, where being a Corsican speaker is still closely associated with speaking a Corsican from a very specific geographical somewhere.

The underspecification of what counts as minority language competence, combined with the persistence of balanced bilingualism as an ideal, also carry some risks for minority language planning. First of all, that underspecification can lead to a diffuse or fragmented focus in policy and practice (particularly in education). The absence of clearly articulated or shared goals can lead to disappointment with the results of language planning. In education in particular, when goals and outcomes remain vague, people harbour unrealistic expectations that schooling can create an ideal balanced bilingual. General acceptance of the notion that bilingualism is a cognitive benefit probably don't affect how that balance is conceived of, since it is difficult to measure metalinguistic competence and overall cognitive agility. This leaves people free to imagine what balanced bilingualism might be. They tend to view it as an exact equivalence that is difficult to achieve in ideal circumstances (of elite bilingualism with extensive societal support) and even less accessible in minority language contexts.

Finally, the shift of focus, in the advocacy of minority language education, towards the general benefits of bilingualism may or may not create long-term support for *minority* language bilingualism. This is because this discourse represents all bilingualisms as equal, whereas everyone knows that they are not. Not only are there hierarchies between different languages, but there are hierarchies between different varieties of the same language. The French that is valued in a global economy is not just any French, it is a standardized, normalized French (international or Canadian) (see for example Boudreau and Dubois 2005 and Kahn and Heller 2005). That is, the positioning of the minority language as a stepping stone for plurilingual competencies needed in a global economy potentially opens a discursive space for people to make the same kinds of choices they made in the past that led to language shift – by choosing a direct rather than indirect path to the dominant languages that work in the global economy. In addition, in many globalized contexts, the value of linguistic products is often classic (unchanged from the 'pre-global' economies in which minority languages faltered): that is, as an index of an essential, bounded identity. That means that in fact, in some sectors of the global economy, bilingual individuals are not always called upon in their capacities as bilinguals, but rather, in their capacities to perform as monolinguals within two different domains of practice (that are projected as closed and homogeneous). The truly 'bilingual' skills that people need are often underspecified, left to chance, and not the target of recruiting or training (Kahn and Heller 2005). In short, minority language speakers' access to *bilingual* skills which involve cultural, political and ideological sensibilities are, for the most part, left out of discourses of globalization. In short, these globalizing discourses may not fully support some of the perspectives legitimating minority language bilingualism seen above.

In summary, the complexities of what it means to be (or become) bilingual in a minority language context are clearly related to the impact of histories of minority language shift and revitalization on practices and attitudes. In this respect, they are distinct. At the same time, bilingualism in the context of minority language movements throws into relief tensions in the representation and experience of bilingualism and its advocacy that apply to many other contexts where – at least at face value – bilingualism seems more straightforward.

notes

1. In the late 1990s, when I was conducting research on audience responses to the use of Corsican in the media, one of the recordings I played to Corsicans I interviewed was a comedy sketch that involved code-switching and contact-influenced mixing from Corsican to French. One middle-aged interviewee said, 'I wish I could just laugh, but I can't.' That is, she could still recollect the stigma attached to limited French competence in her parents' generation (Jaffe 2000, 2005).
2. It is not certain whether or not the reference to 'Le Grand Dérangement' was meant to evoke the historical event of the same name in which Acadians were expelled from their territories in the mid eighteenth century. However, since the Corsican nationalist movement has always situated itself in the context of a world-wide struggle against oppression of minorities, it seems likely that the reference was intentional.
3. See Jaffe (forthcoming), 'Discourses of endangerment: contexts and consequences of essentializing discourses', to appear in *Discourses of Endangerment: Interests and Ideology in the Defense of Languages*, edited by Alexandre Duchêne and Monica Heller, Continuum Publishing Group. Here 'Whorfianism' or 'neo-Whorfianism' refers to variants on the idea that cultural values and beliefs are somehow directly embedded in linguistic form.

references

Académie de Corse (1998). *Charte des sites, filières et classes bilingues des écoles de l'Académie de Corse*, LCC/RA/IDM N003–1998. Retrieved 10 September 2005, from <http://nuticiel.ac-corse.fr/admi/exec/edit.php3?id_webzine=7&id_art=584>.

Arrighi, J. (2004: October). *Discours de clôture*. Presentation at conference on bilingualism, Corté, France.

Assemblée de Corse (1984: November). *Rapport du Président de l'Assemblée sur la promotion et la développement de la langue corse*. Ajaccio, France.

—— (1997) *Présence et Avenir de la Langue Corse*. Déliberation of 20 November, Ajaccio, France.

—— (2005). *Délibération No. 05/112 AC de l'Assemblée de Corse Approuvant les Orientiations Stratégiques pour le Développement et la Diffusion de la Langue Corse*. Retrieved 10 September 2005, from <www.corse.fr/documents/Assemblee/delib/delib_corse.pdf>.

A Sciolilingua (2004a: October). *Introduction à l'atelier no. 1: pédagogie du projet et enseignement bilingue*. Presentation at conference on bilingualism, Corté, France.

—— (2004b: October). *Réflexions et perspectives pour l'enseignement de la LCC dans le premier degré*. Presentation at conference on bilingualism, Corté, France.

Boudreau, A., and L. Dubois (2005: 20–23 March) *Bilingualism and the New Economy in Moncton, New Brunswick: Good Morning Moncton Bonjour*. Paper presented at the Fourth International Symposium on Bilingualism, Barcelona, Spain.

CCECV (Conseil de la Culture, de l'Education e du Cadre de Vie) (1989). *Rapport du groupe de travail: Lingua Corsa*. Ajaccio, France: Assemblée de Corse.

Cristofari, M. (2004: October). *Bilinguisme et alterité*. Presentation at conference on bilingualism, Corté, France.

Duverger, J. (1996: 26–27 October). *Enseignement bilingue: analyse de la problématique du point de vue pédagogique*. Paper presented at the 10th Annual Conference of the FLAREP, Rostrenen. Retrieved 1 October 2005, from <http://www.geocities.com/Athens/Forum/2401/maen3.html>.

—— (2004: October). *Du monolinguisme au bilinguisme*. Paper presented at conference on Bilingualism, Corté, France.

Front Régionaliste Corse (FRC) (1971). *Main basse sur une île*. Corbara: Accademia d'I Vagabondi.

Jaffe, A. (1999). *Ideologies in Action: Language Politics on Corsica*. Berlin: Mouton de Gruyter.

—— (2000). Comic performance and the articulation of hybrid identity. *Pragmatics* 10(1): 39–60.

—— (2005). L'évaluation de la radio: perspectives corses sur le purisme linguistique. *Langage et Société* 112: 79–97.

—— (forthcoming). Discourses of endangerment: Contexts and consequences of essentializing discourses in and out of academe. In A. Duchêne and M. Heller (eds), *Discourses of Endangerment: Interests and Ideology in the Defense of Languages*. Continuum Publishing Group.

Kahn, E., and M. Heller (2005: 20–23 March). *Ideologies and Practices of Multilingualism in Quebec: Struggles and Shifts in a New Economy Site*. Paper presented at the Fourth International Symposium on Bilingualism, Barcelona, Spain.

Ministère de l'Education Nationale (1995). Circulaire 95–086, 7 April. *Enseignement des Langues et Cultures Régionales*.

Ministère de l'Education Nationale/Ministère de la Recherche (2001) *Bulletin Officiel* 33, 13 September. *Langues et Cultures Régionales*.

Unione di u Populu Corsu (1991) *Autonomia*. Supplement to weekly news journal *Arritti*.

4
bilingualism and the nation-state in the post-national era[1]

joan pujolar

introduction

Languages have always played a central role in the construction of modern national identities through the *one language / one culture / one nation paradigm*. Nation-states have always felt the need to create and protect a national speech community as a social base and to ensure that the national language effectively constituted and occupied the public space. But nowadays this monolingual and monocultural agenda is increasingly difficult to carry through. Public spaces (the media, politics, education, the workplace, tourist sites) are becoming increasingly globalized and hence multilingual. International organizations such as the European Union (EU), the European Council or UNESCO are also producing their own discourses on language, which means that nation-states no longer have the political monopoly over their cultural policies (see Muehlmann and Duchêne, this volume). Immigration is fostering cultural diversity and indigenous linguistic minorities keep striving for recognition (see Moyer and Martín Rojo, this volume, and Patrick, this volume). The authority of the state is further undermined by neoliberal policies. The privatization of public industries and services, together with trends towards deregulation, effectively erode the influence of state administrations over public and economic matters (Castells 1997, 1998). In addition to all this, the New Economy involves language (now in a wider sense) in ways that are substantially different from the fordist-based or traditional industrialist forms of production and consumption. The key industries of the contemporary world are those that trade with content, i.e. texts (the media, the cultural industries), and with other text-based services (insurance, financial services, marketing). This means that language has moved towards the centre of economic processes, both in terms of the products being offered and of the *processes* of production, distribution and consumption. In this context, the

71

political and economic bases of nationalism are threatened as social sectors develop new globalized and globalizing lifestyles, discourses and political strategies (Bauman 1998).

In this chapter, I shall explore how these post-national scenarios and post-nationalist ideologies and practices are emerging and how they affect public language policies, the interests and strategies of social groups in relation to language and in relation to the traditional ideologies that constructed languages as separate, immanent systems, and that delegitimized bilingual practices and non-standard varieties.

in what sense are nation-states being challenged?

Theoretical and political debates on nationalism and post-nationalism are rich, complex and involve a degree of conceptual elaboration that is not possible to reproduce here. However, it is necessary to spell out some of the basic principles that have traditionally been considered as constitutive of nation-states and which are increasingly questioned or challenged. The term 'nation-state' itself encapsulates a fundamental duality that has historically accumulated many layers. Its conceptual birth is commonly placed in eighteenth-century France, where revolutionary factions combined (a) the new rationalist political models proposed by Locke and Rousseau (the state as expression of a popular sovereignty based upon a contract between free citizens) with (b) received notions about a 'historical nation'. The rationalist models involved concepts and principles intended to apply in a universal manner, such as the concepts of equality and freedom, or the principle that popular sovereignty was indivisible and unalienable, which was obviously aimed at denying any aristocratic claims to patrimony or power.[2] As the French revolutionaries proceeded to create their new order, they adapted these models by transposing the idea of royal sovereignty for that of a 'national' sovereignty. They claimed that the new state embodied the new political values within French territory and for the 'French people'. As Kearney points out, 'the sovereign people now becomes identified with a sovereign nation embodied in an organized, centralized state' (1997: 18).

This dual foundational origin of nation-states is what classical nationalist discourses have sought to conceal by claiming that both components, nations and states, are one (Gellner 1983; Hobsbawn 1990), hence the endeavours of states to construct a public space that projected the 'historical nation' as it came to be understood, namely as a population sharing a common culture. Language was generally seen as a key component of culture, which explains why linguistic unification was pursued so consistently (Gal and Woolard 2001). But there were many other consequences of this 'statalization' of language, as ideas about language became intimately bound up both with discourses about culture (involving evolutionism and the stigma of hybridity – and hence of bilingualism) and with rationalist management (standardization, hygienization) (Portes and Rumbaut 1990). As Bourdieu (1982) has aptly argued, these discourses provided the ground for struggles over 'the legitimate language' as part of wider social struggles over access to material and symbolic resources. These struggles constitute what we could call 'the secret life' of nations, that is, the unofficial processes and agendas that legitimize the cultural capital (including the linguistic capital) of some groups over others in society, and which may be just as fateful for individuals as official procedures to attain citizenship or statutory entitlements, as immigrants know well.

In any case, this paradigm has never worked smoothly. In principle, it is vulnerable to any threat to state sovereignty or control, any event that visibly contradicts the official vision of the nation, any displacement of discourses on culture that may raise questions about the equation between state and nation or about the nature of language. And the vulnerabilities have produced well-known and recurrent debates: the dichotomy between 'civic' and 'ethnic' nationalism, issues of citizenship and immigration, individual rights versus collective rights, and so on. Issues of language and identity fall naturally within this scope, either when (for example) the state fails to ensure the functioning of a monolingual public space or when particular social processes or new critiques of culture are seen to threaten or affect the integrity, legitimacy or continuity of the linguistic community as it is constructed at a particular historical juncture. Thus, globalization, together with liberalization and the *linguicization* of the economy, are potential threats to the nation-state paradigm too, and they affect its legitimacy from many quarters and at unprecedented scales.

post-national processes and discourses

Post-national processes and discourses are those that question in specific ways the fundamental ideological architecture of nation-states. The questioning can affect both issues of sovereignty, i.e. the state's political supremacy, and of nationhood. And this casts doubts on the legitimacy of the state, as its isomorphism with the national community is problematized. These processes generally mean that social actors find themselves organizing their lives (communicating, working) with people and in contexts that do not really constitute or are constituted by the national public sphere that nation-states have historically sought to articulate on the basis of cultural commonality and the fundamental political contract. The internationalization of the economy is one such process, as it involves corporations organizing production (and hence workers), commercialization strategies (targeting clients) and alliances that transcend state boundaries (and hence cultural and linguistic ones). The articulation of an international political sphere is another, as it questions the idea that the state is the sole source of public rights and legitimate political participation, while international institutions are typically multilingual and multicultural. Migration and other forms of mobility are also creating increasingly diverse communities at the local level. Information and communication technologies (ICTs) push these processes further by providing the technological infrastructure to create and manage transnational networks (of individuals, organizations, institutions) and global contexts of communication, as well as the basis of operation for new types of economic exchange where language is essential. Finally, liberalization constitutes the particular political paradigm that is gradually redefining the relationship between public institutions and the economic sector, on the one hand, and public institutions and citizens on the other. From this perspective, although liberalization is intimately connected with globalization in its present form (it produces it and is produced by it), it has political and cultural implications not reducible to it.

Most of the situations, conditions or processes that discredit the nation-state paradigm are not, strictly speaking, new or characteristic of our time. However, the pace, scale, intensity, frequency and degree of concurrence of all these conditions is probably what justifies the impression that 'complex mobilities and interconnections', as Inda and Rosaldo (2002: 2) describe it, are really changing the ideological foundations of our political systems. And what is also new is the way in which language is implicated in these processes by virtue of its traditional value as symbol of national identity, its increasingly central position within the economy and its insertion in processes of technological development.

nationalists within global markets

In February 1998, Juan Villalonga, president of the recently privatized Telefónica de España SA, was delivering a speech at Tribuna Barcelona, a series organized by one of the city's leading newspapers. In the colloquium that followed, one entrepreneur asked whether the company intended to provide service to customers in Catalan. By way of a response, Villalonga compared the situation of Catalans to that of the 'hundreds of thousands' of British and German retirees in Spain, implying that the company could not possibly take on board the aspirations of such diverse groups of clients. The comment was taken as sarcastic, was widely publicized and got negative reactions from Catalan cultural and political groups. A few weeks later, the Catalan government put out the telephone service for its offices to tender, and Mr Villalonga signed an agreement that ensured the provision of customer services in Catalan (La Vanguardia 1998a, 1998b; Airob 1998).

This case is a good example of how being an actor in the global marketplace makes it difficult to display nationalism. It also exemplifies the fact that newly privatized industries cannot project the type of cultural militancy associated with state services. Telefónica was in the process of expanding to Latin American markets and Portugal (Telefónica 2005). In 2005, the company was reported as the world's fourth largest telecommunications company in terms of capital assets (Cinco Días 2005). Thus, Mr Villalonga's shareholders were arguably not concerned about Spain's national identity in the way that the previous 'owner', the Spanish state, had been. His audience, moreover, represented an influential section of the Catalan market, which was an important basis on which to expand to other markets and to develop other services (mobile communications, internet provision, satellite and cable radio and television). In fact, *Telefónica*'s R&D spin-off, *Telefónica I+D*, had been working for many years to develop various speech technologies for a variety of languages, including Catalan (Telefónica I+D 1997).

The difficulty of engaging the company in Spanish nationalist agendas was mirrored by the difficulties of Catalan authorities to ensure that the company provided its services in Catalan. The privatization of the company had meant that it was no longer bound by regulations affecting state services (see below for more on the implications of liberalization). Although the regulatory powers of Catalan authorities could still impose some conditions of operation to the company, there was a new criterion emerging, namely that of the market significance of the language.

Thus, both Mr Villalonga and the Catalan authorities were learning how to navigate in a post-national scenario. The scenario was not new in the strict sense that transnational companies and entrepreneurs have been around for a long time, although they used to be associated with a few large companies. With globalization, the transnational condition has become a standard for middle-sized, and even for many small-sized, businesses. Mr Villalonga's position could therefore be seen as representative of the large numbers of entrepreneurs and workers that are investing (economically and culturally) in the global marketplace when, just a few years ago, their scope would have been primarily national. For the global or international company, language is no longer a natural, taken-for-granted medium of operation and organization, but a component of markets that has an economic accountability in terms of costs and resources. In this global marketplace, languages increasingly acquire their value as a function of their economic significance, while their value as national symbols and as resources for social identification and differentiation become secondary. This situation effectively erodes the capacity of nation-states to control public linguistic practices, define their conditions of social legitimacy and, as a result, to maintain the procedures for the enactment and reproduction of the national speech community. It is from this perspective that we can understand the reaction of some governments, such as the French and the Danish, to limit the public uses of English, although the measures in place appear already anachronistic (Viaut 2004; Aguilar 2005).

languages in international relations

International politics provides multiple forms and avenues of limitation over state sovereignty, some of which can affect cultural and linguistic policies very significantly. From this perspective, two main areas can be identified: international law and international institutions. It is apt to observe here that the term 'international' generally means more accurately 'inter-state', which means that it already contains the assumption that 'state' and 'nation' are synonyms. From this perspective, the international arena is structured over political and ideological assumptions that are all but post-national. However, participation in the 'international community' has important effects on the ability of states to pursue their 'nationalizing' policies. According to Kearney (1997), international law constitutes a *de facto* limitation of state sovereignty that started with the 1898 and 1907 Hague conferences and continued with the Covenant of the League of Nations and the charter of the United Nations. International institutions and fora (the UN, the EU, the Council of Europe, the IMF, the World Bank, the European Central Bank, UNESCO), treaties (NATO, NAFTA, EFTA, GATT), summits and military alliances constitute new spaces for decision and policy making where nation-states no longer appear as the supreme authority, but just as participants in multilateral structures. According to Castells (1998), this new political space involves a trade-off for states between losing sovereignty and gaining influence in the global stage.

Language was not explicitly mentioned in the first round of covenants, conventions and declarations that spelled out fundamental human rights, except for the typical phrase granting general rights 'without distinction of race, sex, language or religion' in the UN Charter or the UNESCO constitution (Vernet, Pons, Pou, Solé and Pla 2003; UNESCO 1945). No references were made to rights of individuals or groups *as speakers* of particular languages, until the International Covenant on Civil and Political Rights, which stated that minorities 'should not be denied the right...to use their own language' in their community (UN 1976: 179). After this, dozens of initiatives have appeared to promote international linguistic legislation, with a particular focus on the European Union and the Council of Europe. These initiatives present two interlocking lines of argumentation, one seeking to define the rights of minorities (e.g. the 1992 UN Declaration on the Rights of Persons Belonging to National or Ethnic, Religious and Linguistic Minorities), the other seeking to connect linguistic rights with human rights more generally (Vernet et al. 2003).[3] UNESCO supported the process that led to the 'Universal declaration of linguistic rights',[4] promoted by a group of NGOs (in which Catalan organizations played a prominent role) and provided, incidentally, a good example of how some minority groups can effectively reorientate their strategies towards international political contexts (see also Muehlmann and Duchêne, this volume). One of the Council of Europe's most interesting contributions to international linguistic legislation is the European Charter for Regional or Minority Languages, which commits states to detailed principles in relation to their own territorial language groups (Council of Europe 2005). Although the Council cannot enforce its recommendations, it does put some states under political pressure to abide by the principles of the charter.

International pressure to protect minority languages (that is, languages other than that of the state), combined with the political pressure exerted by linguistic minorities, is effectively shifting standard policies from assimilation to bi- or multilingualism. Minority language education is now becoming the standard policy in the territories inhabited by linguistic groups other than that of the state. The Council of Europe has actually become a champion of multilingualism and foreign language teaching through the elaboration of the 'Common European Framework of Reference for Languages', a set of methodological and evaluative standards that is being adopted by administrations and language schools throughout Europe in the design and implementation of the foreign language curricula. The Council of Europe is therefore developing into a continental language planning agency that promotes legislation, establishes standards of practice and monitors policies at all levels (Beacco and Byram 2003).

The multilingualism of international political fora does not contradict, in principle, the monocultural and monolingual conception of nation-states, as these fora are constitutively multilateral spaces. However, as these develop their own multilingual institutions and bureaucracies, their very existence raises questions about the states' internal monolingualisms. This is not to deny that these languages may still be under enormous pressure from national or even international languages, but the discourses of old that stigmatized them or stigmatized the bilingualism of their speakers are no longer legitimate. However, this situation is also consolidating political regimes and structures based on linguistic pluralism that emerge as alternatives to monolingual and monocultural conceptions of governance and nationality.

To summarize, international law is gradually incorporating language policy issues in ways that introduce limitations to state sovereignty and legitimize principles of linguistic pluralism. The states' prerogative of regulating linguistic usages internally is thereby qualified, as it incorporates principles developed by legislators, NGOs and academics active in international fora, what Curtin (1997) considers to be equivalent of international civil society. The creation of multilateral international organizations provides an operational enactment of these principles and further strengthens the case for linguistic pluralism within states. This contradicts traditional unitary conceptions of nation-states. In fact, most European and North American states have gradually adopted such pluralistic policies in the last decades of the twentieth century. Additionally, international linguistic legislation and policies have important conceptual implications that have so far received little attention, namely the fact that they imply a shift from seeing language as an issue of territorial sovereignty and national identity to constructing it as a 'civil rights' issue that may be connected with the struggles of other social groups (women, ethnic minorities, non-heterosexuals, workers and so on).

This is not to say that all these new discourses on linguistic pluralism and diversity are necessarily progressive, that inequalities between language groups are being solved and that states as such are becoming effectively multilingual. It just means that it is increasingly difficult for nation-states and for national elites to draw on the old discourses on language to maintain their legitimacy, and that this forces them to develop new ideological frameworks, strategies and tactics to maintain their dominant position. Most international declarations and regulations are abstract enough to avoid engagement with minority speakers themselves and the historical, social and political economic processes that affect them. In this sense, one significant element is the notable underdevelopment of the linguistic rights of immigrants in comparison with that of (mostly European) territorial minorities (Skutnabb-Kangas 1996, 2002). Moreover, international linguistic legislation and many pluralistic policies draw on essentialist notions of language as independent systems constituting distinct cultures or nations, i.e. the same linguistic ideologies that supported classical nation-state building although interpreted and applied in different ways (see Muehlmann and Duchêne, this volume, and Patrick, this volume). As Beacco and Byram (2003) point out, not all states and social groups understand multilingualism and multilingual competence and practice in the same way or value multilingualism for the same reasons. Multilingual policies may be devised in ways that ensure the privileged position of dominant groups who foster the knowledge of powerful 'foreign' languages in their standard forms but delegitimize or ignore other languages and other forms of multilingual competence and performance (e.g. code-switching, heterogeneous skills).

cultural diversity and transnational experience

During the 1980s and 1990s European societies generally came to realize that cultural diversity is becoming a permanent phenomenon in the contemporary social landscape. Immigration is largely an urban phenomenon that has changed the human landscape of 'global cities' (Sassen 1991). It has turned the city's physical public space into a constant re-enactment of a culturally diverse community, which cannot be used to construct the imagined, unified, national community that now seems a thing of the past (Anderson 1991). Territorial indigenous minorities were rarely able to acquire this visibility in the past, as most were relegated to marginal, rural areas. Moreover, as the improvements in transport and telecommunications have undoubtedly contributed to the acceleration of population movements in the world, these same improvements also involve more possibilities to *keep in touch* with the community left behind through seasonal travel, telephone and email, commercial relationships, satellite television and other forms of circulation of cultural products. Immigration no longer involves (if it ever did) a total or major disconnection with the community of origin, which gives rise to what sociologists and anthropologists have called *transnational* experiences and identities (Basch, Glick and Szanton-Blanc 1994; Kearney 1995; Rouse 1995) or what Appadurai (1996) calls 'ethnoscapes'. This transnational experience, which was formerly associated with political and economic elites, is increasingly available to larger sections of the population. The transnational paradigm is in many ways a break with classical visions of identity as something pre-inscribed in consciousness, unified, compact and territorially-based (Inda and Rosaldo 2002).

How can states project and support identities that are in constant redefinition and change, in constant movement? Transnationalism at this scale fosters a dissociation between citizenship and nationality (or national belonging); that is, a separation between the state's administrative procedures to define individuals as full citizens *and* the social processes of integration and recognition as members of the national group. This dissociation bespeaks the generalized experience of first, second or third generation immigrants who may have the country's passport but do not encounter the same opportunities for social and economic advancement. Debates on language and immigration are very much a consequence and a response to this situation, as language (together with religion, race and class) plays a key role in the processes whereby social actors are granted legitimate membership as nationals, i.e. are treated socially as 'truly' French, Spaniards, Catalans or Danes. Linguistic competence and performance is thus increasingly activated to construct or reinforce differences underpinned by other forms of social categorization (Blommaert 1999; Blommaert and Verschueren 1998; Heller 1999; Rampton 2003).

With respect to more established immigrant communities, hegemonic linguistic ideologies still contribute to the devaluing of the speech forms associated with immigrants: accents, particular speech styles or varieties, as well as bilingual practices, such as code-switching, code-mixing and contact phenomena (Lippi Green 1997; Heller 1999; Zentella 1997). As Heller (1999, 2000, 2005) has pointed out, social and economic markets tend to value the various kinds of bilingualism or bilinguals in different ways. Besides the elite bilingualism based on the standards learnt in foreign language classrooms, there is a mass bilingualism of economically disadvantaged communities whose skills find no recognition in the markets (Roy 2003).

In the future, sociolinguists should keep an eye on the processes of reproduction of these ideologies. It is by no means obvious how generalized negative attitudes towards accents, bilingualism and hybridity will persist in the face of increased mobility amongst the middle classes. From this perspective, tourism is also a phenomenon of increasing importance. It is becoming the most important industry in the world, as it represents 7 per cent of world exports and 30 per cent of exports within the services sector. In the period 1975–2000, world tourism grew an average of 1.3 points above the global GNP increase (World Tourism Organization 2004). Taken together, the migration of low-skilled workers, more affluent sectors and tourists contribute to the creation of multilingual public spaces and private networks, and the circulation of services and cultural products in various languages, which increasingly configures a set of everyday life scenarios that are in contrast with the monocultural, monolingual public space that European nation-states have worked so hard to construct. As transnational and translinguistic experience becomes a generalized phenomenon and is shared by more affluent social groups (students, academics, executives), some classical prejudices must generally change, although not necessarily by granting more recognition to the linguistic resources of deprived groups. Sociolinguists, in any case, will have to focus on the language practices and experiences of more unstable, delocalized, constituencies than they have done in the past, as anthropologists have recently realized (Clifford 1997; Inda and Rosaldo 2002; Kearney 1995).

the new economy

Sociological approaches to globalization and the New Economy very rarely mention linguistic issues (see, for example, Castells 1997 or Giddens 1999). Conversely, linguists and sociolinguists have theorized very little about the role of language in the New Economy. Many studies project a concern about the spread of English and other international languages in many areas of life, and a significant number of linguists has invested a lot in the cause of 'endangered languages'[5] (Hill, Dorian, England, Fishman and Hinton 2002). A more elaborated argument is that of Rassool (2000), who argues that new forms of inequality (both linguistic and social) may be arising as 'world languages' mediate access to ICTs, mass communication and the increasingly cross-cultural social spaces in which cosmopolitan elites control the flows of capital and the organization of production at a global scale.

However, most analysts fail to appreciate the extent to which the New Economy is a 'linguistic' economy in that there is little in it that does not involve language in a central way (Heller 1999, 2003a). ICTs promote networked forms of organization and relationships (Castells 1996); and these operate basically through language. The traditional service sector has characteristically included language-intensive activities and products, data management and social interaction (insurance, financial services, consulting, education, health care, legal support, administration). Moreover, as delocalization pushes the production of manufactured goods towards developing countries, advanced industrial economies tend to concentrate more and more in product design and commercialization, activities that either require or actually constitute communication themselves. Most ICTs acquire their value precisely because they provide new conditions for human interaction and data transfer to take place, which is what actually triggers many of the social processes that are transforming the contemporary world. The new digital environments are also the ideal support for the *content* industries, the media and the cultural industries, that increasingly exploit the possibilities of multimedia and hypertextual expression. Even in cases where end-products are not primarily linguistic (and we do not consider their process of marketization), these products stem from processes of production where language and communication is given much more weight than in traditional, fordist-style industries. Cameron (2000) and Gee, Hull and Lankshear (1996) have documented how new ideologies and practices of corporate organization stress collaborative forms of project management, involving prominently language skills (and thus language skills training) based on teams that operate in less hierarchical ways.

Beyond the argument that language and communicative practices are at the core of the information age, the relevant question here is how linguistic diversity is affected by these transformations: in what ways are different *languages* and bilingual practices inserted in these processes? How does this affect the traditional relationship to language entertained by nation-states?

In the New Economy, language and languages have become strategic economic assets in themselves, that is, they now feature at the centre of struggles over economic resources in society and at a global scale. The main implication of this is that the private sector is developing into a counterpower of the state in the regulation of access to languages and in the management of linguistic resources in the public arena. Media groups can oppose and seriously endanger orthographic reforms that were previously the sole concern of academic institutions and educational authorities. Orthography is, however, just the tip of the iceberg in a process whereby models of language usage are increasingly to be found outside academic and official domains. ICTs provide new contexts (the internet, videogames, mobile phones) for social participation and for the development of new forms of linguistic practices that differ from the traditional language forms and communicative genres that the school has always favoured. These practices involve new literacies, multimedia genres and, as cultural diversity increases, multilingual forms of communication that the traditional monolingual, canonical text-based curriculum does not include (Cazden, Cope, Cook, Fairclough, Gee, Kalantzis, Kress, A. Luke, C. Luke, Michaels and Nakata 1996; Snyder 2002). This means that the role of the school in the inculcation and recognition of the legitimate forms of linguistic expression (Bourdieu and Passeron 1970; Bourdieu 1991) is going to encounter further difficulties as students find alternative forms of communication and competing sources of legitimacy outside the school. The time when public literacy practices were controlled by governments and managed by classical printing industries that clung scrupulously to grammatical and generic propriety are long past. The new contexts of communication created through digital technologies are eminently beyond the control of state bureaucracies. Even manifestly criminal uses of the world wide web (e.g. for drug dealing, terrorist activity, child pornography) are remarkably difficult to tackle by police forces. Control over language choices, uses of speech styles, linguistic hygiene and orthographic propriety is (in a large section of the digital world) simply beyond question.

This does not mean that the new contexts of communication provided by ICTs constitute the ultimate, unconstrained, free, equal, communicative paradise. In these contexts, other conditions and processes may constrain communication and create social hierarchies and inequalities. For instance, despite the fact that the internet is open for the use of official bodies, non-governmental organizations and individuals, the most important spaces for participation are run by private companies. Thus, transnational media, communications and software corporations can take important decisions as to how the cyberspace is used and for what purposes.

Additionally, language technologies (LT), as a specific component of ICTs, constitute an important new phenomenon too. Technologies for speech recognition, speech synthesis, automatic and assisted translation and language support software (e.g. spelling and grammatical checks, lexical support) allow for the development of new forms of human-to-machine interaction and computer-mediated communication. As the development of this type of software requires a huge investment in R&D, it is creating new hierarchies between language groups. This can affect bilingual communities in specific ways as the different varieties of their repertoire become associated with asymmetrical sets of LT resources. In fact, any piece of software can be regarded as a linguistic application from the perspective of its user interface, which is why so many groups fight about the language versions for operating systems and the most popular office packages.

However another aspect of interest to sociolinguists in relation to the New Economy should be to find out what strategies minorities – and their elites – develop to protect their own sources of value and legitimacy. One possibility is that, even if a dominant language is needed for interaction with the actual technology, access to the technology may be controlled in given contexts by particular social groups speaking other languages. Heller's (2002) view is that minorities react to globalization by developing a 'globalizing nationalism' that abandons, in many aspects, the focus on nation-state institutions and searches for resources and power in international markets and institutions. One component of these strategies is to turn language into a commodity on the basis of its value either as a skill or as a brand of authenticity in the cultural industries or in tourism (Heller 2003a; Pujolar, 2006). In these economic sectors, minorities can play the game in the majority language while preserving key spaces for the social and economic development of minority members.

liberalization

Liberalization has played a key role in the articulation of the global economy as liberal governments and transnational corporations have put pressure on all states to 'open up' their local economies. One important policy line has been to privatize services that were typically run by state monopolies such as telephones, airlines, gas, water, electricity, fuel, in some cases health care, pensions, railways, mail, and so on. The above-mentioned case of the Spanish Telefónica SA illustrates some of the implications of such privatization for linguistic minorities. Castells (1998) also argues that this process erodes in a general way the *social* legitimacy of the states, particularly because of its effects on welfare provision. The need to create 'better environments' for investment presses states to lower taxation and devise strategies to reduce production costs, including the cost of the workforce. This has resulted, on the one hand, in spending cuts that have affected the capitalization of services such as health care, unemployment insurance, pensions and education and, on the other hand, in policies of labour-market 'flexibilization'. These policies weaken the commitment to national institutions of large sections of the lower and middle classes who benefited from the welfare state.

However, this process has not simply involved transfers of public property, restructuring of services or legislative adjustments. Neoliberal ideologies have impregnated virtually all areas of public life, thus bringing about the discourses and practices of corporate capitalism into the public sector (Fairclough 2004; Fairclough, Graham, Lemke and Wodak 2004). This new politics of state (dis)engagement has been carried out by reportedly furthering the autonomy of operating units (hospitals, schools), attaching funding to particular performance indicators and evaluation procedures, and otherwise leaving decisions to the units' managers' ability to operate within their own 'markets' (Lankshear 1997; Mautner 2005; Strathern 2000).

These moves can have important implications for language policies and bilingual communities. For instance, Heller (2003b) documents how the new criteria for funding provision and auditing imposed by the Canadian government on one francophone cultural institution effectively created the conditions for important changes to take place: a) a generational change of the institution's leadership and b) a discursive change that emphasized effective management and accountability. In such neoliberal scenarios, bilingual and minority language institutions (particularly schools and universities, but also hospitals and other services) will be set to compete in markets dominated by major languages. A possible consequence of this could be that educational institutions (or their users or 'clients') may increasingly tend to frame bilingual education in terms of its economic value rather than in terms of its former function as a site for the reproduction of particular cultural groups, a tension that Heller (1999) detected in a francophone school in Toronto. Thus, liberalization transforms the field of struggles for linguistic minorities, and pushes them to substitute strictly political strategies and discourses for economic strategies invested with the discourses and practices of corporate capitalism.

globalizing and post-national discourses

Another crucial condition of globalization and post-nationalism is the very fact that it makes sense for many social groups (including academics) to construct it or interpret as such, i.e. to develop *discourses on globalization* as a process or set of processes that transcend nation-states as the supreme frame of reference for the organization of social participation and economic activity.

Discourses on globalization compete with national or nationalist perspectives and become themselves globalizing, that is, they are both constitutive and performative in that they participate in bringing about the very process that is treated as the referent. Discourses on globalization are descriptive/productive in the same way that discourses on 'the nation' have contributed to create the nations concerned. Now ideas and discourses on globalization can be mobilized to further strategic interests of particular groups against others. As Bauman (1998) and Friedman (1997) have argued, globalization is also a way of creating new hierarchies between 'cosmopolitans' and 'locals' in particular contexts as social actors creatively draw on available discourses to legitimize their particular interests and delegitimize those of others.

Spain provides numerous examples of how both Spanish and Catalan nationalists reformulate their arguments within the framework of globalizing discourses. One line of argumentation, which can be found prominently throughout the spectrum of the Spanish media, both progressive and conservative, is that Catalan nationalism is outdated simply because globalization and international cooperation render national frames of reference increasingly irrelevant. Pro-Catalan sectors would therefore constitute the 'local' end of the dichotomy, with the Spanish side on the cosmopolitan, globalizing one. Such discourses started circulating almost immediately after Spain adopted its present constitution in 1978 after 40 years of a Catholic fundamentalist, ultra-nationalist dictatorship. The following citation comes from a lecture delivered by the director of *El País*, Spain's most influential newspaper, which has a social democratic orientation.

> Catalonia witnesses a rebirth of its political nationalism at the cost of losing its universalistic ambitions [...] Madrid is presently the most defined centre of cultural, artistic and sociological interest in Spain. (Cebrián 1984; my translation)[6]

Cebrián's argument is but a recasting of old debates on 'provincialism' or 'irredentism', which sought to delegitimize minority movements as conservative and traditionalist in the face of the modernization processes brought about by nation-states (Grillo 1989; Hobsbawn 1990). In fact, struggles between 'modernizing' and 'globalizing' orientations can be found, as Heller (2002, 2003b) has shown, within competing sectors of linguistic minority movements too. Thus discourses on globalization can also be used to disqualify the nationalist ideas and movements of some groups in the benefit of others; they can be used to create hierarchies between social or cultural groups, as well as to construct new linguistic hierarchies that distinguish between 'global/cosmopolitan' and 'national/local' languages (see next section).

The linguistic correlate of these discursive struggles would be the emergence of a dichotomy between 'local' and 'global' languages, which is indeed the issue discussed in the next section.

post-national strategies, linguistic and not

I would not wish the reader to believe, or to believe that I believe, that the time of nation-states is past and that nationalisms are on their way to social oblivion. States, for all the challenges to sovereignty and legitimacy they are experiencing, are still the primary source of political and military power in the world. The social groups that have traditionally benefited from the control of state apparatuses are still there and are still using states to further their own interests. Nationalist groups, state-backed or not, remain alive and well. However, the developments spelled out in the previous section create new conditions that question the isomorphism between nation and state, cast doubts on the condition of states as expressions of national communities and question the desirability or viability of cultural and linguistic uniformization. This state of affairs leads social actors, groups and organizations to work out new strategies to pursue their interests, i.e. obtain and/or maintain positions of power and access to resources. These strategies may not openly or primarily acknowledge their nationalist base, but nationalist agendas still lurk under discourses and policies presented as pluralistic or purely technocratic.[7]

Thus, there may be policy decisions not openly aimed at promoting cultural uniformization, but aimed at creating the conditions for this uniformization through indirect means. The most typical example affects regulations affecting the mass media sector. In Spain, for instance, autonomous administrations can create and manage television channels. The Catalan government created its own TV channel in 1983 when only two Spanish public channels existed. Seven years later, the Spanish government started issuing licences for private television channels. At the same time, satellite television was introduced. The possibility of licensing channels for the specific territories where languages other than Spanish were spoken was never contemplated. In this way, the Spanish government was creating the conditions for Castilian-based media groups to dominate the Spanish market, conditions in which the articulation of Catalan, Basque or Galician media groups became extremely difficult. The state was implementing a hidden nationalist agenda by preventing competition from within the state, and by helping to consolidate the local industry against foreign competitors before full liberalization was established.

Post-national strategies are characteristically about tactical intervention in economic markets, no matter how 'liberal' or committed to 'free competition' governments may be. The Catalan government's above-mentioned reaction to Telefónica's resistance to the use of Catalan is another example of this. The New Economy, because of its reliance on language-based activities, has pushed administrations and minority groups to develop language-related economic strategies to attract resources for their particular constituencies (however these may be defined or delimited). Thus, for example, Canadian authorities (at local or provincial level) have sought to attract the call-centre sector to capitalize on workforce bilingualism in economically declining areas

(Roy 2003). Canadian and Welsh authorities foster rural development projects that seek to reconstitute local identities as commodities in tourist markets in which language plays an important role (Heller 2003b; Pujolar 2006).

Beyond these initiatives that are typically devised to cope with globalization or to relocate social groups and sectors within globalizing markets, the most visible strategies consist of what I call 'language power blocs'. Language power blocs involve alliances of nation-states (as well as sometimes associated minorities and quasi-nation-states such as Quebec) that pursue linguistic/cultural agendas previously focused on national constituencies or colonial subjects, and now presented as 'international cooperation'. These new agendas constitute the linguistic correlate of the new roles that states are assuming in the context of globalization. As Castells (1998) has argued, nation-states respond to their loss of sovereignty and legitimacy (traditionally based on democratic participation, public order and welfare provisions) by plugging into the complex set of international networks, institutions and alliances that allow them to negotiate their interests and strive for a share of power in the global arena. As their international agendas take precedence over the management of strictly internal, national, affairs, states concentrate in the projection of their own economic sectors in global markets.

English-speaking countries constitute the strongest language power bloc stemming from the British Empire and later the Commonwealth (with the important complement of the United States of America). The founding of the British Council in 1934 attests to the remarkable foresight of British authorities in identifying the role that language could play in international relations (Phillipson 1992). The Organisation internationale de la Francophonie (OIF), created in 1970, stemmed from a more recent assessment of the implications of globalization, including an increasing awareness of the economic and political importance of languages in the contemporary world. This process certainly builds on the experiences of institutions such as the Alliance Française (founded in 1883) or the Goethe Institut (1951), or the network of Institutes of Italian Culture. The larger linguistic power blocs are also characteristically led by former imperial states now projecting their cultural policies in the form of international cooperation over their former colonial subjects. Thus, they allow these states to exploit cultural and economic relationships stemming from the imperial period in a way that masks the colonial dimension of these alliances.

One such bloc, which I will discuss in some detail in order to illustrate some of the processes involved in this repositioning of nation-states in the globalized marketplace, is being articulated around the Spanish language. Del Valle (in press a) has dubbed it *la Hispanofonía* (to differentiate it from the failed, old-fashioned idea of *Hispanidad*). *Hispanofonía* attests to the strategy initiated by the Spanish government in the late 1980s and which combines economic and linguistic elements. A significant moment was the 1992 celebrations of the 500th anniversary of Columbus' 'discovery' of the American continent.

The strategy involved a new 'discovery' of Latin American markets by the strategic sectors of the Spanish economy, which were encouraged to expand internationally through these markets. Telefónica SA also has been one of the flagships of this new 'discovery'. The privatization of the energy sector (oil, gas, electricity) and the state-sanctioned consolidation of the financial sector were additional strategies for ensuring the capacity of the Spanish economy to operate and compete in international, primarily Spanish-speaking, markets (see Casilda 2001; Martín Municio 2003). These recent reflections of the Spanish Minister of Foreign Affairs (a social democrat) can help to exemplify the orientation of this policy:

> Iberoamerican Summits have achieved more than other international organizations based on similar criteria of identity, such as the Commonwealth or the Francophone Community, with whom the Iberoamerican Community advantageously resists [sic] any comparison, maybe because, amongst other reasons, its signs of identity are more solid and the shared values more numerous and homogeneous. (Moratinos 2005; my translation)[8]

Leaving aside the fact that many criteria of comparison would not necessarily reflect on the alleged advantage of Iberoamerican cooperation over that of other linguistic blocs (nationalist discourses are generally and characteristically unimpressed by facts), what is interesting here is to appreciate the extent to which such discourses partially involve a simple transposition of nationalist themes into the international scene. This is remarkably apparent in new discourses on Spanish as a *lengua sin patria*, 'a language without a fatherland'. Del Valle (2005) argues that this theme is centrally developed in the recent discourses of Spanish intellectuals, as part of their claim that the Spanish language has ceased to operate as a symbol of national identity and has become a common resource for many peoples; they say that as a result no single community (read Castilian Spaniards) can stake a claim to symbolic ownership. What is interesting in these texts is (a) that their authors belong to the characteristic class of linguists/philologists traditionally involved in the production of national language ideologies (see Pujolar in press); (b) that most have a clear record as old-style nationalists; and (c) that most still seek to delegitimize linguistic minority movements within Spain, which shows the extent to which such discourses still involve tactical repositionings in traditional nationalist struggles within nation-states. Thus, what the evidence suggests is not so much that nationalisms are waning as a result of globalization, but rather that nationalists are revising their discourses and strategies as political and economic conditions change.

Nonetheless, as national elites manoeuvre to 'save the furniture', as the Spanish saying goes, discourses and policies concerning language must necessarily change. The case of the *Hispanofonía* provides again interesting examples, namely what del Valle (in press b) calls the 'moderate prescriptivism' of the Spanish Royal Academy (Spain's linguistic authority since 1713). This moderate prescriptivism consists of relaxing the most authoritarian or purist stances that traditionally considered only the forms of Iberian Spanish as correct, and of accepting variation and change as something valuable and positive, thus legitimizing linguistic forms accepted by other national academies of the Spanish-speaking world. One example of these changes can be found in the projects of a new working group created by the various academies of the Spanish language, and led by Dr Víctor García de la Concha, the director of the Spanish Royal Academy. After creating a *Diccionario Panhispánico de Dudas* [Pan-Hispanic dictionary of difficulties], the group is now working on a new Pan-Hispanic grammar which, according to its leader, 'shall be the first without a unified norm', 'non-peninsular', reflecting a 'polycentric norm' (Ruiz, 2005). This approach is reportedly aimed at 'making Spanish an international language'. Dr García de la Concha, who produced these statements in a speech at the Iberoamerican Summit, reportedly went on to state that 'the Spanish language was born and bred as a *mestizo* language'[9] as (still according to the reporter Jesús Ruiz) he was intently looking at the Portuguese Nobel laureate José Saramago in the audience, thus suggesting in an eminently ambiguous fashion that the Portuguese language might somehow be involved in this reconstitution of an Iberoamerican linguistic identity.

Now it is by no means clear whether these rhetorical gestures really inaugurate a new paradigm as to the ways in which language has been traditionally constructed and managed by governments and academic authorities. In fact, other 'mestizo' languages such as Spanglish are not so well received (Del Valle in press a). Rather, it seems that the Spanish Academia and other intellectuals are constructing a new discursive position under the new conditions of globalization. This position consists of presenting the language as not nationally situated in order to gain legitimacy in contexts formally characterized by multilateral, not hierarchical, relations. But the varieties such as Spanglish which lack a voice in these fora (in the form of a state-backed academic sector) cannot expect the same recognition. This cooperative articulation of linguistic models can also be presented as not inherently privileging the former imperial power, who nevertheless obtains the legitimacy to further its plans of economic expansion in all Spanish-speaking markets (ibid.).

De la Concha's vague wink to Portuguese-speaking cultural leaders also points to the possibility of some form of interlinguistic alliance that has not yet been defined or developed. There are, in other contexts, incipient examples of this kind of multilingualism, which appears to belong more to the field of declarations of principle than to specific policies and practices. For example, in the Council of Ministers of the Association of Caribbean States in 1998, in the face of the recent advances of English as a regional lingua franca, it was agreed that members would deploy policies to develop the competence of citizens in second and third languages (particularly French and Spanish) 'on the basis of a recognition of the plurilingual reality of the Caribbean space and of the need for a regional identity project' (Dahlet 2000; my translation).[10] The OIF has a strategic line of action called *les langues partenaires*. The documentation about these linguistic *partnerships*[11] suggests that the OIF seeks to present itself as sharing the concern of the governments of some former colonies (particularly African ones) for their own local languages. However, it is not clear how this formal support is translated into policy. Thus, what we presently see here is an investment in multilingualism as a principle in order to legitimate the use of widespread international languages such as Spanish or French instead of English.

Thus, developments within the Spanish and French linguistic blocs point towards an incipient post-national strategy that converges around the concept of *multilingualism* and which is now gathering the support of forceful social, political and economic sectors; much more powerful, at least, than its traditional supporters amongst minority activists and linguists. This does not mean, again, that all supporters of multilingualism are destined for a new linguistic Arcadia. Rather, it probably points towards new scenarios of struggles as to who gets to decide what multilingualism is about, how it is to be managed and evaluated and what the implications are for the social groups or linguistic communities targeted, ignored or otherwise affected by language policies.

conclusions

Globalization is turning the globe into the supreme stage for all types of social, economic and political changes. The implications of these changes for language practices, for the speakers of different linguistic varieties and for linguistic diversity are profound. Now that companies may have plants, workers and markets all over the world, now that international political bodies and fora increasingly grow in influence, now that populations are increasingly diverse and globally interconnected, states find it increasingly difficult to sustain a legitimacy that was based on territorially-bound cultural and linguistic uniformity, particularly when they are adopting policies that tend to leave public services at the mercy of markets. Moreover, as the service and informational sectors of the economy grow in importance, language emerges as a key economic asset and becomes the object of formidable interests for economic actors. From the perspective of the services and information industries, their products are always linguistic (or at least communicative), and so are their markets. Beyond their traditional value in the construction of identities, languages now have costs and benefits and language skills or applications can be bought and sold in contexts that are increasingly different from the national linguistic markets that Bourdieu (1991) so aptly described. Nation-states are no longer the main shareholders of their own national languages.

Dubbing the contemporary world as 'post-national' does not mean that nations, nationalism or nation-states are no longer relevant or are receding in favour of an international, transnational or cosmopolitan era characterized by an egalitarian multilingualism. There are, in fact, strong arguments to contend that nationalism is on the increase (Castells 1997). As I have argued above, what states and nationalist elites are doing is redrawing their strategies, seeking international alliances and influence to adapt to new economic and political conditions. Languages and linguistic ideologies are also being mobilized to support these strategies. However, the linguistic ideologies of the past (based on standard monolingualism) are also loosing their legitimacy and this means that a post-national linguistic order is emerging where ideological struggles converge around the management of multilingualism.

Bilingual practices and skills have had an uneasy fit in the traditional linguistic order. Firstly, bilingual communities were often seen as a threat to cultural unification. 'Local', 'regional' or 'home' languages were often presented as a barrier for access to the national languages. Bilingual practices, especially code-switching and code-mixing, also threatened the conception of languages as separate and autonomous and were treated with the common prejudices associated with cultural and racial hybridization. Only elite 'polyglottism' enjoyed a certain prestige. Nowadays, the tide seems to be on the side of multilingualism. The question is: what multilingualism(s)? Political institutions and the more linguistically-based sectors of the economy are pressing towards a multilingual framework that keeps the basic notion of unified sanitized standard varieties, whereas the more informal social spaces tend to promote increasingly fluid forms of cultural and linguistic hybridization. The tension can probably be felt in liminal spaces or points of confluence, such as the cultural markets that need to offer 'authenticity' (and hence hybrid experience) and, at the same time, standardized products designed for mass audiences. There is therefore a struggle not only to legitimate particular hierarchies between languages, but also between the most 'sanitized' and the most translinguistic language practices. Bilingual practices are at the core of these struggles: bilingual/multilingual skills are gaining market-value and are subject to processes of commodification and marketization. All in all, the old monolingual markets are undergoing a profound transformation and the new struggles over language seem to be focusing on what types of multilingual skills and practices are legitimate in an increasingly internation-alized economy and transnational experience.

The development of sociolinguistics as a discipline, and particularly of interactional sociolinguistics, has contributed to a critique of the language component of nationalism, particularly of linguistic purism and the prejudices towards bilingualism. It was the work of Gumperz that first presented code-switching as an accomplishment rather than as a result of faulty competence or performance (Blom and Gumperz 1972; Gumperz 1982). This has inspired a generation of discourse-analytical work on linguistic alternation (Auer 1998; Myers-Scotton 1998). Another sociolinguistic strand, inspired by the ideas of Barth (1969), has notably been busy deconstructing the link between language and ethnicity (Heller 2002; Rampton 1995; Woolard 1989) and, drawing from Bourdieu, making visible the ways in which language is used by social actors to construct categorizations and legitimize ideologies. Sociolinguistics is thus active in the deconstruction of modern nationalist discourses and, hence, in the production of post-national discourses where bilingualism, code-switching, code-mixing, borrowing or linguistic 'interference' are seen as productive strategies of expression and not as deviant practices. The challenge for sociolinguistics in the twenty-first century is precisely to find the ways to disseminate its findings and its critique so that they permeate the multiple social spaces and practices where the modern ideology of language is still hegemonic, and particularly wherever linguistic ideologies are mobilized in ways that intentionally or unintentionally produce exclusion and reproduce relationships of domination.

notes

1. I am thankful to José del Valle for his helpful comments on drafts of this chapter.
2. Some of these principles were not necessarily put in practice by French revolutionaries first. The indivisible character of state sovereignty had actually informed the policies of absolutist monarchs and Enlightenment elites. Here I am simply trying to summarize the basic principles underlying the historical development of nation-states.
3. The UNESCO website provides a comprehensive analysis of the 'International Legal Instruments' to further linguistic rights: <www.unesco.org/most/ln2int. htm#UN2>.
4. <www.linguistic-declaration.org>.
5. UNESCO Red Book of Endangered Languages (<www.tooyoo.l.u-tokyo.ac.jp/ Redbook/>).
6. Original text: 'Cataluña asiste al reverdecer de su nacionalismo político a costa de la pérdida de sus vocaciones universalistas [...], que es Madrid hoy el núcleo de interés cultural, artístico y sociológico más definido de España.' The author has also published a book called *El futuro no es lo que era* (Madrid: Editorial Aguilar, 2001) in collaboration with former Spanish president Felipe González.
7. I do not discuss the phenomenon of new movements and legislative initiatives to protect national languages such as French in France, Danish in Denmark or English in the US. Although it can be argued that these initiatives constitute a particular response to phenomena associated with globalization (such as immigration or global advertising), they appear to be constituted on the basis of old-fashioned nationalism.
8. Original text: 'las Cumbres Iberoamericanas han hecho más que otras organizaciones internacionales basadas en criterios de identidad similares, como la Commonwealth o la Comunidad francófona, con las que la Comunidad Iberoamericana resiste ventajosamente cualquier comparación, quizá, entre otras razones,

porque sus señas de identidad son más sólidas y los valores compartidos más abundantes y homogéneos'.
9. Original: 'Será la primera sin una norma única', 'hacer del español una lengua internacional', 'la lengua española nació y creció mestiza'.
10. Original: '[...] sur la base d'une reconnaissance de la réalité plurilingue de l'espace caraïbe et des exigences d'un projet identitaire régional'.
11. <www.francophonie.org/actions/francais/index.cfm>.

references

Aguilar, Laura (2005). Multilingüisme, etnicitat i qüestió nacional a Dinamarca: dinàmiques sociolingüístiques d'inclusió i exclusió socials. Unpublished dissertation. Universitat Autònoma de Barcelona.

Airob, David (1998). Convenio entre Telefónica y la Generalitat para catalanizar sus servicios a los usuarios. La Vanguardia, 1 April: 29.

Appadurai, Arjun (1996). Modernity at Large: Cultural Dimensions of Globalization. Minneapolis: University of Minnesota Press.

Anderson, Benedict (1991). Imagined Communities: Reflections of the Origin and Spread of Nationalism (rev. edn). London: Verso. 1st edn 1983.

Auer, Peter (ed.) (1998). Code-switching in Conversation. London: Routledge.

Barth, Fredrik (1969). Introduction. In Fredrik Barth (ed.) Ethnic Groups and Boundaries: The Social Organization of Culture Difference, pp. 9–38. Oslo: Scandinavian University Press.

Basch, Linda, Nina Glick and Cristina Szanton-Blanc (1994). Nations Unbound: Transnational Projects, Postcolonial Predicaments, and Deterritorialized Nation-States. Langhorne, PA: Gordon & Breach.

Bauman, Zygmunt (1998). Globalization: The Human Consequences. Cambridge: Polity Press.

Beacco, Jean-Claude, and Michael Byram (2003). Guide for the Development of Language Education Policies in Europe. From Linguistic Diversity to Plurilingual Education. Draft 1 (rev.) April 2003. Strasbourg: Language Policy Division of the Council of Europe.

Blom, Jan-Petter, and John J. Gumperz (1972). Social meaning in linguistic structures: Code switching in Norway. In John J. Gumperz and Dell H. Hymes (eds), Directions in Sociolinguistics: The Ethnography of Communication, pp. 407–34. New York: Holt, Rinehart and Winston.

Blommaert, Jan (ed.) (1999). Language Ideological Debates. New York: Mouton de Gruyter.

Blommaert, Jan, and Jef Verschueren (1998). Debating Diversity: Analysing the Discourse of Tolerance. London and New York: Routledge.

Bourdieu, Pierre (1982). Ce que parler veut dire. Paris: Fayard.

—— (1991). Language and Symbolic Power. London: Polity Press.

Bourdieu, Pierre and Jean-Claude Passeron (1970). Éléments pour une théorie du système d'enseignement. Paris: Les Éditions de Minuit.

Cameron, Deborah (2000). Good to Talk: Living and Working in a Communication Culture. London: Sage.

Casilda, Ramón (2001). Una década de inversiones españolas en Iberoamérica (1990–2000). El Español en el Mundo. Anuario 2001. Barcelona: Instituto Cervantes – Plaza & Janés.

Castells, Manuel (1996). *The Rise of the Network Society. The Information Age: Economy, Society and Culture.* Volume I. Massachusetts: Blackwell.

—— (1997). *The Power of Identity. The Information Age: Economy, Society and Culture.* Volume II. Massachusetts: Blackwell.

—— (1998). *End of Millennium. The Information Age: Economy, Society and Culture.* Volume III. Massachusetts: Blackwell.

Cazden, Courtney, Bill Cope, James Cook, Norman Fairclough, Jim Gee, Mary Kalantzis, Gunther Kress, Allan Luke, Carmen Luke, Sarah Michaels and Martin Nakata (The New London Group) (1996). A pedagogy of multiliteracies: Designing social futures. *Harvard Educational Review* 66(1): 60–92.

Cebrián, Juan Luis (1984). Cataluña vista desde el resto de España. *El País*, 8 January.

Cinco Días (2005). Telefónica cuarta 'teleco' del mundo por capitalización. *Cinco Días*, 11 October: 3.

Clifford, James (1997). *Routes: Travel and Translation in the Late Twentieth Century.* Cambridge, MA: Harvard University Press.

Council of Europe (2005) European Charter for Regional or Minority Languages. Application of the charter in Spain. Document: ECRML (2005) 4. Strasbourg, 21 September.

Curtin, Deirdre (1997). *Postnational Democracy: The European Union in Search of a Political Philosophy.* The Hague and Boston: Kluwer Law International.

Dahlet, Patrick (2000). Adhésion à la diversité et qualifications francophones dans la Caraïbe. *DiversCité Langues.* Vol. V. Online publication. Retrieved from <www.teluq. uquebec.ca/diverscite>.

Del Valle, José (2005). Lengua, patria común. In Roger Wright and Peter Ricketts (eds), *Studies on Ibero-Romance Linguistics.* Dedicated to Ralph Penny. Newark, Delaware: Juan de la Cuesta Monographs (Estudios Lingüísticos no.7).

—— (in press a). U.S. Latinos, la hispanofonía, and the language ideologies of high modernity. In Clare Mar-Molinero and Miranda Stewart (eds), *Globalisation and Language in the Spanish-Speaking World.* Palgrave Macmillan.

—— (in press b). Embracing diversity for the sake of unity. In Alexandre Duchêne and Monica Heller (eds), *Discourses of Endangerment: Interest and Ideology in the Defense of Languages.* London: Continuum International.

Fairclough, Norman (2004). Critical discourse analysis in researching language in the new capitalism: Overdetermination, transdisciplinarity and textual analysis. in Lynne Young and Claire Harrison (eds), *Systemic Functional Linguistics and Critical Discourse Analysis*, chapter 5. New York: Continuum International.

Fairclough, Norman, Phil Graham, Jay Lemke and Ruth Wodak (2004). Introduction. *Critical Discourse Studies* 1(1): 1–7.

Friedman, Jonathan (1997). Global crises, the struggle for cultural identity and intellectual porkbarrelling: Cosmopolitans versus locals, ethnics and nationals in a era of de-hegemonisation. In Pnina Werbner and Tariq Modood (eds), *Debating Cultural Hybridity*, pp. 70–89. London: Zed Books.

Gal, Susan, and Kathryn Woolard (2001). *Languages and Publics: The Making of Authority.* Manchester, UK: St Jerome's Press.

Gee, James Paul, Glynda Hull and Colin Lankshear (1996). *The New Work Order: Behind the Language of the New Capitalism.* Boulder, CO: Westview Press.

Gellner, Ernest (1983). *Nations and Nationalism: New Perspectives on the Past.* Oxford: Basil Blackwell.

Giddens, Anthony (1999). *Runaway World: How Globalization is Shaping our Lives.* London: Profile Books.

94   bilingualism, nation, state and capitalism

Grillo, Ralph (1989). *Dominant languages: Languages and Hierarchy in Britain and France.* Cambridge: Cambridge University Press.

Gumperz, John J. (1982). *Discourse Strategies.* New York: Cambridge University Press.

Heller, Monica (1999). Ebonics, language revival, la qualité de la langue and more: what do we have to say about the language debates of our time. *Journal of Sociolinguistics* 3(2): 260–6.

—— (2000). Bilingualism and identity in the post-modern world. *Estudios de Sociolinguistica* 1(2): 9–24.

—— (2002). *Éléments d'une sociolinguistique critique.* Paris: Didier.

—— (2003a). Globalization, the new economy, and the commodification of language and identity. *Journal of Sociolinguistics* 7(4): 473–92.

—— (2003b). Actors and discourses in the construction of hegemony. *Pragmatics* 13(1): 11–32.

—— (2005). Language, skill and authenticity in the globalized new economy. *Noves S-L Revista de Sociolingüística*, Winter. Available at <www.gencat.net/presidencia/llengcat/>.

Hill, Jane H., Nancy C. Dorian, Nora C. England, Joshua A. Fishman and Leanne Hinton (2002). Examining the language of language endangerment: An exchange. *Journal of Linguistic Anthropology* 12: 119–56.

Hobsbawm, Eric (1990). *Nations and Nationalism since 1760.* Cambridge: Cambridge University Press.

Inda, Xavier, and Renato Rosaldo (eds) (2002). Introduction. In *Anthropology of Globalization. A Reader.* Malden, MA: Blackwell.

Kearney, Michael (1995). 'The local and the global: The anthropology of globalization and transnationalism. *Annual Review of Anthropology* 24: 547–65.

Kearney, Richard (1997). *Postnationalist Ireland.* London: Routledge.

Lankshear, Colin (1997). Language and the new capitalism. *International Journal of Inclusive Education* 1(4): 309–21.

La Vanguardia (1998a). Quien no llora no mama. *La Vanguardia*, 25 February: 22.

—— (1998b). Villalonga, Pujol y 'El País'. *La Vanguardia*, 2 March: 18.

Lippi-Green, Rosina (1997). *English with an Accent*, chapters 2 and 3. London: Routledge.

Martín Municio, Ángel (ed.) (2003) *El valor económico de la lengua española.* Madrid: Espasa-Calpe.

Mautner, Gerlined (2005). The entrepreneurial university: A discursive profile of a higher education buzzword. *Critical Discourse Studies* 2(2): 95–120.

Moratinos, Miguel Ángel (2005). El nuevo espacio iberoamericano. Más que la Commonwealth o la francofonía. *El País*, 12 October: 15.

Myers-Scotton, Carol (ed.) (1998). *Codes and Consequences: Choosing Linguistic Varieties.* New York: Oxford University Press.

Phillipson, Robert (1992). *Linguistic Imperialism.* Oxford University Press.

Portes, Alejandro, and Rubén Rumbaut (1990). *Immigrant America: A Portrait.* Berkeley: University of California Press.

Pujolar, Joan (2006). *Language, Culture and Tourism: Perspectives in Barcelona and Catalonia.* Col·lecció Monografies sobre Turisme Urbà 2. Barcelona: Turisme de Barcelona.

—— (in press). The future of Catalan: Language endangerment and nationalist discourses in Catalonia. In Alexandre Duchêne and Monica Heller (eds), *Discourses of Endangerment: Interest and Ideology in the Defense of Languages.* London: Continuum International.

Rampton, Ben (1995). *Crossing: Language and Ethnicity among Adolescents*. London: Longman.

—— (2003). Hegemony, Social Class and Stylisation. *Pragmatics* 13(1): 49–84.

Rassool, Naz (2000). Contested and contesting identities: Conceptualising linguistic minority rights within the global cultural economy. *Journal of Multilingual and Multicultural Development* 21(5): 386–98.

Rouse, Roger (1995). Questions of identity: Personhood and collectivity in transnational migration to the US. *Critique of Anthropology* 15(4): 351–80.

Roy, Sylvie (2003). Bilingualism and standardization in a Canadian call center: Challenges for a linguistic minority community. In R. Bayley and S. Schecter (eds), *Language Socialization in Multilingual Societies*, pp. 269–87. Clevedon, UK: Multilingual Matters.

Ruiz, Jesús (2005). El próximo Congreso de la Lengua Española trabajará en una nueva gramática. *El País*, 15 December: 4.

Sassen, Saskia (1991). *The Global City: New York, London, Tokyo*. Princeton, NJ: Princeton University Press.

Skutnabb-Kangas, Tove (1996). The colonial legacy in educational language planning in Scandinavia: From migrant labor to a national ethnic minority? *International Journal of the Sociology of Language* 118: 81–106.

—— (2002) Marvelous human rights rhetoric and grim realities: Language rights in education. *Journal of Language, Identity and Education* 1(3): 179–205.

Snyder, Ilana (ed.) (2002). *Silicon Literacies: Communication, Innovation and Education in the Electronic Age*. London: Routledge.

Strathern, Marilyn (ed.) (2000). *Audit Cultures: Anthropological Studies in Accountability, Ethics and the Academy*. London: Routledge.

Telefónica (2005). Acerca de Telefónica: Descripción del Grupo: Cronología e historia: Historia. <www.telefonica.es/acercadetelefonica/esp/1descripcion/cronologiahistoria/historia.shtml>. This is an official website of the company Telefónica SA.

Telefónica I+D (1997). Telefónica I+D entrega la versión 4.02 del software vocal a Telefónica. Web News Reports of Telefónica I+D. <www.tid.es/noticias/a97/oct/softvocal/vocal.html>.

UNESCO (1945 [2002]). Constitution of the United Nations Educational, Scientific and Cultural Organization. In *Manual of the General Conference*, pp. 7–22. Paris: UNESCO.

UN (1976) *International Covenant on Civil and Political Rights*. United Nations General Assembly Resolution 2200A [XX1]. 16 December 1966. U.N.T.S. (United Nations Treaty Series) No. 14668, vol. 999 (1976): 171–346.

Vernet, Jaume (coord.), Eva Pons, Agustí Pou, Joan-Ramon Solé and Anna-Maria Pla (2003). *Dret Lingüístic*. Tarragona: Cossetània Edicions.

Viaut, Alain (2004). La Charte européenne des langues régionales ou minoritaires: particularités sociolinguistiques et configuration française. Documents de treball 15. Barcelona: <www.ciemen.org>.

Woolard, Kathryn (1989). *Doubletalk: Bilingualism and the Politics of Ethnicity in Catalonia*. Stanford: Stanford University Press.

World Tourism Organization (2004). Retrieved from <www.world-tourism.org> on 1 December 2004.

Zentella, Ana Celia (1997). *Growing up Bilingual*. Oxford: Blackwell.

5
beyond the nation-state: international agencies as new sites of discourses on bilingualism

shaylih muehlmann and alexandre duchêne

introduction

Since the rise of the nation-state in the nineteenth century, issues of bi/multilingualism have generally been debated within the context of nation-states and their institutions. This explains historical emphases on constitutional rights for linguistic minorities within specific nations, and on implementation of structures of regulation of bi/multilingualism in state-run institutions. In the last several decades, however, the nation-state has been displaced as the major site of discursive production on bi/multilingualism. In its place supranational organizations such as the United Nations (UN), and non-governmental organizations (NGOs) such as Linguapax, Terralingua and the Foundation for Endangered Languages are emerging as the primary sites at which debates on multilingualism are taking place.

In this chapter, we will focus on a genealogy of supra- and paranational agencies and their involvement in the production of discourses and ideologies about bi/multilingualism, with a focus on exploring the interests of participants in the spaces they are helping to create. We will also examine how this shift in the sites of discursive production is accompanied by a shift in discourses of bi/multilingualism, from an emphasis on constitutional rights to human rights, and from language diversity as connected to national or cultural identities, to linguistic diversity as connected to universal values of linguistic science or biodiversity. Finally, we will explore how, despite apparent intentions of going beyond the essentializing ethnocultural dimensions of nation-state discourses by appealing to universal values, supra- and paranational agencies in fact reproduce forms of essentialism and reification which may re-inscribe the very relations of power they set out to undo.

In order to examine how the shift in the sites of discursive production related to linguistic diversity, endangered languages or linguistic minorities has transpired we will trace how this shift takes place historically, describe the institutional forms it takes, and explore links among the various institutions involved. We will also describe what emerge as language issues to be addressed, and the new forms of regulation of those issues, which these agencies develop. This chapter will, through this exploration of the genealogy of international sites of discourse production, answer the question of why these agencies appear or acquire new positions and new visibility in the space of discourse on bi/multilingualism; why this phenomenon emerged when it did; and why it has taken the forms it has.

To emphasize the links between discourses and institutions we will examine the forms that current discourses on multilingualism take as well as the political economic conditions of their development. Accordingly, we will examine the institutional contexts from which these discourses emerge as well as the symbolic and praxeological spaces these discourses help to create. Drawing on Foucault's (1971) understanding of discourse as a jointly constitutive and constraining practice, we examine how emerging discourses on multilingualism are conditioned by historical and institutional processes while simultaneously participating in their construction. Our focus is less on the discourses produced in these institutions (see Patrick, this volume; Muehlmann 2007) and more on the way those discourses emerge at specific historical situations and particular institutional spaces.

In tracing the interrelations between institutional architecture and discourse (Foucault 1969), we build on works in institutional and linguistic anthropology (Bellier and Wilson 2000; Heller 1999a; McElhinny 1998; Smith 1990), by retracing the genealogy of particular discursive and institutional sites. This is an important task because the institutions from which discourses on multilingualism are now emerging are powerful political actors, which, by their very structural composition, are constraining the discourses produced. As a result these sites also constrain the possibility of action on language issues by influencing world policy, global laws, and ultimately, resource allocation. By examining the discourses on multilingualism produced at these sites, as structurally bounded and historically situated, we will show how the discourses that have emerged have done so at a specific political and historical moment and at a time when the changing face of the global economy had an impact on the dominant language ideologies produced.

the changing face of the sites of discourse production: from national to international sites of production

Because the nation-state was constructed on the premise of cultural, linguistic, even racial homogeneity, multilingual issues have traditionally been debated in those state-built institutions responsible for establishing this homogeneity.

The school in particular, has been a key space for the production of discourses on monolingualism, because it constructed languages as homogeneous, bounded units in the service of producing citizens of the nation-state (Heller 1999b; Heller and Martin Jones 2001). To be a citizen of the state was to act in ways consistent with the image of the state, including speaking the language of the State. This linguistic homogeneity, assumed by the nation-state formation, has problematized the role of those who could not speak the state language. This has resulted in ongoing debates on the constitutional rights of minority language speakers (Grillo 1989; Heller 1999a; Jaffe 1999; McDonald 1989).

The more nation-states expand their economic networks, however, the more they are integrated into an international capitalist system that undermines the control of any given state. It is through this erosion of state control that the new, 'globalizing' economy has called into question the role of nation-states, as emerging tensions between state based and corporate identities, and between modern nation-states and supranational structures, draw attention to an internationalizing of global activity. This expansion of nation-state economies, and the simultaneous strengthening of the private sector, has also resulted in greater articulations between local, national and supranational identities, as goods, people and information begin moving across boundaries at a new pace (Giddens 1991; Castells 2000).

In this transnational landscape certain sites have gained new visibility: organizations such as the United Nations (UN) have emerged as the legitimate positions from which 'global' interests are articulated. As a result, the nation-state has been displaced from its position as the authoritative voice on issues of multilingualism and as the most relevant interlocutor on multilingual matters. Instead, supranational organizations such as the UN and the United Nations Educational, Scientific and Cultural Organization (UNESCO), and international NGOs like Linguapax, Terralingua and the Foundation for Endangered Languages, become newly legitimate voices on issues of multi-lingualism. These kinds of organizations gain new visibility because NGOs and supranational organizations structurally have more legitimacy in an international context.

While the sites that have gained new visibility since the 1990s are often international governmental or non-governmental organizations, it is important to recognize that international organizations are not, in themselves, a new phenomenon. In order to understand the new roles these organizations play, we have to understand their historical emergence.

old sites and new visibility: the un and unesco

The history of nation-states and nationalism is intrinsically connected with the creation of various discursive spaces where economic as well as political interests have been at stake. The development of supranational agencies is but one step in this historical topology. Supranational agencies were the product of two movements that took place in the nineteenth century: the development of international conferences, and the emergence of international unions which offered a specific site of international cooperation (Abi-Saab 1981).

The League of Nations was a product of these movements and can be seen as a prototype for the supranational agencies, such as the UN, that were to follow. Created after World War I (WWI), the League of Nations moved beyond the construction of temporary spaces of regulation, which were achieved through international conferences, and instead provided an institutional space, with a specific physical location and permanent organizational structure. The League of Nations was conceived as a structure that would maintain peace by promoting the democratic foundation that would prevent conflicts. The League of Nations was a leader in regulating the new landscape, notably by regulating the boundaries built on the Allies' victories, and indeed it was explicitly structured in order to give the Allies ultimate decision-making authority.

The failure of the League of Nations in 1946 was due to several difficulties the organization encountered over the course of its existence, including a failure to enforce its sanctions, ineffective decision-making procedures, and a lack of a stable vision for the goals of the organization. Perhaps most critically, it was unable to recruit all of the world's leading powers: the United States, which had originally helped conceive of the League, was a particularly notable absence, but the USSR was also only belatedly incorporated in 1934. This weak membership culminated with Italy and Japan's shift from ally to enemy, and their subsequent defying of the League in a move that contributed to the outbreak of World War II (WWII). The war was the beginning of the end for the League, as it symbolized the League's failure to meet its original mission of maintaining peace.

The plan to construct a supranational agency for maintaining peace was not abandoned with the failure of the League of Nations, but it was clear that for such an agency to be effective it would have to be much more powerful than the League of Nations had ever been (Tardy 2000). With the tragedies of WWII very fresh in their minds, the victors were convinced of the need for an efficient international organization, and proposed a new structure that became the UN. The UN was designed to be useful beyond the specific historical contingency of the aftermath of WWII, specifically in order to avoid the limited effectiveness that resulted from the League of Nations' exclusive focus on the specific concerns of the immediate aftermath of WWI. The UN achieved this versatility by profiling itself as, above all else, a universal structure. The UN's intention to create a universalizing programme was expressed through two primary goals: to recruit all nations as members, and to create a set of universal rules that would apply to all member nations. The ethical and philosophical framework that underwrites the goals of the UN was based on the conviction that all human beings possess a set of inalienable and universal rights.

The UN's adoption of the human rights framework as the dominant paradigm has several explanations. The concept of 'human rights' legitimated an institutional logic that aimed to establish rules that could be applied transnationally by defining rights that override cultural differences. The framework also distinguished the UN's universalizing perspective from the League of Nations' bilateral one by establishing international laws, as opposed to individual treaties. And finally, the adoption of a human rights perspective legitimized the UN by providing specific standards for denouncing the atrocities committed during WWII.

Language issues only became relevant for the UN within this context of a human rights perspective. Specifically, language issues emerged along with the problem of minorities. The notion of the 'minority' has had a complicated history within the UN, which has shown ambivalence towards minorities since its creation (Bokotola 1992; Duchêne forthcoming). Minorities represent resistance to the hegemonic state and, thus framed, to speak of their protection necessarily gives rise to ambivalence. Furthermore, because the UN defined human rights as universal (understood in this case as both inclusive and individual), the recognition of minorities was initially considered redundant, since the human rights regime explicitly includes all humans; thus, individual members of minority groups are *de facto* incorporated into this framework. The human rights forum allowed the member states to officially recognize the existence of minorities without this recognition posing any risk or any limitations to the member states of the institution. This ideological stance was responsible for the deliberate absence of any reference to minorities in the Universal Declaration of Human Rights (UN 1948), allowing the occidental powers to argue that problems of minorities are in fact solved by the general application of these rights.

If minority issues were meant to be primarily solved through the framework of human rights and the Declaration, structurally minorities were nonetheless officially included within the framework of human rights with the creation of the 1947 Sub-Commission for the prevention of discrimination and the protection of minorities (including linguistic minorities). This sub-commission was created because it was not politically possible to completely phase out the issue of minorities since the UN was founded partially in response to the atrocities committed against minority groups during WWII. The sub-commission was therefore created as a secondary branch of the UN, and has little institutional power because it was designed as an expert space entirely subjugated to the political authority of the Human Rights Commission. Minority language rights did not explicitly appear in an international instrument until 1966, when an article on minority rights was formulated in the Covenant of Civil and Political Rights (UN 1966), article 27. It was not until 1992 that a specific declaration, the Declaration on the

Rights of Persons Belonging to National or Ethnic, Religious and Linguistic Minorities (UN 1992), was formally devised. However, while minorities are progressively becoming more legally recognized within the UN, this very recognition has also functioned as a mechanism for limiting their rights. For example, article 27 (the right for individuals from minorities to practise their own religion, enjoy their own culture and use their own language) is ineffective in nations that do not recognize the existence of minority groups in the first place, since it specifies these rights only 'in States where minorities exist'. The marginal legal recognition of minorities has been maintained by continually subjugating minority interests to the prerogatives of the member states. Therefore, the human rights forum allowed the member states to reconcile the paradox inherent in the need to officially recognize the existence of minorities, without allowing this recognition to impose limitations on the member states of the institution.

It is within this political and ideological climate that language issues emerge in UN discourses. Therefore, the issue of language is inseparable from the notion of minorities and human rights in the UN's framework. Language is only of interest to the UN insofar as it is seen as one specific characteristic of minorities (on the same level as such characteristics as religion and ethnicity). The language, minority and human rights triptych is significant because it constitutes a series of constraints on the actions of nation-states, which are seen as the dominant players in the model of international relations as envisioned by the UN.

The language, minority, and human rights triptych also constrains the discourses of other facets of civil society that interact with the UN. This is particularly visible in the practice and discourse of UNESCO, which was created in 1946 as a special agency of the UN. This agency's primary function is to fund studies and to create conventions and directives that deal explicitly with culture, heritage, science and education, with a mandate to collaborate with organizations representative of civil society, which are non-governmental and non-profit-oriented in nature; UNESCO therefore provides an interface between NGOs on the on hand, and the UN on the other. UNESCO profiles itself in two areas involved in language issues: multilingual and multicultural education, and cultural diversity as part of world heritage.[1] In this way UNESCO actively participates in the proliferation of NGOs on both symbolic and financial levels, but not without imposing significant constraints: 'such organizations must adhere to the ideals of the Organization, concern themselves with matters falling within its fields of competence, and have the means, and the will to contribute to the realization of its objectives'.[2]

Therefore while institutions such as the UN have gained a new visibility in a world increasingly fascinated with international flows, the discourses produced at the UN have remained largely static. The UN's particular take on language issues, which we have argued is based squarely on the concepts of minorities and human rights, has also shaped the discourses produced at relatively new international institutions, specifically, NGOs.

new sites and old discourses: the ngo

The shift in sites where discourses on bilingualism are produced is evident in the proliferation of a number of NGOs in the1990s that emerged to protect the biocultural or biolinguistic diversity of the earth and linguistic human rights. These include, but are not limited to the following: Linguapax, established in 1987; the Foundation for Endangered Languages, established in 1994, and Terralingua, established in 1996. These sites became important in debates on multilingualism for a number of reasons: because NGOs were playing an increasingly active role in UN activities, because NGOs offered a strategic position from which projects could benefit from multiple funding sources, and because NGOs were internationally positioned such that 'world-wide', as opposed to nation-state, language issues could be addressed.

The emergence of international NGOs in the past half-century (and especially the last two decades) has paralleled the expanding role of inter-governmental organizations in the political sphere. In the last half-century, NGO involvement in the United Nations system has become increasingly important, comprising a number of activities including information dissemination, awareness raising, policy advocacy, joint operational projects, and collaborating with UN agencies and programmes.

While non-governmental organizations have been active in the United Nations since its founding, several specific twentieth-century events formalized and intensified NGO participation in the UN. Article 71 of the UN Charter formalized the consultative status of NGOs within the UN. The creation of the Conference of non-governmental organizations in Consultative Status with the Economic and Social Council (CONGO) in 1948 established a coordinating body to guard UN interests in the consultative system. Additionally, the intensification of NGO interactions at the UN Conference on Environment and Development (UNCED) in 1992 had the effect of loosening restrictions on consultative status and, ultimately, in the agenda adopted at the Earth Summit in Johannesburg in 2002.

While the participation of NGOs at the UN has increased in the past half-decade, it is important to recognize that despite these advances, NGOs (and the civil society these organizations are understood to represent), have a distinctly subordinate role in the institutional structure of the UN. One of the consequences of this weak institutional position is that NGOs in dialogue with the UN draw explicitly on the UN's discursive orientation.

This is particularly evident in those NGOs that have a direct connection to the UN and UNESCO. For example, the Linguapax Institute is a non-governmental organization located in Barcelona that was created in 2001 to provide an institutional structure for a series of meetings organized by UNESCO. The basic orientation of the Linguapax Institute is the 'promotion of policies that protect language diversity and that foster the learning of several languages'.[3] Linguapax's recommendation for the role of languages in international governance has close ties to the philosophy put forth by the UN as well as by UNESCO. A central tenet of Linguapax's ideology is that a context of multiple linguistic contacts and language learning can become a way of achieving intercultural understanding and peace. However, unlike the international institutions from which Linguapax emerged, Linguapax focuses explicitly on the issue of languages. In doing so, Linguapax has been able to legitimize the importance of language rights by providing a UN affiliated institution through which to argue that languages, not just minorities, are implicated in potential conflict. Through this position language has become an explicit object of regulation.

Terralingua is an organization that has cast its web of institutional affiliations much wider than Linguapax. In fact, its website claims that in the short time since its founding in 1996, the '"Terralingua perspective" has gained a foothold all over the world, from the halls of the UN down to the grassroots' (Harmon 2000). Indeed, Terralingua is the most well known of the organizations that have recently emerged to protect biolinguistic diversity and linguistic human rights. It is a non-profit, international organization, that is composed of a group of academics, researchers, administrators and managers working in the fields of anthropology, linguistics, biodiversity conservation, and human rights. According to Terralingua's mandate these professionals share a fundamental belief: 'the challenge of protecting, maintaining, and restoring the diversity of life on earth is the challenge of supporting and promoting diversity in nature and culture'.[4]

Despite the wide range of disciplines represented at Terralingua, linguists have been the key actors in this institution: Luisa Maffi and Tove Skutnabb-Kangas are among those linguists who have played primary roles since Terralingua's inception. Their academic works have actively defended endangered languages through various conceptual frameworks including linguistic human rights, traditional ecological knowledge and biological or biolinguistic diversity (Maffi 2001, 2005; Skutnabb-Kangas 2000; Skutnabb-Kangas, Maffi and Harmon 2003). The discourses produced by Terralingua show clear links to these research priorities.

Terralingua has collaborated with a range of NGOs and other organizations dedicated to conservation and human rights, including: the World Wide Fund for Nature (WWF), Conservation International (CI), the United Nations Environment Programme (UNEP), the International Union for the Conservation of Nature (IUCN), the Convention on Biodiversity, the Millennium Ecosystem Assessment, UNESCO, and the UN Centre for Human Rights. Terralingua has also established partnerships with various academic and educational institutions such as the National Geographic Society, the Field Museum of Natural History, the Smithsonian Institution, Northern Arizona University, and the University of Florida. Additionally, Terralingua has worked on a variety of research, education and policy projects with all of these organizations. These projects have been funded by a wide array of institutional sources, including private foundations such as the Christensen Fund and the Ford Foundation, government agencies such as Canada's International Development Research Centre, as well as some of the world's largest conservation organizations including the WWF and The Nature Conservancy (TNC).

The international positioning of NGOs, achieved through both their participation in the UN system and their institutional alliances with other organizations, has had two noticeable effects on the discourses about language they produce. One effect is that the discourses produced have appealed to the legitimacy of ecological discourses by drawing on the paradigm of biodiversity conservation that had gained such success in the environmental movement (Conklin and Graham 1995). Another effect is that these NGOs have also drawn on discursive elements of UN documents, which emphasize a human rights framework. The incorporation of ecology and human rights discourses has shifted language policy debates from an emphasis on 'linguistic rights' to what is now more often formulated as 'linguistic human rights', and from 'linguistic diversity' to 'biolinguistic', or 'biocultural' diversity. We will further explore the nature of this discursive shift in the next section.

international organizations as new possibilities for discourse production

The shift in the sites of discursive production, away from nation-state institutions and towards international ones, appears to be accompanied by a shift in discourses of bi/multilingualism. While a discourse of language rights as constitutional rights was the dominant framework for discussions of multilingualism in the 1980s (Skutnabb-Kangas and Phillipson 1986, 1989), in the 1990s the rubric of biolinguistic diversity became increasingly visible in discussions of multilingualism (Harmon 2002; Posey and The United Nations Environmental Program, 1999; Skutnabb-Kangas et al. 2003). This shift in discursive frameworks entailed moving from emphasizing language rights as constitutional rights, to an emphasis on language rights as human rights, and from a concern with language diversity linked to national or cultural identities, to a concern with linguistic diversity in the context of world-wide ecological and cultural sustainability. However, while it looks like a new set of discourses on language emerges along with this shift in sites, the essentializing language ideologies that were dominant in nation-state discourses have in fact been reproduced, along with the particular discursive traps these discourses created.

As sociolinguists have documented, minority movements took over the very discourse of the centralized homogeneous nation-states which marginalized them, and created them as a category in the first place (Heller 1999a, 2002; Jaffe 1999, this volume). These movements have done so by claiming collective rights to political autonomy, in terms that are generally considered legitimate because they underlie the legitimacy of existing states whose power is being contested (Heller 2002: 19). Heller emphasizes that the successes of linguistic minority movements have also necessitated a recognition of the relations of inequality within the boundaries of what is understood as the minority. She highlights the fact that these are some of the problems faced by linguistic minority movements which adopt a discourse of collective political rights based on the ideology of the nation-state, at a time when the nation-state itself is being called into question.

Much like the discourses produced by linguistic minority movements, the discourses that have emerged from supra- and paranational agencies have also failed to move beyond the essentializing ethnocultural dimensions of nation-state discourses, despite the international positioning of these agencies. While the international organizations and NGOs we have profiled have focused on human rights as opposed to constitutional rights, these institutions continue to frame language issues within the problem of minority protection. The notion of linguistic human rights is contingent upon the concept of the linguistic minority, that is, a social group which is marginalized from centres of power on the basis of linguistic difference. In turn, the concept of the linguistic minority depends on the discursive formation of the nation-state understood as linguistically and culturally homogeneous. Therefore, the human rights framework persists as the dominant ideology through which minorities and linguistic minorities are understood in these institutions.

Despite the focus on 'biolinguistic' diversity in NGOs such as Terralingua, these organizations also ultimately reproduce nation-state ideologies. Like its counterpart in the notion of biodiversity, the notion of linguistic or biolinguistic diversity appears to highlight the interconnectedness of the 'global world', including connections between culture, nature and language. In this respect, the framework of biolinguistic diversity seems to provide a clear departure from the nation-state ideology of language, which constructed the unit of language through the formation of the nation-state. However, the discourse of diversity not only reproduced this ideology of language but also reproduced the paradoxical forms of resistance to it that were problematic for minority language movements. One manifestation of this is the technique of enumeration, which has been one of the primary discursive tactics NGOs have used to express the threat to language diversity (Hill 2002). For example, UNESCO claims that of the 6,000 languages in the world today up to 50 per cent will become extinct in the next century. The Foundation for Endangered Languages and Linguapax cite similar statistics on their websites.

The technique of enumeration initially emphasized languages, as opposed to dialects or any other category reflecting linguistic diversity, as the basic unit of linguistic diversity to be protected, borrowing the notion of autonomous languages from the ideology of the nation-state. But in developments similar to those which emerged from the challenges that were waged against the nation-state's homogeneous ideology of state-languages by minority language groups, new forms of linguistic autonomy are now being claimed by language endangerment NGOs. The argument for protecting 'endangered dialects' is particularly noteworthy because it takes the form of the discourses on language endangerment but applies it to a different scale of linguistic differentiation. For example, 'Terralingua declares: that every language is inherently valuable and therefore worthy of being preserved and perpetuated, regardless of its political, demographic, or linguistic status.' Terralingua sets forth the following goals: 'to help preserve and perpetuate the world's linguistic diversity in all its variant forms (languages, dialects, pidgins, creoles, sign languages, languages used in rituals, etc.) through research, programs of public education, advocacy, and community support'.[5] The irony in the argument for protecting endangered dialects is that it appeals to the inherent value of 'dialects', borrowing the same homogenizing logic used to gain support for 'languages'. Of course it was this logic that facilitated the exclusion of dialects from the endangered language canon in the first place.

Therefore, while supranational agencies create discursive spaces that address language questions on an international level, the ideology of these institutions shows that the nationalist perspective remains dominant and continues to shape discourses on multilingualism. What both the emerging endangerment discourses in the UN and language NGOs, and national school discourses demonstrate, is what Heller refers to as 'the inherent fragility of discourses of homogeneity' (2002: 16). In linguistic minority movements against the dominant nation-state language, this is evident in the recognition of internal fragmentation into more minority claims. In the discourses of NGOs such as Terralingua, this fragility is evident in the emerging discourses on the endangerment of dialects and intra-language variation. In both cases this fragmentation has a potential of infinite recursion, reproducing the mechanism of exclusion, which these groups initially set out to challenge.

shifting sites: consequences and possible challenges

Tracing the genealogy of these institutions provides a window onto the workings of the discourses they produce and how these discourses are partially shaped by shifting political economic conditions. By exploring the sociohistorical conditions linked to evolving ideologies of language we get a glimpse of why a discourse of biolinguistic diversity and linguistic human rights emerged at the time that it did, why it has taken the shape that it has, and how we, as sociolinguists, are implicated in this process.

What a genealogy of the new discursive sites of multilingualism has revealed is that, while the concept of language rights and constitutional rights made sense while the nation-state was the primary interlocutor, the discourse of universal human rights and of biolinguistic diversity has gained more salience in the context of the 'global world' where international organizations become the primary discursive sites. Consequently, the shift in sites from nation-state institutions towards international organizations has been accompanied by a parallel move towards discourses that mirror the international structure of the sites. Universal human rights are those that all of humanity ought to recognize, not just the nation-state, and biocultural diversity is a necessary condition for the health of the entire world ecosystem, not just individual nations.

As we have argued, however, this new discourse is not exactly new. The appeal to linguistic biodiversity and human rights incorporates an older discourse of linguistic rights but emerges in a way that takes a different shape. It can also be seen as a means of preserving ethnonationalist linguistic minority movements at a time when the discourse of the homogeneous nation-state is losing credibility (see Duchêne and Heller 2007; Cameron forthcoming; Heller 2002).

In fact, it is interesting to note that the same scholars who brought the issue of language rights into the field of sociolinguistics in the 1980s and 1990s, notably Robert Phillipson and Tove Skutnabb-Kangas (Phillipson and Skutnabb-Kangas 1995; Skutnabb-Kangas 2000; Skutnabb-Kangas and Phillipson, 1995) have now incorporated the discourse of language diversity into their work (Skutnabb-Kangas et al. 2003), and have instigated the shift of emphasis to linguistic human rights (Skutnabb-Kangas 2000).

Therefore, while the shift in the sites of discursive production on multi-lingualism is accompanied by an internationalizing of discursive strategies, there has been a fundamental continuity in this shift: the key linguistic experts have remained the same, and the underlying language ideologies have endured, although their legitimacy is articulated on different grounds.

The basis of legitimacy of the agencies have become linked to two domains of authority: science and international law, which in turn rely on developing structures that produce expert discourses drawing on these domains. Sociolinguists have played prominent roles in this process, in some ways legitimating the institutional and discursive spaces that have emerged. Because of the legitimacy that international organizations glean from these domains of authority, these organizations are also a strategic site for linguists to occupy for disseminating their own interests and promoting their own prescription for action.

The involvement of experts in linguistic activism is not new (Cyr 1999; Heller 1999b; Laforest 1999; Rickford 1999); however, the role that linguists have taken on in the context of the NGOs and supranational organizations we describe is noteworthy because it is a distinctly universalizing stance. In the context of a 'world-wide' threat to language, linguists are speaking on behalf of all dominated language communities. Therefore, an inherent asymmetry skews this discourse, as the subjects it addresses – the speakers of the languages to be protected – are further and further removed from the production of the discourses that emerge, ostensibly on their behalf.

This raises a series of questions about the role of the sociolinguist as a public intellectual, the value attributed to what we say, and the nature of the knowledge our discipline produces: Whose interests do we serve when we participate in public debates about language? What are the consequences of linguists endorsing reifying and essentializing notions of language?

Identity politics always involves projecting representations that reduce intragroup diversity to idealized homogenized images (Conklin and Graham 1995). The politics of language is perhaps not different in this respect. However, the question of whether essentializing language is an inevitable component of effective political action has not been fully explored.

When linguists participate in producing essentializing ideologies of language, we also risk obscuring the fundamental role that language plays in the construction of social inequality. What contemporary debates on multilingualism and language endangerment show is that language plays a central role in the processes of categorization, which regulate access to resources. If we cannot place our understanding of language in this context – as a central player in the social construction of inequality – we risk reproducing the very ideologies of language which marginalize some language groups in the first place.

We are not convinced that it is necessary to take this risk for effective political action on multilingual issues. In order to determine what alternatives might exist, however, a series of questions must be addressed: under what conditions could emerging networks of institutional structures provide a new platform for the discussion of multilingualism? How could this platform maintain a recognition of the role of language in the construction of inequality while avoiding essentializing ideologies? Through what mechanisms could international institutions make it easier for language minorities to by-pass the state in order to rally support among more international and perhaps more sympathetic audiences?

While answering these questions is beyond the scope of this chapter, we have instead attempted to trace the sociohistorical processes that have made it necessary to ask these questions at this time. The transnational institutions we have described deploy language ideologies to imagine the nation-state in only slightly different ways from institutions centrally involved in the construction of state hegemony. Indeed, the flow of language ideologies from nation-state institutions to transnational ones has, in fact, re-imagined state hegemonies on transnational scales. The emerging sites and modes for regulating language are thus an important institutional and discursive terrain on which social inequality is constructed, maintained, and crucially, potentially mitigated.

acknowledgements

We would like to thank the editor of this volume, Monica Heller, for her comments on earlier drafts of this chapter. Part of the research for this article has been facilitated by a individual research grant from the Swiss National Science Foundation (Alexandre Duchêne PNE1–102747).

notes

1. <www.unesco.org/most/ln2lin.htm>; <http://portal.unesco.org/culture/en>, accessed 4 May 2005.
2. <www.unesco.org/most/ln2lin.htm>, accessed 14 April 2005.
3. <www.linguapax.org/en/homeang.html>, accessed 2 May 2005.
4. <www.terralingua.org/AboutTL.htm>, accessed 1 March 2005.
5. <www.terralingua.org/SOP%20Translations/English.htm>, accessed 21 July 2004.

references

Abi-Saab, G. (1981). Introduction: The concept of international organization: a synthesis. In G. Abi-Saab (ed.), *The Concept of International Organization*, pp. 9–24. Paris: UNESCO.
Bellier, I., and T. Wilson (2000). Building, imagining and experiencing Europe: Institutions and identities in the European Union. In I. Bellier and T. Wilson (eds), *An Anthropology of the European Union: Building, Imagining and Experiencing the New Europe*, pp. 1–27. Oxford and New York: Berg.
Bokotola, I. (1992). *L'Organisation des Nations Unies et la protection des minorités*. Bruxelles: Etablissements Emile Bruylant.
Cameron, D. (2007). Language endangerment and verbal hygiene: history, morality and politics. In. A. Duchêne and M. Heller (eds), *Discourses of Endangerment: Ideologies and Interests in the Defense of Languages*, pp. 268–85. London and New York: Continuum International.
Castells, M. (2000). *The Information Age: Economy, Society and Culture*. Oxford: Blackwell.
Conklin, B., and L. Graham (1995). The Shifting Middle Ground: Amazonian Indians and Eco-Politics. *American Anthropologist* 97(4): 695–710.
Cyr, D. (1999). Metalanguage awareness: A matter of scientific ethics. *Journal of Sociolinguistics* 3(2): 283–86.
Duchêne, A. (forthcoming). *Language, Ideologies and International Organizations*. Berlin and New York: Mouton de Gruyter.
Duchêne, A. and M. Heller (2007). *Discourses of Endangerment: Interests and Ideology in the Defense of Languages*. London and New York: Continuum International.
Foucault, M. (1969). *L'archéologie du savoir*. Paris: Gallimard.
—— (1971). *L'ordre du discours*. Paris: Gallimard.
Giddens, A. (1991). *Modernity and Self-Identity: Self and Society in the Late Modern Age*. Cambridge: Polity Press.
Grillo, R.D. (1989). *Dominant Languages: Language and Hierarchy in Britain and France*. Cambridge and New York: Cambridge University Press.
Harmon, D. (2000). Invitation to join Terralingua, <www.undp.org.vn/mlist/develvn/012000/post69.htm>. Accessed 25 May 2005.
Harmon, D. (2002). *In Light of Our Differences: How Diversity in Nature and Culture Makes Us Human*. Washington, DC: Smithsonian Institution Press.
Heller, M. (1999a). Alternative ideologies of la francophonie. *Journal of Sociolinguistics* 3(3): 336–59.
Heller, M. (1999b). Sociolinguistics and public practice. *Journal of Sociolinguistics* 3(2): 287–88.
Heller, M. (2002). Language, education and citizenship in the post-national era: notes from the front. *The School Field* 13(6): 15–31.

Heller, M., and M. Martin Jones (eds) (2001). *Voices of Authority: Education and Linguistic Difference*. Westport, CT: Ablex Publishing.

Hill, J. (2002). 'Expert Rhetorics' in Advocacy for Endangered Languages: Who Is Listening, and What Do They Hear? *Journal of Linguistic Anthropology* 12(2): 119–33.

Jaffe, A. (1999). *Ideologies in Action: Language Politics on Corsica*. Berlin and New York: Mouton de Gruyter.

Laforest, M. (1999). Can a sociolinguist venture outside the university? *Journal of Sociolinguistics* 3(2): 276–82.

Maffi, L. (2001). *On Biocultural Diversity: Linking Language, Knowledge, and the Environment*. Washington, DC: Smithsonian Insitute Press.

Maffi, L. (2005). Linguistic, cultural and biological diversity. *Annual Review of Anthropology* 29: 599–617.

McDonald, M. (1989). *'We are not French': Language, Culture and Identity in Brittany*. London: Routledge.

McElhinny, B. (1998). 'I don't smile much anymore': Affect, gender and the discourse of Pittsburgh police officers. In Jennifer Coates (ed.), *Language and Gender: A Reader*, pp. 309–27. Malden, MA: Blackwell.

Muehlmann, S. (2007). Defending diversity: Staking out a common, global interest? In A. Duchêne and M. Heller (eds), *Discourses of Endangerment: Interest and Ideology in the Defense of Languages*, pp. 14–34. New York: Continuum International Publishing.

Phillipson, R., and T. Skutnabb-Kangas (1995). Linguistic rights and wrongs. *Applied Linguistics* 16(4): 483–504.

Posey, D.A., and the United Nations Environmental Program (UNEP) (1999). *Cultural and Spiritual Values of Biodiversity*. London: Intermediate Technology.

Rickford, J.R. (1999). The Ebonics controversy in my backyard: A sociolinguist's experiences and reflections. *Journal of Sociolinguistics* 3(2): 267–75.

Skutnabb-Kangas, T. (2000). *Linguistic Genocide in Education – or Worldwide Diversity and Human Rights?* Mahwah, NJ: L. Erlbaum Associates.

Skutnabb-Kangas, T., L. Maffi and D. Harmon (2003). *Sharing a World of Difference: The Earth's Linguistic, Cultural and Biological Diversity*. Paris: UNESCO, WWF, Terralingua.

Skutnabb-Kangas, T., and R. Phillipson (1986). Denial of linguistic rights: The new mental slavery. In R. Phillipson and T. Skutnabb-Kangas (eds), *Linguicism Rules in Education*, pp. 416–65. Roskilde: Roskilde University Centre.

—— (1989). *Wanted! Linguistic Human Rights* (Vol. 44). Roskilde: Roskilde University Centre.

—— (1995). *Linguistic Human Rights: Overcoming Linguistic Discrimination*. Berlin: Mouton de Gruyter.

Smith, D. (1990). *Texts, Facts, and Feminity: Exploring the Relations of Ruling*. London and New York: Routledge.

Tardy, T. (2000). L'héritage de la SDN, l'espoir de l'ONU. Le rôle de l'ONU dans la gestion de la sécurité internationale. *Revue Etudes internationales* 31(4): 691–708.

UN (1948). Universal Declaration of Human Rights. Adopted and proclaimed by General Assembly resolution 217 A (III) on 10 December 1948, United Nations.

—— (1966). International Covenant of Civil and Political Rights. Adopted and opened for signature, ratification and accession by General Assembly resolution 2200A (XXI) on 16 December 1966 (*entry into force* 23 March 1976).

—— (1992). Declaration on the Rights of Persons Belonging to National or Ethnic, Religious and Linguistic Minorities. Adopted by General Assembly resolution 47/135 on 18 December 1992.

6
language endangerment, language rights and indigeneity

donna patrick

introduction

Bilingualism, and the ideologies associated with it, are closely tied to social, political and economic circumstances. This is both because the linguistic practices that characterize bilingualism arise out of particular social conditions, which lead people to interact in particular ways in order to live together, and because bilingual practices in turn shape new social identities and new ways of interacting socially, culturally, politically and economically. This understanding of bilingualism can shed light not only on such well-studied cases as that of French-English bilinguals in Canada or Catalan-Spanish bilinguals in Spain, but also on the lesser-known cases that are the subject of this chapter: those involving Indigenous groups around the world. These groups speak both their 'traditional' language and a 'dominant' language, associated with a current or former colonizing power. This chapter will provide an analysis of this form of bilingualism, which has arisen in situations of language contact between Indigenous and larger colonizing or dominant languages.

A key to this analysis will be the observation of changing patterns of language use and their link to political and socioeconomic shifts among Indigenous groups. These in turn are related to larger economic and state processes that have their origins in the European mercantile expansion of the fifteenth century and colonialism. From the earliest days of contact, Indigenous people have been faced with the dispossession of their lands and have resisted and/or accommodated to new forms of power and the rise of state regulation and control. This means that they have adopted certain material things and concepts that have been useful to their survival, while actively engaged in struggles to control their lands and retain their political, social and cultural autonomy. These struggles have been crucial not only to combat marginalization and reduced standards of living among Indigenous peoples, but to also gain recognition and equitable treatment within the nation-state. While struggles over territory, language and culture have been intensely local (and national) affairs, they have now become global struggles. That is, they have become framed by global concerns around neocolonialism, neoliberal economic expansion and the destruction of the environment. As we shall see, this global intensification has arisen with the proliferation of international discourses on rights, social justice and indigeneity in the twentieth century.

In addition to territorial struggles, Indigenous peoples have also engaged in mobilization to 'protect' and promote their language and culture. This mobilization has generally been associated with the desire to assert Indigenous values, beliefs and practices – that is, Indigenous ways of life, cosmologies and relationships associated with land and the natural resources found there. In this way then, language struggles have become linked to material struggles over territory in complex ways. As we shall see, this complexity is manifested in contemporary discourses on language rights and language endangerment, that have drawn on 'modern' Western concepts of 'language', 'rights' and 'nature' to advocate for the protection of Indigenous language and culture. At the heart of these discourses is the following contradiction: appeals to maintain Indigenous languages are linked to the maintenance of 'pre-modern' values associated with 'traditional' life on the land; yet, to make these appeals requires one to discursively adopt a modern, reified notion of 'language' and to promote unifying and homogenizing kinds of language use. In other words, the rhetoric of modern nationhood, as built on 'one language and one people' is paradoxically taken up in efforts to resist modern cultural and linguistic domination. These language endangerment discourses, as we shall see, are shaping the ways in which bilingualism in dominant and minority languages is promoted, which ultimately serve the interests of some members of Indigenous groups but not others.

Recent international appeals for the 'protection' of language, culture and other forms of 'intangible' heritage have become useful discursive and rhetorical tools to further Indigenous goals to regain political and cultural autonomy and engage in other processes of decolonization. The promotion of both language rights and a greater awareness of language endangerment has figured prominently in the work of various supranational organizations, both governmental and non-governmental, as can be seen from the declarations, covenants and other documents emanating from these organizations (see Muehlmann and Duchêne, this volume). Discussion of these issues internationally has included discussion of language ecology, which we can understand as the economic, environmental and community contexts in which languages thrive, and the related issue of protecting biocultural diversity, the range of cultural and linguistic practices associated with these different contexts. Movements to promote language rights and language ecology have become popular ways for language groups and language advocates to mobilize in order to protect smaller languages. The interests of Indigenous groups have become a part of these language movements, as language advocates have found new ways to promote community-based interests in raising the status of Indigenous language usage and securing resources for language maintenance.

In what follows, we shall be examining the content of these discourses and some of their consequences for bilingual Indigenous communities. Among these consequences is that the promotion of one particular language variety and language group is often at odds with the complex and messy ways that languages are used in day-to-day life, especially in contexts of bilingualism and rapid social change. It also means that in struggles for equality and social justice, certain language varieties and speakers will nevertheless fare better than others. Despite these problems, movements to promote language rights and Indigenous languages have come to play a major role in the lives of many people. It is therefore imperative for scholars of language to look more closely at what is involved in these movements in order to understand the implications of these discourses, not only in the struggles over symbolic and material (land) resources, but also in relation to the intended and unintended consequences for the speakers involved.

The first section of this chapter explores the notion of 'indigeneity' and Indigenous languages. Indigeneity, which is closely tied to the process of contact between Indigenous people and European and other colonizing forces, involves assertions of Indigenous identities that are shaped by Indigenous social and economic practices, beliefs, and notions of place and territory. These aspects of Indigenous life have arisen out of centuries of contact with dominant groups and resistance to the efforts of these groups to assimilate them into dominant nation-states and to inculcate mainstream values and practices. As such, these Indigenous identities, beliefs and practices continue to mark both Indigenous 'difference' and diversity among Indigenous peoples. Indigenous languages are a significant part of these practices. These languages, like many other minority or smaller languages, are often seen as 'endangered', largely because of economic and cultural transformations and state policies. For Indigenous peoples, these policies have involved everything from land appropriation to residential schools, where use of native languages was forbidden. Indigenous languages have thus become the object of language preservation efforts reflected in the rise of Indigenous and language rights discourse.

The themes of language endangerment and language rights are explored in subsequent sections of this chapter. The second section examines the universalizing Western discourses of language rights and linguistic human rights. The section after that examines the endangered language and language ecology movements, and the appeals made for protection of the world's biodiversity and traditional knowledge, of which language is a part; and the fourth section offers a critique of these discourses and discusses four problems associated with the language rights and language ecology movements. The final section offers a summary and some conclusions.

While the focus of this chapter is Indigenous groups, it should be noted that national minorities (such as the French in Canada, Welsh in Great Britain and Catalan in Spain) have also adopted the ideologies of the nation-state and mobilized around language and culture to assert their own 'national' status and autonomy in their respective countries. Other minority groups, including people who may have migrated en masse across geopolitical borders and resettled within new nation-states, have also mobilized around language rights.

While there are similarities between the discursive strategies used by minorities and those used by Indigenous groups to promote their languages, there are also differences. Language minorities, for the most part, want access to modern state organizations and structures and wish to embrace modernity in order to gain access to social, political and economic structures on a par with the dominant culture that surrounds them. For Indigenous groups, however, language and territorial struggles are more complex. For these groups, there is a greater tension between the desire (even need) to modernize, in order to increase their standard of living and life expectancy, and the need to retain particular 'pre-modern' relationships to the land, people, waterways and animals – relationships which are central to 'non-Western' ways of life.

For both minority and Indigenous groups, discourses on language rights and language endangerment are part of the process of seeking full recognition and equitable treatment within the nation-state. However, for Indigenous groups, the links between language, land and culture have particular significance and are crucial to continuing processes of resistance and decolonization.

european expansion, indigeneity and the nation-state

We can understand Indigenous peoples as inhabitants of 'independent countries' who are 'descen[ded] from the populations which inhabited the country, or a geographical region to which that country belongs, at the time of conquest or colonization or the establishment of present state boundaries'[1] (International Labour Organization 1989, cited in Hughes 2003: 14–15).[2]

For Indigenous peoples, notions of 'indigenousness' or indigeneity are rooted in historical relations to territory, 'tradition' and environment. These relations have shifted over time throughout histories of conflict and accommodation found in the patterns of colonization. The chronology of colonization is similar for many groups. First came the arrival of 'foreign' mercantile explorers and traders, followed by the introduction of diseases, violent 'conquest' and/or other forms of colonial subjugation, the arrival of missionaries and other settlers, increased political and economic domination, and the continued encroachment upon and dispossession of Indigenous lands. Accompanying these material aspects of colonization were colonial discourses which privileged certain forms of knowledge over others. These included discourses of religious/moral, 'rational' and social superiority, which legitimized racial hierarchies, marginalization and the 'desettlement' of Indigenous peoples from their lands, which were rapidly resettled by the colonial population.

Throughout these processes, it is important to note that Indigenous people were not 'acted upon', but were active agents, adopting new technologies and concepts that had been useful (and often crucial) to their survival. These have included tools, machines, foodstuffs and dry goods that have become integrated into Indigenous ways of living. In addition, discursive practices such as literacy, schooling and forms of knowledge have been crucial in the mobilization of Indigenous groups in order to gain title to particular tracts of lands and to manage and control the resources on that land. These struggles for Indigenous control over land and resources have been necessary to combat the devastating effects of colonization and unwanted 'development', including social marginalization, high levels of unemployment, and other forms of economic 'underdevelopment'. And, as discussed in the introduction, these political movements to make material inroads have now been accompanied by appeals to 'protect' and maintain symbolic resources, including Indigenous languages and the cultural and spiritual beliefs associated with them.

patterns of indigenous bilingualism

As speakers, we value, and share meanings about, the languages that we speak in our interactions with people and participation in day-to-day activities. Our interpersonal relationships, and the languages that we use (or wish to use) in pursuing them, are shaped by particular historical, political and economic contexts. That is, our identities and social positions are constructed in large part through historical relationships and the conflicts and accommodations that have arisen between particular social groups and the state. For Indigenous groups, the historical processes and changing relationships have been crucial in the formation of social and political identities and patterns of bilingualism.

Colonizing powers bring with them colonizing languages, or dominant forms of literacy and ways of speaking. This form of contact results in different kinds of bilingualism for different groups. Thus, in countries such as India and many parts of Africa and Asia, local languages thrived alongside English, French, Spanish or other European languages. For many Indigenous groups, however, who maintained Indigenous harvesting (i.e. hunter-gatherer) economies, not only were their languages devalued (and seen as 'primitive' and 'backward') but their whole way of life was often at odds with the colonial forces, which sought land for settlement, economic exploitation and 'development'. In many cases, therefore, language contact between Indigenous groups and speakers of more dominant, powerful languages has often resulted in (1) bilingualism, whereby the Indigenous speakers learn the dominant language rather than the other way around; and (2) patterns of language shift towards the dominant language – which can involve not only an increased use of the dominant language in various domains of use, but dramatic vocabulary and grammatical changes in the Indigenous language.

Not all Indigenous groups, however, have experienced such forms of bilingualism and shift. Some Indigenous people were either pushed off large tracts of their traditional lands, or retained their livelihoods on remote frontier lands (unattractive to colonial exploitation), and have been able to maintain cultural and economic practices which have favoured the use of an Indigenous language. This is the case in more remote regions of Central and South America, and in northern regions of Canada, where a number of Indigenous languages (Cree, Ojibwe, Inuktitut, and some of the Athabaskan languages) are still being taught to children, but where English, as the language of power and 'modernity', is becoming more and more prevalent in everyday conversation. Other Indigenous groups have not fared so well, having been unable to recover in numbers from the devastation of war and/or disease. In other geographical regions, state policies such as residential schooling – often taking young children far away from their parents and communities to spend a childhood where speaking their Indigenous language was strictly forbidden – have drastically hastened the process of language shift. In all these cases, whether or not and to what extent a language shift takes place depends largely on the historical, cultural and political economic circumstances of speakers. In other words, there is no one factor responsible for people moving towards speaking a dominant language over an Indigenous one, but rather a number of social circumstances and ideological conditions.

indigeneity and social change

As noted above, processes of contact, resistance and accommodation for Indigenous groups began with the economic expansion of Europe in the fifteenth and sixteenth centuries and the resultant linkages between 'continents, societies, economies, and social actors' (Wolf 1982: 17). Through this expansion of web-like global connections, Indigenous material culture was transformed, as were notions of moral regulation, forms of governance through state structures, and the rise of various ethnic and national collectivities. Shared symbolic and ritualistic practices shaped notions of collectivity and belonging, from local communities to broader forms of imagined nationhood (Anderson 1991; Hobsbawn 1990: 59–62). Although Indigenous groups responded differently to the experience of colonization in different continents and centuries (see e.g. Wright 1992 for some examples from the Americas), they each retained a sense of 'indigeneity' – of profound attachment or primordial 'belonging' to their homelands, communities and the knowledge systems associated with these territorial and environmental attachments. Thus, through colonization, Indigenous peoples have constructed forms of 'difference' and maintained their distinctiveness, as reflected, for example, in their linguistic, cultural and spiritual practices.

As nation-states and the ideologies underpinning them developed and spread across Europe and beyond, so too did the policies and practices that defined rights, responsibilities and citizenship. Since European nationhood was rooted in the Romantic essentialization of language, culture and territory – that is, of one people being united in speaking one language in one territory – the languages of Indigenous groups that were 'brought into' the nation were put at risk. State policy to eradicate native language was ideologically justifiable through appeals to democratization, unification and citizenship through the institutionalization of and formalization of the dominant language. Here the development of literacy, institutionalized education, and standardization of written language worked against oral cultures and language use linked to traditional governance and land use practices. Ultimately, states have had the power to manage the social groups and to control the granting of rights to these groups within their borders. Different Indigenous groups have been subjected to these homogenizing forces of nation-building and new forms of social organization and have responded in different ways to them. These groups have also experienced varying degrees of linguistic and cultural assimilation, loss and revitalization. However, regardless of the degree of shifting among speakers to the dominant languages with which they have come into contact, their attachment to the lands on which they have hunted, fished, gathered or farmed since time immemorial has endured.

This attachment to the land is often seen as the heart of belonging to an Indigenous group. Yet, what for many Indigenous peoples is also at the heart of this belonging is their traditional language – which for some groups has meant mobilization around language issues and engaging in movements and discourses that seek to 'promote and protect' these and other 'endangered' languages. Language endangerment discourse has drawn largely on appeals to understand languages as 'living entities' that have been 'dying' world-wide in the twentieth and twenty-first centuries as a result of the colonization and neoliberal economic expansion, shifting peoples and their languages into new political economic realities.

indigenous and other endangered languages

One of the many texts which comprise language endangerment discourse is the *Red Book on Endangered Languages*, a web-based UNESCO (the United Nations Educational, Scientific and Cultural Organization) document cataloguing threatened languages. Similar to other writings on the subject, it notes that by the end of this century, at least half of the world's languages, the majority of them Indigenous, will have very few or no speakers left.[3] Other reports have appeared in academic books and articles, websites, and the popular media, that have presented statistics and other facts about the precarious nature of Indigenous and other smaller, lesser-used languages, and some of the measures used to promote and 'save' these languages including recording, documenting and teaching them.[4] Although important cultural, social and linguistic reasons have been claimed for these measures, including the urgent need to document the world's linguistic and cultural diversity, the documentation often notes that resources allocated to this vast enterprise have been insufficient. Moreover, what reports about these languages all seem to indicate is that the increased amounts of money devoted to them have done little to alter the fact that the majority of the world's 'languages' risk falling into disuse.[5]

The discourse of language endangerment has focused largely on the 'loss' of languages, and the lack of resources to document (largely) Indigenous languages as speakers shift to dominant language varieties which offer more economic and social power. This process of shift has been labelled a 'crisis' and forms the rhetorical (and often alarmist) basis for garnering international support for language documentation and revitalization (Krauss 1992). Key to this discourse is its inherent depoliticization, since it is abstracted away from the political economic context of speakers. That is, rather than focusing on the speakers themselves and their shifting political and economic relations, the discourse turns towards the grammatical features of these languages and the cultural knowledge that they encode, and the risks of 'losing' these forms and knowledge forever. There is thus a disconnect between this largely depoliticized language endangerment discourse and the increased politicization of Indigenous groups and the Indigenous movements that have emerged in the latter half of the twentieth century.

indigenous languages and political struggle

The rise of postcolonial independence after World War II brought with it an array of mobilizing strategies for Indigenous peoples, which have included the development of a group consciousness and collective identities, the recognition of centuries of resistance and engagement in new forms of resistance, and the construction of a politics of 'difference' (Smith 1999; Feldman 2001). Significantly, language has figured prominently in all of these processes; and political struggles – whether to achieve equality for Indigenous peoples, to gain greater political recognition or some form of autonomy, or to reclaim territory – are usually intertwined with language struggles, even if this linkage has not always been made explicit.

Given this connection between Indigenous languages and politics, we can just as easily say that language struggles are usually tied to political struggles, even if the former are not always seen that way. We can then begin to understand how depoliticized discourses on language endangerment and language survival, and actions taken to 'save' languages, can have unintended consequences for the language groups and speakers involved in them. One such consequence is the increased politicization of language groups, who make strategic use of language rights and survival discourse to advance particular political goals. Another is increased competition between groups, as divisions between groups become exacerbated through the increased rights or resources gained for the language variety of one group but not others. A third such consequence is the creation or promotion of a group identity which may not even have existed before actions were taken to 'save' the language (see e.g. Whaley 2004). A final unintended consequence of such discourses, and particularly the discourse of biocultural diversity, is the essentialization of language, culture and environment, which creates an inextricable link between them. This can have significant implications for Indigenous people themselves, in their efforts to gain more control over development on their lands. This is because notions of 'authenticity' – of who counts as an 'authentic' Indigenous person or representative – can become linked in a timeless past to traditional clothing, language use and other cultural practices, which then become the only 'legitimate' forms of indigeneity, and the only ones recognized as 'authentic' by the dominant group. The danger here is that those whose linguistic or cultural practices do not accord with these notions of authenticity might have no legitimacy as representatives of Indigenous people, making suspect any claims that they might make for the need to 'save' Indigenous language and culture. Given the power associated with these discursive constructions, it may become difficult to step beyond such stereotypes. All of these unintended consequences of language endangerment discourse, which we shall be examining in detail in the following sections, suggest the great difficulties associated with this discourse as mobilization enters global as well as local and national arenas.

rights discourses and the protection of the world's languages

In the late twentieth century, rights have become a widely discussed issue in the broader language endangerment discourse. This is not only because they are important for the protection and support of Indigenous and minority languages, but also because of the push for the recognition of universal linguistic human rights (see e.g. Capotorti 1979; Thornberry 1991; de Varennes 1996; Kontra, Skutnabb-Kangas, Phillipson and Varady 1999; Kymlicka 1995; Phillipson 1998, 2003; Skutnabb-Kangas 2000, 2002; Skutnabb-Kangas and Phillipson 1994). This proliferation of work on rights has in turn led to increased sociolinguistic discussion and critique and has attracted the attention of sociolinguists, language planners and sociologists of language. In fact, it is useful to examine these critiques if we are to understand the claims that have been made to grant language rights to Indigenous and other minority language groups and the consequences of doing so (see May 2005a, Freeland and Patrick 2004, and Wiley and Ricento 2002 for overviews of some of these issues).

language rights and linguistic human rights

A good place to start our investigation of language rights is by examining rights more generally. One way to think about rights is as entitlements or privileges to something for which one has a just claim. Rights can be granted to people by other, usually more powerful, people or by institutional, state or other governance structures. They can also be, and often are, recognized in law.

Among the rights that have been widely recognized are human rights, which embody the 'natural rights' stemming from the European Enlightenment and the liberal ideal of individual liberty. Natural rights derive from the 'law of nature' and are part of what it means to be able to live fully as a human being – for example, being able to work, having an adequate standard of living, and having access to education. Human rights are also conceived of as 'inalienable rights', which are absolute in the sense that they are not granted by humans and cannot be transferred or taken away. Both of these concepts of rights have moral appeal for nation-states, which either have, or are aspiring to have, related liberal principles.

Since rights can be recognized in law, it is important to note that any law that grants language rights has a regulatory function. That is, its goal is to regulate or 'manage' language conflicts, including those that arise in situations of bi- or multilingualism as a result of social injustice, exclusionary practices, and other inequities in the production and distribution of linguistic resources (see Patrick 2005). In other words, language rights become the means for working out 'language problems', which are usually part of larger political problems within nation-states. This regulatory nature of rights is often overshadowed by their moral dimension, particularly when rights are invoked in recognizing minority or Indigenous groups and in addressing issues of equality.

The pressure on states to recognize Indigenous and minority peoples has emanated from and been reinforced by the production and circulation of Western rights discourses in supranational organizations, most notably the United Nations and two of its organizations: UNESCO and the International Labour Organization (ILO). Among the key declarations and covenants produced by these organizations are the *Universal Declaration of Human Rights* (1948), the *International Covenant of Civil and Political Rights* (1966, 1976), the *Declaration on the Rights of Persons belonging to National or Ethnic, Religious and Linguistic Minorities* (1992), the ILO *Convention 169 concerning Indigenous and Tribal Peoples in Independent Countries* (1989), the United Nations *Draft Declaration on the Rights of Indigenous Peoples* (1994), and the *Draft International Convention on the Protection of the Diversity of Cultural Contents and Artistic Expressions* (2005). These universal discourses have been crucial for Indigenous and other minority groups, who have rallied around them in order to gain recognition, material and symbolic support, and protection within nation-states.

Significantly, however, there is no specific reference in these discourses to language rights, which has motivated some language scholars to advocate for linguistic human rights (LHR) as a kind of inalienable human right. The language rights movement that has emerged has drawn support from the larger language endangerment or language ecology movements (May 2005b: 319), to be discussed in more detail below.

While the goal of espousing LHR is to help protect the languages of particular groups by appealing to universal principles and to the international community, the appeal to such rights is not without problems. Most glaring among them is that, despite these efforts to override the interests of particular nation-states, the recognition of human and other rights remains very much a matter for nation-states, so that linguistic human rights are almost as much at the mercy of national interests as any state laws are. There is thus something deeply paradoxical in the conception of 'human rights' as inalienable rights, as noted by Asad (2003, cited in Patrick 2005: 372):

> [T]he notion that inalienable rights define the human does not depend on the nation-state because the former relates to a state of nature, whereas the concept of citizen, including the rights a citizen holds, presupposes a state that Enlightenment theorists called political society. Human rights, including the moral rules that bind humans universally, are intrinsic to all persons irrespective of their 'cultural' make-up. Yet the identification and application of human rights law has no meaning independent of the judicial institutions that belong to individual nation-states (or to several states bound together by treaty) and the remedies that these institutions supply – and therefore of the individual's civil status as a political subject. (Asad 2003: 129)

As this passage suggests, any role that human (and other) rights can have in eliminating social injustice depends on their being officially recognized by nation-states; accordingly, such rights are severely limited both in their moral appeal and in their effectiveness in eliminating such injustice. This is particularly the case because nation-states act in their own interests when they grant rights and enact laws – as reflected, for example, in who counts as what kind of political subject with what kinds of rights. This means that a nation-state's own interests may conflict with its granting of language and other rights to Indigenous or minority groups (Patrick 2005: 372).

Notwithstanding the difficulties just described, some language groups will continue to fight for their right to be educated in their language, to have their language officially recognized, and to garner resources to revitalize and protect their languages. This is because some form of recognition or protection of their language – and by extension, of the cultural and other interests of the language group itself – is better than none. For many Indigenous groups, the mobilization and recognition of language issues is part and parcel of other forms of mobilization to gain political and cultural autonomy and some form of increased territorial control.

In sum, language rights and the promotion of linguistic human rights have been important for speakers of Indigenous and other 'small' languages. Discriminated groups have come to rely on the power and appeal of universal discourses to legitimately demand that a language variety associated with the group, and in turn the group itself, receive protection against symbolic domination within state and supra-state structures.

Of course, our discussion of language rights so far has not addressed various other important questions about these rights. These include how such rights are granted by particular state structures and how they become policy or law, enacted to 'manage' language conflicts in bi- and multilingual settings. These also include questions about sociolinguistic realities on the ground and social effects on actual speakers, when rights are granted and language policies are implemented. Before turning to these issues, however, we need to examine the language ecology and biocultural diversity movements with which the LHR movement is associated, which have become basic to international mobilization for language rights, language revitalization and language protection more generally.

language ecology and biocultural diversity movements

While many Indigenous and minority language groups have sought protection for their languages in the international arena, there has been increasing interest in the links between biodiversity and the preservation of language and culture. This issue has been framed in terms of language ecology and biocultural diversity, which have given rise to global movements.[6] Language ecology is broadly conceived as the way in which a language interacts with its environment, including the various activities that speakers of the language engage in, the institutional support that a language receives, and the encoding of ecological systems (Mühlhäusler 1996, 2000). Similarly, biocultural diversity involves the relationship between language, knowledge and the environment – a relationship often thought to be breaking down 'under the pressure of "modernization"' (Maffi 2001: 3).

Both language ecology and biocultural diversity rely crucially on the metaphor of languages as living things or 'species', which is consistent with metaphorical talk of languages 'living', 'surviving' and 'dying'. While certain problems arise in conceiving languages as 'species', as will be discussed below, the biological and ecological associations that this discourse invokes have had considerable rhetorical appeal for Indigenous language movements.

The ecological linguistic approach 'investigates the support system' of a language (Mühlhäusler 1996: 313), which can be conceived of as a 'habitat' consisting of the social and economic conditions that allow languages to thrive. Thus, languages are 'lost...as a result of the loss of their non-linguistic support system' (ibid: 322) and 'new self-sustaining ecological systems can be created, combining indigenous and introduced species' (ibid: 323). As long as the 'Indigenous' language species can coexist with an 'introduced' predator language, a new ecological balance can be struck in which bilingualism and diversity will thrive. Diversity is thus seen as a human 'good', since it ensures economic and social well-being – in other words, the maintenance of a healthy habitat (Mühlhäusler 1996, 2000).

The loss of traditional 'habitats' or economic systems, such as hunting and other harvesting activities, coincides with the loss of biodiversity due to encroaching development and modernization and a parallel loss of language. This link between the environment, language and traditional ecological knowledge about plants and animals and the spiritual, cultural and healing practices related to them is key to the 'biocultural diversity' perspective. That is, an Indigenous group, living in a particular ecosystem, will organize information and knowledge about this ecosystem in their language.

Closely tied to the promotion of biocultural diversity is the notion that languages should be revitalized because of their intimate connection to traditional ecological knowledge (TEK). This notion has provided a useful strategy for Indigenous groups, who can thus appeal to national and international covenants and law in seeking to protect the environment and biological diversity. Appeals can also be made to the need to protect 'intangible heritage', of which TEK and Indigenous languages are a part. International conventions, declarations and covenants, such as the UNESCO (2003) *Convention for the Safeguarding of the Intangible Cultural Heritage* and the *Universal Declaration of Cultural Diversity* (2001), have accordingly become useful tools in lobbying for such protection.

The key to understanding these claims from an Indigenous perspective is that the link between biodiversity and TEK depends crucially on the link between languages and 'the land'. In fact, we might say that the restitution of land taken through colonization has become a key issue, to which language and cultural issues have become associated (see Patrick forthcoming). This is not to undermine the significance of language and culture, but simply to highlight the material importance of land and its relation to linguistic and cultural practices. As such, appeals to international conventions on Indigenous rights, such as the ILO *Convention 169 concerning Indigenous and Tribal Peoples in Independent Countries* (1989) and the United Nations *Draft Declaration on the Rights of Indigenous Peoples* (1994), become as relevant to the protection of language as the *Convention on Biological Diversity* (1992).[7]

Just as the appeal to language rights has provided a political means for Indigenous groups to fight for resources to promote and legitimize particular language varieties, so too does the appeal to biodiversity and its link to language. The international arena in which these appeals are made has thus become a political space in which Indigenous groups can seek support and gain moral clout in dealing with language and cultural issues within their own national structures.

critiques of the 'species' metaphor

In spite of the rhetorical and strategic power achieved by linking language to environmental issues, as is evident in the national and international campaigns just alluded to, there are very basic problems with metaphors that liken 'languages' to 'species' and 'linguistic diversity' to 'biological diversity', creating a distorted view of languages and language endangerment. These problems have been discussed at length in Freeland and Patrick (2004) and Patrick (2004), and the remarks that follow are based on these studies.

There are at least three basic problems with the 'language as species' metaphor at the heart of this language preservation discourse. One problem is that it reinforces the belief that languages can be viewed as 'discrete', bounded objects. Even if we accept this metaphor and recognize that there is always biological variation within species, the fact remains that the category 'species' predisposes us to see language as a well-defined 'object'.

A second problem is that this metaphor has the effect of sidelining the actual speakers of endangered languages – a rather troubling fact, given that it is the speakers of a language who live and die, rather than the languages that they speak. This problem highlights the need for an approach to language study that shifts the focus from languages as 'species' or objects in the world to language speakers themselves, who use languages in multiple ways and in particular social, political, cultural and geographical contexts. As these contexts alter the patterns of living languages, they also create new ways in which languages are used, as people form new social networks and allegiances. Thus, while speakers' linguistic practices may change, markers of 'difference' and particular cultural meanings and ideologies do not necessarily 'die'. Such considerations ultimately lead us to investigate to what extent cultural continuity and new identities among Indigenous groups are manifested in new forms of language use.

A third, closely related, problem with this metaphor is that language varieties do not 'disappear' in the same way that 'endangered species' do. Although one language variety may fall out of use, new forms may be created that contain the discursive, lexical or pragmatic features of the old variety. In other words, a language variety, unlike our commonly-held conceptions of an 'endangered species', does not completely disappear. Likewise, a language's falling into disuse does not generally result in speakers' linguistic repertoires being 'out of balance' in the same way that an ecosystem might be with the extinction of a species; instead, the linguistic repertoires of speakers will continue to change and develop. An even more problematic aspect of the idea that languages 'die' just as other species do is the slippery slope from this idea to a 'survival of the fittest' view of language varieties, where the 'strongest' among them survive because of greater ability to 'adapt' to the environment – a view that is at odds with the way language and power interact with historical processes to create dominant languages (see e.g. Grillo 1989). It is not the 'strength' of a language in and of itself which accounts for its dominance, but rather the political and economic conditions in which its use is embedded.

These considerations suggest that we should move away from a view of languages as biological species and focus on actual language speakers and the social and political economic conditions in which languages are used. If we are to make use of this biological analogy at all, it would make more sense to focus on linguistic 'habitats', and how these sustain linguistic practices, than on language 'species' *per se*. Languages change and shift depending on the social context – including the economic, cultural and political milieu in which speakers find themselves. What this means is that speakers, as social actors, as well as the political economic context in which they live, need to be part of the language–power–survival equation.

As we have just seen, the 'species' metaphor of 'language survival', though rhetorically powerful, can obscure the fact that new forms of language are constantly developing in increasingly complex social and cultural relations. These new forms include the language of younger speakers and mixed language forms, which are often considered illegitimate, as well as revived forms of language, which might be considered to lack authenticity. This makes the study of bi- and multilingualism a complex one. Local and global forces are at play, situating speakers in particular sociocultural, historical and economic environments. As students of bilingualism, we need more sophisticated ways of relating language to context, not just through an analysis of registers and genres, but by understanding that there are different ways of 'doing language' and of linking new language forms to culturally meaningful and socially significant practices.

One way to move forward in our understanding of language endangerment and its relation to Indigenous and minority-language groups is to address some of the other problems that arise when these groups attempt to revitalize their 'endangered' language, as we shall do in the next section.

problems in language rights and language endangerment discourse

In the previous section, we dealt with certain problems associated with the 'language as species' metaphor at the heart of current language endangerment discourse. Here, we shall be dealing with a different, though closely related, set of problems: namely, those that arise when rights are granted, languages are promoted and language policies are implemented. Since it is important to foster a dynamic relationship between language 'experts' and the Indigenous and minority groups that they serve, it is especially important for academics, language activists, supranational and state organizations, and others concerned with language endangerment to recognize the consequences of the discourses and practices that they engage in. These consequences include the ways that this discourse can shape conceptions about language, culture and Indigenous people and how it interacts with the desires and goals of people belonging to smaller language groups. If Indigenous and other groups are to benefit from interventions and other processes related to language 'survival', language rights and state policy, we need to consider what is involved, and what is at stake, in these processes.

Four interrelated critiques of language rights and language ecology/ endangerment discourses can serve to raise our awareness of the difficulties associated with the promotion of endangered languages. These are as follows:

1. Language endangerment discourse tends to romanticize language and cultures.
2. Language issues in language endangerment/rights discourses are often treated as cut off from the historical, political and economic context in which speakers find themselves.
3. The notion of mobility, and its geographic and social complexity for speakers, is often sidelined in rights and endangerment discourse.
4. Nation-building and the related codification of language within the nation-state are unifying and homogenizing processes, which risk excluding and marginalizing minorities or people from less powerful groups.

The rest of this section will elaborate upon these four critiques and how they are related to indigeneity and the issues surrounding Indigenous languages in particular. We will then consider how we might transcend these conceptual problems and come to a better understanding of the nature of bilingualism in the context of a discourse of Indigenous language endangerment.

the romanticizing of languages and cultures

The idea of 'saving' the world's smaller, less-used languages has often been criticized as reflecting an overly romantic or sentimental view of 'pristine' past cultures. Among the difficulties noted for the romanticizing of languages and cultures are (1) that it is simply naïve to romanticize smaller languages while failing to recognize the inevitable shift to more useful, dominant ones (see May 2005b: 321); and (2) that this romanticism risks essentializing not only language, culture, territory and a 'people', but also the links between language, culture and traditional knowledge. For Indigenous people, and for any 'traditionally'-based minority language group for that matter, the latter point is particularly important. Linking a language to a people and a 'tradition' is often not in the interests of all speakers. In fact, linking people to particular 'traditional' identities and practices can be detrimental and at odds with the goals to improve life conditions. This is particularly important given the contradictory position of many communities that need to 'modernize' to gain the infrastructure and social conditions to better their living conditions, and at the same time, desire some form of bilingualism, maintaining the 'traditional' language.

The 'romantic' ideas that have been targeted by this criticism of endangerment discourse are ones that evolved from the eighteenth- and nineteenth-century philology and the romantic philosophy of Johann Gottfried Herder, who viewed 'tradition' and folklore, and the languages that expressed them, as 'pure' and 'natural' expressions of the *Volk* (Bauman and Briggs 2003). This not only glorifies folklore as somehow 'superior' in moral character, but also essentializes language, culture and 'peoplehood', located in a timeless past.

Despite the force of these criticisms, a reasonable response to the claim outlined in (1) above, that the romanticizing of smaller languages is simply naïve, is that various contexts in which bilingualism continues to thrive demonstrate that there is, in fact, nothing inevitable about a shift of smaller (minority or Indigenous) languages to dominant ones (see May 2005a for discussion). In places like Quebec, Wales, France and Spain, where language rights have been granted and language has become politicized, minority and Indigenous languages are in daily use (see e.g. Heller 1999a, 1999b; Patrick 2003; May 2000; Woolard 1989; Jaffe 1999). Thus, there is still considerable motivation for Indigenous groups to use the political spaces offered by language rights discourses to further their aims for more local, political and cultural autonomy.

A forceful response to the criticism outlined in (2), however, is more difficult to come by, since the 'essentializing' of languages and cultures seem to have a largely negative effect on them. When 'pristine' cultures are situated in a utopian past – at the expense of other, more contemporary representations – speakers can be locked into fixed or essentialized notions of identity, 'authenticity' and place, which provide no recognition of mobile, postcolonial speakers. This can also undermine the political credibility and 'authenticity' of Indigenous leaders who, in their capacity as representatives of their people, wish to present themselves as astute and politically sophisticated negotiators who can deal with multinational and state officials (see Blaser 2004 for a discussion of this problem in the Latin American context).

A final problem for romanticized notions of language and culture is that such notions may gain recognition in state laws, thereby excluding other Indigenous practices and understandings of indigeneity. Various recent Supreme Court of Canada decisions about Aboriginal rights appear to have done just that – defining Indigenous practices as 'authentic' only when they are continuous with a pre-contact past, and thus effectively determining for legal purposes what it means to be Indigenous and when an Indigenous 'right' should be granted (see Patrick 2005).

ahistoricism and lack of political economic context

The second basic criticism of language endangerment and language rights discourses, as noted above, is that they tend to treat language ahistorically – as removed from time and space and from the political economic context in which language speakers find themselves. Although colonization and modernization are often cited as the root causes of language loss (see e.g. Mühlhäusler 1996; Maffi 2001), the discussion of language endangerment has overlooked both historically situated resistance strategies and the more recent political goals of Indigenous groups – particularly those of land 'ownership' and increased political and economic control over development on that land within the nation-state.

We can see the problematic nature of this ahistorical perspective more clearly if we observe that it largely overlooks Indigenous perspectives – which, on the one hand, highlight the importance of the land and of traditional land-based practices; and, on the other, recognize emerging, and largely urban, cultural and social practices. Since the roles that language and culture play in contemporary Indigenous society are so socially and historically contingent, it seems that an ahistorical approach to them cannot avoid misrepresenting fundamental aspects of this society and of its goals for the future.

the issue of mobility

A third, related, criticism of language rights and language endangerment discourses is that they have failed to acknowledge the geographic and social mobility of Indigenous and minority language speakers. Increasingly, these language speakers, like other individuals all over the world, are choosing (or are sometimes 'pushed') to move to urban centres and to make language choices that might lead to greater employment opportunities and social mobility. While these new sociolinguistic realities must be taken into account in any serious consideration of language use among these groups, language rights and language endangerment discourses have conspicuously failed to do so.

Although such economically driven language choices among Indigenous and minority languages speakers must be acknowledged, it must also be emphasized that these choices need not necessarily lead to language shift, as demonstrated by healthy speech communities around the world where bilingualism and multilingualism continue to flourish. As such, the worry expressed by some critics of language rights discourse that the continued attachment of speakers to smaller languages only hinders their adoption of a dominant language and thus their integration into dominant economies and forms of social life (May 2005b: 333–7) seems to be misplaced.

homogenization of nation-building and related linguistic practices

A final criticism of language rights and language endangerment discourses is related to nation-building and the related codification and standardization of languages within the nation-state. To the extent that the discourses in question promote such processes, which serve to unify and homogenize nation-states and the languages spoken within them, they risk excluding and marginalizing minorities and members of less powerful groups.

Processes of nation-building commonly go hand in hand with the construction of a national language, which reflects the ideology of linguistic homogeneity in nationhood. Thus, even when nation-building includes the granting of rights to minority or less powerful language groups within the nation-state, these rights will always be circumscribed by an ideology of linguistic homogeneity, and linguistic diversity will thereby be compromised (see Freeland and Patrick 2004: 4–6). Although linguistic homogeneity is largely 'imagined' (i.e. constructed) through the process of print capitalism (Anderson 1991; Irvine and Gal 2000: 76), the ideology permeates our way of thinking about language 'difference', language hierarchy, and variation within a speech community. This is particularly so because homogeneity is further reinforced through codification and standardization of the nation-state's dominant language variety, and through its use in institutional arenas (which is part of the process of print capitalism). Thus, the 'national language' is given a prominence far greater than that of other varieties or 'dialects' spoken within the same nation-state, which accordingly become marginalized or even denigrated. Yet, these standardizing processes, in creating discrete, 'bounded' languages, lead to linguistic forms that are artificial in much the same way as the 'authentic' cultural practices that are the product of essentializing discourses about culture.

Nation-state ideology thus creates two major paradoxes concerning Indigenous languages, 'indigeneity', and Indigenous mobilization for territorial control. First, there is a central paradox in the promotion of Indigenous and minority language rights in a discourse based on equality, individual liberties and national unity. This is that the promotion of such rights effectively challenges the founding ideologies of these states, and even their integrity, and can succeed only insofar as states are willing and able to reconceptualize themselves. The second paradox is more important to the overall argument of this chapter. This is that Indigenous groups that are mobilizing for rights and political and cultural autonomy within nation-states ultimately need to use the same nation-state ideologies to further their goals. These include ideologies about unified linguistic and cultural practices, which are not only antithetical to Indigenous notions of language and culture, but which promote Western concepts and forms of knowledge which the mobilization is trying to resist in the first place. It is a paradox that characterizes contemporary language movements and is key to understanding the inherent tensions and challenges facing Indigenous politicization of language and culture.

conclusion

This chapter has focused on the ideological nature of bilingualism and the ways in which changing patterns of language use are tied to larger historical, political and economic processes. These processes as related to Indigenous groups include contact and trade with colonizing powers and economic shift, as well as those of state formation, nation-building, and cooptation through political and economic control and state regulation. Significantly, different forms of bilingualism and multilingualism, and associated beliefs about different language varieties, can be seen to have arisen in response to these larger shifts and social changes. However, the increasing encroachment of dominant languages, which have been part and parcel of state domination and control, has led Indigenous and smaller language groups to appeal to international discourses of language rights and language ecology and the larger concern with language endangerment to halt the decline of their own languages.

In general, what we have found is that while language rights and language ecology discourses offer important strategic tools to empower and strengthen Indigenous communities, they are nevertheless fraught with complications and contradictions. This is because the terms on which language rights are granted – the romantic essentialization of language, culture and territory, the power and control that states have in managing rights and social groups within their borders, and the homogenizing forces in nation-building processes – often run counter to sociolinguistic realities 'on the ground' and may be more of a hindrance than a help to those whose language varieties and ways of speaking are excluded. Moreover, the biological metaphors in which language ecology discourse has been couched, according to which 'saving' a language is akin to saving an endangered 'species' from extinction, create their own set of problems. While such metaphors, which link language revitalization to environmental conservation, are strategically powerful, they also tend to reify (or objectify) language, leading us away from current Indigenous language practices and the lived realities of language speakers themselves.

Thus, while language rights and language ecology discourses have helped Indigenous and minority groups to gain power and to create new political spaces both nationally and internationally, they are nevertheless fraught with complications. While universalist discourses on rights and links of language to biological diversity are both morally and rhetorically compelling, they are just two discourses among many that Indigenous groups can draw upon to garner support and resources for their languages. In fact, what falls under the rubric of language endangerment and revitalization discourse is a complex interplay of local, national and international ideologies and rationales, which vary as much from one nation to another as they do from one locale to another.

acknowledgements

I wish to thank Monica Heller and Benjamin Shaer for helpful discussion on earlier versions of this chapter and Huamei Han for very useful editorial advice.

notes

1. This 'official' definition from the ILO Convention No. 169 *Concerning Indigenous and Tribal Peoples in Independent Countries* (1989) is one of many definitions of 'Indigenous peoples'; see Hughes (2003) and Niezen (2003).
2. In some cases, it might be difficult to define language groups categorically, and 'self-identification' might be used to distinguish 'indigenous' from 'national minority' languages or groups mentioned in the introduction.
3. See UNESCO, *The Red Book on Endangered Languages*, at <www.unesco.org>.
4. See e.g. Robins and Uhlenbeck (1991), Krauss (1992), Hale et al. (1992), McCarty and Zepeda (1995), Henze and Davis (1999), Nettle and Romaine (2000), Crystal (2000), Hinton and Hale (2001), Maffi (2001), Fishman (2001), Gibbs (2002); websites include <www.ethnologue.com> (Summer Institute of Linguistics, SIL); <http://jan.ucc.nau.edu/~jar/TIL.html> (Teaching Indigenous Languages); <www.indigenous-language.org> (Indigenous Language Institute); and <www.ogmios.org/home.htm> (Foundation for Endangered languages).
5. Here it is important to emphasize the problematic use of 'language' in this discourse, and the reification of 'language' as a fixed entity. First, it is difficult to define what precisely constitutes a 'language' (or a 'language variety'), a point which is reflected in different numbers given for the 'world's languages'. While 5,000 is said to be a conservative estimate, sources such as Ethnologue cite over 7,000. Politics and the challenges of using normative criteria to define 'languages' from 'dialects' is clearly at play. What is more troublesome, however, is the fact that as a language falls into disuse, new ways of speaking and new 'language varieties' are formed.
6. The edited volume by Luisa Maffi (2001) offers an excellent overview of language ecology and biocultural diversity. The Terralingua website <www.terralingua.org> and the newsletter 'Langscape' provide further information on this movement. See also Muehlmann and Duchêne, this volume.
7. For an example of how Indigenous groups have strategically used international conventions and declarations in arguing for the protection of endangered languages, see the Task Force on Aboriginal Languages and Cultures report (2005): *Towards a New Beginning: A Foundational Report for a Strategy to Revitalize First Nation, Inuit, and Métis Languages and Cultures*. Available at <www.aboriginallanguagetaskforce.ca>.

references

Anderson, Benedict (1991). *Imagined Communities: Reflections on the Origin and Spread of Nationalism*. London: Verso.

Asad, Talal (2003). *Formations of the Secular: Christianity, Islam, Modernity*. Stanford, CA: Stanford University Press.

Bauman, Richard, and Charles L. Briggs (2003). *Voices of Modernity: Language Ideologies and the Politics of Inequality*. Cambridge: Cambridge University Press.

Blaser, Mario (2004). 'Way of life' or 'who decides': Development, Paraguayan indigenism and the Yshiro people's life projects. In Mario Blaser Harvey Feit and Glenn McRae (eds), *In the Way of Development: Indigenous Peoples, Life Projects, and Globalization*, pp. 52–71. London/New York: Zed Books.

Capotorti, Fransico (1979). *Study on the Rights of Persons Belonging to Ethnic, Religious and Linguistic Minorities*. New York: United Nations.

Crystal, David (2000). *Language Death*. Cambridge: Cambridge University Press.

de Varennes, Ferdinand (1996). *Language, Minorities and Human Rights*. The Hague: Kluwer Law International.

Feldman, Alice (2001). Transforming peoples and subverting states. *Ethnicities* 1: 147–78.

Fishman, Joshua (2001). *Can Threatened Languages be Saved? Reversing Language Shift Revisited: A 21st Century Perspective*. Clevedon: Multilingual Matters.

Freeland, Jane, and Donna Patrick (eds) (2004). *Language Rights and Language Survival*. Manchester: St Jerome Press.

Gibbs, W. Wayt (2002). Saving dying languages. *Scientific American*, August 2002: 79–85. <www.sciam.com>.

Grillo, Ralph D. (1989). *Dominant Languages: Language and Hierarchy in Britain and France*. Cambridge and New York: Cambridge University Press.

Hale, Ken, Michael Krauss, Lucille Watahomigie, Akira Yamamoto, Colette Craig, La Verne Masayesva Jeanne and Nora England (1992). Endangered languages. *Language* 68(1): 1–42.

Heller, Monica (1999a). *Linguistic Minorities and Modernity: A Sociolinguistic Ethnography*. London: Longman.

—— (1999b). Heated language in a cold climate. In J. Blommaert, *Language Ideological Debates*, pp. 143–70. Berlin and New York: Mouton de Gruyter.

Henze, Rosemary, and Kathryn A. Davis (guest eds) (1999, March) *Anthropology & Education Quarterly* 30(1). Theme issue, Authenticity and identity: Lessons from indigenous language education.

Hinton, Leanne, and Ken Hale (eds) (2001). *The Green Book of Language Revitalization in Practice*. San Diego: Academic Press.

Hobsbawm, Eric (1990). *Nations and Nationalism since 1780: Programme, Myth, Reality*. Cambridge: Cambridge University Press.

Hughes, Lotte (2003). *The No-Nonsense Guide to Indigenous Peoples*. Toronto: New Internationalist Publications/Between the Lines Press.

Irvine, Judith, and Susan Gal (2000). Language ideology and linguistic differentiation. In Paul Kroskrity (ed.), *Regimes of Language*, pp. 35–84. Sante Fe: School of American Research Press.

Jaffe, Alexandra (1999). *Ideologies in Action*. Berlin and New York: Mouton de Gruyter.

Kontra, Miklos, Tove Skutnabb-Kangas, Robert Phillipson and Tibor Varady (eds) (1999). *Language: A Right and a Resource. Approaches to Linguistic Human Rights*. Budapest: Central European University Press.

Krauss, Michael (1992). The world's languages in crisis. *Language* 68(1): 4–10.

Kymlicka, Will (1995). *Multicultural Citizenship: A Liberal Theory of Minority Rights*. Oxford: Clarendon Press.

McCarty, Teresa, and Ofelia Zepeda (eds) (1995). Indigenous language education and literacy. *Bilingual Research Journal* 19(1). Special issue.

Maffi, Luisa (2001). *On Biocultural Diversity: Linking Language, Knowledge, and the Environment*. Washington, DC: Smithsonian Institution Press.
May, Stephen (2000). Accommodating and resisting minority language policy: The case of Wales. *International Journal of Bilingual Education and Bilingualism* 3: 101–28.
—— (ed.) (2005a). Debating Language Rights. Theme issue of *Journal of Sociolinguistics* 9(3).
—— (2005b). Language rights: Moving the debate forward. *Journal of Sociolinguistics* 9(3): 319–47.
Mühlhäusler, Peter (1996). *Linguistic Ecology: Language Change and Linguistic Imperialism in the Pacific Region*. London and New York: Routledge.
—— (2000). Language planning and language ecology. *Current Issues in Language Planning* 1: 306–67.
Nettle, Daniel, and Suzanne Romaine (2000). *Vanishing Voices: The Extinction of the World's Languages*. Oxford: Oxford University Press.
Niezen, Ronald (2003). *The Origins of Indigenism: Human Rights and the Politics of Identity*. Berkeley: University of California Press.
Patrick, Donna (2003). *Language, Politics, and Social Interaction in an Inuit Community*. Berlin and New York: Mouton de Gruyter.
—— (2004). The politics of language rights in the Eastern Canadian Arctic. In J. Freeland and D. Patrick (eds), *Language Rights and Language Survival*. Manchester: St Jerome Press.
—— (2005). Language rights in Indigenous communities: The case of Inuit in Arctic Quebec. *Journal of Sociolinguistics* 9(3): 369–89.
—— (forthcoming). Indigenous language endangerment and the unfinished business of nation-states. In Monica Heller and Alexandre Duchêne (eds), *Discourses of Endangerment: Interest and Ideology in the Defense of Languages*. London: Continuum International Publishing Group.
Phillipson, Robert (1998). Globalizing English: Are linguistic human rights an alternative to linguistic imperialism? *Language Sciences* 20: 101–12.
—— (2003). *English-Only Europe: Challenging Language Policy*. London: Routledge.
Robins, Robert H., and Eugenius M. Uhlenbeck (eds). (1991). *Endangered Languages*. Oxford and New York: Berg.
Skutnabb-Kangas, Tove (2000). *Linguistic Genocide in Education – or Worldwide Diversity and Human Rights*. Mahwah, NJ: Lawrence Erlbaum.
—— (2002). Marvellous human rights rhetoric and grim realities: Language rights in education. *Journal of Language, Identity and Education* 1(3): 179–206.
Skutnabb-Kangas, Tove, and Robert Phillipson (1994). *Linguistic Human Rights – Overcoming Linguistic Discrimination*. Berlin and New York: Mouton de Gruyter.
Smith, Linda Tuwahui (1999). *Decolonizing Methodologies: Research and Indigenous Peoples*. London and New York: Zed Books.
Thornberry, Patrick (1991). *International Law and the Rights of Minorities*. Oxford: Clarendon Press.
Whaley, Lindsay (2004). Can a language that never existed be saved? Coming to terms with Oroqen language revitalization. In J. Freeland and D. Patrick (eds), *Language Rights and Language Survival*, pp. 139–49. Manchester: St Jerome Press.
Wiley, Terrence G., and Thomas Ricento (eds) (2002). Language rights and educational access at the crossroads, past and present. Theme issue, *Journal of Language, Identity, and Education* 1(3).
Wolf, Eric (1982). *Europe and the People Without History*. Berkeley: University of California Press.

Woolard, Kathryn (1989). *Double Talk: Bilingualism and the Politics of Ethnicity in Catalonia*. Stanford, CA: Stanford University Press.

Wright, Ronald (1992). *Stolen Continents: The 'New World' through Indian Eyes*. Toronto: Penguin Canada.

part two
the state, the economy and their agencies in late modernity

7

language, migration and citizenship: new challenges in the regulation of bilingualism[1]

melissa g. moyer and luisa martín rojo

introduction

At the start of the twenty-first century one in every 35 people is an international migrant.[2] The movement of populations across national boundaries is emerging as one of the main challenges for nation-states. Monolingualism as a universal criterion for citizenship in a nation-state cannot be sustained anymore in the face of the language diversity of migrants and national linguistic minorities. In addition, in this era of globalization, migration is no longer understood as a one-time displacement. The connectedness of today's societies brought about by the development of communication technologies, and by cheaper and easier communications, makes physical mobility and contact with a country of origin easier for migrants. At the same time, liberal democratic states must deal with diversity in language, culture and identity in ways consistent with their political philosophy. These changes are bringing about a shift in ideologies, in particular, in the way bilingualism is understood, constructed and practised. Multilingual practices in monolingual institutional contexts can no longer be considered an exception. The tensions that exist in public institutions as a result of the diversity brought by immigration elicit contradictions between the democratic commitment of modern states to citizenship rights and the restrictive homogeneous views still in place about who counts as a citizen.

The present chapter looks at migration and the role of language in the control and regulation of citizenship. Using data from the sites of a health clinic in the Catalan-Spanish bilingual city of Barcelona and a Spanish secondary school on the outskirts of Madrid, we illustrate the ways migrants are regulated in both a material and symbolic sense, with consequences for the definition of who counts as a qualified citizen, at least in those domains.

We focus specifically on the dimensions of material access to health and education provided to migrants, as well as on the manner and type of services delivered. Language, both choice of code and professional discourses addressed to migrants by social actors in the sites studied are some of the symbolic means by which ideologies about immigration, the regulation of bilingualism and the production of categorization and exclusion are (re)produced.

The interest in the study of a specific country such as Spain is its location as a nation-state with ethnolinguistic minorities in the European Union context. It is a case that is traversed by tensions around internal homogeneity, challenged at once from above by supra-national entities (see Pujolar, this volume), and from below by the mobility of people across national boundaries. Migrants are presently understood to be subjects for socialization into citizenship and into the languages, behaviour and knowledge of the nation-state. A close-up look at two state agencies, the school and the health clinic, shows how linguistic and cultural ideologies of homogeneity and standardization are played out in everyday practices.

The following section presents the challenges posed by transnational migration to nation-state ideologies of monolingualism/bilingualism and citizenship. The section after that takes up the role of institutions (medicine, education, law, welfare) as localized sites where the state constructs and regulates citizens with respect to both mind (what they are allowed to think, the ways they are supposed to learn) and body (how to behave, how to take care of oneself as well as one's physical appearance). The conflicts that arise from the linguistic diversity brought by migrants and their language practices are discussed in the fourth section. The relation to nationalist views of language as an element in the construction of identity is also raised here. The questions raised in these sections are then presented in relation to examples of a school and a health clinic. The conclusions highlight new ways migration is changing traditional nation-state conceptions of language and citizenship from below.

transmigration and citizenship

Citizenship has traditionally been closely linked to nationality and to the way modern nation-states have defined membership. Basic to this notion of membership is the idea of a single shared culture where language is a key element (Gellner 1983). The connection between nationality and citizenship is being questioned by processes of migration and by the increased role played by supranational organizations. Presently, states have to recognize rights (previously limited to territorially based populations) of persons who speak various languages and who come from other places. Linguistic minorities within nation-states like Spain have received an important degree of recognition. This recognition has been less forthcoming with respect to migrant minorities who seek the right to express their linguistic, cultural and religious heritage in public domains and the opportunity to participate in the economic and political life of the host country (May 2001). The citizen rights of foreigners in the Spanish context are doubly regulated by the European Union and the Spanish foreigners law (or *ley de extranjeria*). Both the Maastricht Treaty and the European Constitution make a distinction between persons who are citizens of the nation-states that comprise the EU and persons from third countries.[3] In addition to specific legislation designed to define the conditions upon which foreigners can have access to the material resources (i.e. health, education, employment) of a nation, there are also symbolic means by which citizenship is regulated, and which include language practices and public discourses about difference that are carried out locally in institutional contexts. Habermas sums up the challenge migrants pose for the hegemonic construction of the modern nation-state:

> A liberal version of the system of rights that fails to take this connection into account will necessarily misunderstand the universalism of basic rights as an abstract leveling of distinctions, a leveling of both cultural and social differences. To the contrary, these differences must be seen in increasingly context-sensitive ways if the system of rights is to be actualized democratically. (1994: 116)

Discourses about citizen rights in pluralist societies have primarily centred on private spaces and the right to identity practices involving language, religion and cultural traditions in the home, as long as they do not interfere with public policies of the nation-state. The practice of diversity in private domains does not pose a threat to conceptions of homogeneous citizens of the nation-state. Visibility and participation of minority groups' culture and language in the public sphere is the real challenge faced by present-day pluralist democracies.

The mobility of people across national boundaries is closely related to the needs of domestic nation-state labour markets. Economic migrants are either formally admitted under quota systems to undertake technical and specialized jobs that pay well, or they are employed at low-skilled, high risk and poorly paid jobs. An additional feature of transmigration today is the possibility of multiple identities and citizenships, due to facility in communications and mobility of persons and services between host country (or countries) and the country (or countries) of origin. New identities are emerging from new contexts that are not tied to a single location or a single language.

In the case of Spain, migration is a relatively recent phenomenon. Up until the 1970s, Spaniards migrated to the industrial centres of Spain (notably to Barcelona) and Europe, such as Germany and France. When Spain joined the EU in 1986, it was drawn into European discussions of migration. Only very recently has it come to experience and to understand migration as a matter of consequence within Spain itself. Spain's first-generation newcomers come primarily from developing countries; they fill the niche of poorly paid lower-scale jobs, often in an underground economy (e.g., in agriculture, construction and domestic work). In spite of the three regularization processes undertaken in 2000, 2001 and 2005, by which many migrants became documented and officially recognized, migration to Spain has largely been illegal. This has had important consequences for the way these new minority groups are perceived, and it also helps to understand the delay in the recognition of migrants' health and educational rights, as well as in the assignment of public resources to facilitate integration. Spain's migration policies are more reactive than meditated or planned. This positioning – or, rather, the lack of positioning – by the Spanish state has left an open terrain where nationalist discourses that portray migration as a threat to the standard language/s and culture/s have remained unchallenged.

the state through its institutions

The state in a plural democratic society relies on institutions to implement its policies and to regulate its citizens. It is in this respect that institutions play a key role in the (re)production of a particular social order. The universalizing ideology that inspires state activities gets taken up in the way benefits are dispensed on the basis of uniform and homogeneous conceptions of citizenship. The functioning of institutions and the way social order gets reproduced and naturalized (cf. Giddens 1984; Dimaggio and Powell 1991) is through routine as it is carried out by knowledgeable social actors. The interactions that take place among social actors in ritual institutional encounters are the locus where the policies of the nation-state get implemented (Goffman 1988). The roles doctors or teachers must perform in the clinic or the classroom are instantiated in tasks that have been carefully set out and authorized by the state. Performing as a doctor or a teacher requires living up to a conventionalized and routinized way of presenting oneself in public. It involves imparting culturally established forms of knowledge, behaviours, as well as ways of taking care of the body. Furthermore, institutions are considered webs of interrelated rules and norms that regulate social relationships (Nee 1991: 8); they include the formal and informal social constraints that shape the choices available to social actors. As such, institutions naturalize routine conduct that embodies the interests and preferences of the members of a group or a community.

In the institution of the health clinic, a practice of boundary construction or 'othering' of the migrant is carried out through language, but also through the way medical practices are delivered. Health care providers (doctors, nurses and administrative staff) play a key role in regulating access to health services and treatment. They are also responsible for teaching migrants the proper way to take care of their bodies. Standard ways of giving instructions to patients can represent a problem for several reasons: language barriers, or unfamiliarity with culturally standard medical practices, dietary customs, or ways of talking about illness.

In the school, practices of 'othering' also involve the construction of deficiency with respect to institutional norms. The school is perhaps the most important institutional arena available to the state to create and regulate citizens. Language figures in a prominent role in this site. It is the 'ideal standard language' (Lippi-Green 1997) as defined by school authorities that must get transmitted in the educational process. By 'standard language' what is meant is the monolingual norm, as opposed to a more diverse bi/multilingual view, and also a specific normative, educated and regional variety, which excludes vernaculars or other geographically based varieties. In addition to the regimentation of language, there is also control over knowledge; this includes control over the type of knowledge, at what point in time that knowledge is taught and how it is learned. Schools regiment the mind by defining what it is citizens are supposed to know and how they are supposed to express that knowledge. Institutional processes are constructed around the concept of an 'ideal imagined citizen' (Anderson 1983), one who shares a way of talking, a common knowledge and experience, as well as a collective understanding of the way to conduct oneself in both a physical sense as well as for communicative purposes. Diversity and multilingualism challenge long-established institutional routines that were created for a particular type of citizen with a set of features and 'needs' understood to be shared by the community at large. (See also Martin-Jones, this volume, for further discussion of bilingualism and education.)

The diversity brought by migrants who have settled in Spain constitutes a new reality that still needs to be addressed by schools if they wish to provide equal opportunities for all students. Changes in the school curricula, alternative conceptions of learning and making use of knowledge are still to be implemented in spite of the fact that immigration in Spain has existed for more than fifteen years.

language and languages

What usually underlies officially monolingual and bilingual nation-states is the assumption of a one-to-one relation between language and its group of speakers (Billig 1995). Changes in the economy and the commodification of language (Heller 2002, 2003) are changing this univocal relationship; speakers are discovering the economic benefits of learning the language of the majority or minority groups. At the same time, English (and to a lesser extent, former languages of empire such as French and Spanish) as a global world language used by postcolonial societies, supranational organizations and in communications technologies, also calls into question the monolingual language practices of nation-states. Migrants are the new social actors challenging the hegemonic linguistic construction of the nation-state from below in different ways. Access to health, law and education require a presence of migrant languages in the public sphere in order to guarantee rights and equal access to these resources, but a pluralist system must also be able to guarantee the chances of migrants to participate fully in the host society and at the same time to maintain their linguistic, cultural and religious heritage.

Heller (2003: 473) points out that the globalized new economy is bound up with transformations of language and identity. The mobility of persons for work and tourism, or the development of language industries (translation and language teaching) are just some examples where language and culture have been brought to the forefront of the present day economy. Knowledge of languages is a form of social capital and as such its unequal distribution is tied to real life chances for the people who possess this valuable resource. From the perspective of new migrant minorities, who arrive to participate in domestic nation-state economies, filling either well-paid, technical and highly skilled jobs, or the opposite, low-skilled, high risk and poorly paid jobs, knowledge of a country's language constitutes linguistic capital. It allows a person to gain access to basic material and symbolic resources by providing a means by which people can communicate with and understand each other.

Nation-state ideological discourses also get constructed by the European Union. With regard to language, European institutions give official recognition to the languages of each member state that comprises the Union, and a form of acknowledgement to the languages of minorities within these states. Part of the European project to promote multilingualism and the learning of languages (especially other European Community languages) does not take into account the languages originally brought and still spoken by second and third generation migrants residing in the nation-states of the European Union (see the 1994 European Parliament *Resolution on the Linguistic Minorities in the European Community*). It was not until 2003 that the European Commission incorporated a more global and positive vision of linguistic diversity, by designing a plan for promoting the learning of languages that brings together all the languages spoken in the Union, whether official, regional, nation-state minority, migrant minority, or sign (McPake, Martyniuk, Aarts, Broeder, Latomaa, Mijares, Tinsley 2006; Beacco and Byram 2003). At the present time, the European Union promotes the acquisition and use of 1+2 languages (first language and two more languages); these languages may be official languages of an EU member state, languages spoken within a region of one of those states (e.g. Welsh, Catalan, Frisian), languages spoken in various parts of Europe (e.g. Romany, Yiddish), languages brought into Europe via immigration (e.g. Turkish, Arabic) or, finally, sign languages. Even though migrant languages have recently been accepted alongside with European nation-state languages, resources and steps have not been taken to promote their learning and development.

Nonetheless, different linguistic policies aimed at the acquisition and use of what Europe has defined as patrimonial languages, which include the languages of the state and of the regions within states, are set apart from the policies for the non-patrimonial languages of migrants. One set of language teaching practices aims at facilitating the return of 'migrant workers' to their countries of origin (even when the children in question were born in the host country). These programmes, some of which still exist today, are supported by the European Union and developed through bilateral agreements between a European state and a third country which finances them (see 1987 European Parliament *Resolution on the Languages and Cultures of Regional and Ethnic Minorities in the European Community*). These classes are not open to the public in general, since the main goal of the funding countries is to promote and maintain the identity of origin of its citizens; furthermore, they are organized as extracurricular activities. (Morocco and Portugal are the only countries who have taken up this initiative in Spain.)

Only at the end of the 1990s does the teaching of heritage languages start to be seen as a bridge between cultures, that is, an essential part of intercultural education, rather than a way to keep open the possibilities of return. However, this new orientation does not enjoy any financing (Bekemans and Ortiz de Urbina 1997), nor indeed, any official recognition from the EU (Eurydice 2004: 71). EU discourse on intercultural education remains ill-defined, and in general the EU accords more attention to dominant languages as means to integration. One result is the perpetuation over generations of the category 'immigrant'.

Just as the speakers of immigration-origin languages are seen as short- or long-term residents and not as European citizens, their languages are seen as 'resident languages', and not patrimonial. This is due to the fact that the motivations for their acquisition and use are linked preferentially to reasons of identity (that even open the path of return to the country of origin) and are not understood as a resource for a multilingual and multicultural society (for example, a resource for increasing commercial relations and exchanges of all kinds; for a development of these approaches and what they imply, see May 2001). The distinctions made by European laws reveal the different values attributed to languages, and they also illustrate the way language programmes and policies are traversed by nationalist ideologies, both on the part of the nation-states that comprise the European Union, and that of the migrants' countries of origin.

The connection between citizenship and language is not just a question of knowing the language of the host society (e.g. Spanish or Catalan). Whether a person's linguistic resources get valued or not is closely tied to interactional relations of power and the way migrants get positioned. For unskilled workers or for children at schools, knowledge of the host language is more than speaking and understanding it in a specific way; it means knowing the standard language and how to use it. Non-standard speech, including accented or semi-grammatical expressions, is often the basis upon which migrants are categorized and excluded from participation in citizenship.

ideologies of homogeneity in the school

Schools are well known for their homogenizing role. They are a key site for teaching and transmitting a standard language, and also a place where common knowledge and values get established. Schools are sites where there is a specific distribution of social capital, which endows that context with a particular logic of its own (Bourdieu 1984, 1990). It is a place where a constant evaluation of the social, cultural and linguistic resources of students shapes hierarchical or power based relationships. Teachers are in a position to assign value to other languages and cultures within the school. The practices of authorized social actors and the way social capital (Willis 1977) gets distributed has an effect on social processes of inclusion and exclusion in the school context. The different values that get assigned to students' resources establish differences in social capital; they therefore also produce power differences among the students. One historical role of schools has been to act as a key agent of social selection, accomplished by constructing those students whose cultural and linguistic resources are different as instead having deficient or non-existent resources, and therefore as 'bad' or 'incompetent' students. This process of delegitimization or erasure reflects ideologies that value monolingualism, standardized language and cultural homogeneity.

At the present time, universal education is recognized as one of the main cornerstones of democratic societies, as well as one of the main instruments available to nation-states for fabricating the ideal citizen. Social scientists have long recognized that pedagogic actions are a primary means of reproducing and legitimizing dominant social and cultural values of a country. It is through education and the pedagogic actions it involves that absence of linguistic, cultural and behavioural diversity gets constructed and passed on.

In the academic year 2000–01, Madrid was the autonomous region (the equivalent of a province) of Spain with the greatest number of migrant children in its schools (Broeder and Mijares 2004). The right of migrants to an education under the same conditions as Spanish citizens is recognized both in national Spanish laws, and in the laws of the autonomous regions.[4] In Madrid, the language of instruction is Spanish, which is both the language of the autonomous region of Madrid and the language of Madrid as the capital of the state (as opposed to autonomous regions with more than one official language, i.e., Catalonia, or the Basque Country). Language practices at schools in the autonomous region of Madrid follow the monolingual formulations of the nation-state, as stipulated in article 3 of the Spanish constitution, which affirms that Castilian is the official language of the state. This is reinforced by the (now widely internalized) article of the constitution, which affirms that 'all Spaniards have the duty to know and the right to use Spanish' (Constitución Española 1979: 20). This article has historically applied to linguistic minorities in Spain; in the case of Madrid schools, the presence of a wide variety of the world's languages is making the reproduction of linguistic homogeneity a difficult task.

In Madrid, Spanish coexists together with over fifty languages (Broeder and Mijares 2004; Martín Rojo, Alcalá, Garí Pérez, Mijares, Sierra, Rodríguez 2003).[5] Nothing seems to indicate that this diversity of languages will continue to be a part of the linguistic repertoires of their speakers, even in the case of young children who arrive at school without any previous knowledge of Spanish. Broeder and Mijares (2004) show how indices of linguistic vitality are low among migrant students. For young children, the languages of origin are mainly used at home and to a lesser extent with siblings and friends. Spanish is the language that is most common; this is also the case for adolescents who have not received any formal instruction or support in their language of origin. There is no policy in place as in other European and North American countries where efforts have been made to introduce measures to foster this diversity, such as (a) programmes to guarantee knowledge of the school language; (b) programmes to support languages of the country of origin; or (c) to a lesser extent, measures that regulate and promote coexistence rather than competition among languages (such as intercultural education and some immersion programmes that promote addition rather than substitution, or an emphasis on balancing knowledge of various languages). The view that standard Spanish in school is the main criterion for integration of migrants does not account for the practical issues that arise when students arrive at school for the first time without any knowledge of this language.

Classrooms in Madrid are still for the most part monolingual spaces; there has been no attempt to remedy the clear failure to apply the European directive from 1977 that requires schools to teach the language of origin. No bilingual programmes have been started in which migrant languages such as Arabic are included, even when the number of Arabic-speaking students in schools would justify such a measure. Spain is just another example of the way language policies have been implemented in Europe. Rather than considering them an asset, these languages are treated as an obstacle to integration. This is demonstrated by the fact that educational actions and resources are directed preferentially to ensuring the teaching of monolingual norm. The efforts to maintain the pre-eminence of a school language can be observed in the reception programmes (or *aulas de enlace*) where migrant children are segregated in a special school in another part of the city, and where they are taught Spanish as a second language. A policy of diversity would involve providing support in the mainstream classroom where migrants are not singled out as lacking knowledge of the language and culture of the nation-state, but where autochthonous students would also need to develop knowledge of their migrant classmates. In addition, these special centres often do not help to foster ties with the school where foreign students will continue their instruction. When coordination between reception class schools and mainstream schools is lacking, students who attend these special programmes feel lost, and are categorized as difficult and problematic learners. The practical results of this segregation policy are negative for three reasons: it separates students from a context of Spanish-speaking students where peer interaction takes place; it labels and marginalizes those who do not know the language, institutionally problematizing the situation; and it generates competition between languages, since the contexts of use are separated and the students are pressured to substitute one language for another.

Language homogeneity in the school context in Madrid not only applies to the sole use of Spanish for instruction (as opposed to inclusion of other languages spoken by students), but it also refers to the imposition of a standard orthographical, lexical and pronunciation norm. This norm, which is based on the prescription by the Royal Academy of the Spanish Language (*Real Académia Española de la Lengua*) of a standard language, is said to represent the language of an educated sector of society. The objective of schools is to teach this norm as the gateway to upward social mobility and to integration as a Spanish citizen. The unequal social distribution of linguistic capital (in this case Spanish) has consequences for social mobility, since it can facilitate access to different social spaces, or, on the contrary, make this possibility difficult to realize, creating social exclusion. The standardized norm contributes to reinforcing the belief that in order to be integrated one cannot be different or speak differently. The assumption that a language or an element like pronunciation can have drawbacks, occurs only when the language in question is not valued (if the pronunciation showed signs of an English accent, perhaps such a claim would not be made). There are many indications that such a negative evaluation has an impact on the academic success of the student and the access she may have to valuable social resources.

The pedagogic practices by which dominant language ideologies get reproduced in the classroom setting is illustrated by a tightly constrained turn exchange episode where the norm gets established through explicit correction by the teacher.

example 1

- – Teacher's question
- – Student's answer
- – Teacher's correction, where imposition of linguistic norm takes place
- – Student's reformulation, where a student's answer is substituted for linguistic form in accordance with the standard norm

If the reformulation is difficult or not possible for the student, a new adjacency pair involving an alternative correction by the teacher and a new reformulation by the student takes place. This act of correction not only imposes a norm but also is an event in which a student is singled out from among other students for speaking unacceptably.

The regulation of language in the school not only establishes this site as an almost exclusive space for Spanish, where there is little or no visibility of the many other languages brought by students, but it is also a place where the variety or type of Spanish is dictated. For students of Latin American origin, it is not sufficient to know the language; they must also learn the standard forms of that language (i.e. vocabulary and standard pronunciation). To count as a citizen, knowing the Spanish language is not enough. Linguistic differences reveal themselves as differences in capital, which establishes a principle of asymmetry among the students that is perceived by all of them and has repercussions for their relations with one another. Recordings carried out in the school have shown the great frequency with which foreign students are challenged to *'say it right'* or *'say it in Spanish, so it's understood'*.

In interviews, teachers said they considered the emphasis on normative behaviour part of their understanding about the role of school in the regulation of difference, that is the correction of student deficit. Teachers justify this position as a way to provide students with the linguistic and cultural capital they need to integrate and progress in Spanish society. The actual classroom practices illustrated above, and the ideologies that render these practices legitimate, are tied to liberal democratic views regarding the role of education as one of the main mechanisms for eliminating social inequality. While the goal of producing homogeneous citizens with equal life chance opportunities through education is still upheld in theory by teachers and educational institutions, what prevails in schools is a diversity of languages, behaviours and cultures that are formally unrecognized and even actively suppressed in instructional processes.

Despite this, in example 2 (below) we see how a minority of teachers do find ways to treat linguistic differences more inclusively, ways which value the linguistic capital of both local and migrant students and make them aware of linguistic differences without stigmatizing them. In the example, we see the way a teacher can focus on linguistic variation. Lexical variants are equated with local forms, instead of being labelled as 'incorrect uses'. This variation is presented as the normal outcome of the geographic spread of the Spanish language. This particular teacher is aware that students from Latin-American backgrounds could feel, by means of this strategy, more represented and valued in the classroom.

example 2[6]

Profesor: o cuando hay una frase hecha / típica de aquí / propia de España / les pregunto por sus frases correspondientes / no sé/ recordando ahora por ejemplo salado / había una vez en un texto era un chico muy salado/ y los ecuatorianos / al menos la mayoría había entendido que era- /

Teacher:	... or when there's a fixed expression / typical of here / specific to Spain / I ask them for their corresponding expressions / I don't know / remembering now, for example, 'salado' (witty) / there was a time in a text that there was a very 'salado' boy / and the Ecuadorians / at least the majority of them had understood it to mean- /
Investigadora:	que tenía mala suerte.
Researcher:	... that he was unlucky.

The present linguistic order in the school domain is oriented towards substituting the language of origin for a new one. Bilingualism or bidialectalism is still considered an exception, except for the special multilingualism of the 'educated' or 'intelligent'. Our data and fieldwork experience reveal that coexistence is not a problem for speakers. However, the attempt to substitute one language for another generates competition, it forces one to choose and to reproduce ideologies and practices of homogeneity. The social consequences are clear: students who own a valued resource (namely, knowledge of the language of classroom instruction) because of their social and regional origin, are considered normal participants who are legitimate in the social space of the school.

This particular understanding of bilingualism explains some decisions that have been made in schools, and not only in traditionally monolingual zones like the regional community, and the elimination of a third language in the curriculum of these students (a practice quite distant from the 1+2 model of the EU). In some schools, in order to 'facilitate the acquisition of Spanish', students are not allowed to enrol in French or English courses offered to other students, despite the fact that these are subjects in which many of them could have excelled. European colonization of their countries make them familiar with these languages to some degree (French for the Moroccan or Algerian population; English for people from India or Pakistan).

example 3[7]

'Porque claro, al final, estos críos que te vienen de fuera, tienen una mezcolanza que no se aclaran. Entre el suyo, el de aquí, más otra tercera lengua que les metemos...que al final, para mí, que no saben ninguna.'

'Because, of course, in the end, these kids that come to you from another place, have a mixture that they can't sort out. If you count their own (language), the one from here, plus another third language that we impose on them...that in the end, in my mind, well, they don't learn any of them.' (Interview with teacher)

In the bilingual regional communities of Spain that have linguistic minorities, a similar tendency occurs involving one of the three policies: (a) the elimination of the third language from these students' curriculum (Nussbaum 2005); (b) the maintenance of the programmes in Castilian, for all students of foreign origin, or (c) the selection of Castilian as the language of exchange with them, inside and outside the classroom (Ruíz Bikandi 2003). These linguistic options, built on the same prejudice about the impossibility of bilingualism or trilingualism, have a harmful effect on students, since they establish a dynamic of confrontation between their presence and the socially shared goal of reinforcing and maintaining the official languages of the community. Testimonies are frequent among teachers in the Basque Country, Catalonia and the Balearic Islands, in which they reveal their fear that the presence of these students works to the detriment of maintaining the regional minority languages. Meanwhile, in monolingual areas like the regional community of Madrid, we find teachers who do not see the preservation and use of other languages as something normal; rather, they see students' use of them as 'unfair', presuming students use it just as a strategy to conceal meaning and exclude outsiders, that is, as a premeditated strategy for secrecy and deception (equivalent to those traditionally attributed to jargons; see Martín Rojo 1997). This view presents the use of L1 as a 'strategy that constrains and even impedes communication', excluding outsiders; it is thus not seen as a spontaneous form of speech, or as a 'language'.

Underlying the 'impossibility' of bilingualism is a vision of linguistic competence as compartmentalized knowledge that is monolingual, and subject to being supplanted by other monolingual knowledge during the learning process. Molina and Maruny (2003) show how, from a normative and ethnocentric perspective, people can *not* value linguistic and communicative competence among speakers who know several languages and know how to take advantage of their communicative strategies. This view of competence impedes understanding a good number of practices, such as distinguishing between languages in terms of contexts, or, on the contrary, alternating their use; mixing them or using them interchangeably; or using them in a creative way to increase expressivity or create complicity. In Madrid schools, teachers mainly struggle to maintain the monolingual norm of classroom interaction and knowledge production, a norm to which the institutional arrangements made for the education of immigrants strongly contributes (see Martín Rojo and Mijares 2006).

language diversity and categorization in a health care context

State and national discourses about citizenship have an important impact on health policies and on the access migrants have to national health care schemes. Citizenship is a form of regulation by the state that distinguishes between those who can make legal claims for protection and benefits, as opposed to foreigners or those positioned as non-citizens (Sharma 2006: 18). In the case of France, for example, a universalizing conception of citizenship is the basis for the way public services, and in particular health care, get delivered in the same way to everyone, regardless of their country of origin. This stems from the French state's denial of difference (Moreno 2003; Jaffe 1999), and from its universalizing laws that disregard any sort of political mechanism for recognizing concrete interests that may interfere with the notion of the ideal individual citizen and her/his relation to the Republic. An alternative understanding of citizenship, as in Great Britain, acknowledges the various multicultural collectivities and their distinct sets of needs. This way of contemplating difference with respect to the benefits provided by the state has given ethnic minorities the legitimacy they need to organize and to articulate explicit demands around specific issues such as health.

After 40 years of dictatorship, Franco's death opened up debates about the nature of Spanish citizenship and the way to incorporate historical linguistic minorities.[8] In the midst of these debates, the issue of immigration has recently come to the fore. The categorization of foreigners regardless of their status as residents or undocumented migrant workers, is how the state legally organizes exclusion and controls the right to resources that are available to Spanish citizens. The organization of health care under Franco was highly centralized, with important inequalities generated by rural–urban and socioeconomic differences. Everyone was entitled to health care whether or not they were employed, but the type of coverage depended on their socioeconomic status. During the first Socialist government, Felipe Gonzalez universalized the right to have health assistance for all citizens. Until the law changed in the year 2000, migrants who were not legally employed were only entitled to medical attention at an emergency room of state hospitals, at charity hospitals, or at an NGO. At present, health care is provided to people who can prove that they reside in Spain, regardless of their citizenship or legal status (Moreno 2004; Jansà and Villalbí 1995; Solé 2004).

Undocumented migrant workers are invisible to the state and to the European Union in spite of their physical presence and visibility at local institutional levels such as the health clinic. This often creates tensions between institutions, local administrations such as the Catalan government and the Spanish state, over funding and resources to provide the type of services required to attend to newcomers. In addition, the state's failure to legislate regarding migrant resident rights allows it to eliminate any discussion of citizenship and diversity. This reluctance to deal with migration was observed in the past regional elections of 2003, in which Catalan politicians agreed to leave the topic of immigration out of the political debate. This pact of silence on immigration reflects politicians' concerns about addressing the issue of what it means to be Catalan, especially since they risk appearing racist by capitalizing on anti-immigrant sentiment. The consequence of this decision is the hiding of migrants, not only their voices and their presence in Catalonia but also the silencing of information about the conditions in which they live (Colectivo Ioé 1992; Fundació Jaume Bofill 2001).

The health care clinic we discuss here is a public institution responsible to the Catalan Department of Health, *Institut Català de la Salut*. Legislation formally establishes Catalan and Spanish as the two official languages but most internal activities (i.e. meetings, written documents, interactional exchanges, and brochures) of the Catalan public administration are produced in Catalan.[9] The medical and administrative staff are also required to know Catalan in order to work at this institution. The linguistic ideologies that guide the choice of languages (Catalan and Spanish) at the clinic are similar to the language practices in other spheres of Catalan life where Spanish rather than Catalan is typically addressed to outsiders. As Pujolar (2007) points out, Catalan embodies national identity as well as a type of cultural capital that ensures access to networks of power and employment. The meaning and the value of Catalan today must be understood in the light of specific historical circumstances that assume the repression of national identity under the Franco regime, the economic leadership within Spain, and the centre of attraction for internal migration.

Migration to Catalonia is not a new phenomenon. During the industrial boom of the late 1950s and the 1960s migrants from within Spain's borders found work there in the industries, and they settled in towns that have come to be known as the working class neighbourhoods of Barcelona. These neighbourhoods are today mainly Spanish-speaking, even though the people who live there, now in the second and third generation, have been educated in Catalan schools (Vila i Moreno 1996; Woolard 1989). The arrival of new migrants and the challenges they pose in terms of different cultural, religious and language practices has revised thinking about migration from within Spain as a successful process but migration from outside is being constructed as a threat to the survival of Catalan language and identity. Health providers who use Spanish with migrants are reproducing language ideological practices that have long been present in Catalan society. Today, Spanish is typically used to interact with people who were once called 'the other Catalans', namely, the working class from the regional communities of Andalusia and Extremadura who understand and speak the language after having resided in Catalonia since the industrial boom of the 1960s. Citizenship rights for these migrants were guaranteed because of their national origin. The electoral slogans of the Catalan conservative nationalist party, *Convergència i Unió*, in the 1990s, 'som sis millons' [we are six million], or 'tothom qui viu i treballa a Catalunya es català' [everyone who lives and works in Catalonia is Catalan] use the inclusive first person plural pronoun in order to gain the support of migrants from inside Spain. Whether such inclusive slogans will be used in future campaigns to include the language, culture and religious diversity brought by migrants from outside Spain's borders and who are currently living in Catalonia will be linked to the government's ability to reach a consensus over a more pluralistic and a less essentialized conception of citizenship.

Locally situated social practices at the health care site in Barcelona illustrate some of the ways migration is currently contesting nation-state ideologies about bilingualism and citizenship, and the contradictory ways authorized institutional actors are dealing with these challenges (Blommaert, Collins and Slembrouck 2005). The linguistic diversity medical providers encounter at the clinic has changed, and with that, so have routine practices. In particular, daily language practices are no longer strictly based on a choice of either Catalan or Spanish. Challenges to the institutional linguistic norm are carried out in the daily practices of the health centre where certain bilingual practices are regulated.

Rather than dwell on strategies for facilitating or negotiating meaning, the practices that take place in the clinic show how social categorization and inequality get (re)produced through language (Collins and Slembrouck 2004). The habitual choice of Spanish, or of an international language such as English or French rather than Catalan has certain consequences for migrants. It is a practice that categorizes them not only as outsiders, but as members of the working class which, in Catalonia, has historically been Spanish-speaking.

The examples that follow illustrate how the state leaves the delivery of health care for migrants to the medical staff's own devices. The lack of resources and support for improving communication in the clinic is a consequence of the state refusing to formally recognize the diversity and the specific needs migrants bring. The multilingual practices observed show typical interactions where no single language dominates the everyday practice of medicine. Understanding is achieved, as example 4 demonstrates, but it is achieved by code-switching or combining English and Spanish (which goes counter to the notion that ideal communication is monolingual).

example 4

Situation: A Pakistani man (UH1) comes to the front desk and asks for Dermatology. A young male researcher (INV) and a middle-aged female member of the administrative staff (SM6) respond. English in bold letters.

1 UH1: hola estoooo **skin** # esto # otro otro # **skin**
%tra: *hello thiiis skin # this # other other # skin*
2 SM6: **skin?**
3 UH1: ehhh # dermatologia la segunda?
%tra: *ehh # dermatology the second?*
4 INV: **the second floor.**
5 UH1: **second floor?**
6 INV: **second floor**
7 UH1: gracias
%tra: *thank you*

Example 5 (below) sheds light on the type of interactions that take place in a new globalized world order where English has come to play a dominant role. The English from a postcolonial context has become an important social resource for the Pakistani patients in a new situation brought about by migration, and it meets the English of Barcelona clinic staff, acquired in the context of globalization.

example 5

Situation: There are three participants: a male patient from Pakistan (PAT), a female researcher (INV), and a male doctor (DOC). The interaction takes place in the doctor's office. The patient comes in with an itchy scalp. English in bold letters.

1 PAT: hola
   %tra: *hello*
2 INV: hola
   %tra: *hello*
3 DOC: sienta # sienta +...perdona un momento eh@i
   %tra: *sit # sit # +...excuse me a moment*
4 PAT: no # no # no. no **worry**
5 DOC: bueno. jamir
   %tra: *well. Jamir*
6 PAT: **yeah**
7 DOC: dime
   %tra: *tell me*
8 PAT: **speak English and +...?**
9 DOC: si # si # si
   %tra: *yes # yes # yes.*
10 PAT: **OK # OK. my problem is the forehead # night # ten o'clock # eleven o' clock # it** *pipili* **[=?] and then like +...**

In example 6 (below), French does not work as well as a common language as English did in the previous example. The fallback language then remains Spanish. The researcher's knowledge of French is not sufficient for bridging the communication gap. The result of not achieving understanding has important consequences for the patient who leaves the clinic after she was asked to wait in order for the nurse to check her blood pressure and to write up her medical history.

example 6

Situation: There are three participants: a female patient from Tunisia (UH1), a male doctor (DOC), and a female researcher (INV). The interaction takes place in the doctor's office. The patient comes in seeking a prescription for a chronic heart condition. French in bold.

1	DOC:	a ver. alima. es la primera vez que viene?
	%tra:	*Let's see alima. Is this the first time you've come?*
2	UH1:	alima.
3	DOC:	vale. bueno # alima # yo soy el doctor alvarez. doctor
	%tra:	*ok. good # alima # I am doctor alvarez. doctor*
4	UH1:	doctor alvarez **ici**
	%tra:	*doctor alvarez here*
5	DOC:	yo
	%tra:	*I*
6	UH1:	**oui**
	%tra:	*yes*
7	DOC:	doctor alvarez
8	UH1:	**oui # ça va bien**?
	%tra:	*yes # how are you?*
9	DOC:	**ça va**. alima # tu hablas # castellano?
	%tra:	*fine alima # do you speak # castilian ?*
10	UH1:	(silence)
11	DOC:	no. frances?
	%tra:	*no. french?*
12	UH1:	frances # **un peu**
	%tra:	*french # a little*
13	DOC:	y castellano # español ?
	%tra:	*and castilian # spanish?*
14	UH1:	no.
15	DOC:	nada # perfecto
	%tra:	*nothing # perfect*
16	UH1:	frances
	%tra:	*french*
17	DOC:	solo frances. yo no hablo frances alima
	%tra:	*only french. I don't speak french alima*
18	DOC:	tu hablas frances? [directed to the researcher]
	%tra:	*do you speak french?*
19	INV:	yo hablo un poquito # si
	%tra:	*I speak a little # yes*

The everyday multilingual practices that appear in the above extracts become meaningful if we ask why languages other than global ones, or bilingual practices involving Catalan, are not present. These extracts illustrate the way language is regimented by Catalan health providers who choose English or Spanish over Catalan. It is in the everyday provision of health care services by situated actors that ideologies about Catalan and its boundaries get reproduced.

Another example of how multilingual practices are regulated at the clinic involves an episode with a member of the administrative staff. Montse is a Catalan woman who speaks both Urdu and Punjabi. Her job at the reception desk – as she explained it – consisted in providing information to patients and setting up appointments for them with the attending social worker, medical doctors and nurses. Many of the patients were Pakistani mothers with their babies. Their knowledge of Catalan or Spanish was limited. In the absence of any institutional documentation in a language they could understand, Montse voluntarily prepared handwritten posters in Urdu and Punjabi explaining the institutional procedures for getting an appointment, seeing a specialist, as well as general recommendations about vaccinations, diet or what to do if a child runs a fever. These information posters lasted a short time before they were taken down from the wall and the author reprimanded. The explanation for taking the posters down offered by the person in charge of this clinic was that Catalan patients would complain about seeing signs in a language they could not understand, and that the presence of these signs would give the impression that it was a health centre only for migrants. In this particular case, the way institutional ideology was played out and justified is rather alarming. When enquiring about this event with other health providers, reasons relating to personal character were given to delegitimize Montse's actions. For some people at the health clinic Montse was cast as a difficult person whose life choices went against widely held beliefs about what constituted the ideal citizen. In particular, what people mentioned about Montse was that she had married a Pakistani man who already had a wife and children in Pakistan, and, furthermore, she had converted to Islam and at work she often wears 'ethnic dress'. This example illustrates national ideologies about what counts as the acceptable language/s and what is an appropriate lifestyle.

While language is one dimension of categorization in the clinic, it combines with other ways in which immigrants are constructed as Other, and as subject to institutional control (Moyer and Codó 2002). We see this, for example, in health education classes directed to migrant women who had recently given birth. The classes were organized by one of the paediatricians at the health centre and her attending nurse. It is also through the paediatrician and her nurse that a small group of Pakistani mothers were recruited for a post-natal class. These classes consisted in doing exercises on a floor mat and learning how to stand and hold one's body in order to avoid back pain. The purpose of the gathering, according to the doctor, was also to provide an acceptable space for these women to meet outside their home and where the husbands would let them come. The language used by the native Catalan-speaking nurse in these classes was again Spanish, and there were no native Catalan/ Spanish-speaking women who would arguably also benefit from participating in these classes. The underlying assumption in practically all interactions between patients and health providers is that migrants do not or perhaps cannot know Catalan. Despite attempts at civic nationalism, on the ground we see the reproduction of ethnonational boundaries, often accompanied by the construction of immigrants not only as the Other, but as deficient.

conclusions

The mobility of persons across nation-state borders is no longer an isolated one-time experience, nor a limited one. The present chapter has explored the way a particular nation-state and its institutions are coping with this new diversity and in particular with the linguistic diversity brought by migration. The two cases studied show how health clinics and schools in Spain construct diversity as a problem, or at best a deviation from the norm. The social and cultural configuration of institutions has changed; the population is no longer homogeneous. Institutional practices have not adapted yet to serve the new population. In fact, the definition and understanding of the social categories of identification has not changed. Distinctions continue to be made between 'normal' and 'foreign' or 'migrant' citizens, and this difference is often in addition seen as a scale ranging from proficiency to deficiency.

Our present understanding of language, and one that is assumed in this chapter, is as a means to gain access to both symbolic and material resources in a community. The construction and reproduction of social structure and relations of power are also carried out through routinized language practices. Migrants from different language backgrounds constitute a challenge for traditional nationalist discourses and ideologies that are still present in the institutions of pluralist democratic states. Public health services and the educational system need to take into account the multilingual reality if they intend to be inclusive. As it stands, multilingual reality comes up against national ideologies of monolingualism and homogeneity, and institutional ideologies of inclusion.

As a result, knowledge and use of the standard variety of Spanish function as criteria of belonging to the community (as may be the case for the official languages of the bilingual autonomous communities). Language is, in principle, an element that can facilitate integration: if one doesn't know a language it can be learned, and its presence or absence can be modified, unlike physical features or one's birthplace. Nevertheless, by introducing the local norm as an exclusive criterion (you speak it or you don't speak it), by imposing educational models that promote monolingualism or 'European bilingualism', or by using a language such as Spanish both as a bridge and as a national border (we Catalans vs. you Others), language comes to be treated as a defining feature that either immediately separates, or on the contrary becomes hegemonic, hiding any trace of difference. We again find the domination of homogeneity in the face of diversity. What is more, diversity is seen as a threat to the language of the community, whether because it 'corrupts' or 'dismembers' (with vulgar and incomprehensible variations), or because it limits the success of a now-dominant linguistic minority movement.

The resulting contradictions are left to actors on the ground to resolve, with the resources and expectations they bring to that encounter. Our cases show, however, that the strict separation of languages which is part of our operationalization of nation-state based ideologies of bilingualism may be harder and harder to accomplish as mobility increases.

notes

1. The authors wish to acknowledge the support from the Ministerio de Ciencia y Tecnologia, Plan Nacional de la Ciencia I+D+I through the project BFF2001–2576 and the project BFF 2003–04830.
2. 16 March 2006, Fact-file Global Migration at the address <http://news.bbc.co.uk>.
3. Third country is a term used in European institutions and documents to refer to countries that are not members of the Union.
4. For more information see the LODE (Ley Orgánica de Educación), the LOGSE (Ley Orgánica General del Sistema Educativo), and the LOPEG (Ley Orgánica de la Participación, la Evaluación y el Gobierno de Centros Docentes) which regulate the rights and the delivery of education in Spain.
5. The data collected on schools in Madrid is from the European project on 'Multilingual Cities' led by the University of Tilburg in the Netherlands, and by the Taller de Estudios Internacionales Mediterráneos (TEIM), of the Universidad Autónoma de Madrid. Laura Mijares directed this project in Madrid where a survey was done to obtain a representative sample of language practices from Madrid schools. The results can be consulted in Broeder and Mijares (2004). Another project titled 'Diversidad Cultural y Lingüística: Una Propuesta de Estrategias y Recursos para la Educación', led by Luisa Martín Rojo, was carried out in conjunction with the above-mentioned European team.
6. This extract was obtained from an interview carried out by Adriana Patiño with the language teacher at the IES Evangelista School in 2004.
7. This is an extract from an interview carried out by Esther Alcalá with a teacher in the Public School Los Santos in 2001.
8. At present, different national projects are under debate in Spain. There is a centralist model inherited from Franco and still present in the discourse of right-wing groups; an autonomous model (administrative decentralization), adopted after Franco's death, which represents a half-way model reached by consensus; a federal model (involving political decentralization), defended by some autonomous regions in Spain and left-wing groups; and, finally, a model that sustains self-determination (confederation or independence) of the regions and 'historical nationalities'. These political projects promote different forms of compatibility or incompatibility between nation-state and regional-national identities. The centralist and independentist political positions are linked to a lack of compatibility between regional and national identities; while autonomy and federalist projects accept both identities as compatible. Spain is seen, in this case, as a plurinational state, and this understanding of the nation could be potentially more open to diversity even though this is not always the case.
9. See the language policy law, *Llei 1/1998* from 7 January and published in the *Diari Oficial de la Generalitat*.

references

Anderson, Benedict (1983). *Imagined Communities: Reflections on the Origin and Spread of Nationalism*. New York: Verso.

Beacco, Jean-Claude, and Michael Byram (2003). *Guide for the Development of Language Education Policies in Europe: From Linguistic Diversity to Pluralingual Education.* Strasbourg: Council of Europe, Division of Linguistic Policies.

Bekemans, Leonce, and Ortiz de Urbina (1997). *The Teaching of Immigrants in the European Union.* Working Document. Luxembourg: European Parliament. Education and Culture Series.

Billig, Michael (1995). *Banal Nationalism.* London: Sage.

Blommaert, Jan, James Collins and Stef Slembrouck (2005). Polycentricity and interactional regimes in global neighbourhoods. Manuscript.

Bourdieu, Pierre (1984). *Distinction: A Social Critique of the Judgement of Taste.* London: Routledge.

—— (1990). *In Other Words: Essay Towards a Reflexive Sociology.* Cambridge: Polity Press.

Broeder, Peter, and Laura Mijares (2004). *Multilingual Madrid: Languages at Home and at School.* Amsterdam: European Cultural Foundation.

Colectivo Ioé (1992). *La inmigración en Catalunya.* Barcelona: Institut Català d'Estudis Mediterranis.

Collins, James, and Stef Slembrouck (2004). 'You don't know what they translate': Language contact, institutional procedure, and literacy practice in neighbourhood health clinics in urban Flanders. *Working Papers on Language, Power and Identity,* no.19. <http://bank.rug.ac.be/lpi/>.

Constitución Española (1979). Madrid: Ministerio de Asuntos Exteriores.

Dimaggio, Paul J., and William Powell (1991). *The New Institutionalism in Organizational Analysis.* Chicago: Chicago University Press.

European Parliament (1987). *Resolution on the Languages and Cultures of Regional and Ethnic Minorities in the European Community.* Strasbourg: European Parliament. <www.ciemen.org/mercator/UE21-GB.HTM>.

—— (1994). *Resolution on the Linguistic Minorities in the European Community.* Strasbourg: European Parliament. <www.ciemen.org/mercator/UE23-GB.HTM>.

Eurydice (2004). The Academic Integration of the Immigrant Student Body in Europe Bruselas Eurydice (Comisión Europea: Dirección General de Educación y Cultura). <http://eurydice.org>.

Fundació Jaume Bofill (2001). *Anuari de la Immigració a Catalunya.* Barcelona: Editorial Mediterrània.

Gellner, Ernest (1983). *Nations and Nationalism.* Oxford: Blackwell.

Giddens, Anthony (1984). *The Constitution of Society.* Berkeley: University of California Press.

Goffman, Erving (1988). *Exploring the Interaction Order.* Boston, MA: Northeastern University Press.

Habermas, Jurgen (1994). Struggles for the recognition in the democratic constitutional state. In Amy Guttman (ed.), *Multiculturalism: Examining the Politics of Recognition,* pp. 107–48. Princeton, NJ: Princeton University Press.

Heller, Monica (2002). Actors and discourses in the construction of hegemony. *Pragmatics* 13(1): 11–32.

—— (2003). Globalization, the new economy and the commodification of language and identity. *Journal of Sociolinguistics* 7(4): 473–92.

Jaffe, Alexandra (1999). *Ideologies in Action: Language Politics on Corsica.* New York: Mouton de Gruyter.

Jansà, J.M., and J.R. Villalbí (1995). La salud de los inmigrantes y la atención sanitaria primaria. *Atención Primaria* 15 (31): 320–7.

Lippi-Green, Rosina (1997). *English with an Accent: Language Ideology and Discrimination in the United States*. London: Routledge.

McPake, Joanna, Waldemar Martyniuk, Rian Aarts, Peter Broeder, Sirkku Latomaa, Laura Mijares and Teresa Tinsley (2006). *Community languages in Europe: Challenges and opportunities*. Manuscript.

Martín Rojo, Luisa (1997). Jargon. In J. Verschueren, J.-O. Östman and J. Blommaert (eds), *Handbook of Pragmatics*, vol. 2, pp. 2–19. Amsterdam: Benjamins.

Martín Rojo, Luisa (dir.), Esther Alcalá, Aitana Garí Pérez, Laura Mijares, Inmaculada Sierra and M. Angeles Rodríguez (2003). *¿Asimilar o integrar? Dilemas de las políticas educativas ante los procesos migratorios*. Madrid. CIDE no. 154. <www.mec/cide/>.

Martín Rojo, Luisa, and Laura Mijares (eds) (2006). *Voces del Aula*. Barcelona: Gedisa.

May, Stephen (2001). *Language and Minority Rights: Ethnicity, Nationalism and Politics of Language*. Harlow, UK: Longman.

Molina, Monica, and Luis Maruny (2003). Motivacions, funcionalitat i usos lingüístics en l'adquisició de competència plurilingüe. In Joan Perera, Luci Nussbaum and Marta Milian (eds), *L'educació lingüística en situacions multiculturals i multilingües*, pp. 235–46. Barcelona: Institut de Ciències de l'Educació, Universitat de Barcelona.

Moreno, Francisco Javier (2003). *Análisis comparado de las políticas sanitarias hacia las poblaciones de orígen inmigrante en el Reino Unido, Francia y España*. Madrid: Instituto Juan March de Estudios e Investigaciones.

—— (2004). *The Evolution of Immigration Policies in Spain. Between External Constraints and Domestic Demand for Unskilled Labour*. Madrid: Instituto Juan March de Estudios e Investigaciones.

Moyer, Melissa, and Eva Codó (2002). Language and dynamics of identity among immigrants: Challenging practices of social categorization in institutional settings. In Xoan Paolo Rodríguez Yañez et al. (eds), *Proceedings for the Second University of Vigo International Symposium on Bilingualism*. Vigo: University of Vigo. <http://webs.uvigo.es/ssl/sib2002/>.

Nee, V. (1991). Sources of the New Institutionalism. In Mary G. Brinton and Victor Nee (eds), *1998. The New Institutionalism in Sociology*, pp. 1–15. New York: Russell Sage Foundation.

Nussbaum, Luci (2005). Dilemas y desafíos de la educación lingüística. In Luisa Martín Rojo, Luci Nussbaum and Virginia de Unamuno (eds), *Escuela e Inmigración. Estudios de Sociolingüística*, vol. 5(2) 2004: 19–25.

Pujolar, Joan (2007). The future of Catalan: Language endangerment and nationalist discourses in Catalonia. In Alexandre Duchêne and Monica Heller (eds), *Discourses of Endangerment: Interest and Ideology in the Defense of Languages*. London: Continuum.

Ruíz Bikandi, Uri (2003). Formación del profesorado: Necesidades nuevas en una nueva época. In Joan Perera, Luci Nussbaum and Marta Milian (eds), *L'educació lingüística en situacions multiculturals i multilingües*, pp. 113–35. Barcelona: Institut de Ciències de l'Educació. Universitat de Barcelona.

Sharma, Nandita (2006). *Home Economics: Nationalism and the Making of Migrant Workers in Canada*. Toronto: University of Toronto Press.

Solé, Carlota (2004). Immigration policies in Southern Europe. *Journal of Ethnic and Migration Studies* 30(6): 1209–21.

Vila i Moreno, Xavier (1996). When the classes are over: Language choice and language contact in bilingual education in Catalonia. Unpublished PhD thesis, Vrije Universiteit Brussel.

Willis, Paul (1977). *Learning to Labour: How Working Class Kids Get Working Class Jobs.* Farnborough: Saxon House.
Woolard, Kathryn A. (1989). *Double Talk: Bilingualism and the Politics of Ethnicity in Catalonia.* Stanford: Stanford University Press.

8
bilingualism, education and the regulation of access to language resources

marilyn martin-jones

introduction

What kinds of bilingualism should be developed through education in different social contexts? What kinds of bilingualism can be developed in and through education? What languages should be promoted within the foreign language curriculum and why? What medium of instruction policy should be adopted in multilingual settings? Should regional vernaculars be used in teaching and learning in postcolonial settings along with national and official languages? Should minority languages be included in the curriculum within a national education system? Should some form of bilingual education be adopted? If so, how should it be organized and in what sectors of education: at pre-school, primary and secondary levels? At college or university level? In adult basic education or literacy programmes? What are the consequences of such educational interventions in multilingual settings? For well over half a century, questions such as these have surfaced over and over again in public debates about language in education in bilingual and multilingual settings. They have been posed by researchers, educational practitioners, parents, journalists and language activists in relation to very different forms of language education provision, in very different historical conditions.

Over the same time span, forms of educational provision in multilingual settings have become increasingly diverse. They now include different kinds of programmes developed specifically for indigenous groups or first peoples; bilingual (or monolingual) pathways through education for learners from linguistic minority groups who are positioned on the political and economic periphery of nation-states; diverse forms of language education intervention for children and adults of migrant and refugee origin and special forms of educational provision, such as immersion programmes, that are designed so as to give access to bilingualism for children from dominant linguistic groups whose histories have been characterized by investment in monolingualism. In addition, there are local debates about the precise form that each type of provision should take and what the goals of that provision should be. Take, for example, the diverse forms of intervention that have emerged in the United States for linguistic minority groups of migrant origin, including transitional bilingual programmes, programmes aimed at first language maintenance and, more recently, dual language or two-way programmes. In Canada, immersion education has also taken diverse forms, including, for example, early partial immersion, total immersion and late immersion programmes. These types of educational intervention have also been exported to other countries. There now exist a vast array of different arrangements for the management of linguistic diversity and for the promotion of particular kinds of bilingualism across the world. These arrangements are, for the most part, made in and through public education systems, though, increasingly, new forms of bilingual education provision are being developed within a globalized private education sector (e.g. within international schools or European schools) and within a highly localized, often neighbourhood-based voluntary sector, such as in heritage language programmes organized by parent groups or community language classes.

Distinct but interlocking strands of research have been built up around these different forms of educational provision, notably research on second language learning and teaching, bilingual education and language policy and language planning. Research evidence has even been a key point of reference in language policy debates. Take, for example, the significance given to research findings pointing to 'positive outcomes' in the case of French immersion programmes in Canada (Harley 1991; Johnson and Swain 1997; Mejia 2002). Across these fields of research, there have been three main preoccupations: firstly, a preoccupation with the description and classification of different language policies and bilingual education programmes; secondly, a preoccupation with documenting the outcomes of different kinds of educational intervention; and, thirdly, a preoccupation with the development of learners' linguistic proficiency. The cultivation of particular forms of bilingualism within national education systems has tended to be seen as tied to taken-for-granted goals of economic or political development.

In this chapter, I start out by unpacking these preoccupations and by providing a genealogy of some of the discourses underpinning these fields of research – discourses about bilingual education which remained dominant until the late 1980s. I then go on to trace the development of alternative approaches to linguistic and cultural diversity in education. I focus first on the turn towards interpretive research in multilingual school and classroom settings and on the intersecting influences of ethnomethodology, interactional sociolinguistics and ethnography on this research. I then show how critical perspectives were incorporated into these strands of interpretive work and I outline the significant advantages that accrued from this.

The main aim of the chapter is to make the case for conducting critical, interpretive research on language in education in bilingual and multilingual settings. I argue that it is only through this kind of research, in specific local educational sites, that we can begin to address, in an adequate way, the questions posed at the beginning of this chapter. Critical, interpretive approaches enable us to link insights from the close study of the interactional and textual fine-grain of everyday life in educational settings with an account of specific institutional regimes, the wider political economy and the global processes of cultural transformation at work in contemporary society. Critical studies of bilingualism in education foreground the role of education in nation-building, in the shaping of the identities of citizens and workers and in the definition of a national culture. They also highlight the specific ways in which, in different multilingual contexts, education serves as a means of assigning value to language and literacy resources and, at the same time, as a means of regulating access to them. The lenses that are used for observing these processes are, on the one hand, the everyday rituals and communicative practices of teachers and learners in schools, adult literacy programmes or universities and, on the other hand, wider policy discourses as they are articulated in policy documents and in interviews with key players in policy debates.

Having made my case for conducting research of a critical, interpretive nature, in the concluding section of this chapter, I then offer some reflections on different dimensions of change that have been ushered in by globalization, on the impact these have had on language-in-education policies and on the scope for further critical, interpretive enquiry related to these dimensions of change.

bilingualism in education:
discourses long-dominant in research and practice

From the 1950s to the 1980s, researchers and practitioners working on bilingualism in education had three main preoccupations: (1) comparing and classifying language policies and forms of bilingual (and monolingual) educational provision; (2) documenting the educational outcomes of language policy decisions and patterns of enrolment in different kinds of educational programmes; (3) describing and assessing learners' linguistic competence in the first and second language. Three types of discourse developed out of these preoccupations: a discourse about 'models' of bilingual education; a discourse about bilingual education and achievement, and a discourse about language competence and 'balanced bilingualism'. These discourses were taken up in both research and practice and are still widely articulated in textbooks for students on bilingual education courses or in-service teacher education programmes. In this section of the chapter, I will consider each of these discourses in turn, showing how they have guided thinking about bilingualism in education, how they have given rise to particular kinds of research questions and, hence, to particular kinds of research endeavours.

Throughout the chapter, I will use the term 'bilingual education' to refer to all forms of provision for bilingual learners, including minimal forms of support for learning in and through two languages. This is a convention widely followed in the research literature. However, I do not include under this label different types of programmes for teaching English as a second or additional language.

a discourse about 'models' of bilingual education

From the 1960s onwards, we saw the emergence and wide dissemination of taxonomic discourses about bilingual education. The first typologies of bilingual education were devised by sociolinguists and social psychologists working within a broadly structural-functionalist view of society (e.g. Fishman and Lovas 1970; Mackey 1972; Spolsky and Cooper 1978). As I have noted elsewhere, this view of society dominated sociolinguistic research on bilingualism throughout the 1960s and 1970s (Martin-Jones 1989). Other typologies, developed later, attempted to introduce a critical perspective and draw attention to the ways in which particular forms of education provision contribute to the reproduction of social relations of inequality between dominant and minority language groups (e.g. Skutnabb-Kangas 1984; Hornberger 1991, which provides a useful overview of typologies, and Baker 2006).

Nevertheless, this discourse about 'models' is now well established in the general research literature on bilingual education and in educational practice. 'Models' are compared according to various criteria, such as programme goals, types of learners recruited (i.e. learners from linguistic minority groups versus learners from dominant majority groups); arrangements for the use of languages (e.g. across the curriculum or across academic timetables). Taxonomies vary in complexity depending on the number of criteria employed. 'Models' of bilingual education are represented as if they were discrete, fixed entities and readily transplantable, like neutral technologies, from one sociolinguistic context to another.

This taxonomic discourse, and the terminology associated with it, derives primarily from the specific and highly charged debates about forms of bilingual education provision that have taken place, over the years, in the United States and in Canada (for details of the debates in the United States, see Crawford 1995 and Freeman 1998, and for the debates in Canada, see Tardif and Weber 1987, Olson and Burns 1983 and Heller 1990). This discourse has now been taken up in other bilingual and multilingual contexts and still circulates widely. Thus, researchers and practitioners in two different contexts in Europe – in the Swedish-speaking region of South West Finland (Björklund 1997) and in Catalonia (Artigal 1997) – describe Swedish-medium provision and Catalan-medium provision respectively, as immersion-style education, evoking the Canadian immersion 'model', widely hailed as the most successful 'model' of bilingual education.

A good deal of the early research on bilingual education was policy-driven and so the focus was on issues related to programme design and implementation, on the development of teaching/learning materials and on classroom practice. 'What' and 'how' questions predominated, instead of 'why' questions. Major concerns included, for example: what model of bilingual education is most appropriate in this context? How should the bilingual programme be organized? What percentage of the academic timetable should be devoted to instruction in Language A and Language B? Few questions were asked about wider issues, such as: why do particular types of bilingual education get introduced in particular social and historical contexts? In whose interests? And with what consequences?

A salient feature of bilingual education programmes devised from the 1960s onwards was the strong preference for the construction of parallel, monolingual spaces for learning, with strict monitoring of those spaces for their monolingualism. A distinction was made in the research literature between a 'language separation' approach and a 'concurrent' language approach (Faltis 1989; Jacobson and Faltis 1990). In the former approach, the languages used in a bilingual programme were confined to different days or to different areas of the curriculum. In the latter, both languages were used by teachers and learners in all activities of the programme and code-switching was, thus, a salient feature of classroom interaction. This was seen as problematic. The orthodoxy of the language separation approach was reinforced by the dominant discourse of the time, in applied linguistics, about keeping to the use of the 'target language' in the classroom. This discourse was particularly salient in immersion programmes, since the classroom was the only space in which learners could gain access to bilingualism. In the 1980s, the principle of 'bilingualism through monolingualism' was put forward by those who advocated the 'language separation approach' (e.g. Swain 1983). A much-cited article, entitled 'Bilingualism without tears' (ibid), set out the rationale for espousing this principle. One of the reasons given was that a language separation approach in a bilingual education programme provides a better guarantee that equal time will be assigned to both the languages.

a discourse about bilingual education and achievement

Another type of discourse that has persisted since the 1960s and that has now become increasingly prevalent is a discourse of achievement. This derives from the preoccupation with the outcomes of the bilingual policies and programmes put in place in particular sociolinguistic contexts. Again, the research in this area has been largely policy-driven, speaking to the concerns of policy-makers and, in the case of immersion programmes, parents. The kinds of research questions addressed have been along the following lines: what are the consequences of organizing educational provision for learners in bilingual and multilingual contexts in particular ways, employing different 'models'? What kinds of educational programmes foster second language development or the development of 'full' bilingual competence? What is the impact of bilingual education on patterns of achievement across the curriculum (e.g. in maths and science as well as in language)?

Inevitably, these kinds of questions have given rise to large-scale research, with particular cohorts of students, involving the use of standardized tests and the generation of quantitative findings of the type that policy-makers find compelling. This research has sometimes had a comparative dimension, focusing on the outcomes of different kinds of programmes. Thus, for example, in the United States, in the mid-1970s, there was a brief spate of research comparing the outcomes (in terms of students' performance on standardized tests) of bilingual education programmes using a language separation approach and those using a concurrent approach (Legarreta 1977; Wong Fillmore 1980). In Canada, there has been a long tradition of comparing, in a similar manner, the outcomes of different types of immersion programme (e.g. early partial immersion, total immersion and late immersion) (Swain and Lapkin 1982; Harley 1991). In recent years, in the United States, even larger scale research has been undertaken, generating statistical evidence across school districts, as a means of countering the official backlash against bilingual education and in an attempt to demonstrate that there is 'added value' in bilingual education programmes (Thomas and Collier 2002).

discourses about linguistic competence and 'balanced bilingualism'

Particular discourses about language learning and about linguistic competence predominated for a couple of decades, from the 1960s to the 1980s, in popular and academic writing on bilingual education. These discourses and the preoccupation with learners' linguistic proficiency was partly due to the dominance, at the time, of narrowly conceived, cognitive approaches to research on second language acquisition (see McCarthy 2001 for a fuller account of these approaches). Teaching and learning were characterized in equally narrow terms, with the emphasis being on identifying ways in which classroom practice could be oriented to providing 'comprehensible input' (ibid). For example, in immersion contexts, there was a particular concern with what came to be known as the 'plateau effect' (Swain 1985). While surveys showed that second language learners of French were developing linguistic competence comparable to that of 'native speakers' in understanding spoken French, their speaking skills apparently remained at a level below that of a 'native speaker'.

Ever since the 1960s, various metaphors have been used to characterize bilingual competence by those advocating different kinds of bilingual education programmes and 'mother tongue' programmes. One of the most common of these is a 'container' view of competence which is manifested in terms like 'full bilingual competence', 'balanced bilingualism', 'additive bilingualism' and 'subtractive bilingualism'. These particular terms emerged from the early Canadian research (e.g. in the work of Lambert and Tucker 1972). Certain types of educational provision, such as the 'submersion' or 'sink-or-swim' model, where only the second language is used as a medium of instruction, were said to lead to subtractive bilingualism, that is, a shift on the part of the learner to his or her second language and subsequent loss of his or her first language. In contrast, immersion education was said to lead to 'additive bilingualism'. 'Balanced bilingualism' (in effect, two full containers, side-by-side) was the idealized benchmark against which the developing linguistic capabilities of all learners were assessed. Those who argued for 'strong models' of bilingual education, where the aim was to support the development of the learner's first language, alongside the second language (e.g. Skutnabb-Kangas 1978; Cummins 1979) introduced the contrasting notion of 'semilingualism' or 'double semilingualism' in the 1970s, also drawing on a container metaphor of competence (for a fuller discussion of the debates about this concept, see Martin-Jones and Romaine 1986, and Stroud 2004).

researching language in bilingual education practice: the turn towards interpretive work

The 1980s saw the beginning of a major shift in research on bilingual education, towards interpretive work and towards the incorporation of theoretical and methodological perspectives from ethnomethodology, interactional socio-linguistics and the ethnography of communication. While large scale surveys and statistical analyses of patterns of achievement among bilingual students were still being undertaken, research of a qualitative, interpretive nature gradually came to occupy the centre ground. The shift towards interpretive work on bilingual education was, of course, part of a broader theoretical and methodological turn across the social sciences towards dialogic interaction and social constructionism. There were also other motivations for this shift which were specific to the field of bilingualism in education. Firstly, there was a growing awareness of the explanatory limits of the large scale survey work that had dominated research on bilingual education since the 1960s. Secondly, there was a new interest in the negotiation of meaning in and through interaction and a strong inclination towards research in educational settings which put teachers and learners centre stage, paying close attention to the ways in which they made sense of the daily round of activities in bilingual classrooms. Thirdly, there was a move away from the generalizing taxonomies of the bilingual education literature and idealized 'models' to the specificity of the arrangements and communicative practices observable in particular bilingual and multilingual contexts. And, lastly, there was a growing consensus about the limitations of research which was confined to a focus on the linguistic proficiency of learners and which drew on relatively narrow approaches to second language acquisition.

This was a period when concern about the processes contributing to the construction of school failure for children from linguistic minority groups was widely articulated. Researchers began to ask different kinds of questions: about the nature of the school experience for minority students; about the organizational and discursive routines in bilingual and multilingual classrooms; about the ways in which these routines contributed to the construction of the institutional order of schools; about the processes of social categorization and selection taking place in different educational sites and about the consequences of these processes for minority students. Some researchers approached these questions through the lens of language and literacy socialization, following students from their local life worlds to the classroom. Others focused on the interactional order of classrooms, with a view to building an understanding of the processes involved in the construction of the institutional order. The interpretive work that was conducted over the following decades provided a wealth of insights into the nature and significance of communicative practices in schools and classrooms in bilingual and multilingual contexts. Intersecting strands of influence were clearly discernible in this work. I will briefly trace some of these influences in the paragraphs below.

Many of the early studies were conducted in bilingual education programmes based in urban schools in the United States (e.g. Mehan 1981; Zentella 1981). They built explicitly on the ethnomethodological tradition, investigating the institutional order of particular schools and classrooms through detailed description and analysis of bilingual classroom interaction between teachers and learners. The focus was generally on the sequential structuring of bilingual classroom talk, on the management of turn-taking in more than one language and on the local interactional routines established for accomplishing this. These studies emphasized the need to understand that, on entering bilingual schools and classrooms, students not only have to get acquainted with a new interactional order and orient themselves to 'learning lessons' but they also have to learn the local routines for the management of multilingual resources and repertoires.

Other early studies were conducted in a primarily ethnographic vein, foregrounding 'culturally distinct' interactional practices, narrative styles and aspects of non-verbal communication (e.g. conventions around silence in conversational interaction). The contexts for this research included indigenous education programmes in the United States (Philips 1983) and Canada (Erickson and Mohatt 1982), and schools in postcolonial contexts (e.g. Watson Gegeo and Gegeo 1986). This work grew out of a concern about the failure of educational institutions to take account of the linguistic and cultural resources that children were bringing to the learning process (e.g. Moll, Amanti, Neff and Gonzalez 1992). The focus of some of this empirical work was on language and literacy socialization practices at home and at school. Researchers worked across domains, following children from home to school. Detailed accounts were built up of children's experiences of talk and texts in different domains, using key ethnographic concepts such as 'speech event' (Hymes 1972) and 'literacy event' (Heath 1982). The latter concept provided a key unit of analysis for the study of the ways in which talk unfolded around texts within the interactional routines of daily life at home and at school.

Other ethnographic research concentrated primarily on classroom-based interaction between teachers and learners with different linguistic and cultural backgrounds (e.g. Cazden, Carrasco, Maldonado-Guzman and Erickson 1980; Erickson and Mohatt 1982). In these studies, both verbal and non-verbal aspects of interaction were studied in minute detail. The aim was to identify some of the ways in which interactional synchrony and reciprocity were (or were not) achieved in particular teaching/learning episodes. In these detailed accounts, often involving analyses of video-recorded episodes, we saw the influence of the micro-ethnographic approaches developed by researchers such as Fred Erickson.

A third group of researchers drew on both of the traditions mentioned above, blending early work on the ethnography of communication (e.g. Hymes 1974) with conversation analytic and ethnomethodological perspectives. This is the area of research that came to be known as interactional sociolinguistics. It remains closely associated with the work of John Gumperz (1982, 1986). Gumperz himself was particularly concerned with the processes of social stereotyping and selection at work in educational institutions and with the ways in which judgements are made about people based on the way they talk. Drawing on conversational analysis and early work in pragmatics, he developed an approach to the study of interaction which focused on the ways in which meanings are exchanged in classroom talk and on the ways in which situated inferences are made as that talk unfolds.

One of the notions that Gumperz employed in his studies of talk in multilingual contexts was that of 'contextualization cue' (1982: 131). It served as a key analytic concept for investigating the situated nature of talk, particularly talk that involves quite rapid alternation between two or more languages. According to Gumperz, contextualization cues are any choice of verbal or non-verbal resources within a communicative repertoire that interlocutors recognize as 'marked', that is, choices that depart from an established or expected pattern of communication. They range from phonological or lexical or syntactic choices to different types of code-switching and style-shifting. They also operate at the prosodic, paralinguistic, kinesic and gestural level. An interactional sociolinguistic approach to classroom discourse thus foregrounds the ways in which teachers and learners draw on contextualization cues and on the background knowledge that they bring to different teaching/learning events (background knowledge is characterized as frames, scripts, schemata, structures of expectation or members' resources).

These cues and knowledge resources are seen as the key means by which participants in bilingual teaching/learning events negotiate their way through an interaction, making situated inferences as to what is going on, working out their respective discourse roles and evaluating the contributions made by other participants.

The 1990s saw an intensification of interest in the close study of bilingual classroom discourse. The analytic approach developed by John Gumperz provided an important impetus for this research. There was also a significant diversification of research sites. Research now began to be undertaken in a range of contexts where schools were officially constructing monolingual spaces for learning while, in practice, two or more languages were being used on a daily basis by either teachers or learners (or both). The vast majority of studies carried out in this decade were in postcolonial settings, where a former colonial language was still being used as a medium of instruction (e.g. Arthur 1996; Bunyi 2001; Canagarajah 1995; Chick 1996; Hornberger 1988; Lin 1996; Martin 1999; Rubagumya 1994). Work was also undertaken in urban settings where some form of bilingual educational provision was being made for learners of migrant or refugee origin (Jørgensen 1998; Martin-Jones and Saxena 1996; Mondada and Gajo 2001; Rubinstein-Avila, 2002). Some studies were carried out with teachers and learners from regional minority groups (Heller 1994, 1996, 1999; Jaffe 1999; Vila i Moreno 1996). Research on bilingual talk was also conducted in immersion programmes (Mejia 1998), lifting the veil on communicative practices in settings where, as I indicated earlier, there has long been a dominant discourse about sole use of the 'target language'.

Over the last two decades, we have come a long way from the discourses about idealized 'models' of bilingual education that predominated in the 1960s and 1970s. From this preoccupation with education models and outcomes, the focus has shifted to classroom processes and communicative practices. We now know much more about how multilingual resources are managed in different educational contexts, and we have a greater understanding of the kinds of discursive routines (bilingual and monolingual) that emerge in particular kinds of sociolinguistic conditions, when particular kinds of bilingual arrangements are ushered in with new educational policies. Focusing on the dynamics of interaction has made us aware of the range and complexity of communicative processes at work in bilingual and multilingual classrooms and of the ways in which discourse practices are indexically oriented to wider ideologies (e.g. about sole use of the language of instruction in class) (see Martin-Jones 2000 for further details).

the critical study of bilingual education practice

It is to the critical strand of research on communicative practices in bilingual education contexts that I now turn in this section. Following Tollefson (2002),

I am using the term 'critical' here in the sense of aiming to reveal links between local discourse practices (bilingual or monolingual), the everyday talk and interactional routines of classrooms and the wider social and ideological order. I will first say a word or two about the origins of current critical approaches to the study of bilingual education practice. I will then go on to outline some of the ways in which the critical project has been defined.

origins of critical approaches

Predictably, perhaps, the critical study of bilingual education practice was first developed by two broad groups of researchers: those of us who were working with learners from linguistic minority groups (e.g. Blackledge 2001; Creese 2002; Heller 1994, 1999; Jaffe 1999; Martin-Jones and Saxena 1996; Mondada and Gajo 2001; Rubinstein-Avila 2002) and those working in post-colonial contexts (e.g. Arthur 1996; Bunyi 2001; Canagarajah 1995; Chick 1996; Hornberger 1988; Lin 1996; Martin 1999; Rubagumya 1994). The commitment to developing a critical approach arose out of a shared concern with the ways in which educational policies *and* classroom practices contribute to the reproduction of asymmetries of power between groups with different social and linguistic resources. The largest contribution to the development of a critical body of work (in terms of the sheer number of studies) has come from researchers based in postcolonial contexts. This is remarkable given the lack of research resources in the countries of the South. However, the new perspectives brought by these researchers and their powerful critique of the neocolonial discourses about language planning and bilingual education that circulate in such countries has provided and continues to provide significant input to the development of the critical project (e.g. Stroud 2003; Lin and Martin 2005).

linking the interactional order with the social and institutional order

The main empirical concern for those of us engaged in critical, interpretive research has been with developing different strategies for linking ethnography (mostly participant observation and ethnographic interviews) with analysis of audio- and video-recordings of bilingual teaching/learning events. Drawing on the conceptual frameworks and analytic approaches developed in previous interpretive work in monolingual and multilingual classes, we were able to provide fairly fine-tuned descriptions of the interactional routines of particular classes in particular sociolinguistic and educational contexts. But we also felt the need to go beyond these descriptions of regularities in the cycles of communicative life in the classrooms we were observing. We found that it was not possible to explain these interactional routines solely on the basis of data from these sites. So we began to seek ways of linking the local situated practices and our detailed accounts of the interactional order of the classroom with analyses of institutional and historical processes, with wider discourses about language and about the role of schooling in the context of linguistic diversity. The approach was essentially a bottom-up one: starting from an analysis of local discursive practices and trying to provide an account of the ways in which these practices were embedded in the wider social and historical contexts we were concerned with (see Martin-Jones and Heller 1996; Heller and Martin-Jones 2001 for more detailed accounts of this approach).

Our main theory-building strategy was to focus on two main ways in which schools operate as institutions linked to the state: firstly, the ways in which schools serve as spaces within which specific languages (national, official languages) and specific linguistic practices (ways of speaking, reading and writing) come to be inculcated with legitimacy and authority; secondly, the ways in which schools function as spaces for selecting and categorizing students, for assessing performance (including linguistic performance) and providing credentials that are ultimately tied to positioning in the world of work, along with the ways in which these categorization processes are bound up with wider processes of social stratification along the lines of ethnicity, class and gender.

The work of the late Pierre Bourdieu proved to be of particular relevance in pursuing these lines of theory-building, particularly his notion of 'legitimate language' (Bourdieu 1991). Bourdieu provided a detailed account of the social, political and economic conditions he deemed to be necessary for a language to gain legitimacy within a particular linguistic market. For him, language legitimation takes place through the institutions of the state, and especially through education. He saw education as a key site for social and cultural reproduction and for the imposition of a particular symbolic order. Rather more controversially, Bourdieu also characterized the educational and linguistic market as being 'unified'. What he had in mind was social and economic contexts where the labour market plays a key role in determining the value of dominant languages and certain ways of speaking and writing, and where schools provide access to these linguistic resources and, hence, to social and occupational mobility. Aligned to this is the fact that schools are also social spaces where students are ranked on the basis of their performance. Access to the highly prized symbolic resources which can determine their eventual position within the labour market is unevenly distributed.

Bourdieu has provided us with one of the most comprehensively theorized accounts of the processes involved in the (re)production of legitimate language and of the role of schools in these processes. His model is clearly relevant to the project of developing a critical, interpretive approach to bilingual education practice. However, processes of language legitimation are highly contingent and context-specific. Studies in specific historical contexts have drawn attention to some of the problems with Bourdieu's model (e.g. Heller and Martin-Jones 2001). I will briefly discuss two problems here. The first has to do with Bourdieu's focus on symbolic domination and with the bleakness of his vision. For him, symbolic power saturates consciousness and remains uncontested. However, the imposition of power in institutions such as schools is primarily accomplished in and through interaction. One of the main insights from ethnomethodology is that because it is interactionally constructed, the institutional order is always indeterminate. There are always possibilities for challenging and even modifying it. At the same time, it is clearly not possible to argue that the practices of teachers and learners in schools are completely unconstrained. It is necessary to see them as being socially positioned and, at the same time, actively responding to the constraints and to the possibilities open to them in particular school and classroom sites.

The second problem with Bourdieu's model pertains to his claims about the unified nature of the educational and linguistic markets. We know that, in her research in Catalonia, Kathryn Woolard (1985) found that Bourdieu's predictions regarding the role of education and unified markets in language legitimation were not borne out. When Woolard conducted her study in Catalonia in the early 1980s, Catalan showed considerable vitality across a range of domains despite the continued promotion of Castilian within the institutions of the Spanish state. Clearly, Bourdieu's claims about the unified nature of education and linguistic markets were overstated. Moreover, he did not provide a way of accounting for change over time. The conditions for the valuation and legitimation of a language and for the exercise of symbolic power are always changing. For each of the settings where we wish to investigate the practice of bilingual education, we need to build a sociocultural and historical account of these conditions.

I turn now to two examples of studies in which Bourdieu's theory of symbolic power has been relevant. In a series of ethnographic studies of French language minority schools in Ontario, Canada, which were carried out over the best part of a decade, Monica Heller (1994, 1996, 1999) built upon and extended Bourdieu's model to take account of students' responses to the symbolic order of the school, including in-class practices of collusion and contestation. The notion of legitimate language was central to her account. She provided a detailed analysis of the interactional means by which teachers in the schools defined what counted as 'good French', showing, for example, that the teacher feedback within the typical Initiation-Response-Feedback routines of teacher-centred classrooms, provided multiple opportunities for defining legitimate language: in this case, monolingual performance in standard Canadian French. She also showed how, in the daily rounds of communicative life in class, secondary students in the university-bound streams colluded with the symbolic order of the school and the imposition of the dominant discourses about what counted as 'good French'; while those in streams oriented towards the job market either contested their placement or challenged the content of the school curriculum, including the language content of the curriculum.

Working in a postcolonial context, Angel Lin (2001) has conducted research of a critical, interpretive nature in Hong Kong schools where English is the language of instruction, although teachers and learners all have Cantonese as a first language. She explains why English has come to be valued by the Hong Kong elite, not only as a means of maintaining Hong Kong's privileged position in world markets but also as a means of access for individuals to economic and educational resources in English-speaking countries. She then goes on to demonstrate that the linguistic market in Hong Kong has remained largely unchanged in the post-1997 situation, since decolonization. The Chinese administration introduced a linguistic streaming system in 1998 that retained a tier of over one hundred elite English-medium schools, along with the general Chinese-medium provision. The same values are still associated with English, and the elite English-medium schools in Hong Kong are still seen as key sites for access to English and, eventually, to the predominantly English-medium higher education institutions. In addition, Lin describes the force of pervasive ideologies of language that devalue hybrid language practices. This ideology heightens the pressure for a particular way of using English in the classroom, that is, in ways that mirror English-language education in monolingual settings. Drawing on classroom-based research conducted in English-medium schools during the colonial era, Lin describes the consequences of these ideological pressures for teachers and learners and for language use in Hong Kong classrooms, demonstrating how students of the dominant group who already have knowledge of English from outside school are positioned advantageously in comparison to poorer students who do not have this access. The code-switching practices of these classrooms serve to reproduce existing relations of dominance.

language-in-education practices as a window on wider social, political and ideological processes

Comparison of the findings of critical, interpretive studies such as these throws into sharp focus the role of education in constructing particular regimes of language and in regulating access to language resources in multilingual settings. The field of bilingual education has certainly moved on from the days when the main concern was with choices between 'models' or types of educational programme and with monitoring learners' developing linguistic competence. In 2001, Monica Heller and I co-edited a volume which brought together studies in multilingual settings that had been conducted in a critical interpretive vein. Drawing on the insights gleaned from these studies, we made the following observation:

> Educational choices in such settings, whether regarding structures, programs, practices, or materials, are clearly much more than choices about how to achieve linguistic proficiency. They are choices about how to distribute linguistic resources and about what value to attribute to linguistic forms and practices. They are choices that are embedded in the economic, political and social interests of groups and that have consequences for the

life chances of individuals as well as for the construction of social categories and relations of power. (Heller and Martin-Jones 2001: 419)

A critical, interpretive approach brings several new dimensions to the investigation of the regulation of bilingualism within the domain of education. Firstly, it provides penetrating insights into the processes at work in everyday classroom life, building on the research approaches honed and refined within the interpretive traditions described above. It does this in three main ways: it lays bare the ways in which language values and discourses about language and language learning are produced and reproduced in and through the daily interactional rituals in classrooms; it reveals the complex ways in which classroom participants draw on the linguistic resources available to them as they collaborate with or resist the interactional order and the institutional order in which it is embedded; and it illuminates the consequences of these practices for the construction of different social categories.

Secondly, a critical interpretive approach provides a window on wider social, political and ideological processes and offers greater depth of explanation. Working in this way enables us to bring out connections between developments at different points in the history of language-in-education policies in a particular nation-state and between local struggles over language in urban or rural areas with different sociolinguistic histories. Starting from the assumption that education is a key site for the creation of the monolingual spaces of a nation-state (or indeed of an empire, with all its colonies) and for the definition of 'legitimate language' (the standardized, 'pure' and natural language), we can see what the consequences of this might be for speakers of other languages or other varieties of the 'same' language. One consequence, well documented in decades of sociolinguistic research, is the devaluing or stigmatization of other languages and varieties. Moreover, educational institutions contribute to the stigmatization of minority languages, regional dialects and the languages of colonized peoples whilst, at the same time, providing access to other highly valued forms of bilingualism, for example, through the teaching of major European languages, as part of the foreign language curriculum. These more prestigious forms of bilingualism are, of course, consistent with class interests and with the interests of international trade and diplomacy. The stigmatization of minority languages or the languages of colonized peoples can also lead to the mounting of challenges to the role of education as an agency for producing the monolingual order of nation-states, particularly as political and economic conditions change, as they did in the 1960s, and as particular groups are mobilized around their language. These challenges give rise to some of the different forms of bilingual education already mentioned in this chapter, along with new discourses about what counts as 'legitimate language' and about creating monolingual spaces for learning.

Thirdly, critical interpretive work on language-in-education in multilingual settings gives us a window on the contemporary processes of change ushered in by globalization and by the emergence of a new world order. In some contexts, attempts have been made, since the late 1980s, to forge new educational landscapes through educational 'reforms', in response to these changing political, economic and cultural conditions. This process has, inevitably, been characterized by tensions, by a shifting politics of identity and by the emergence of new discourses about language-in-education. The tensions arising out of different dimensions of globalization are only beginning to be explored in critical, interpretive research on education in multilingual settings (e.g. Harris, Leung and Rampton 2002; Heller 2003; Stroud 2003; Lin and Martin 2005; McEwan-Fujita 2005). I will outline three of these here. All are likely to be key foci for future research on bilingualism in education that is conducted in a critical, interpretive vein.

The first dimension of globalization that poses a challenge for national education systems is the rapid expansion of the new economy. The balance in education has already shifted towards the demands of free market capitalism, transnational corporations and the new knowledge-driven economy. There is a new emphasis on language and literacy 'skills' and on the creation of a new generation of skilled workers, alongside the older discourses about instilling notions of democracy and citizenship. Processes of social stratification and access to the labour market have always been tied to education and to the valuation of the language and literacy resources that learners bring to education. However, the stakes are now even higher. New kinds of language and literacy resources, including new foreign language skills, are required for entry to the labour market in most post-industrial societies where the service sector and new media are expanding rapidly (see Block and Cameron 2002; Cameron 2002; Gee, Hull and Lankshear 1996 and Cope and Kalantzis 2000, for more detailed description of these new language and literacy resources). Moreover, as Heller (2003) has argued, languages are increasingly being seen as 'commodities' on an international market. According to Heller, 'the commodification of language…renders language amenable to redefinition as a measurable skill, as opposed to a talent, or an inalienable characteristic of group members' (2003: 474). This process of commodification, both within education and within the new work order, is dislodging traditional discourses about language being iconic of national, regional or ethnic identity and constructing new systems of assessment and social selection.

The second dimension of globalization that presents major challenges for education systems is what Appadurai (1990) refers to as changing 'ethnoscapes': that is, the increasing population flows of immigrants, refugees, migrant workers and elite workers moving within the global capitalist system. Sociologists and anthropologists have drawn our attention to the nature and significance of new diasporic identities and networks as part of a process of 'globalization from below' (Portes 1997). They have also highlighted the emergence of global cities, centres of finance, transport and commerce, whose populations include an increasingly wealthy transnational elite and low paid workers in what is often an invisible economy. Comparing the new 'ethnoscapes' created by globalization with nineteenth-century visions of the links between identity and territoriality, Cohen (1997) makes the following remark:

> What nineteenth century nationalists wanted was a 'space' for each 'race', a territorializing of each social identity. What they have got instead is a chain of cosmopolitan cities and an increasing proliferation of subnational and transnational identities that cannot easily be contained in the nation-state system. (1997: 175)

However, from the late 1980s to the present, educational policy-makers in many economically advanced, post-industrial nation-states have responded to these significant demographic changes by introducing or consolidating language and literacy education policies that are designed to impose uniformity and by asserting the value of languages seen as the carriers of their national traditions. These processes have been well documented in the case of England, where standard English was reinserted at the heart of the National Curriculum, as part of a planned project, after the passing of the Education Reform Act (ERA) of 1988 (see Cameron and Bourne 1988 for details). There have been similar reflexes elsewhere. As Harris, Leung and Rampton (2002) have observed:

> England is not alone in its inability / reluctance / failure to engage con-structively with the effects of globalisation, with the realities of the global city and new diaspora relations. A broadly comparable pattern of educational policy reactions can be found in the USA, Canada and Australia. (2002: 41)

The third dimension of globalization that has had a significant impact on education systems world-wide is the relentless spread of English, along with the perception that gaining access to the language will lead to increased prosperity. As Lin and Martin (2005) put it, English is seen as part of a 'package' bound up with other dimensions of 'modernization':

> English has often been perceived as an indispensable resource which many post-colonial peoples and governments seek for themselves and their younger generations in their respective socioeconomic contexts. This is often infused with a strong desire for economic development, technological and material modernisation, and human-resource capital investment for current and future successful participation in the new global economic order...Such capital includes English communication skills, information technology, business management and commercial know-how. (2005: 3)

There has been considerable interest among applied linguists in language-in-education policy developments spurred on by globalization and, in particular, in the rapid proliferation of bilingual education programmes involving the use of a national language and English and the rapid expansion of private sector provision of English-medium education. Studies of a critical, interpretive nature, combining critical analysis of policy developments with detailed accounts of language practices in sites where such policy interventions are taking place are still few and far between. Notable exceptions are recent studies by Valencia (2004), in Colombia, and Martin (2005), in Malaysia.

These dimensions of globalization not only present challenges to education systems within individual nation-states. They also present challenges to research and to theory-building in the field of language-in-education in bilingual and multilingual settings. We now know a good deal about the direction of the changes triggered by globalization and about what might be at stake for different social and linguistic groups. But we still know relatively little about what is happening 'on the ground', as it were, in particular local educational sites where policies, shaped by changing political and economic conditions, are being implemented. Adopting a critical, interpretive approach and providing detailed accounts of language and literacy practices in such sites gives us a means of drawing attention to the disjunctures between the contemporary realities of life in multilingual classrooms and communities and the types of discourses and language-in-education policies that I have discussed above. It is in this way that we can provide the necessary educational critique and begin to define a future vision for language and literacy education that takes account of increasing local diversity and global connectedness.

references

Appadurai, A. (1990). Disjuncture and difference in the global cultural economy. In M. Featherstone (ed.), *Global Culture: Nationalism, Globalisation and Modernity*. London: Sage.

Arthur, J. (1996). Codeswitching and collusion: Classroom interaction in Botswana classrooms. *Linguistics and Education* 8(1): 17–34.

Artigal, J.M. (1997). The Catalan immersion program. In R.K. Johnson and M. Swain (eds), *Immersion Education: International Perspectives*, pp. 133–50. Cambridge: Cambridge University Press.

Baker, C. (2006) (fourth edition). *Foundations of Bilingual Education and Bilingualism*. Clevedon, UK: Multilingual Matters.

Björklund, S. (1997). Immersion in Finland in the 1990s: A state of development and expansion. In R.K. Johnson and M. Swain (eds), *Immersion Education: International Perspectives*, pp. 85–101. Cambridge: Cambridge University Press.

Blackledge, A. (2001). The wrong sort of capital? Bangladeshi women and their children's schooling in Birmingham, UK. *International Journal of Bilingualism* 5(3): 345–69.

Block, D., and D. Cameron (eds) (2002) *Globalization and Language Teaching*. London: Routledge.

Bourdieu, P. (1991). *Language and Symbolic Power.* Cambridge, MA: Harvard University Press.

Bunyi, G. (2001). Language and educational inequality in primary classrooms in Kenya. In M. Heller and M. Martin-Jones (eds), *Voices of Authority: Education and Linguistic Difference*, pp. 77–100. Westport, CT: Ablex.

Cameron, D. (2002). Globalization and the teaching of 'communicative skills'. In D. Block and D. Cameron (eds), *Globalization and Language Teaching*, pp. 67–82. London: Routledge.

Cameron, D., and J. Bourne (1988). No common ground: Kingman, grammar and nation. *Language and Education* 2(3): 147–60.

Canagarajah, S. (1995). Functions of codeswitching in ESL classrooms: Socialising bilingualism in Jaffna. *Journal of Multilingual and Multicultural Development* 16(3): 173–95.

Cazden, C., R. Carrasco, A.A. Maldonado-Guzman and F. Erickson (1980). The contribution of ethnographic research to bicultural bilingual education. In J.E. Alatis (ed.), *Current Issues in Bilingual Education: Georgetown University Round Table on Languages and Linguistics.* Washington, DC: Georgetown University Press.

Chick, K. (1996). Safe-talk: Collusion in apartheid education. In H. Coleman (ed.), *Society and the Language Classroom*, pp. 21–39. Cambridge: Cambridge University Press.

Cohen, R. (1997). *Global Diasporas.* London: University College London Press.

Cope, B. and M. Kalantzis (eds) (2000). *Multiliteracies: Literacy Learning and the Design of Social Futures.* London: Routledge.

Crawford, J. (1995) (third edition). *Bilingual Education: History, Politics, Theory and Practice.* Los Angeles: Bilingual Educational Services. See also: <http://ourworld.compuserve.com/homepages/JWCRAWFORD>.

Creese, A. (2002). The discursive construction of power in teacher partnerships: Language and subject specialists in mainstream schools. *TESOL Quarterly* 36(4), 597–616.

Cummins, J. (1979). Linguistic interdependence and the educational development of bilingual children. *Review of Educational Research* 49: 222–51.

Erickson, F., and G. Mohatt (1982). Cultural organization of participant structures in two classrooms. In G.D. Spindler (ed.), *Doing the Ethnography of Schooling: Educational Anthropology in Action.* New York: Holt, Rinehart and Winston.

Faltis, C.J. (1989). Codeswitching and bilingual schooling: An examination of Jacobson's 'New Concurrent Approach'. *Journal of Multilingual and Multicultural Development* 10: 117–27.

Fishman, J.A., and J. Lovas (1970). Bilingual education in sociolinguistic perspective. *TESOL Quarterly* 4: 215–22.

Freeman, R. (1998). *Bilingual Education and Social Change.* Clevedon, UK: Multilingual Matters.

Gee, J.P., G. Hull and C. Lankshear (1996). *The New Work Order: Behind the Language of the New Capitalism.* Boulder, CO: Westview Press.

Gumperz, J.J. (1982). *Discourse Strategies.* Cambridge: Cambridge University Press.

—— (1986). Interactional sociolinguistics in the study of schooling. In J. Cook-Gumperz (ed.), *The Social Construction of Literacy*, pp. 45–68. Cambridge: Cambridge University Press.

Harley, B. (1991). Directions in immersion research. *Journal of Multilingual and Multicultural Development* 12 (1 & 2): 9–19.

180   the state, the economy and their agencies in late modernity

Harris, R., C. Leung and B. Rampton (2002). Globalization, diaspora and language education in England. In D. Block and D. Cameron (eds), *Globalization and Language Teaching*, pp. 29–46. London: Routledge.

Heath, S.B. (1982). Protean shapes in literacy events. In D. Tannen (ed.), *Spoken and Written Language: Exploring Orality and Literacy*, pp. 91–117. Norwood, NJ: Ablex.

Heller, M. (1990). French immersion in Canada: A model for Switzerland? *Multilingua* 9(1): 67–85.

—— (1994). *Crosswords: Language, Education and Ethnicity in French Ontario*. Berlin: Mouton de Gruyter.

—— (1996). Legitimate language in a multilingual school. *Linguistics and Education* 8(2), 139–57.

—— (1999). *Linguistic Minorities and Modernity: A Sociolinguistic Ethnography*. Harlow, UK: Longman.

—— (2003). Globalization, the new economy and the commodification of language and identity. *Journal of Sociolinguistics* 7(4): 473–92.

Heller, M., and M. Martin-Jones (eds) (2001). *Voices of Authority: Education and Linguistic Difference*. Westport, CT: Ablex.

Hornberger, N. (1988). *Bilingual Education and Language Maintenance*. Dordrecht: Foris Publications.

—— (1991). Extending enrichment bilingual education: Revisiting typologies and redirecting policy. In O. García (ed.), *Bilingual Education: Focusschrift in Honour of Joshua A. Fishman* (vol. 1). Amsterdam and Philadelphia: John Benjamins.

Hymes, D. (1972). Models of the interaction of language and social life. In J.J. Gumperz and D. Hymes (eds), *Directions in Sociolinguistics*, pp. 221–8. New York: Holt, Rinehart and Winston.

—— (1974). *Foundations in Sociolinguistics*. Philadelphia, PA: University of Pennsylvania Press.

Jacobson, R., and C. Faltis (eds) (1990). *Language Distribution Issues in Bilingual Schooling*. Clevedon, UK: Multilingual Matters.

Jaffe, A. (1999). *Ideologies in Action: Language Politics on Corsica*. Berlin: Mouton de Gruyter.

Johnson, R.K., and M. Swain (eds) (1997). *Immersion Education: International Perspectives*. Cambridge: Cambridge University Press.

Jørgensen, J.N. (1998). Children's acquisition of codeswitching for power-wielding. In P. Auer (ed.), *Codeswitching in Conversation: Language, Interaction and Identity*, pp. 237–58. London: Routledge.

Lambert, W., and R. Tucker (1972). *Bilingual Education of Children: The St Lambert Experiment*. Rowley, MA: Newbury House.

Legarreta, D. (1977). Language choice in bilingual classrooms. *TESOL Quarterly* 1: 9–16.

Lin, A.M.Y. (1996). Bilingualism or linguistic segregation? Symbolic domination, resistance and codeswitching. *Linguistics and Education* 8(1): 49–84.

—— (2001). Symbolic domination and bilingual classroom practices in Hong Kong. In M. Heller and M. Martin-Jones (eds), *Voices of Authority: Education and Linguistic Difference*, pp. 139–68. Westport, CT: Ablex.

Lin, A.M.Y., and P.W. Martin (eds) (2005). *Decolonisation, Globalisation: Language-in-Education Policy and Practice*. Clevedon, UK: Multilingual Matters.

Mackey, W.F. (1972). A typology of bilingual education. In J.A. Fishman (ed.), *Advances in the Sociology of Language*, pp. 413–32. The Hague: Mouton.

Martin, P.W. (1999). Bilingual unpacking of monolingual texts in two primary classrooms in Brunei Darussaalam. *Language and Education* 13: 38–58.

—— (2005). 'Safe' language practices in two rural schools in Malaysia: tensions between policy and practice. In A.M.Y. Lin and P.W. Martin (eds), *Decolonisation, Globalisation: Language-in-Education Policy and Practice*, pp. 74–97. Clevedon, UK: Multilingual Matters.

Martin-Jones, M. (1989). Language, power and linguistic minorities: The need for an alternative approach to bilingualism, language maintenance and shift. In R. Grillo (ed.), *Social Anthropology and the Politics of Language*, pp. 106–25. London: Routledge.

—— (2000). Bilingual classroom interaction: A review of recent research. *Language Teaching* 33: 1–9.

Martin-Jones, M., and M. Heller (1996). Language and social reproduction in multilingual settings. (Introduction to two special issues on 'Education in multilingual settings: Discourse, identities and power') *Linguistics and Education* 8(1): 3–16 and 8(2): 127–37.

Martin-Jones, M., and S. Romaine (1986). Semilingualism: A half-baked theory of communicative competence. *Applied Linguistics* 7: 26–38.

Martin-Jones, M., and M. Saxena (1996). Turn-taking, power asymmetries, and the positioning of bilingual participants in classroom discourse. *Linguistics and Education* 8(1): 105–23.

McCarthy, M. (2001). *Issues in Applied Linguistics*. Cambridge: Cambridge University Press.

McEwen-Fujita, E. (2005). Neo-liberalism and minority-language planning in the Highlands and islands of Scotland. *International Journal of the Sociology of Language* 171: 155–71.

Mehan, H. (1981). Ethnography of bilingual education. In H.T. Trueba, G.P. Guthrie and K.H. Au (eds), *Culture and the Bilingual Classroom: Studies in Classroom Ethnography*. Rowley, MA: Newbury House.

Mejia, A-M de. (1998). Bilingual story-telling: Codeswitching, discourse control and learning opportunities. *TESOL Journal* 7(6): 4–10.

—— (2002). *Power, Prestige and Bilingualism*. Clevedon, UK: Multilingual Matters.

Moll, L., C. Amanti, D. Neff and N. Gonzalez (1992). Funds of knowledge for teaching: Using a qualitative approach to connect homes and classrooms. *Theory into Practice* 31(2): 132–41.

Mondada, L., and L. Gajo (2001). Classroom interaction and the bilingual resources of migrant students in Switzerland. In M. Heller and M. Martin-Jones (eds), *Voices of Authority: Education and Linguistic Difference*, pp. 235–68. Westport, CT: Ablex.

Olson, C.P., and G. Burns (1983). Politics, class and happenstance: French immersion in a Canadian context. *Interchange* 14(1): 1–16.

Philips, S. (1983). *The Invisible Culture: Communication in Classroom and Community on the Warm Springs Indian Reservation*. Prospect Heights, IL: Waveland Press.

Portes, A. (1997). *Globalization from Below: The Rise of Transnational Communities*. Oxford: Transnational Communities Working Paper, WPTC – 98 – 01. Online. Available at <www.transcomm.oxford.ac.uk>.

Rubagumya, C. (ed.) (1994). *Teaching and Researching Language in African Classrooms*. Clevedon, UK: Multilingual Matters.

Rubinstein-Avila, E. (2002). Problematizing the 'dual' in a dual-immersion program: A portrait. *Linguistics and Education* 13(1): 65–87.

Skutnabb-Kangas, T. (1978). Semilingualism and the education of migrant children as a means of reproducing the caste of assembly line workers. In N. Dittmar and U. Teleman (eds), *Papers from the First Scandinavian-German Symposium on the Languages of Immigrant Workers and their Children*. Roskilde: Roskilde Universitet Center, Linguistgruppen.

—— (1984). *Bilingualism or Not: The Education of Minorities*. Clevedon, UK: Multilingual Matters.

Spolsky, B., and R.L. Cooper (eds) (1978). *Case Studies of Bilingual Education*. Rowley, MA: Newbury House.

Stroud, C. (2003). Postmodernist perspectives on local languages: African mother tongue education in times of globalisation. *International Journal of Bilingual Education and Bilingualism* 6(1): 17–36.

—— (2004). Rinkeby Swedish and semilingualism in language ideological debates: A Bourdieuan perspective. *Journal of Sociolinguistics* 8(2): 196–214.

Swain, M. (1983). Bilingualism without tears. In M. Clarke and J. Handscombe (eds), *On TESOL '82: Pacific Perspectives on Language Learning and Teaching*. Washington, DC: Teachers of English to Speakers of Other Languages (TESOL).

—— (1985). Communicative competence: Some roles of comprehensible input and comprehensible output in its development. In S. Gass and C. Madden (eds), *Input in Second Language Acquisition*. Rowley, MA: Newbury House.

Swain, M., and S. Lapkin (1982). *Evaluating Bilingual Education: A Canadian Case Study*. Clevedon, UK: Multilingual Matters.

Tardif, C., and S. Weber (1987). French immersion research: A call for new perspectives. *Canadian Modern Language Review* 44(1): 67–77.

Thomas, W.P., and V.P. Collier (2002). *A National Sudy of School Effectiveness for Language Minority Students: Long Term Academic Success*. Final Report, Project 1.1. Santa Cruz: Center for Research on Education, Diversity and Excellence.

Tollefson, J.W. (2002). *Language Policies in Education: Critical Issues*. Mahwah, NJ: Lawrence Erlbaum.

Valencia, S. (2004). English language teaching in Colombia: Changes in policy and practice viewed through a regional case study. Unpublished PhD thesis, University of Wales Aberystwyth.

Vila i Moreno, F.X. (1996). *When Classes are Over: Language Choice and Language Contact in Bilingual Education in Catalonia*. Brussels: Vrije Universiteit Brussel.

Watson-Gegeo, K.A., and D.W. Gegeo (1986). Calling-out and repeating routines in Kwara'ae children's language socialization. In B.B. Schieffelin and E. Ochs (eds), *Language Socialization across Cultures*, pp. 17–50. New York: Cambridge University Press.

Wong Fillmore, L. (1980). Language learning through bilingual instruction. Unpublished mimeo. Berkeley: University of California.

Woolard, K. (1985). Language variation and cultural hegemony: Toward an integration of sociolinguistic theory and social theory. *American Ethnologist* 12: 738–48.

Zentella, A.C. (1981). Ta bien, you could answer me en cualquier idioma: Puerto Rican codeswitching in bilingual classrooms. In R. Duran (ed.), *Latino Language and Communicative Behavior*. Norwood, NJ: Ablex.

9

bilingualism and the globalized new economy: the commodification of language and identity[1]

emanuel da silva, mireille mclaughlin and mary richards

introduction

Globalization: a big word that is meant to account for a multiplicity of processes and practices, namely an increase in quantity and rapidity of the circulation of people, identities, imaginations and products across borders. At the heart of globalization are discursive struggles over positioning and repositioning of actors as a result of the changing conditions of production and consumption of goods and identities. One of the driving forces of trans-nationalism is the tertiarization of the economy, that is, its transformation to a concentration in service and knowledge-based activities. As a result of tertiarization, we are currently witnessing a shift between two ideological systems when it comes to the organization of the relations of power which structure social, linguistic and identity practices. Indeed, the tertiarization of the economy is transforming the economic bases which organize the reproduction of social groups, and the associated management of linguistic and cultural difference.

The first ideological system, currently challenged by economic globalization, is bound up in the processes linked to the legitimization of the nation-state as the dominant model of governance – involved, that is, in the naturalization of a bounded, homogeneous group. Within this naturalization of 'national' powers, language was and continues to be a terrain upon which are fought struggles for control over who gets to define the content and boundaries of the groups and the symbolic and material resources they value (see Pujolar, this volume). Collective and individual practices of bilingualism and the 'integration' of immigrants within these bounded national entities have also been highly problematic within this system (see Moyer and Martín Rojo, this volume). These processes raise questions about who is considered a legitimate speaker possessing the 'right' bilingual skills, and about what is the basis of this legitimacy (Bourdieu 1982).

The second ideological system emerges today, as the material and discursive conditions that have allowed for the reproduction of nation-states and quasi-nation-states (like Quebec or Acadie) are eroding in the face of a restructuration of economic and symbolic flows. Indeed, the conditions of the new economy are bringing about a reconfiguration of the links between language, identity and 'territory-body-personhood': language is being commodified as a skill in sites such as the language industry, and ethnic identity is being produced and commercialized for global markets through tourism and cultural, artistic and crafts production.

But on the ground, language and identity are not so easily reified, and so it is the discursive (re)organization of the links between them both that we wish to explore in this chapter. We will argue that these shifting conditions have allowed for the creation of markets where the value of language(s) and the old ways of doing identity and citizenship are subjected to processes of commodification. The question is: can any speaking body, anywhere, provide the legitimate linguistic and cultural performances? Does commodification somehow require that the individuals providing the linguistic and cultural skills have access to resources that are anchored somewhere? In the new economy, which linguistic forms, which performances of language, culture and identity are rendered legitimate? Who and what gives them value, with what consequences for the actors involved?

the new economy and the commodification of language

Many authors have argued that capitalism and the ways it structures the distribution of resources (material or symbolic) have been transformed by what Harvey (1990) calls 'time-space compression'. He argues that we are witnessing faster movements of capital, products and people across the globe, just as the networks sustaining these movements are morphing and multiplying, thus reducing spatial and temporal distances in an increasingly 'smaller', yet still unequally interconnected world. This occurs at a time when a primarily production-based global economy is shifting to an economy of consumption which relies more and more on niche marketing. These processes help shape, and are themselves shaped by the ways nation-states and linguistic minorities manage linguistic and cultural diversity as languages and identities become commodified.

This chapter focuses on francophone minority communities in Canada, and draws from ongoing ethnographic, sociolinguistic research[2] primarily in Acadie and Ontario, the two major areas of Canada where Francophones reside outside of Quebec. Linguistic minority spaces such as these are particularly revealing of the changes we wish to discuss here, for several reasons. First, as minority nationalist movements, they tend to have observable traces of nationalist discourses, and therefore of the challenges to them (see Jaffe, this volume). Majority spaces can exercise symbolic domination in ways which mask interests and discourses; minority spaces are challengers, and render things more explicit. Second, having always been on the periphery of national markets, minority spaces experience the shifts in conditions which sustain them perhaps more directly. Finally, they have always had to invest in one form or another of multilingualism, and are hence particularly well-positioned to rethink and re-evaluate what multilingualism means. In particular, as we shall see, they are directly involved in the commodification of language and identity which emerges out of the repositioning of national and regional markets, out of the collapse of primary- and secondary-resource based markets which sustained peripheral communities, and out of the emergent tertiarized economy.

Thus, the changing social conditions linked to postmodernity or globalization have enabled the emergence of new or 'non-traditional' linguistic and cultural sites for representing and doing francophone identity, such as the language industry; cultural, artistic and crafts production; and tourism. These sites allow us to examine discursive tensions over access to symbolic and material resources. Many of these tensions revolve around the question of authenticity. Who counts as a 'good' Francophone? What counts as 'good' French and 'good' bilingual practices? Why? How? Who decides? And what are the consequences?

We are witnessing a shift towards a tertiarization of the economy where product branding, and the concomitant importance of customer service, are all the more emphasized, just as the technologization of all sectors of the economy (from extraction to services) are relying more and more on information technologies and language in the course of daily activities. This tertiarization of the economy creates an increased demand for 'language workers', that is, individuals hired to act as the voices or the cultural brokers of enterprises, negotiating the inherent multilingualism of global business practices. What does this mean for language, linguistic practices and our understanding of bilingualism? In an economy which increasingly emphasizes global customer service, we witness the commodification of language and its disentanglement from 'personhood' (Adkins 2005). This means that language, as a commodity, is no longer an inherent quality of certain individuals or something that individuals own, but something that is separate and external to their personhood. In the new economy, linguistic practices can be seen as resources which, in an effort to cater to markets and consumers, are mobilized by actors to produce and reproduce a multiplicity of social identities.

The 'success' of these identity and language practices depends largely on whether or not others consider them authentic. As Coupland (2003) points out, we are currently in a discursive regime where authenticity matters. Yet authenticity results from social processes, and it is embedded in unequal power relations that link certain practices with certain markers of group identity. In fact, when authenticity is used in the commodification of identity, we witness the tensions produced by transnationalism, as various actors try to (re)produce the (now unsustainable?) national markets as bounded entities.

In addition, language has also been considered a bounded entity. As Heller mentions in the introduction to this volume, bilingualism has been predominantly conceived as 'the coexistence of two separate linguistic systems' within the field of linguistics and sociolinguistics. This conceptualization of bilingualism as a double or parallel monolingualism emerged from and structured the ideology of the modern nation-state, which equates one language with one nation, race or people (Blommaert 1999; Hobsbawm 1990). However, the 'traditional' model of bilingualism does not enable us to deconstruct the hybridity and multiplicity of linguistic practices and their social and contextual embeddedness. We argue for a dismantling of the systemic categorizations of languages and identity, and adopt instead an approach which views language as a social action. The theoretical and methodological tools provided to us by critical sociolinguistics (Heller 2001) and social theory (Giddens 1984) allow for a different conceptualization of bilingualism (see Heller's introduction to this volume).

Our approach focuses on language as a social practice embedded in processes of social structuration, and it allows us to better understand how the commodification of linguistic practices and identities creates tensions between the constitution of local, national and transnational identities in today's global economic conditions. In the following sections, we will first study the commodification of language and the emergence of the language worker in fields such as the language industry and, more specifically, the call centre industry. We will show that the new economy has brought forward a new discourse where languages are disentangled from personhood and community, thus bringing minority francophone communities and institutions in Canada to reposition their 'national' identity as a commodifiable resource in the interconnected fields of tourism and cultural production, which will be discussed in the second half of this chapter. This highlights the power struggles at play in the maintenance of the boundaries of a collective identity. All in all, we will show that practices and processes of commodification of language and identity emerge from the creation of new markets within the new economy, and bring about a new discursive regime where the links between languages, nation and citizenship are being reworked.

the commodification of language

language and the new economy

This section examines different sites where language is at the centre of commodification processes stemming from recent shifts from a modern, industrialized economy to a globalized one based on services, information and communication. With this new focus, the bilingual language practices of minority francophone communities are seen as a new and plentiful resource to draw from, by actors within these communities as well as by the different levels of government involved in community development. In the context of the privatization of the public sector and the Canadian government's shift from the preservation of cultural heritage to the push for economic development and accountability, bilingualism (traditionally seen as a personal characteristic without much economic value in the 'old economy', except for the elite) became valued as a skill to be honed and as a commodity to be traded on a national and global market. In what follows, we will explore the commodification of language as a resource through the expansion of the 'language industry' and the emergence of the 'language worker', as well as the legitimating ideologies behind these terms and behind the concepts of bi- and multilingualism, before reflecting on what all of this means for a critical perspective on bilingualism.

the language industry

From a historical perspective, the existence of a 'language industry' *per se* is not an entirely recent phenomenon, since international trade has existed for thousands of years and its success has depended largely on the need to speak different languages, and, more specifically, on the existence of techniques and actors specialized in language. However, what is new about this language industry is its particular forms of institutionalization, as a result of the reconfiguration of the globalized new economy, and the consolidated state-sponsored effort to support an entire 'industry' set up to maintain and develop language as a resource. Today, language is still used in the process of selling products (as a communicational tool), but more importantly it has also become a product itself (that is, a marketable resource). Those whose jobs involve the management and production of language are considered 'language workers' (Heller 2005b), working on and with language as if it were a physically tangible resource (like lumber or steel). As Heller (2003: 474) points out, this marketable commodification of language renders it 'amenable to redefinition as a measurable skill, as opposed to a talent, or an inalienable characteristic of group members'. In this light, languages do not necessarily need to be part of the individual's ethnolinguistic background, which means that they can be commodified by people who stake no claim to identity.

In order to better understand the language industry in Canada, we need to begin with the government's *Action Plan for Official Languages* (Government of Canada 2003). This policy statement and action plan was designed to renew and update the commitment to the principle of English and French as the two official languages of Canada[3] by focusing on four main areas: education, community development, public service and the language industries. The services provided by the language industries (originally referred to in the plural) are considered essential to Canada's ability to function as a bilingual country[4] and include translation, interpretation, language training and technology. These have since been consolidated under a representative trade association, known as the *Association de l'industrie de la langue / Language Industry Association* (AILIA), created by a \$5 million pledge from the Canadian government in an effort to support, promote and coordinate the 'industry'. The *Action Plan* hopes that as a result 'our language industries will be better equipped to support a bilingual Canada in its efforts to take full advantage, now more than ever, of its linguistic duality' (Government of Canada 2003: 59).

The advantage is primarily economic.[5] Since linguistic resources are involved in every sector of the economy, from tourism to communications and information technology to the marketing of goods and services, the language industry is 'at the heart of international markets'. Canada, for its part, is portrayed as 'a leader in this burgeoning sector' and 'a key player in the global language marketplace' (AILIA 2005).[6]

But what is it about Canada that would make it such a global leader or key player in the language industry? Maurice, a business development agent for an AILIA-related research centre, explained in an interview:[7]

> Maurice: évidemment au Canada on pense bilinguisme [Anglais-Français] / mais le mandat du centre de recherche et les groupes de recherche / c'est le multilinguisme (...) et on veut profiter du multilinguisme au Canada[8]

> Maurice: obviously in Canada we think bilingualism [English–French] / but the mandate of the research centre and the research groups / is multilingualism (...) and we want to profit from Canada's multilingualism [our translation]

We see here that, contrary to what one might expect given Canada's 'linguistic duality', inherited from its 'founding people' (the English and French), it is multilingualism and not just bilingualism that is valued and commodified. This value, however, is not institutionalized because Canada remains 'officially' bilingual and 'unofficially' multilingual – a linguistic reality the state refuses to recognize for fear of discrediting its nationalist roots.[9] It does, however, officially recognize the current multicultural make-up of the country, but chooses to frame it in an imaginary bilingual space. And so, out of the ambiguity of these competing ideologies, Canada's language industry profits from the historic legitimacy of bilingualism as well as the multilingual 'by-products' of multiculturalism, as AILIA's promotional document (AILIA 2005) so clearly points out:

> This exceptional multilingual expertise is a by-product of Canada's rich, well-nurtured tradition of multiculturalism and is thus rooted in a very concrete understanding of the cultural and linguistic reality of the various groups to be served throughout the world.

When asked how he thought the language industry defines languages, Maurice responded:

> Maurice: ben ce sont les langues de communication on revient au concept de communication finalement / l'importance là-dedans c'est pas la langue en tant que telle / c'est la langue en tant qu'outil de communication // et la raison pour laquelle l'industrie de la langue (...) est plus visible / c'est parce qu'avant c'était euh / quelque chose qu'il fallait faire parce qu'on parlait une langue ou l'autre pis fallait faire une traduction / mais là avec la mondialisation / les échanges commerciaux à l'international qui augmentent énormément / et (...) aussi les échanges en communication en général comme par internet le web etc. // donc on a besoin de faire le pont / linguistique entre deux langues / donc pour nous les langues sont toutes les langues parlées a priori euh / qui sont utilisées en communication à travers le monde

> Maurice: well they're languages of communication in the end we come back to the concept of communication / the important thing isn't the language itself but the language as a communicational tool // and the reason why the language industry (...) is more visible now / is because back in the day um / it was something you had to do because we spoke one language or another and we had to translate / but now with globalization / the commercial exchanges the enormous growth of international trade / and (...) also communicational exchanges in general with the internet the web etc. // so we need to build linguistic bridges / between two languages / so for us language includes all languages *a priori* um / that are used to communicate throughout the world

This excerpt begins with Maurice stressing the use of language as a communicational tool (a useful metaphor in an industrial space), completely avoiding any distinction among linguistic varieties. He goes so far as to say that 'the important thing isn't the language itself', which seems to contradict the view of language as something concrete with which the 'specialists' in the language industry work. If language, as seen through 'the concept of communication', is at the heart of the language industry, then one could expect that code-switching, language mixing, 'foreign' borrowings and neologisms (all characteristics of vernacular bilingualism) would be accepted because they are authentic means of communication. But they are not. In fact, these forms of communication pose problems for those in the language industry, because they work with languages as separate systems (e.g. machine translations which are programmed to work with 'standard' languages).

When Maurice stresses the need to 'build linguistic bridges between two languages', he highlights the linguistic binary vision that characterizes the language industry. Inherent to translation (and the dominant discourse surrounding bilingualism in general) is the notion of two well-defined and separate languages or systems between which translators must navigate. It is commonly believed that the best translations are done into a person's 'mother tongue' (almost always in the singular) because it is seen as the one that the person knows best and is most comfortable with. This brings us to a point of intersection between conflicting ideologies: language as an external or neutral system vs. language as an internal possession of 'native' speakers.

Having touched on some of the language ideologies of bilingualism that are present in the language industry, let us turn to the individuals that propel the industry: the language workers. There are various types of language workers, including: translators, interpreters, language editors and proofreaders, language planners and language teachers. In the following subsection, however, we focus primarily on call centre employees and their language managers because the call centre industry clearly exemplifies the commodification of language brought about by the new economy.

the language worker and call centres

Although the language industry, in a general sense, may not be an entirely new reality, call centres and the language workers they employ are the result of recent changes brought about by the globalized new economy. The ability to offer, for example, instant interpretation from English into more than 150 languages would not be possible without globalization and language workers at the front lines, or rather the phone lines. Language Line Services (LLS)[10] is an example of a company which profits from the commodification of language as a skill:

> As the leading provider of over-the-phone language interpretation, LLS employs professionally trained and tested interpreters who **are far more than just bilingual speakers** [emphasis added]. Successful applicants (proficient in English and at least one other language) are trained in the business concepts and terminology of the clients they serve, which allows them to interpret meaning-for-meaning and not just word-for-word. (...) This synergistic combination of global reach and home-based talents feels like the perfect business fit. (Retrieved 3 March 2006 from LLS website)

This raises at least two interesting questions: what does it mean to be 'more than just bilingual'? And what is it about the global and the local that makes LLS' approach 'the perfect business fit'? Firstly, for some reason bilingualism is perceived as insufficient or incomplete, because it is assumed to be a literal interpretation of two languages and disconnected from culture. Thus, through language training, a person can improve their skills to interpret 'meaning-for-meaning and not just word-for-word'. Beyond a literal understanding of two languages, bilingual language workers need to be well versed in the particular cultural/contextual vocabulary relevant to the client's needs. Not only that, but call centre operators are taught specific communication styles: how to use an 'agreeable' tone of voice, to use a 'caring' or expressive intonation, how to 'smile' on the phone, or use minimal but supportive questions and answers. Cameron (2000) argues that these are all characteristics of a speech style that is associated, in the popular imagination as well as in some empirical research, with the speech of women rather than men. It is no surprise then, that the call centre industry (much like the new economy) is a highly gendered space (see Heller in press). Call centres, particularly those in customer service, are extremely feminized places of work, and the commodification of language is also in some sense the commodification of a quasi-feminine service persona (Cameron 2000). The few men that are present are usually found in specialized, often more technical services, or in upper management where they do not answer phones (Roy 2002).

This gendered reality applies not only to how the language workers do their work, but also where they do it. In the promotional case-study of one of its 'teleworking language interpreters', Pura Carlson,[11] Language Line Services stresses its flexibility in letting people work from home. This allows LLS to tap into the market of bilingual 'stay-at-home' parents – especially mothers. Pura, who reportedly followed her husband to a small town, can 'be the hands-on parent she wants to be, spend quality time with her family and still be a productive professional. (...) Her small son and daughter have become experts on the dual roles she takes on at home: Mom in her office means Mom is at work.' This kind of home-based 'teleworking' language interpretation is quite different from the dynamics of a larger call centre. For example, it is very likely that Pura lacks the support often found in larger group settings and in contact with co-workers.

In contrast, the call centre data we use come from Ontario and New Brunswick (the only officially bilingual province in Canada) where the sound of heavy machinery that once characterized the working conditions of most Francophones has now been replaced, for the most part, by the sound of voices. As Heller (2004: 30) describes it, the call centre represents '... a new economy production line, but the crash and bang of the factory floor is replaced by the low hum of a hundred voices'. In this new call centre industry, bilingualism is very clearly valued as a skill – but not just any kind of bilingualism. The professional, standardized, well-structured image that companies want to transmit is expected to be performed through a language (or languages) that is (are) also seen as 'professional'. And professional in this case means having a near perfect mastery of each individual (standard) language and not mixing them together – this bilingualism is thus seen as what Heller (1999) calls 'parallel monolingualisms'. It is unclear whether or not the bilingual skills of the workers (in this case from francophone minority settings) correspond exactly to the ideology of parallel monolingual-ism and the image that companies want to portray through the voices of their operators. For example, the operators' vernacular bilingualism, which may be a marker of their authentic French-Canadianness, may portray a more local image than the company wishes to transmit. Conversely, it might provide the 'personal touch' that the customer wants or which sets the company apart from its competition.

In the end, however, there is no such thing as a neutral language. This is why companies like JPT, an international employment agency, cater their (linguistic) services to the needs of their customers. Below, Nicole explains why some of her Canadian clients specifically ask for *Québécois* French and not Parisian, European, African or Acadian French.

> Nicole: we usually get requests for bilingual candidates and bilingualism is French of course / generally the *Québécois* (version) and employers will specifically say to you that they want to make sure that it is *Québécois* French (...) they're concerned that they're going to irritate their customers (...) the customers are from Québec and they're intolerant (...) and they've got somebody on the phone who just doesn't understand what they're saying but they're both speaking the same language[12]

This excerpt reveals certain ideologies of bilingualism in Canada. Firstly, we have the view that 'bilingualism is French': this implies that everyone speaks English by default, and that French is the 'added value'.[13] Secondly, we see that that bilingualism traditionally means speaking two different (standard) languages, which are seen as unified wholes, not two varieties of 'the same (neutral) language' – like *Québécois* or *Acadien*. This excerpt also reveals the ambivalence of competing ideologies: language as a neutral or professional skill vs. language as an authentic personal touch.

Given the global scope and profit-driven mentality of the call centre industry, operators do not actually have to be themselves 'authentically' local; companies often train their operators to accommodate to the way the clients speak by pretending to be from their local area and introducing some elements of the local speech or culture (expressions, vocabulary, accents, etc.). As a result, the language worker must quickly negotiate between different language practices and identities while at the same time provide the customer the professional service they require.

In some circumstances the frames of reference associated with each language collapse, for example in talk between operators (see the data from the New Brunswick call centre below). This distances the operators from the professional image the company would like to portray. Yet, the language workers resolve this problem by distinguishing between spaces that are public (or online, with clients or business partners) and private (offline, among operators or between operators and their immediate supervisors). Another strategy used by the language workers to manage their different identities in order to turn in 'believable' performances as speakers of both English and

French is to assume the corresponding versions of their first name (*Mary* one instant, and *Marie* the next).

Both strategies are employed in the following example where a female operator calls a female 'bridge' (supervisor) to ask for information regarding a cancellation; the bridge then phones a hotel.[14]

Bridge:	allô c'est Marie	*hello this is Marie*
Operator:	allô c'est XX	*hello this is XX*
Bridge:	salut	*hi*
Operator:	[rires] euhm peux-tu *bringer up* une *reservation* pour moi?	*[laughs] um can you bring up a* reservation *for me?*
Bridge:	oui	*yes*
Operator:	[en riant] c'est trop *funny* [rires]	*[laughing] it's too* funny *[laughs]*
Bridge:	vas-y	*go ahead*
[...]		
Bridge:	*stop laughing at me*	stop laughing at me
[...]		
Operator:	[prénom et nom de la cliente] [rires] elle veut canceller [rires]	*[client's first and last name] [laughs] she wants to cancel [laughs]*
[...]		
Bridge:	c'est quoi sa raison là?	*what's her reason?*
Operator:	euhmm pas de *clue*	*umm I don't have a* clue
[...]		
Hotel:	Zenith [XX] [first name] *how may I direct your call?*	
Bridge:	*is it possible to have the front desk please?*	
Hotel:	*thank you*	
Bridge:	*thank you*	
[a short pause followed by the phone ringing]		
Front desk:	*front desk this is* [first name] *how can I help you?*	
Bridge:	[XX] *Mary calling from the bridge at ZZZ how are you today?*	
Front desk:	*good how are you?*	
Bridge:	*good good / I was wondering / do you have two seconds?*	
Front desk:	*yes*	

Although language workers have some stylistic choices (as seen in the example above), they often give a verbal performance following a 'script' that a hired external firm has written and that others (a 'language' manager?) observe and survey. Not including their co-workers, language workers effectively have two audiences: they speak directly to the customer and indirectly to their supervisor(s) who enforce(s) linguistic and other norms through surveillance. This produces a market in which bilinguals, and especially bilingual women, sell their voices and construct their identities in ways which neutralize professional pressures as well as pressures to establish personal links with clients. Ultimately, the language workers' linguistic performance is treated as a controlled commodity (along with other aspects related to the individual, like physical appearance and dress), as part of what organizations are selling to their customers.

what does this mean for bilingualism?

We have seen the tensions between some of the competing ideologies that arise from the commodification of language which view it on the one hand as a neutral skill, disconnected from identity and culture, and on the other as a marker of socially situated local authenticity. These tensions make it extremely difficult to answer such seemingly common-sensical questions such as: what does it mean to be bilingual? What counts as good bilingualism? What can a person (not) do with their bilingualism? Recent intensified global competition has sharpened awareness of bi- and multilingual language practices as valuable commodities and a source of 'competitive advantage' which, according to governments and industry leaders, needs to be 'managed' in order to be sustainable or profitable. Nevertheless, although this plurilingualism is valued, it is still done so through the essentialist and reductionist frame of monolingualism. What is it about globalization and the tertiarization of the economy that creates the conditions of commodification?

From what we have observed, virtually all forms of management (be it of languages, services, natural resources, etc.) are driven by some kind of standardizing forces. Variability is organized into identifiable and manageable pieces, and so linguistic performances are also considered divisible – breaking bilingualism down into parallel monolingualisms. Thus, despite the ongoing changes brought about by the globalized new economy, there is an attempt by those in positions of power to maintain the same ideologies of uniformity from previous discursive regimes. The difficult task of negotiating the various tensions discussed above fall squarely on the shoulders of each individual language worker.

In the old economy of primary resource extraction and industrial transformation, the working class was not made up of language workers. Instead, it was management that relied heavily on language and communication as they made their rounds around the job site, conducted meetings and produced reports, for example. Today, one of the main features of the new economy is the major role that language plays at all levels of work (and social class?). The language industry, through the call centre industry and the economic rationalization of its other sectors, is emerging as a working class sector. The different ways that the social, linguistic and other tensions between the management and the working class of the old economy get played out in the new economy deserve further investigation. One hypothesis is that the elite use language norms, on the one hand, to hide and naturalize relations of power (and symbolic domination) by focusing on language (bilingualism) as an innate talent when it benefits them and, on the other, to define the language (bilingualism) of the working class as an objective, measurable and learnable skill.

the commodification of ethnic and linguistic identity

linguistic identity on the terrain of the new economy

We have seen in our fieldwork in call centres and the language industry that there is an attempt to maintain an ideology of language as bounded, separate and separable entities. This grants us an interesting perspective into the ways that today's linguistic markets are structured by economic processes while still being tied up in the social, cultural and linguistic ideologies which were prevalent during the emergence of the nation-state as a mode of governing economic growth, and of managing linguistic, ethnic and social differences.

The multiple ways in which actors, through various social practices such as language, operate to reproduce identities and to construct and maintain boundaries are being restructured by globalization. The changing economic and discursive conditions bring forward not only a commodification of language, but also a commodification of identities – a commodification in which linguistic practices are often mobilized to mark cultural authenticity. One notable example is the use of regional linguistic practices and forms in tourist sites as a way to accentuate and thereby render exotic one's practices in order to attract a global public. In this section we will focus on how these concomitant commodifications of language and identity challenge the 'national' boundaries which constituted 'francophone minority communities' within francophone Canada.

We argue that we are witnessing an attempt, made by linguistic minority elites in the face of the commodification and depersonification of language, to maintain the symbolic markets which have organized linguistic identities (understood as linking cultural and linguistic practices as bearers of identity) as sites of power, as a means of producing these identities as a form of capital. But as social actors mobilize to reproduce the structures through which they have gained social mobility in the modern economy, they are confronted with and reconstituted by the conditions of the new economy, the same ones that structure the commodification of language as a skill. In the field of Canadian francophone minority communities, it becomes clear that social actors have a sense of the ways capitalism, local nationalism and discourses legitimating Canada as a nation-state, converge to make, reproduce and dismantle social categories. The social actors who have come to wield a certain amount of power within the politico-linguistic structures of Canada through the insti-tutionalization of the official language communities are feeling the pressure of the new conditions of the economy. As a result, they are expanding into tourism as a way to maintain their constitutive discourses of community by investing in the production and circulation of 'Franco-Canadian' products.

So how do identity, nationality and commodification come together? Let's start with a simple example: maple syrup. It travels the globe, from 'rustic' camps in Canadian forest-side villages to festivals and commercial fairs in Japan, France or Germany. In France, we observed it being sold in commercial fairs attended by *Québécois* sale representatives clad in nineteenth-century costumes who would use a marked *Québécois* accent to lure their clientele to the stand. The sales strategy relied on the performance of national identities to market the product. This is just one of the signs that in a world of niche markets (Gee, Hull and Lankshear 1996), ethnic and national identities sell. They sell many different ways for many different reasons, sometimes with more success than others – all various modes of mobilizing (tapping, resisting) power through available resources. National and quasi-national identities are used as an added value for certain products or to construct and target certain publics for the sale. Why and how do identities sell? Which identities are produced for whom, when and how? Who participates in producing these identities, why and how? What is the link between the challenging of the idea of identities as the symbolic property of individuals indexing their anchoring in a specific set of social ties, and their commodification? These are some of the questions we will explore below.

Cultural tourism and cultural productions are fields where revealing tensions emerge in regard to how groups perform their identities as commodities. Elyachar (2002: 512) states that: 'Much of the world's population might be left with only its cultural practice as a means of survival.' Here lie some of the tensions emerging as to the access and attribution of value to resources, tensions embedded in the complex heritage of nationalisms as bearers of identities and citizenship in a global world. Indeed, the vestiges of the essentialized ways we have come to know ourselves in the present are recuperated in the new economy through practices such as tourism and cultural production. These practices, often meant to save constituted 'ethnic' symbolic markets (which allow for the conversion of symbolic capital into material capital; Bourdieu 1982), take hybrid forms, as strategies meant to reproduce the discourses legitimating the traditional (modern) distribution of symbolic and material resources at a time when the economic foundations of these markets are changing. In an economic context which relies increasingly on transnational flows, tensions emerge as to the traditional, modernizing and now globalizing ways in which Franco-Canadians have come to understand their identities (Heller and Labrie 2003).

We will focus on three sites where we can see a shift brought about by the global economy on the discourses of linguistic identities, their interplay with nationalism and the processes of their commodification: a Franco-Ontarian blockbuster play, an Acadian musical show and the Acadian World Congress. The tensions emerge in regard to the stories that are told and the markets that are targeted as the public for these events. We will focus on how, where, when and why social actors mobilize 'linguistic minority' identities to maintain control over, or contest, the boundaries of the symbolic markets that are being redefined by the new economy.

tourism, the state and the redefinition of linguistic minorities

In policy such as the *Action Plan for Official Languages* (2003), the Canadian federal state redefined its involvement, both financial and structural, in francophone minority communities, at the same time as it prioritized the commodification of language as a skill. It moved from policy and practice aimed at sustaining French language and culture through support for lobbying groups and social and cultural associations, to a focus on economic development. The interdepartmental government–community partnership that ensued from a nation-wide multi-sectorial consultation process (FCFA 1998), now known as the *Réseau de développement économique et d'employabilité*[15] (henceforth RDEE), highlighted four sectors in which francophone communities, economic agencies and federal departments should invest to ensure the reproduction of the francophone minorities: tourism, the knowledge-based economy, youth in economic development and rural development. The following is an excerpt from their first Annual Report, with concise explanations as to why these priorities were chosen:

- Tourism, because the last three National Forums of Francophone Business People unanimously agreed on its importance;
- The knowledge-based economy, because the world-wide trend in this regard is clear;
- Rural development, because half of the Francophone and Acadian communities are located in rural areas and there is consensus on the need for a national development strategy;
- The integration of youth in economic development, to bring along the next generation of business leaders. (RDEE 1998, English in original)

As francophone minorities cope with globalization, the neoliberal turn taken by the government brings forward tensions as to the modernizing discourses constitutive of francophone identity (rurality, transmission and vitality) (Heller 2005a) and the economic interests of business communities and their representatives (such as the Western Economic Diversification Canada or the Atlantic Canada Opportunities Association). In its 1998 report, the 'Francophone Economic Development in Western Canada' programme, an initiative of Western Economic Diversification Canada (WED) (itself a partner in the RDEE), clearly identifies tourism as the most viable economic development strategy for francophone communities:

Les minorités de langues officielles de l'Ouest ont déterminé que le tourisme était le secteur qui leur offrait les plus grandes possibilités de développement économique. DEO travaille activement dans ce secteur. (DEO 2000)

The official language minorities from the West determined that tourism was the sector that offered them the greatest possibilities of economic development. WED is working actively in this sector. (WED 2000)

What does this emphasis on tourism mean for francophone minorities on the ground? It involves, first of all, a restructuration of the political economy of these minorities through a shift from local, primary-resource based economies once protected by the state to transnational markets. It means, as we will see, a reliance on an essentialization of francophone and national identities and debates over the 'authenticity' of these identities, debates surrounding the legitimacy of the products as well as debates as to who should get to perform identity, how and when. It positions certain actors as producers of culture, others as performers, some as 'authentic' representatives and others as guests/tourists within the new markets. It also creates tensions as the new conditions of the market, and the commodification of language and identity, open up new discursive positions which come into conflict with the once dominant discourse of linguistic minority rights.

language as practice, authenticity and the new economy

As we have already mentioned, old ways of mobilizing the discourse constructing the French language as an entity belonging to and protected by a collectivity are unravelling as francophone linguistic minorities in Canada are moving from a legal and political discourse of 'oppression', 'struggles' and 'rights' to an economic discourse of 'sustainability', 'added value' and 'accountability'. It is language that is being redefined from a right to a resource, but francophone 'communities' remain an operational site for the distribution of this resource. This shift means that social actors who were involved in the struggles to establish the political status and institutional spaces of linguistic communities are now caught between discourses which constitute them as homogeneous, bounded quasi-national communities and discourses which constitute their identity as a commodity. These tensions emerge particularly strongly in the junction where 'nationalist' cultural production meets the logic of tourism and commerce, in sites such as *L'Echo d'un peuple* [The Echo of a People], a blockbuster play which chronicles 400 years of francophone presence in Ontario. Modelled after other such plays in France and Quebec that tell elements of local history to a 'global' public, *L'Echo d'un peuple* was developed as a tourism strategy to attract Franco-Ontarian, *Québécois* and eventually Franco-European publics to the Prescott-Russell region.[16]

The same Franco-Ontarian social actors who, from 1997 to 2002, mobilized to protest against the closure of the Hôpital Montfort, the only French-speaking hospital in Ontario, decided to invest in the development of a community play run almost entirely by local volunteers, as way to ensure a positive (economic and social) impact on the region:

> Simon: **on voulait faire valoir nos talents parce qu'on a beaucoup de talents** (…) des talents musicaux euh d'un bout à l'autre on a des gens de la région ici qui sont au Cirque du Soleil on a des gens qui sont bon à la: à la télé euh / même dans / c'est un projet si on parle de la grande région / Ottawa Cornwall et Hawkesbury pour parler de l'Est ontarien / **ben là on a euh je veux dire que ce soit dans n'importe quelle industrie mondiale / on a des des gens de cette région ici des Franco-Ontariens qui euh / qui laissent leur marque** (…) **donc l'idée c'était bon ben / au lieu d'aller / créer un rayonnement juste ailleurs ben créons un rayonnement ici** / de ces gens-là donc ça c'était un des pis en même temps ben donner une euh / une plateforme aux jeunes aux familles aux gens pour pouvoir grandir / de différentes façons de leurs talents

> Simon: **we wanted to showcase our talent because we have a lot of talent** (…) musical talents uh from one end of the region to the other we have people who are (involved with) with the Cirque du Soleil we have people who are well on: on TV uh / even in / it's a project which if we are speaking about the greater region / Ottawa Cornwall and Hawkesbury to speak of eastern Ontario / **well then we have I mean be it in any global industry / we have people from this region here some Franco-Ontarians who uh / are making their mark** (…) so the idea was well ok / **instead of going / and creating a positive impact elsewhere well let's create a positive impact here** / for these people so that was one and at the same time (we wanted to) give uh / a platform to the youth to the families to the people so that they can grow / many different ways from their talent [our translation; emphasis added].[17]

For reasons we are trying to uncover, the show did not produce the anticipated financial return, but, rather, within two years of existence, ran a deficit. This prompted a journalist to mobilize the discourse of 'struggle' yet again, claiming that: '*L'Echo d'un Peuple* a besoin de vous' ['*L'Echo d'un Peuple* needs you'] (Raîche 2005). From an event meant to represent the long history of the struggles of Francophones in Ontario, *L'Echo d'un Peuple* itself became part of the struggles, and prompted questions not so much about the content and marketing of the product or on the expertise in tourism of the social actors involved, as about the 'vitality' of the community itself. If, as a strategy to ensure the reproduction of the traditional boundaries of the community, the form of the play made sense, as a commercial strategy, its magnitude and national discursive orientation failed to attract publics who were not invested in this particular construction of Franco-Ontarian identity, such as Ontarians who were not included in the 'us' being told, as well as

Québécois and Franco-Europeans. The commodification of Franco-Ontarian identity was perceived by some actors as a means of ensuring the reproduction of the former boundaries of the community itself, but the very insistence on these boundaries meant that a particular type of public was called into the site of the production. More importantly, the failure of the show indicates that there is a mismatch between the working conditions of the new market and a changing discursive regime which transforms the distribution of resources and the value that they have. In short, the essentialized image of Franco-Ontarian identity being recuperated by a modernizing elite is not sellable on a global market.

The boundaries of linguistic minorities are therefore confronted, challenged and reworked by global economic processes. This is of particular relevance to the ideology of the nation-state as the dominant mode of governance. In Canada, investment in language communities is meant to save the structure of the Canadian state and the linguistic market it produces and sustains through its official language policy. The history of language communities in Canada has relied on a discourse which constituted cultural identities and linguistic practices as bounded and homogeneous. In this regard, linguistic practices become salient markers of 'authenticity' in the field of tourism, thus reconstituting the boundaries of self and other within these communities.

In this, actors involved in the new economy can even be brought to consciously perform authenticity by drawing on specific linguistic forms. The following example is taken from an interview with Nadine, a performer in a musical stage play about Acadian history.[18] Mélanie, the interviewer, asks her why, at some moments during the presentation, her regional 'accent' is more pronounced than at others:

Mélanie: pis sur scène quand vous parlez de: chacun vos régions pis vos expériences on / on l'entend [votre accent] vraiment / mais / des fois quand vous parlez des régions / de façon un peu PLUS marquée (...) est-ce que c'est: fait exprès ou c'est juste que comme vous parlez des régions ça vient naturellement ou c'est:

Nadine: l'accent tu veux dire? (...) je pense qu'on s / on / on fait moins attention ou on / on se permet d // d'aller / de de se laisser aller si je peux dire ça là / comme moi par exemple / quand je parle du Sud-Est / de la province je parle de Notre-Dame-de-Cocagne (...) Clément [le metteur en scène] nous avait donné cette consigne là que // laissez-vous aller là dans / dans votre affaire sans exagérer là
(...)
Nadine: un moment donné je vas dire euhm /// on parle d'Évangéline pis je dis euh / on parle d'un arbre pis on dit il est tellement vieux il y a des peteaux [poteaux] qui le tchenne deboutte ben / moi c'est pas comme ça je le dirais (...) nécessairement (...) mais Clément // t'sais disait ah ben

dans la conversation de tous les jours c'est peut-être comme ça que tu le dirais donc / laisse-toi aller t'sais ça fait partie du (...) du spectacle c'est important que les gens entendent / les différents accents

Mélanie: and on stage when you're speaking of: each of your regions and your experiences we / we really hear [your accent] / but / sometimes when you speak of the regions / [we hear it] in a way that's a bit MORE noticeable (...) is that done on purpose or is it just that when you speak of your region it comes naturally or:

Nadine: the accent you mean? (...) I think that we / we / we are less careful or we / we allow ourselves t // to / to go / to to let ourselves go if I can say it like that there / like in my case for instance / when I speak of the South-East [region] / of the province I speak of Notre-Dame-de-Cocagne (...) Clément [the stage director] had given us that directive to // let yourself go in / in your role without exaggeration
(...)
Nadine: at one point I say hmm /// we are speaking of Evangeline and I say uh / we speak of a tree and we say it's so old it has some *sticks* which *hold* it *up* [the words in italics are pronounced in a regional accent] well / me that's not how I would say it (...) necessarily (...) but Clément // you know would say ah well in everyday talk that might be how you would say it / so let yourself go you know it's part of the (...) the show it's important that people hear / the different accents [our translation]

What Nadine expresses in the excerpt above is the tension she feels, related to having to 'let herself go' while performing on stage. In a public performance, she needs to be able to speak with the accent Clément identifies as her 'everyday talk', the one understood to be 'authentic', in a context where, normally, she would choose to speak a more standardized form of French, or at best (from Clément's perspective), would use something else as representative of her everyday talk (albeit apparently not something Clément sees as sufficiently evocative of the local and authentic identity he wants Nadine to perform). Yet it is this recontextualization of what the producers of the show perceive as 'her' authentic practices which is a source of tension: it is not easy learning to speak in what she associates as a 'relaxed' linguistic register while performing on stage, nor is it easy to perform someone else's idea of the vernacular. As Nadine hangs on to notions both of correctness and of linguistic authenticity and 'reality', Clément can only convince her to perform identity through linguistic practices by asserting that they are indeed part of a local repertoire to which she might belong. These tensions emerge on the field of tourism as linguistic identities are being performed for a global public. They stem from intersecting language ideologies associated with linguistic practice: on the one hand, they anchor a certain practice of language to community identity as constructed by national ideology; on the other, the performance of practices as symbolic of identity is reframed for commodification on a global market.

Furthermore, the commodification of identity for tourism implies that this identity is commodified for a public whose boundaries are not necessarily delineated by the practice of a common language. Such is the case for most Acadian tourist products and events, which, to constitute their potential markets, draw upon a long history of migration across the North American continent (because of a series of military and then economic events). In this, there is a tension between the double construction of 'l'Acadianité' as being, on the one hand, a kinship heritage, and, on the other, the practice of French. The trend in tourism has been to capitalize on l'Acadianité as heritage, as the bigger part of the market is constituted by North American 'Acadians' who no longer speak or have never spoken French. As such, events such as the 2004 *Congrès mondial acadien* [Acadian World Congress] framed linguistic authenticity by distributing French monolingual cultural products (such as music and poetry) through a French–English bilingual setting. The on-stage performances of French-only songs and academic presentations were mitigated by some comments, made in English, addressed to the English-speaking public and by the use of simultaneous translation (made available through a radio earphone system).

doing identity in a global economy

As national markets are challenged by the globalization of the economy, the commodification of linguistic identities through tourist practices emerges as a consolidation of the inheritance of the nationalist ways we have come to understand, organize and attribute value to symbolic capital. The commodification of national and quasi-national identities raises many questions. Any telling of national history necessarily encounters contradictions, especially when confronted to a tourist and therefore global market: how does one establish the boundaries of the self and the others? How does one cope with the struggles of others and the multiple interpretations these various others might have of the events being told? How does one account for one's community as an historically nameable and stable object without losing voice and agency in the present, without falling into the very same essentialization that in other contexts one had contested in order to access power? How does a group consolidate the pluralistic strands of its history as monolithic in order to tell oneself to a multifarious public? And how does one neutralize all these tensions in a nicely marketable package?

conclusion

In this chapter, we set out to show how some particular emerging phenomena linked to processes and practices of the globalization of the new economy have forced us to rethink concepts of bi- and multilingualism. We focused on what these processes, linked to the commodification of language and identity, mean for minority francophone Canada to see, in particular, how these new phenomena challenge the pillars of legitimation of minority language institutions. Through data and examples from the call centre industry as well as from tourism development strategies in francophone Ontario and in Acadie, we have outlined how the material and discursive conditions of a restructuring economy bring out tensions between old and new regimes, between competing ideologies of language as a marketable skill and language as an inherent marker of cultural identity.

The conditions of the new economy provide new possibilities for the commodification of language, identity and authenticity, which in turns calls into question who exactly has the right to perform certain linguistic and identity performances. Is it possible that just anyone can perform valued linguistic skills? And who has access to these privileged roles? For example, is it possible that an Indian in India can perform the linguistic as well as the associated cultural performances of an Anglophone in England to meet consumer and employer demands? Can a Francophone in Africa perform essential linguistic and cultural services for a *Québécois* clientele? What is essential in authenticating commodifiable skills? Can anyone perform them or do they somehow need to be geographically bound or socially situated? That is, are skills and performances neutral or are they necessarily contextualized? The same line of questioning applies to the commodification of identity – by and for whom is authenticity defined? Who gets to perform what identities for tourism: the '*heritiers*' or just anyone?

Authenticity is an essential element in strategies to save old structures through the creation of new markets for language and identity. However, as we have seen, the very fact of commodification can be considered destabilizing. Who can position themselves as a producer and/or a consumer? Who are the social actors who circulate within and between the emergent markets of the new economy? And how do these markets function? This leads us to question how, for example, immigration fits into the marketing of minority francophone language and identity within the new economy. Immigration is about mobility. However, with this type of mobility comes competition, not only in terms of access to migration processes but also in terms of competition for jobs where multilingual skills are highly valued. These questions foreground the need to rethink how social actors use linguistic practices to navigate through the social world, especially at a time when the transformations of the economy change the rules regimenting the ways social actors use bilingualism and identity, and the distribution of access to the resources of language and authenticity.

notes

1. We are grateful to Monica Heller and Melissa Moyer for their constant support and insightful comments on the multiple versions of this chapter. Any shortcomings are, of course, our own.

2. This research is part of a project funded by the Social Sciences and Humanities Research Council of Canada (*La francité transnationale: pour une sociolinguistique de la mouvance*; 2004–07). Principal investigators: Monica Heller, Annette Boudreau, Lise Dubois, Normand Labrie and Mathieu LeBlanc; collaborators: Claudine Moïse, Peter Auer and Werner Kallmeyer; research assistants: Emanuel da Silva, Mélanie Le Blanc, Sonya Malaborza, Mireille McLaughlin, Mary Richards and Chantal White.

3. The first Official Languages Act was passed in Canada in 1969.

4. According to the *Action Plan*, not only have the language industries produced official documents in both languages, and strengthened Canadian businesses world-wide, but they have also 'fostered communication between English- and French-speaking Canadians' (Government of Canada 2003: 57).

5. As a way of having some sense of the market share of multilingualism-related jobs, Industry Canada – the federal ministry responsible for 'fostering a growing competitive, knowledge-based Canadian economy' – conducted the first ever *Language Industry Survey* in 2004. In that year, the more than 600 private sector firms that made up Canada's language industry recorded over $400 million in revenues (Government of Canada 2004).

6. Canada reportedly ranks favourably among the top five countries offering translation services (with 10 per cent of the global market) and language training services (approximately 12 per cent) (AILIA 2005).

7. This interview was conducted on 1 February 2005 by Mireille McLaughlin and Emanuel da Silva in Ottawa for the research project 'La francité transnationale'.

8. In our transcriptions we use the following symbols instead of punctuation: / indicates a short pause, // a pause, /// a long pause and : an elongated vowel.

9. 'A country must be faithful to its roots. Linguistic duality is an important aspect of our Canadian heritage' (Government of Canada 2003: 1). The naturalization of this discourse surrounding Canadian bilingualism (and biculturalism) as normal or 'obvious' silences the voice of the indigenous populations and perpetuates the myth of Europeans as nation-builders (Heller 1999; Wolf 1982).

10. This American company claims to be the world's largest and only global language services provider. <www.languageline.com>.

11. Any association to 'purity' (etc.) is purely coincidental as that is the name used in the LLS case study (CBDD 2005).

12. This interview was conducted on 24 April 2002 by Monica Heller in Toronto for the research project which preceded 'La francité transnationale', namely 'Prise de Parole II: la francophonie canadienne et la nouvelle économie mondialisée' (PPII, 2001–04) with Monica Heller and Normand Labrie as principal investigators.

13. From an economic perspective, Nicole notes that while the 'added value' of bilingualism is worth an extra $2 per hour (a 'language premium') for a particular company in Toronto, for example, it is of no 'added value' for the same company's employees in Montreal where the workforce is assumed to be bilingual.

14. These exchanges were observed by Mélanie Le Blanc in a Moncton call centre on 13 November 2002 for the research project 'Prise de Parole II'.

15. There is, as yet, no official translation for the RDEE, but as the federal government is in the process of setting up a similar partnership for Anglophone Quebec, one is surely forthcoming. Loosely, RDEE translates into 'Network of Economic Development and Employability'.

16. Prescott-Russell is an eastern Ontarian community whose mostly dairy-based agricultural economy has undergone important restructuration in the face of neighbouring Quebec's successful attempt at placing its own dairy products as

'produits du terroir' in the national and global markets. <http://francoscenie. ca/>.

17. This interview was conducted on 10 April 2005 by Monica Heller, Mireille McLaughlin and Mary Richards in Northern Ontario for the research project 'La francité transnationale'.
18. This interview was conducted on 2 September 2004 by Mélanie Le Blanc in Moncton for the research project 'La francité transnationale'.

references

Adkins, L. (2005). The new economy, property and personhood. *Theory, Culture & Society* 22(1): 111–30.

AILIA – Association de l'industrie de la langue / Language Industry Association (2005). *Single Point of Contact for the Canadian Language Industry*. Retrieved 3 March 2006 from <www.ailia.ca/documentVault/AILIA-English.pdf>.

Blommaert, J. (1999). *Language Ideological Debates*. Berlin: Mouton de Gruyter.

Bourdieu, P. (1982). *Ce que parler veut dire*. Paris: Fayard.

Cameron, D. (2000). *Good to Talk?* London: Sage.

CBDD – Center to Bridge the Digital Divide (2005). *Language Line Services: Over-the-Phone Language Interpretation*. Washington State University. Retrieved 3 March 2006 from <http://cbdd.wsu.edu/initiatives/ework/pdf/casestudies/LangLine.pdf>.

Coupland, N. (2003). Sociolinguistic authenticities. *Journal of Sociolinguistics* 7(3): 417–31.

Elyachar, J. (2002). Empowerment money: The World Bank, non-governmental organizations and the value of culture in Egypt. *Public Culture* 41(3): 493–513.

FCFA – Fédération des communautés francophones et acadienne du Canada (1998). *Réflexion sur l'évaluation des ententes Canada-Communautés*. Ottawa, 18 June.

Gee, J.P., G. Hull and C. Lankshear (1996). *The New Work Order*. Sydney: Allen and Unwin.

Giddens, A. (1984). *The Constitution of Society*. Cambridge: Polity Press.

Government of Canada (1969). *Official Languages Act*. Royal Commission on Bilingualism and Biculturalism.

—— (2003). *Action Plan for Official Languages: The Next Act: New Momentum for Canada's Linguistic Duality*. Privy Council Office.

—— (2004) *Language Industry Survey*. Industry Canada. Retrieved 3 March 2006 from <www.statcan.ca/Daily/English/060303/d060303a.htm>.

Harvey, D. (1990). *The Condition of Postmodernity*. Blackwell: Cambridge.

Heller, M. (1999). *Linguistic Minorities and Modernity: A Sociolinguistic Ethnography*. London: Longman.

—— (2001). *Eléments d' une sociolinguistique critique*. Paris: Didier.

—— (2003). Globalization, the new economy, and the commodification of language and identity. *Journal of Sociolinguistics* 7(4): 473–92.

—— (2004). Paradoxes of language in the new economy. *Babylonia* 4: 29–31.

—— (2005a). Une approche sociolinguistique à l'urbanité. *La Revue de l'Université de Moncton*, 36(2): 321–46.

—— (2005b). Language, skill and authenticity in the globalized new economy. *Noves SL. Revista de Sociolingüística*, winter. Retrieved 28 May 2006 from <www6.gencat. net/llengcat/noves/hm05hivern/heller1_2.htm>.

—— (in press). Gender and bilingualism in the new economy. In B. McElhinny (ed.), *Words, Worlds and Material Girls*. Berlin: Mouton de Gruyter.

Heller, M. and N. Labrie (eds) (2003). *Discours et identités: la francité canadienne entre modernité et mondialisation*. Fernelmont (Belgium): Éditions modulaires européennes.

Hobsbawm, E. (1990). *Nations and Nationalism since 1780: Programme, Myth, Reality*. Cambridge: Cambridge University Press.

LLS – Language Line Services. <www.languageline.com/>.

Raîche, M. (2005). L'Echo d'un peuple a besoin de vous. *Le Reflet*, 24 August 2005.

RDEE – Réseau de développement économique et d'employabilité (1998). Annual report. <www.rdee.ca/>.

Roy, S. (2002). Valeurs et pratiques langagières dans la nouvelle économie: une étude de cas. Unpublished PhD thesis, University of Toronto.

WED – Western Economic Diversification of Canada (2000). *Plan d'action pour la mise en œuvre des articles 41 de la loi sur les langues officielles*. Government of Canada. <www.wd.gc.ca/rpts/strategies/ola/2000_04Status/3_f.asp/>.

Wolf, E. (1982). *Europe and the People without History*. Berkeley: University of California Press.

10
bilingualism in the mass media and on the internet

jannis androutsopoulos

1. introduction

In *Spanglish*, a Hollywood movie released in late 2004, the mixed code usually referred to as Spanglish is conspicuous by its absence. The movie's title turns out to be a metaphor for the cultural conflicts that arise when a Mexican housekeeper moves in with an Anglo family – and an eye-catcher that exploits the increased media interest in Spanglish for promotion purposes. Current examples of the marketing of Spanish/English bilingualism in the US are not hard to find. Language mixing is no doubt part of the symbolic capital that lifestyle magazines like *Latina* (the 'Magazine for Hispanic Women') and rap stars like N.O.R.E. ('Oye Mi Canto') sell to their audiences. Beyond the US, music with bilingual lyrics thrived in the 1990s, ranging from Algerian *rai* to African hip-hop, from Bollywood soundtracks to Korean pop. While popular music audiences 'seem more receptive to music using other languages than their counterparts of 20 years ago' (Bentahila and Davies 2002: 190), other sorts of bilingual media messages look back to an even longer tradition, such as multilingual advertising (Piller 2003) and the use of English in the fringe media of youth subcultures, which Hess-Lüttich (1978) has termed 'bilingualism as a style resource'. Research findings on various other sites of media discourse strengthen the impression that linguistic diversity is gaining an unprecedented visibility in the mediascapes of the late twentieth and early twenty-first century.

These observations indicate a gradual shift in the sociolinguistic condition of a domain that has traditionally been dominated by ideologies and practices of monolingualism. Historically, the monoglot and standardized linguistic habitus of the mass media results from their primary institutionalization as agencies of construction of the nation-state. The mass media contributed to the constitution of national languages and gave rise to the linguistic ideal of public discourse in the monolingual nation-state: a language as homogeneous as the nation it represents (Anderson 1983; Blommaert and Verschueren 1998; Boyd-Barrett, Nootens and Pugh 1996; Morley and Robins 1996). This strong link between national identity and linguistic homogeneity does not automatically exclude bilingual practices from the public sphere, but rather frames their modality and meaning. Code-switching and language mixing have been at best displayed and narrated as private practices, good enough for the fictional representation of everyday life-worlds but 'naturally' unsuited as legitimate institutional voices.

Yet current processes of sociocultural change create pivotal points for the public display of linguistic diversity. First, there are hallmarks of the globalization process: The transnational flow of populations gives rise to migrant communities that develop their own public spheres, including ethnic minority media (cf. Appadurai 1996; Karim 2003a). The transnational flow of information provides recipients with linguistic and semiotic resources that are appropriated and re-contextualized in local practices of cultural bricolage (Rampton 1999; Urla 1995). The global Anglo-American dominance in science, technology and entertainment is often evoked to account for the use of English in national media (e.g. Phillipson and Skutnabb-Kangas 1999).

A second set of suggestions points to changing conditions of media production and reception. Despite the concentration of media ownership in the globalizing world, access to media production is becoming more accessible to marginalized social groups. Institutional support for minority language media increased in the last decades (e.g. as set down in the European Charter of Regional and Minority Languages; cf. Cormack 1998). Minority media activists exploit non-commercial broadcasting and the internet as affordable means of addressing and engaging their communities. On the other hand, as the commercial media sector is customizing its output for ever smaller target groups, niche media may emerge that exclusively address minority groups or incorporate them in their programme.

On a more micro level, textual and interactional processes in media discourse come into the picture. In the era of digital technologies, the sampling and recontextualization of media content is a basic practice in popular media culture: rap artists sample foreign voices in their songs; entertainment shows feature snatches of other-language broadcasts for humour; internet users engage in linguistic *bricolage* on their homepages. Conversationalization, i.e. the tendency to incorporate conversational speech styles in public discourse (Fairclough 1995), may also foster the public visibility of code-switching, for instance in host–caller radio talk, which is a commonly examined genre in the literature discussed below.

However, with the exception of advertising (cf. Kelly-Holmes 2005; Piller 2003), bilingual media discourse is a little-explored area in sociolinguistics and discourse studies (cf. Boyd-Barrett et al. 1996; McClure 1998; Busch 2004). This neglect seems only in part due to the recentness of the issues.

Another reason might be the tendency to view bilingualism in the media as 'derivative', 'artificial' or 'inauthentic' (cf. Callahan 2004). This seems a natural outcome of its comparison with 'authentic' bilingual speech in spontaneous interaction in a local community. A few media genres seem to approach this authenticity, e.g. live radio talk or computer-mediated interaction; but in advertising, television shows, song lyrics, movies or fashion magazines, the decision to use two or more languages is subject to careful planning, editing and staging. What could be less authentic than that?

The notion of authenticity in sociolinguistics has come under fire as an ideological construct that confines intentional linguistic variability to the margins of sociolinguistic theory (Bucholtz 2003; Coupland 2001). Recent research on sociolinguistic style is moving away from this construct to examine creative manipulations of linguistic resources, and is increasingly concerned with 'the dense interpenetration of local performance with styles of speech that are reflexively designed, produced and disseminated through mass mediated institutional and/or electronic communication systems' (Rampton 1999: 423). From this angle, an *a priori* understanding of bilingualism in the media as something 'less than the real thing' seems anachronistic, and an alternative is called for. As researchers of language mixing in popular music have pointed out, when code-switching moves into the arena of public discourse, it requires a different approach to analysis (Bentahila and Davies 2002; Lee 2004; Sarkar, Winer and Sarkar 2005).

My take on an approach of this kind foregrounds the situated, intentional, and audience-oriented deployment of linguistic resources in media discourse. Rather than measuring them against the yardstick of face-to-face interaction, it seeks to understand how social actors – from media professionals to lay internet users – use their linguistic resources to shape sites of media discourse, and how these sites in turn shape their choices. This is not to deny that code-switching in the media derives its meaning from its association with conversational bilingual speech, nor that it is rarely as structurally 'rich' as prototypical bilingual conversation. The aim is rather to examine the hows and whys of the strategic selection, combination and transformation of linguistic resources in particular discursive spaces of mediated communication. Understanding the nature of these spaces can help us comprehend how the media shape public images of bilingualism (cf. Hill 1999), and how they might be used to challenge and alter these images.

2. analysing bilingual media discourse

This chapter considers bilingual (and in some cases multilingual) practices in the media based on an examination of research findings from a range of speech communities, including my own German-based research. This approach bridges a gap in the literature, Boyd-Barrett et al. (1996) being to my knowledge the only research review available. The research covered here includes printed media, broadcasting, popular music, movies, and public discourse on the internet; it excludes literary fiction, film subtitling/dubbing, and interpersonal computer-mediated interaction. Rather than restricting discussion to e.g. minority language media, this chapter explores the diversity of the subject matter in a variety of linguistic and institutional settings.

The chapter is arranged in two main sections. This one outlines a set of categories for the study of bilingual media discourse, which take into account the local context of bilingual text and talk as well as the institutional organization of the media (cf. Fairclough 1995). I discuss relevant units of analysis (section 2.1), the distinction between societal and impersonal bilingualism (2.2), the impact of different media sectors on bilingual practices (2.3), relevant media genres (2.4), patterns of language contact in media language (2.5), and the relationship of bilingual practices to the performance and design of social identities (2.6). The section after that will provide in-depth discussion of bilingual practices in selected sites of media discourse.

2.1 units of analysis

My approach to bilingualism in the mass media and on the internet focuses on manifest choices and juxtapositions of languages within units of text or talk that are delimited from other similar units in their particular context. The relevant unit of analysis is thus the individual radio show rather than the entire daily radio channel production; the newspaper article rather than the complete issue; the web discussion thread rather than a complete web discussion forum. This working definition does not restrict the juxtaposition of languages to their prototypical sequential proximity in bilingual interaction, but embraces more distant, generically conditioned relationships, e.g. between a headline and its copy text or a song's chorus and its stanzas. Drawing inferences about the language practices of media authors and presenters in other contexts is not part of the scrutiny. Using units of text and talk as a *tertium comparationis* enhances the comparability of the rather disparate research literature; it circumvents a general problem of media language studies, i.e. tracing the authorship of a media item (cf. Bell 1992); and it allows us to focus on processes of code-switching and language mixing.

However, such a focus is largely absent from much work on minority language media (including both indigenous and non-indigenous linguistic minorities; cf. Cormack 1998), which examines language choices at channel and issue level, though without any closer look at actual language use (cf. chapters in Riggins 1992 as well as papers in Danet and Herring 2003; Wright 2004 for this approach in studies of computer-mediated communication). The picture emerging from this line of research is often one of double monolingualism: minority language media offer monolingual output in the minority language (or dedicated slots for minority language content), but languages apparently remain separated. Any closer linguistic encounters that might occur are ignored. In fact, when code-switching, interference or other language contact phenomena are mentioned at all, they are obstacles to a 'clean' broadcast to be erased by editing (cf. Moal 2000: 130), or potential agents of minority language decay (cf. Ní Neachtain 2000). I do not mean to downplay the important findings of this line of research, but only to point out that literature on minority, indigenous and migrant language media rarely provides insights into the focus of this chapter, i.e. bilingualism within a single communicative episode of media discourse.

2.2 societal and impersonal bilingualism

The default case would seem that bilingual text and talk in the media reflect, in some way, bilingual practices of the society in which they are produced and consumed. This is the case in a few available studies on multilingual societies (cf. section 3.1) and in the somewhat better covered area of minority language media (cf. sections 3.2 and 3.3), which includes indigenous minorities (e.g. the Basque Country), immigrant groups (e.g. Turks in Germany) or migration-induced but assimilated ethnic groups (e.g. Welsh descendants in the US).

The counterpart to these reflections of societal bilingualism is a media use of languages that are not anchored in the speech community but understood as belonging to another society and culture. Haarmann termed this 'impersonal bilingualism' in his study of English, French and German use in the Japanese mass media (Haarmann 1986, 1989). The same process is captured in notions such as 'referee design' (i.e. a language style that responds not to the language of the audience, but to an absent reference group; Bell 1992) and 'language display' (the use of out-group language to lay claims to attributes associated with that out-group; Eastman and Stein 1993). Advertising is probably the prototypical site of impersonal bilingualism (cf. section 3.5), but we will also discuss televised performances of intercultural interactions (Jaworski, Thurlow, Lawson and Ylänne-McEwen 2003) and the use of English in the media of non-English speaking countries (section 3.6).

2.3 public, commercial, and non-profit media

Instances of societal and impersonal bilingualism may occur in public media funded by the nation-state (e.g. the BBC), private commercial media (e.g. commercial television), or private non-commercial media (e.g. community radio). Ang (1991) and Busch (2004) argue that each of these three 'media sectors' has its own philosophy that structures the relationship to its audience. Public media conceive of their audience as citizens of the nation-state: they fulfil their mission to inform, educate and entertain citizens by broadcasting a 'meaningful' programme. Private commercial media conceive of their audience as consumers rather than citizens. Broadcasting a meaningful programme is far less important than attracting the attention of potential consumers of the media output *and* of the products and services advertised therein. The emerging 'third sector' of private non-commercial media offers a forum to social groups that have traditionally been excluded from the public sphere (Busch 2004: 48–9). Their relationship to their audience resembles the public sector in that they address citizens rather than consumers, but is egalitarian and emancipatory rather than paternalistic; the borders between production and reception are fuzzy, and audiences are encouraged to participate actively.

Approaching bilingualism in the media from this angle entails asking how the economy of each sector shapes and constrains the public display of bilingualism (cf. Fairclough 1995: 42), and where the potential for challenging monolingual norms lies. Most ethnic minority media covered in Riggins (1992) fall into the third sector, but in this chapter I also discuss commercial ethnic magazines and local commercial radio. Public media increasingly allocate time to minority programmes, but this does not guarantee an encouragement of bilingual practices (cf. Busch 2004). Impersonal bilingualism proliferates in both the commercial and the non-profit sector, its most prominent forms being commercially framed (e.g. popular music, advertising, lifestyle magazines). Thus the situation seems more complex than a straightforward relationship between media sectors and types of bilingual practice, and the internet is increasing this complexity. Uses of the internet by linguistic minorities blend non-profit activism with commercial interest, and sites of vernacular media production are emerging on the internet that partly fit and partly transcend the classic media sectors. This is the case with individual publishing, as in weblogs, and online communities, i.e. networks of individuals who sustain regular interaction on newsgroups or chat-channels. While these are certainly not mass media in the classic sense of the term, they are arguably sites of public discourse; they are cross-linked with mainstream media in manifold ways, and have the potential of gaining regular audiences. The next section of this chapter will discuss how the internet extends the opportunities for societal and impersonal bilingual discourse (cf. sections 3.3, 3.6, 3.7).

2.4 media genres

A broad notion of genre – e.g. language use according to social purpose (Fairclough 1995) or 'a conventionalized orienting framework for the production and reception of discourse' (Bauman 2001: 79) – is useful in grouping together the research literature covered here. In a nutshell, bilingual practices have been repeatedly attested in five groups of (spoken or written) media genres: First, talk between media professionals and members of the audience, especially phone-in radio, which seems the closest equivalent to spontaneous bilingual interaction in the media sphere (cf. sections 2.6, 3.1, 3.2). Second, performance genres such as comedy, movies, television shows and popular music, in which bilingual speech is subject to planning and editing (sections 2.6, 3.1, 3.4). A third genre group is advertising (section 3.5). The fourth group encompasses various non-fictional genres of written discourse in e.g. ethnic, fan or fashion magazines as well as mainstream newspapers (section 3.6); and the fifth group includes computer-mediated interaction in newsgroups, web discussion forums, chat-channels and role-playing environments (sections 3.3, 3.7). The apparent diversity of genres should not distract from the fact that bilingual practices still tend to proliferate in the tradition of fiction, entertainment and advertising.

Understanding bilingualism in media discourse comprises an examination of how the organization of media genres constrains choices of and alternations between languages. For example, the function of English in a German advertisement is different according to its occurrence in the slogan (which encodes the voice of the institution behind the ad) or the headline (which often encodes the voice of the implied addressee; Piller 2001). To take another example, language alternation in pop music is often confined to the chorus, i.e. the most memorizable part that summarizes the song's message. More complex media formats such as entertainment shows and movies may offer several slots for bilingual talk, and understanding the distribution of linguistic resources to participant roles and parts of the plot is a necessary part of the analysis. But the opportunities for bilingualism afforded by a particular genre are realized in different ways across sociolinguistic settings. In the case of radio talk, compare the sparse use of Corsican (Jaffe 2000) to the language mixing attested in settings of stable societal bi- and multilingualism such as Barcelona or Nairobi (Woolard 1988; Horstmann and Alai 2004). Within a speech community, the same genre may provide a site of both commodified and resistance bilingualism (cf. Heller 2000). For example, casting a song's chorus in a different language may draw on a language that has 'value in the global marketplace' or on a minority language in an attempt to fragment the dominant monoglot ideology (Heller 2000: 12). More generally, the staging of 'mixed forms of language and culture' in performance arts can be 'in itself' a form of legitimation of everyday bilingual practice when addressed to a local bilingual audience (Jaffe 2000: 43); but it can also reaffirm cultural stereotypes by stylizing linguistic minorities for the sake of a monolingual audience (Hill 1995).

2.5 from mixing to minimalism: patterns of bilingual text and talk

In her work on English code-switching in Spanish and Mexican newspapers, McClure points out the absence of 'the richness of form and function repeatedly described in studies of spoken language code-switching in bilingual communities' (McClure and Mir 1995: 47). Yet cases of rich code-switching and/or language mixing are attested, for various media genres, in settings of both societal and interpersonal bilingualism. An example for the latter is the use of non-native English in pop music (cf. section 3.6); as for the former, consider the case of *Latina*, the US 'Magazine for Hispanic Women': its predominantly English texts are 'peppered with Spanish nouns, determiner phrases, conjunctions, prepositional phrases', and intrasentential switches (e.g. 'seduce him *en la cocina*') are common (Mahootian 2005).

Such switching and mixing that reflects community norms may blend with deliberate departures from conventional patterns of bilingual speech. For example, a Catalan comedian draws on Spanish interference and borrowing that is frequent in the Catalan speech community, and he also uses Spanish/Catalan code-switching to a much greater extent than the general population does in order to create a fictional world 'where the two languages have found a peaceful coexistence' (Woolard 1988: 71; Woolard 1999). Instances of language mixing as poetic or attention-seeking device are also found in rap lyrics (Sarkar et al. 2005), advertising (Bhatia 1992), and computer-mediated discourse (Androutsopoulos 2006).

On the other hand, several studies report cases in which one language clearly predominates, the other being reduced to a few isolated occurrences, notably chunks and formulaic expressions. Examples include the 'phrasebook dialogues' between presenter and local hosts in British tourism TV shows (Jaworski et al. 2003); the tiny amounts of redundant and predictable Corsican in French radio talk (Jaffe 2000); the 'semantically slight but pragmatically versatile' uses of Welsh in ethnic magazines (Coupland et al. 2003); or the fixed uses of Punjabi in ethnic newsgroups (Paolillo 1996, in press). They can be summarized as instances of minimal or token bilingualism (cf. Kelly-Holmes 2005, and Li 2000: 6 who defines a minimal bilingual as someone 'with only a few words and phrases in a second language'). Minimal bilingualism in media discourse often responds to (factual or assumed) limited language competence on the part of the audience, and exploits the symbolic, rather than the referential, function of language (cf. sections 3.2, 3.6). This is sometimes achieved by its use as a framing device (Coupland et al. 2003: 167): tiny amounts of a second language are positioned at the margins of text and talk units, and thereby evoke social identities and relationships associated with the minimally used language.

Whether bilingualism in media discourse comes in dense code-switching or just in a few 'spectacular fragments of language' (Rampton 1999: 423) is the outcome of strategic decisions at specific historical moments. Consider the case of Algerian *rai* music lyrics (Bentahila and Davies 2002): early *rai* recordings capitalize on an 'insertion style' with frequent incorporation of French nouns and clauses in an Arabic matrix, which bears close resemblance to code-mixing in urban Algerian communities. But in later productions the languages are more separated, their distribution bearing a 'more systematic relationship to the structure of the song' (Bentahila and Davies 2002: 202). Rather than reflecting societal language change, this shift from mixing to a generic separation of languages is motivated by a shift in target audiences: as *rai* music became more popular in France, its artists and producers turned to a more prominent use of French for key phrases, refrains and titles in order to increase its chances of exposure to a French audience.

2.6 performance and design: styling bilingual identities

Media discourse is planned and staged for large audiences. It is therefore characterized by a heightened attention to the perception of these audiences;

an attention to the details of linguistic form; and the conscious inhabiting of professional roles that need a recognizable, hence stereotyped, voice (Jaffe 2000: 42; Jaworski et al. 2003). Rather than always speaking in their 'own voice', media performers use language to stylize an array of social identities, relying for this purpose on the cultural and sociolinguistic knowledge they assume to share with their audience (Coupland 2001). These identities may be claimed by the performers themselves, projected to their audience or ascribed to social types in the bilingual community.

Comedy and singing are celebrated as sites for 'virtuoso performances of linguistic mixing' (Woolard 1999: 22). By skilfully moving across linguistic and cultural boundaries, performers meet generic expectations to 'impress with linguistic virtuosity' (Eastman and Stein 1993: 195), and exploit the associations of linguistic codes to social identities and stances (Woolard 1999; Jaffe 2000; Heller 2003: 167). Consider how these two dimensions of bilingual performance blend in the lyrics of Montreal hip-hop artists, which 'contain many instances of code-switching or code-mixing between the languages or language varieties that are commonly in use in the ethnically and racially diverse urban contexts in which Montreal hip-hop is grounded' (Sarkar et al. 2005: 2058). Based on Quebec French, they draw on words and phrases from various languages to craft their rhymes, and specifically use African-American English to 'assert a certain cultural and ethnic allegiance that identifies them as young *Black* Québécois' (Sarkar et al. 2005: 2066). This example illustrates that the relationship of bilingualism and identity in media discourse may extend beyond the performer's own ethnolinguistic background to practices of language crossing (Rampton 1995), in which speakers appropriate (fragments of) languages that are significant in the local context without necessarily having full command of them. The discussion of English in global hip-hop below (section 3.6) illustrates how this Montreal case resonates with similar practices elsewhere.

Researchers of multimodal discourse define design as the use of semiotic resources 'as means to realize discourses in the context of a particular communicative situation' (Kress and van Leeuwen 2001: 5–6). When media makers devise an advertisement, plan a lifestyle magazine or set up a website, they may select linguistic codes (a second language, a mixed code) just for specific portions of their product, based on anticipations of their aesthetic value, their indexical or symbolic force, and, ultimately, their effects on the audience. In other words, the design of media discourse may entail the strategic allocation of languages to particular generic slots. This is nowhere as clear as with emblems, i.e. items that represent an actor or institution, such as names and headers, section titles, jingles and station signs, website navigation bars. To the extent secondary codes are selected by design for these items, a sort of emblematic bilingualism emerges, which does not challenge the dominant language in terms of informational load, but declares another code as relevant to the 'face' of an institution (cf. Urla 1995: 254).

3. selected sites of bilingual media discourse

Drawing on the categories introduced above, this section discusses bilingual practices in selected sites of media discourse. We begin with two examples that illustrate how dense multilingual talk indexes power relationships in a multilingual society (section 3.1). We then examine strategies of resistance against monolingual norms in minority radio (3.2), the use of migrant languages on the diasporic internet (3.3), and the stylization of immigrants in films addressed to monolingual mainstream audiences (3.4). We enter the area of impersonal bilingualism with its prototypical case, advertising (3.5), proceed to English in the media of non-anglophone countries (3.6), and conclude with a case from transnational computer-mediated discourse (3.7).

3.1 mediated reflexes of societal multilingualism

The two case studies discussed here demonstrate the richness of multilingual media discourse in a multilingual society. The first is concerned with a radio show in Nairobi, Kenya, in which switching and mixing of English, Kiswahili and Kisii (a local language) is common practice (Horstmann and Alai 2004). The speech of 'Caroline', the main presenter, reflects an urban style of mixing Kiswahili and educated urban English. 'Nyambane', the minor figure performed by a professional cabaret artist, stages the villager from the Kisii region, the language of which he speaks, in addition to Kiswahili and non-standard English. There is a clear power differential between the two, Caroline correcting and even insulting Nyambane, but it is he who is occasionally outspokenly critical of the government. The distribution of languages to participant roles here evokes urban stereotypes regarding local languages and their speakers, and at the same time creates a subject position that is able, through its being cast as subordinate, to voice political critique.

The second study is on rap music in Senegal and Gabon (Auzanneau 2001). The linguistic repertoire of these rap artists includes standard and non-standard varieties of French (the official language in both countries) and English; Wolof, the main African language of Senegal; and local languages such as Poular (in Senegal) and Téké (in Gabon). Rappers code-switch between these languages at the intersentential, intrasentential and tag level. They also use a mixed style, i.e. a French matrix with vocabulary from various languages, which reflects linguistic developments in urban vernaculars. Auzanneau shows that language choice and code-switching in these songs are topically motivated. For instance, French is preferred for international and serious topics, whereas non-standard forms of French are selected to narrate African life reality or youth-cultural issues; non-standard forms of English index the values of US hip-hop culture but also provide a means of symbolic emancipation from traditional francophone dominance. Wolof is preferred in Senegal to address issues of African society or Senegalese identity; local languages are confined to matters of cultural tradition and rural African life; and language mixing foregrounds the rappers' difference from the dominant society and their solidarity with their peers. Although mixing might pose comprehension problems to outsiders, rappers use it as a 'we code' (Gumperz 1982) to instigate dialogue with a broader public. But vernacular French, Wolof or a local language may also be cast as 'we code', depending on the social identity of the artist and the social relationships that are enacted in a particular song. Auzanneau suggests that the language choices of these rap artists respond to two different exigencies: the 'local identity logic' demands that local languages be used as an assertion of ethnic identity. The 'commercial logic' favours French and English, because they provide access to an international audience. Using both French and a local language in a song is a solution to this dilemma.

3.2 bilingual strategies in minority language radio

Studies of bilingual radio talk illustrate the effect of dominant monoglot ideologies on the linguistic practices of minority language media. Rather than valuing the bilingual speech of everyday life, their producers and audiences support a separation of languages in the public sphere, and perpetuate the stigmatization of language mixing as a problem of competence (Jaffe 2000: 43; Busch 2004: 127; Bhatia 1992: 196). This leads to the paradoxical situation that media committed to a local minority agenda erase local linguistic practices from their repertoire (Busch 2004: 117). Against this backdrop, any public display of mixed codes has the potential to be read as resistance against monoglot ideologies. Going public with what is usually kept private gives symbolic value to 'the hybrid communicative practices that characterize much everyday interaction' (Jaffe 2000: 44), and helps to assert 'a public identity usually invisible in mainstream communication' (Fjelsted 1999: 42). Such resistance bilingualism may manifest itself in quite small linguistic forms, such as bilingual puns, which are a well-documented strategy of playful and subtle subversion of the authority of the dominant group (Fjelsted 1999: 46; Heller 2003: 167; Zentella 2003).

Even if there is institutional support for a bilingual programme, minority actors must develop strategies for incorporating bilingualism into the genres at hand, taking into account the potential heterogeneity of their audience. These strategies are examined in a recent study of non-profit radio stations in Austria (Busch 2004). These stations allocate airtime to migrant actors and overtly encourage them to alternate between languages. However, this is not equally ratified by listeners, who interpret code-switching and interference not as an indication that the presenter is at home in both languages, but as the first step in a process of language shift (Busch 2004: 127). Bilingual talk is therefore often restricted to an opener in the dominant language, the remainder being wholly in the minority language.

A number of ethnic music shows practice a 'one speaker – one language' distribution: within a multi-ethnic team, each presenter uses her/his own native language, its frequency depending on the current topic and the language preference of guests, and intelligibility being supported by short summaries at speaker takeover. Busch (2004: 143–8) discusses an experimental radio commentary of a football match between Austria and Turkey, in which the Austrian and Turkish presenters invited listeners to shut off the TV sound and follow the radio commentary instead. Almost half of it turned out to be in German and 30 per cent in Turkish, the remainder being sequences of rapid switching or simultaneous talk at moments of excitement. Busch considers this to be a step towards developing strategies of multilingual radio talk that go beyond a tokenistic co-presence of languages. We can also consider it a form of resistance bilingualism (Heller 2000), in that it seeks to de-nationalize what is usually thought of as a national domain, i.e. football, combining for this purpose bilingual commentary with discourse strategies on the propositional level, e.g. a use of 'we' that indexes both nations.

3.3 bilingual practices on the diasporic internet

The internet extends the 'media of diaspora' (Karim 2003a) in various ways, the most analysed one being transnational diasporic communities in newsgroups, mailing lists or discussion forums. Studies of language use in virtual diaspora communities attest to their use of code-switching for various discourse purposes, though not always to a dominance of home or migrant languages. Some studies document dense conversational code-switching and mixing across or within turns at talk, whereas others report a rather minimal use of home languages in settings of English-language dominance, and attribute this to ongoing language shift and to the ethnically mixed audience of the virtual environment (cf. McClure 2001; Paolillo 1996, in press; Androutsopoulos 2006 for a fuller discussion).

A second type of diasporic media on the internet are ethnic websites, which offer edited sections with news, event listings and other cultural resources, as well as discussion forums that are open to registered users free of charge. Their producers explore the potential of the internet 'in overcoming some of the hierarchical structures of traditional broadcast media' (Karim 2003b: 13), but also in catering for niche diasporic markets with customized advertising, merchandising and paid services (cf. Sinclair and Cunningham 2000). The linguistic consequences of this tension between commercial editorial practices and community discourse are examined in research on websites for German-based diasporic groups, notably of Moroccan, Persian, Indian and Greek origin (cf. Androutsopoulos 2006). German clearly predominates across these websites, but the currency and value of migrant languages are quite different in edited sections and discussion forums. In the latter, home languages gain prominence in discussion topics relevant to the home country, and are used in small performances such as quoting homeland poetry or ethnic joke-telling. Alternation between German and home languages is a common practice, covering a range of typical discourse functions of conversational code-switching. There are also instances of purposeful language mixing, which is construed to display linguistic virtuosity or to respond reflexively to debates about ethnic identity. Bilingual speech in these debates is consonant with the complex language-identity relationships discussed above (cf. sections 2.6 and 3.2). Rather than an essentialist use of home language as 'we code' and German as 'they code', participants draw on a variety of code choices to negotiate a multiplicity of identities that are contiguous to diaspora and its virtual space.

By contrast, the edited sections of these websites maintain a clear separation of languages. Their language choices are shaped by their commercial imperatives rather than by a commitment to home language maintenance. Their decision for German responds to assumed language preferences of the diasporic audience as much as to the wish to be accessible to interested members of the dominant group, including advertisers. This does not exclude bilingual design, notably the use of home languages and English for names and slogans. For instance, the Indian website <www.theinder.net> features an alternative Hindi homepage, in which the Hindi language is confined to the navigation bars. At the same time, the website producers assume that Hindi, at least in its native Devanagari script, is not intelligible to the majority of their audience. This is a case of what Coupland et al. (2003) term 'iconising', i.e. the process by which rudimentary amounts of an ancestor language build signifiers of ethnic identity. Thus different interests shape the value of home languages within these multi-layered web environments. Hindi is reduced to 'a ceremonial and celebratory icon' (Coupland et al. 2003: 156) of Indianness in web design, but is used, alongside other languages of India, in bilingual talk in the discussion forums.

3.4 styling ethnic otherness for majority audiences

We now move from in-group bilingual spaces of immigrants to their stylization for mainstream audiences. The arena is film, a prime site for the reproduction of linguistic stereotypes (cf. Lippi-Green 1997: 79–103). Lippi-Green notes that film conventionally exploits assumptions about socially typified speech styles as a means to draw characters quickly, and argues that this linkage of language variation to character distinctions may discriminate against linguistic minorities. Her study of Disney animated movies suggests that non-standard accents are reserved for villains and low status characters; ethnic characters are given stereotypical broad accents, but ethnic protagonists (e.g. Aladdin) have a mainstream accent.

For the purpose of this chapter I examined the use of migrant languages in a number of recent German and US American movies, in which Mexican and Greek migrants in the US and Turkish migrants in Germany are the main subject. They include three US movies (*Spanglish*, a 2004 comedy about a Mexican woman working for an Anglo family; *Real Women Have Curves*, a 2002 drama about Mexican-American teenagers; and *My Big Fat Greek Wedding*, a 2002 comedy about the romance between a Greek woman and an Anglo man); and five German movies (*Kanak Attak*, a 2000 drama about Turkish gangsters; *Kurz und Schmerzlos* or 'Short Sharp Shock', a 1998 drama about young migrants caught in a life of crime; *Gegen die Wand* or 'Head-on', a 2004 drama about the love affair between two German Turks; *Kebab Connection*, a 2004 comedy about the meeting of cultures in Hamburg; and *Süperseks*, a 2004 comedy about a Turkish-language telephone sex hotline).

As migrant languages are presented to an audience assumed to be mainstream monolingual, their use is unsurprisingly restricted to a few rudimentary code-switches in a few scenes, comprehension being supported by redundancy and visual context. However, their distribution among characters and parts of the plot reflects sociolinguistic stereotypes of migrant communities: we witness the parent generation using the home language with each other and with their children, but the younger ones using (an ethnolect of) the majority language with each other. In a mother–daughter dialogue in *Real Women Have Curves*, the mother switches to Spanish for emphatic repetition in an emotional outburst; in *Kanak Attak*, elderly characters switch to Turkish as soon as their argument escalates. In *Kebab Connection* and *Süperseks*, the young Turkish protagonist has a native German accent, and a successful Turkish doctor has a good command of German and only speaks Turkish when emotionally involved, whereas Turkish shopkeepers prefer Turkish and use learner varieties of German. In these two movies, as well as in *My Big Fat Greek Wedding*, longer stretches of migrant language occur either in religious settings or in scenes that are dominated by the concurrent visual event (e.g. fighting, a wedding celebration). *My Big Fat Greek Wedding* features a couple of Greek phrases that recur throughout the story; one of them is positioned as an instance of second-language acquisition at the happy ending.

Overall, home languages are portrayed as being subject to intergenerational language shift, heritage settings and emotional outbursts being their sites of survival. The message about the connection between language choice and social status is clear: the more socially successful a migrant, the more linguistically assimilated and native-like; 'bad guys' speak worse German (and more Turkish) than the characters we are supposed to identify with. I hesitate to say that all this amounts to discrimination against minorities. But it certainly reproduces a folkloristic, highly clichéd image which does not even come close to reflecting the diversity of bilingual speech in migrant communities, in Germany, the US or elsewhere.

3.5 multilingual advertising: ethnosymbolism and beyond

Advertising discourse has a long tradition of 'language display', i.e. the appropriation of out-group language 'to attract potential customers by appealing to their sense of what is modern, sophisticated, elegant, etc.' (Eastman and Stein 1993: 198). Haarmann coined the term 'ethnosymbol-ism' for 'the use of foreign languages as symbols of foreign ethnic groups and their cultures' (Haarmann 1986: 109). Here are two examples: the first, a commercial for German beer, broadcast in Australia, features barely intelligible German in the background, framed by an English voice that states: *You don't need to speak German to enjoy a good beer.* The second is a print advertisement for French cigarette paper in Germany, in which an attractive female is given the headline: *Voulez-vous rouler avec moi?* In the first case, the mere acoustic presence of German, devoid of propositional meaning, alludes to the product's original context of consumption and thereby highlights its authenticity. The second case appropriates a French pop song line to contextualize the main ethnosymbolic value of French in German advertising, i.e. eroticism (cf. Piller 2001).

The 'toolkit' for the analysis of ethnosymbolism in advertising encompasses: the semantics of foreign language chunks; their distribution across the components of an advertisement and the voices of advertising discourse, i.e. narrator (the institution behind the ad) and narratee (the implied recipient); the relation of language choice to types of commodities (product groups); and other verbal or visual features that support ethnosymbolism (cf. Piller 2001; Bhatia 1992; Martin 2002; Cheshire and Moser 1994). Slogans and headlines are the most favoured sites for additional language choices as well as for deliberate language mixing 'which introduces innovative and creative effects' (Bhatia 1992: 196).

English is 'the single most favored language selected for global mixing' in advertising (Bhatia 1992). French, Italian, Spanish and German have an international appeal as well, the use of other languages depending on local setting (e.g. Bhatia documents Persian in Indian ads). What sets English apart is the range of values it can be associated with, and the range of commodities it promotes. It has been attributed symbolic values such as novelty, modernity, internationalism, technological excellence, hedonism and fun, as opposed to the stereotypical restriction of French to elegance and eroticism, Italian to food, German to technology (cf. Piller 2001). German is sometimes selected even for cars not made in Germany (cf. Bell 1992), but it is still confined to a particular type of product that matches the main symbolic value of that language. English, by contrast, illustrates how ethnosymbolism is left behind, as its distribution to types of commodities is more significant than the origin of the commodities themselves.

Cheshire and Moser (1994) suggest that the type of product is a better predictor of language choice than the type of media that hosts the advertisement. Their results show that English in francophone Swiss ads predominates 'for products that are particularly susceptible to passing fashions, and which people may use as part of an expression of social identity' (ibid: 460), such as cigarettes, clothing, shoes, watches and alcohol. Likewise, Androutsopoulos, Bozkurt, Breninck, Kreyer, Tornow and Tschann (2004) found significant distributions of English slogans to product groups across three decades of German advertising: slogans for clothing, tobacco and communications technologies make most use of English, followed by media, cars and cosmetic products. Political ads, which address recipients as citizens of the nation-state rather than consumers, unsurprisingly have the lowest percentage of English slogans in this sample. Yet this did not prevent Germany's Conservative party from using the slogan 'black is beautiful' in the 1970s, exploiting the African-American movement of that era to valorize its own symbolic colour, black. This confirms Bhatia's view that 'no advertisement [...] is likely to escape the influence of language mixing', and his suggestion that restricting English to a closed set of products would 'miss the dynamics of language mixing' (Bhatia 1992: 198, 204). As Bell (1992: 338) argues, there is no categorical connection between language style, type of product, and the stereotype associated with it. Language choice in multilingual advertising can be interpreted, but not predicted.

3.6 non-native english, english from below, and the styling of 'glocal' identities

The use of English in the mass media of non-anglophone countries is traditionally attributed to Englishization, i.e. the infiltration of host societies and cultures by anglophone – in particular American – technology and lifestyle (Phillipson and Skutnabb-Kangas 1999). The traditional focus of this debate is on anglicisms, i.e. lexical borrowings (cf. Gardt and Hüppauf 2004 for German). Yet current uses of English in national language mass media also include one-word code-switching (nonce-borrowings), chunks, formulae, phrases or utterances, as well as English headlines and subtitles (cf. McClure 1998; Haarmann 1989). Their frequency may be limited (for instance, single nouns are the main type of English code-switching in McClure's data), but their very existence calls for the bilingual discourse analysis that was pioneered in studies of advertising (cf. section 3.5).

McClure (1998) suggests that the degree of national language/English code-switching depends on the relationship of the host societies to English-speaking countries. Its higher frequency in Mexican than Spanish newspapers correlates with geographical proximity and a more intense cultural contact to the US, and its discourse functions index the ambivalent relationship of Mexicans to the US (e.g. satirical code-switching that alludes to border relationships). McClure argues that the even lesser degree of English code-switching in the Bulgarian media she examined is a result of the only recent orientation to English-speaking societies and popular culture in Bulgaria, and an index of the still limited number of sufficiently bilingual members of the national audience.

Less attention has been paid to the relationship of Englishization and 'glocalization', i.e. the process by which globally circulating cultural resources are recontextualized in local settings (Robertson 1996). This relationship is foregrounded in Preisler's notion of 'English from below', which he defines as 'the informal – active or passive – use of English as an expression of subcultural identity and style' (Preisler 1999: 241). In contrast to 'English from above', which is promoted 'by the hegemonic culture for purposes of international communication', English from below is motivated by 'the desire to symbolize subcultural identity or affiliation, and peer group solidarity' (Preisler 1999: 241, 246). It is acquired via non-institutional channels, practised in vernacular literacies, and involves styles and varieties of the English language that are associated with particular cultural images, such as African-American English with hip-hop. English from below therefore involves more variation than officially promoted, institutionally transmitted English as a Foreign Language (Preisler 1999: 260; Androutsopoulos 2004; Leppänen forthcoming).

The impact of English from below in media discourse becomes apparent when we turn from nation-wide media to niche, commercial and non-profit media for various contemporary youth-cultural communities and audiences. Their uses of English, some matching the profile of minimal bilingualism outlined above (section 2.5), others involving more dense code-switching and language mixing, challenge the 'overly simple view that English is for intercultural communication and local languages for local identities' (Pennycook 2003: 83; Leppänen forthcoming). I suggest that the identities at stake might best be termed 'glocal', because they gain their meaning as local performances of a global cultural paradigm, and it is precisely this relationship that English contextualizes. Three examples from Germany will illustrate this point: skate-boarding magazines, rap lyrics and hip-hop discussion forums.

In German skate-boarding magazines, short English phrases (e.g. *just skate for fun*; *skate or die*; *in the name of the game*) are used by German actors in editorials, reports and interviews, or left untranslated in interviews with US skaters (Deppermann 2001). These phrases relate their referent or topic, both by content and language choice, to the globally leading US skater scene. They are resources for these magazines' 'rhetoric of authenticity', i.e. their strategy for defining 'real' skater culture and setting off 'authentic' members from imitators and novices. The case of rap lyrics illustrates how Englishization goes beyond propositional demands to the organization of discourse and the refinement of poetic form (Androutsopoulos and Scholz 2002; Auzanneau 2001; Lee 2004; Pennycook 2003; Sarkar et al. 2005). German rappers use (African-American) English discourse markers to signal turn taking, and nonce-borrowings to facilitate rhyme; they code-switch to claim culturally significant attributes; and they sample African-American voices for the intro or the chorus of their songs. Yet the dominant language of these songs is clearly German, and they seldom, if ever, reach international audiences. As in the African and Canadian cases (cf. sections 2.6 and 3.1), the aim of using English is to display poetic skills and cultural affiliation to local audiences rather than to audiences in the culture of origin.

In the discourse of German hip-hop fans on the internet, hip-hop English is appropriated and tailored to new generic demands (Androutsopoulos 2003). Producers of personal homepages pick up linguistic elements from US rap bands to design their navigation bars, page titles and text headings. In web guest books and discussion boards, stylized Black English is a common choice for ritual activities in and through which participants perform being a hip-hopper: greetings to the local crew, ritual appeals to other fans or vows of loyalty to favourite artists. The ample opportunities for phatic communion and performance afforded by these spaces boost the use of short, formulaic English code-switches when compared to printed media (Androutsopoulos 2004). Remarkably, similar processes are encountered on hip-hop sites from Italy and Norway. Thus from a transnational perspective, English from below establishes a symbolic connection between rap and fan discourse on the one hand, and between various localized hip-hop discourses on the other.

3.7 beyond localness: language choices in transnational web environments

In all the cases discussed so far, the backdrop of bilingual practices in the media is the usage and/or ideology of a local community. However, spaces of transnational communication are emerging on the internet, in which the choice of linguistic resources is evaluated against the norms and practices of the virtual community alone. An example that illustrates this process is 'active worlds' (www.activeworlds.com), a multi-user environment of role-playing interaction (Axelsson, Abelin and Schroeder 2003). 'Active worlds' is structured in a multitude of 'worlds', i.e. discourse environments that are organized by theme. Each 'world' has a 'main language', established by its administrator, which is not always identical to the 'majority language', i.e. the one used by most participants in a particular encounter. For instance, Spanish is the main language in the environment called 'mundo hispanico', but the majority language of some interactions is English.

Axelsson et al. (2003) focus on 'introduced languages', i.e. languages other than the main or majority language of a 'world'. They distinguish three main motivations for the introduction of a new language, three types of response to it, and three factors for the acceptance or rejection of the newly introduced language. In particular, users may introduce a new language in order to get in touch with fellow speakers of their language, to initiate language play, or to attract other users' attention, thereby disturbing ongoing conversations. In reaction, the language introducer can be accepted (i.e. responded to in a friendly way), rejected (told to switch to the main language or to leave) or simply met by silence. How the newly introduced language is treated depends on the type of language, the type of environment, and the perceived intention of the language introducer. The authors suggest that English speakers are less tolerant, non-English speakers more willing to accommodate a new language introducer. The acceptance of languages other than English is rather low in general-character 'public worlds' and higher in 'themed worlds', which are frequented by more experienced users. Finally, the tolerance of a new language is higher when the introducer is in search of fellow native speakers and lowest if they are perceived as intrusive. In sum, the case of 'active worlds' illustrates how the interactional meanings and consequences of language choices are shaped by the emergent social structure of virtual communities: localness is recontextualized in virtual rather than physical space.

4. conclusion: bilingual practices in changing media landscapes

Based on a review of transnational research findings, this chapter explored the range of contemporary language encounters in the mass media and on the internet. I argued that in order to understand the complexities and tensions involved in the mediation of bilingual practices, we need to transcend the implicit benchmark of 'authentic' bilingual speech in a twofold way: first, by embedding any comparison between mediated and immediate bilingual speech in an examination of the institutional settings and generic contexts of media discourse; and second, by extending the scope from societal to impersonal bilingualism. This allowed us to consider issues that are largely overlooked in mainstream bilingualism research, and yielded a picture in which bilingualism in the media is ubiquitous rather than exceptional. On this basis, this chapter advances an understanding of bilingualism in the media as a set of processes by which institutional and vernacular media actors draw on linguistic resources from their own inheritance, their social environment and the wider semiotic flows they have access to in order to construct textures and voices that mediate and balance between immediate communicative exigencies, market expectations and loyalties to local and imagined communities.

This inclusive approach did not attempt to conceal the fact that societal and impersonal bilingualism in the media are subject to different processes of change. In minority language media, bilingualism is still constrained by dominant monolingual ideologies, and minority actors develop strategies of resistance against these ideologies (cf. section 3.2). Minority actors disclose new sites of bilingual discourse on the internet (section 3.3), and minority bilingual practices are in some cases promoted to a norm by niche ethnic media (Mahootian 2005). On the other hand, impersonal bilingualism in contemporary media landscapes extends beyond advertising to discourses of 'glocalization', in which 'imported' linguistic resources may gain entirely different and new meanings (sections 3.5, 3.6). Even though impersonal bilingualism is often thought of as a process 'from above', controlled by the commercial interests of global corporations, bilingualism 'from below' in the literacy practices of 'glocal' youth cultures eventually reinforces a *dissociation* of language and nation, as counter-normative uses of non-native English construct imagined alliances with global cultural movements and may well be used to challenge the hegemony of English-speaking countries.

I conclude by summarizing four processes that cut across societal and impersonal bilingualism and seem characteristic of the current proliferation of bilingual discourse in the media. First, bilingualism thrives at the 'periphery' rather than the 'core' of contemporary mediascapes. This applies in terms of frequency and structural complexity as well as in terms of genres and discursive practices: Many linguistic encounters in the public sphere are clearly framed by a dominant language, restricting other languages to 'spectacular fragments' that are 'intricately interwoven with other expressive modalities' (Rampton 1999: 423). To this extent, the public visibility of bilingualism is due to many small ruptures at the margins of monoglot mediascapes rather than to a few radical changes at their centre.

Second, bilingual practices in the media are a means for social actors to establish symbolic values in discourse. This is not a contradiction to their peripheral character, as symbolic values may well be established by designing the 'face' rather than the 'body' of discourse (see sections 2.5 and 2.6). Many instances of bilingualism in the media constitute a response to the tension between the global and the local. One of its manifestations is the wish to make cultural commodities accessible and attractive to distant audiences without sacrificing the symbolic bond to the original, proximal ones; indeed, it is precisely this symbolic bond that authenticates globally circulating cultural commodities. In the case of *rai* music, bilingual lyrics aim at 'a dual effect, conveying both an in-group, solidary tone and a more global, international flavour, without sacrificing the one to the other' (Bentahila and Davies 2002: 204). In diaspora contexts, a fragmented and minimal bilingualism is often the only means of indexing bonds to a distant imagined origin and establishing the symbolic value of a minority language in globalized mediascapes (Coupland et al. 2003). In the realm of impersonal bilingualism, the local value of bilingual practice can only be established against, and would not exist without, a global backdrop. Appropriations of a second code are authenticating devices (Bucholtz 2003; Eastman and Stein 1993), by which participants style themselves as local representatives of global movements.

A third point worth highlighting is the nexus of bilingualism and com-modification. Commercial appropriations of bilingualism discussed in this chapter range from the retention of local minority audiences to stylizations of ethnic otherness in mainstream films. We are here no doubt witnessing the effect of wider processes of change, such as the lead of the commercial sector in the conversationalization of media discourse (Fairclough 1995: 43); the entertainment value assigned to practices of language stylization in media performance (Coupland 2001); and the marketing appeal of hybridity and *bricolage* in the globalizing world. Commodifications of hybridity were traditionally confined to advertising, but the current nexus of bilingualism and commodification seems more multivalent than that. Many celebrations of bilingual or mixed norms in the literature have indeed a commercial bottom line. When ethnic media turn mixed talk into their institutional voice, they legitimize community norms and at the same time exploit the public celebration of a bilingual ethnic 'we' as a strategy of local audience retention (Mahootian 2005; Jaffe 2000). Rap artists may well be commercially successful with their ways of 'subverting language prescriptivism through their own use of language strategies such as multilingual code switching' (Sarkar and Winer 2006: 28). Subversive language practices also depend on marketing to reach their audiences, and commercially framed bilingualism may well challenge monolingual norms of public discourse. We might therefore ask whether the distinction between resistance and commodified bilingualism (Heller 2000) is perhaps better viewed as a continuum rather than as a rigid dichotomy.

Finally, social appropriations of new communications technologies are extending the public visibility of bilingualism, in both societal and impersonal settings. Bilingual discourse is part of the practices by which diaspora populations use the internet as a site for 'the productive construction of new hybrid identities and cultures' (Sinclair and Cunningham 2000: 15). Although the new media are not *per se* sites of language revitalization and maintenance (Sperlich 2005), spaces of online discourse allow for practices of conversational switching and mixing that are qualitatively different from traditional forms of bilingual written discourse, and provide opportunities to establish such practices as the default case.

references

Anderson, B. (1983). *Imagined Communities: Reflections on the Origin and Spread of Nationalism*. New York: Verso.

Androutsopoulos, J. (2003). HipHop und Sprache: Vertikale Intertextualität und die drei Sphären der Popkultur. In J. Androutsopoulos (ed.), *HipHop: globale Kultur – lokale Praktiken*, pp. 111–36. Bielefeld: transcript.

—— (2004). Non-native English and sub-cultural identities in media discourse. In H. Sandøy (ed.), *Den fleirspråklege utfordringa / The multilingual challenge*, pp. 83–98. Oslo: Novus.

—— (2006). Multilingualism, diaspora, and the internet: Codes and identities on German-based diaspora websites. *Journal of Sociolinguistics* 10(4) (Theme Issue, *Sociolinguistics and computer-mediated communication*, ed. J. Androutsopoulos): 524–51.

Androutsopoulos, J., N. Bozkurt, S. Breninck, C. Kreyer, M. Tornow and V. Tschann (2004). Sprachwahl im Werbeslogan. *Networx 41*. Retrieved 7 December 2005, from <www.mediensprache.net/de/networx/docs/networx-41.asp>.

Androutsopoulos, J., and V. Hinnenkamp (2001). Code-Switching in der bilingualen Chat-Kommunikation: ein explorativer Blick auf #hellas und #turks. In M. Beißwenger (ed.), *Chat-Kommunikation*, pp. 367–401. Stuttgart: Ibidem.

Androutsopoulos, J., and A. Scholz (2002). On the recontextualization of hip-hop in European speech communities. *PhiN – Philologie im Netz* 19: 1–42. Retrieved 7 December 2005, from <http://web.fu-berlin.de/phin/>.

Ang, I. (1991). *Desperately Seeking the Audience*. London: Routledge.

Appadurai, A. (1996). *Modernity at Large: Cultural Dimensions of Globalization*. Minneapolis and London: University of Minnesota Press.

Auzanneau, M. (2001). Identités africaines: le rap comme lieu d'expression. *Cahiers d'Études africaines* 163–164, XLI (3–4): 711–34.

Axelsson, A.-S., Å. Abelin and R. Schroeder (2003). 'Anyone speak Spanish?' Language encounters in multi-user virtual environments and the influence of technology. *New Media and Society* 5(4): 475–98.

228   the state, the economy and their agencies in late modernity

Bauman, R. (2001). Genre. In A. Duranti (ed.), *Key Terms in Language and Culture*, pp. 78–80. Malden, MA: Blackwell.

Bell, A. (1992). Hit and miss: Referee design in the dialects of New Zealand television advertisements. *Language and Communication* 12(3&4): 327–40.

Bentahila, A., and E.E. Davies (2002). Language mixing in rai music: Localization or globalization? *Language and Communication* 22: 187–207.

Bhatia, T.K. (1992). Discourse functions and pragmatics of mixing: Advertising across cultures. *World Englishes* 11(1): 195–215.

Blommaert, J., and J. Verschueren (1998). *Debating Diversity*. London and New York: Routledge.

Boyd-Barrett, O., J. Nootens and A. Pugh (1996). Multilingualism and the mass media. In H. Goebl et al. (eds), *Kontaktlinguistik/Contact Linguistics*, vol. 1, pp. 426–31. Berlin and New York: de Gruyter (HSK 12.1).

Bucholtz, M. (2003). Sociolinguistic nostalgia and the authentication of identity. *Journal of Sociolinguistics* 7(3): 398–416.

Busch, B. (2004). *Sprachen im Disput. Medien und Öffentlichkeit in multilingualen Gesellschaften*. Klagenfurt: Drava.

Callahan, L. (2004). *Spanish/English Codeswitching in a Written Corpus*. Amsterdam and Philadelphia: Benjamins.

Cheshire, J., and L.-M. Moser (1994). English as a cultural symbol: The case of advertisements in French-speaking Switzerland. *Journal of Multilingual and Multicultural Development* 15(6): 451–69.

Cormack, M. (1998). Minority language media in Western Europe: Preliminary considerations. *European Journal of Communication* 13(1): 33–52.

Coupland, N. (2001). Dialect stylization in radio talk. *Language in Society* 30: 345–75.

Coupland, N., H. Bishop and P. Garrett (2003). Home truths: Globalization and the iconising of Welsh in a Welsh-American newspaper. *Journal of Multilingual and Multicultural Development* 24(3): 153–77.

Danet, B., and S. Herring (eds) (2003). The Multilingual Internet. Special Issue of *Journal of Computer Mediated Communication* 9:1. Retrieved 7 December 2005, from <http://jcmc.indiana.edu/vol9/issue1/>.

Deppermann, A. (2001). Authentizitätsrhetorik: Sprachliche Verfahren und Funktionen der Unterscheidung von 'echten' und 'unechten' Mitgliedern sozialer Kategorien. In W. Essbach (ed.), *wir/ihr/sie. Identität und Alterität in Theorie und Methode*, pp. 261–82. Würzburg: ergon.

Eastman, C.M. and R.F. Stein (1993). Language display: Authenticating claims to social identity. *Journal of Multilingual and Multicultural Development* 14(3): 187–202.

Fairclough, N. (1995). *Media Discourse*. London: Edward Arnold.

Fjelstad, P. (1999). Language, 'thickness' and popular pride: Tejano radio in south Texas. *Medienjournal* 23(2): Themenheft Medien und Minderheiten, 40–7.

Gardt, A., and B. Hüppauf (eds) (2004). *Globalization and the Future of German*. Berlin: Mouton de Gruyter.

Gumperz, J.J. (1982). *Discourse Strategies*. Cambridge: Cambridge University Press.

Haarmann, H. (1986). Verbal strategies in Japanese fashion magazines: A study in impersonal bilingualism and ethnosymbolism. *International Journal of the Sociology of Language* 58: 107–21.

—— (1989). *Symbolic Values of Foreign Language Use: From the Japanese Case to a General Sociolinguistic Perspective*. Berlin and New York: Mouton de Gruyter.

Heller, M. (2000). Bilingualism and identity in the post-modern world. *Estudios de Sociolingüística* 1(2): 9–24.

—— (2003). *Crosswords: Language, Education and Ethnicity in French Ontario*. Berlin: Mouton de Gruyter.

Hess-Lüttich, E. (1978). Bilingualismus als Stilmittel: Drogenkultur und Sprache. In G. Nickel (ed.), *Rhetoric and Stylistics*, pp. 69–82. Stuttgart.

Hill, J.H. (1995). *Mock Spanish: A site for the indexical reproduction of racism in American English*. Retrieved 7 December 2005, from <www.linguistics.ucsb.edu/faculty/bucholtz/hill/>.

—— (1999). Styling locally, styling globally: What does it mean? *Journal of Sociolinguists* 3(4): 542–56.

Horstmann, S., and N. Alai (2004, 23–25 September). *Inszenierung von Mehrsprachigkeit. Spracheinstellung und Patrizipation im kenianischen Radiosender Kiss 100*. Paper presented at the 35th Conference of Gesellschaft für Angewandte Linguistik, Wuppertal.

Jaffe, A. (2000). Comic performance and the articulation of hybrid identity. *Pragmatics* 10(1): 39–59.

Jaworski, A., C. Thurlow, S. Lawson and V. Ylänne-McEwen (2003). The uses and representations of local languages in tourist destinations: A view from British TV holiday programmes. *Language Awareness* 12(1): 5–29.

Karim, K.H. (2003a). *The Media of Diaspora: Mapping the Globe*. Oxford: Routledge.

—— (2003b). Mapping diasporic mediascapes. In K.H. Karim (ed.), *The Media of Diaspora*, pp. 1–17. Oxford: Routledge.

Kelly-Holmes, H. (2005). *Advertising as Multilingual Communication*. Basingstoke and New York: Palgrave Macmillan.

Kress, G., and T. van Leeuwen (2001). *Multimodal Discourse: The Modes and Media of Contemporary Communication*. London: Arnold.

Lee, J.S. (2004). Linguistic hybridization in K-pop: Discourse of self-assertion and resistance. *World Englishes* 23(3): 429–50.

Leppänen, S. (forthcoming). Youth language in media contexts: Some insights into the functions of English in Finland. *World Englishes* 26 (2007).

Li, W. (2000). Dimensions of bilingualism. In W. Li (ed.), *The Bilingualism Reader*, pp. 3–25. London: Routledge.

Lippi-Green, R. (1997). *English with an Accent*. London and New York: Routledge.

Mahootian, S. (2005). Linguistic change and social meaning: codeswitching in the media. *International Journal of Bilingualism* 9 (3&4): 361–75.

Martin, E. (2002). Mixing English in French advertising. *World Englishes* 21(3): 375–402.

McClure, E. (1998). The relationship between form and function in written national language – English codeswitching: Evidence from Mexico, Spain and Bulgaria. In R. Jacobson (ed.), *Codeswitching Worldwide*, pp. 125–50. Berlin and New York: de Gruyter.

—— (2001). Oral and written Assyrian–English codeswitching. In R. Jacobson (ed.), *Codeswitching Worldwide II*, pp. 157–91. Berlin: Mouton de Gruyter.

McClure, E., and M. Mir (1995). Spanish–English codeswitching in the Mexican and Spanish press. *Journal of Linguistic Anthropology* 5(1): 33–50.

Moal, S. (2000). Broadcast media in Breton: Dawn at last? *Current Issues in Language and Society* 7(2): 117–34.

Morley, D., and K. Robins (1996). *Spaces of Identity: Global Media, Electronic Landscapes and Cultural Boundaries*. London: Routledge.

Ní Neachtain, M. (2000). Competence and minority language broadcasting: A response. *Current Issues in Language and Society* 7(2): 155–8.

Paolillo, J.C. (1996). *Language choice on soc.culture.punjab*. Retrieved 7 December 2005, from <http://ella.slis.indiana.edu/~paolillo/research/paolillo.publish.txt>.

—— (in press). 'Conversational' codeswitching on Usenet and Internet relay chat. In S.C. Herring (ed.), *Computer-Mediated Conversation*. Cresskill, NJ: Hampton Press.

Pennycook, A. (2003). Global Englishes, Rip Slyme, and performativity. *Journal of Sociolinguistics* 7(4): 513–33.

Phillipson, R., and T. Skutnabb-Kangas (1999). Englishization: One dimension of globalization. In D. Graddoll and U.H. Meinhof (eds), *English in a Changing World*, pp. 19–36. Aila Review 13.

Piller, I. (2001). Identity constructions in multilingual advertising. *Language in Society* 30(2): 153–86.

—— (2003). Advertising as a site of language contact. *Annual Review of Applied Linguistics* 23: 170–83.

Preisler, B. (1999). Functions and forms of English in an European EFL country. In T. Bex and R.J. Watts (eds), *Standard English: The Widening Debate*, pp. 239–67. London and New York: Routledge.

Rampton, B. (1995). *Crossing*. London: Longman.

—— (1999). Styling the other: Introduction. *Journal of Sociolinguistics* 3(4) (Theme Issue, *Styling the Other*, ed. B. Rampton): 421–7.

Riggins, S.H. (ed.) (1992). *Ethnic Minority Media*. Newbury Park: Sage.

Robertson, R. (1996). *Globalization: Social Theory and Global Culture*. London: Sage.

Sarkar, M., and L. Winer (2006). Multilingual code-switching in Quebec rap: Poetry, pragmatics and performativity. *International Journal of Multilingualism* 3(3): 173–92.

Sarkar, M., L. Winer and K. Sarkar (2005). Multilingual code-switching in Montreal hip-hop. In J. Cohen et al. (eds), *ISB4: Proceedings of the 4th International Symposium on Bilingualism*, pp. 2057–74. Somerville, MA: Cascadilla Press.

Sinclair, J., and S. Cunningham (2000). Go with the flow: Diasporas and the media. *Television & New Media* 1(1): 11–31.

Sperlich, W.B. (2005). Will cyberforums save endangered languages? A Niuean case study. *International Journal of the Sociology of Language* 172: 51–77.

Urla, J. (1995). Outlaw language: Creating alternative public spheres in Basque free radio. *Pragmatics* 5(2): 245–61.

Woolard, K.A. (1988). Codeswitching and comedy in Catalonia. In M. Heller (ed.), *Codeswitching: Anthropological and Sociolinguistic Perspectives*, pp. 53–76. Berlin and New York: de Gruyter.

—— (1999). Simultaneity and bivalency as strategies in bilingualism. *Journal of Linguistic Anthropology* 8(1): 3–29.

Wright, S. (ed.) (2004). Multilingualism on the Internet. Theme Issue, *International Journal on Multicultural Societies* 6(1) (February 2004). UNESCO Social and Human Sciences. Retrieved 7 December 2005, from <www.unesco.org/shs/ijms>.

Zentella, A.C. (2003). 'José, can you see?': Latin@ responses to racist discourse. In D. Sommer (ed.), *Bilingual Games: Some Literary Investigations*, pp. 51–66. New York: Palgrave Macmillan.

part three
identity practices

11

language socialization and the (re)production of bilingual subjectivities

paul b. garrett

introduction

Language socialization is the human developmental process whereby a child or other novice (of any age) acquires communicative competence (Hymes 1972), enabling him or her to interact meaningfully with others and otherwise participate in the social life of a given community. Language socialization occurs primarily through interactions with older or otherwise more experienced persons (Garrett and Baquedano-López 2002; Ochs and Schieffelin 1984; Schieffelin and Ochs 1986a, 1986b), but also, in most cases, through interactions with peers (Dunn 1999; Farris 1991; Paugh 2005; Rampton 1995a). The child or novice's development of communicative competence through such interactions is largely a matter of learning how to behave, both verbally and non-verbally, as a culturally intelligible subject. While mastering the formal features of the community's language or languages so as to be able to produce grammatically and pragmatically well-formed utterances (Ochs and Schieffelin 1995), the child or novice must also learn how to use language in conjunction with various other semiotic resources as a means of actively co-constructing, negotiating and participating in a broad range of locally meaningful (though largely quite mundane) interactions and activities – a process that Schieffelin and Ochs (1996) characterize as 'the microgenesis of competence'. In practical terms, this involves learning what social roles and categories of identity exist in one's social world, and which among them are potentially viable options for oneself; how one's choices among those options are likely to be interpreted and evaluated by others, and what social consequences are likely to result; how engaging in particular kinds of activities indexes (either directly or indirectly) particular roles, statuses and identities (Ochs 1990, 1993); how one goes about inhabiting or enacting such roles and statuses oneself; and how one manages multiple, shifting identities that overlap and intersect in complex ways, and may sometimes conflict. Just as important, the child or novice must also learn how to recognize and respond to others' verbal and non-verbal 'acts of identity' (Le Page and Tabouret-Keller 1985).

All of these matters tend to be thrown into sharp relief in bilingual settings, where almost inevitably, a speaker's use of particular linguistic resources in a particular context or at a particular moment of interaction will be regarded by his or her interlocutors as meaningful in and of itself. This is attributable in part to semiotic properties and processes that are inherent in language use, especially indexicality, the process whereby a speaker's use of a particular linguistic form or set of forms 'points to', thereby making relevant to the present context or moment of interaction, a particular identity, discourse, set of beliefs, body of knowledge, domain of activity, prior event, etc. Indexicality is a key factor in the ideologically mediated, culturally and politically inflected processes through which the linguistic resources potentially available to speakers within a given 'bilingual' community come to be divided and differentiated into more or less distinct codes in the first place. The sustained coexistence of two (or more) normatively differentiated codes within a particular community is rarely an unproblematic, politically neutral state of affairs; it tends to be a focal point of metapragmatic, discursive and ideological elaboration, and often, of social and political tensions (Garrett 2004; Garrett and Baquedano-López 2002). Certain kinds of linguistic differences may be mapped onto other social categories and divisions based on such notions as ethnicity, nationality, class, race, gender, religiosity, political affiliation and generation; or they may be used as means of marking, reinforcing and policing the boundaries of such categories (Irvine and Gal 2000; Urciuoli 1995). Typically, conflicts or tensions which get played out through language, and on the surface appear to be about language itself, can be shown to be inextricably bound up with other, equally contested issues which are simultaneously being played out on multiple levels, from the household to the state. As they are socialized to use language and to engage in specific communicative practices and activities involving differential use of two or more normatively defined codes (Schieffelin 1994), children and other novices (such as international students and adult immigrants) also develop awareness of these intimately related issues, and of locally preferred and dispreferred ways of dealing with them.

But how exactly does this happen? How do bilingual subjectivities emerge? How do bilinguals learn to use language as a resource for constructing and asserting their identities, and for negotiating their interactions and relationships with others? How do they develop their characteristically subtle, finely tuned sense of when and how to draw upon the linguistic resources at their disposal so as to achieve a variety of pragmatic effects (intimate, distancing, authoritative, poetic, humorous, playful, etc.)? To what extent do they experience their everyday communicative practice as involving the use of two distinct codes (Döpke 2000), and how and why does this vary across contexts (Urciuoli 1995, 1996)? How are speakers' subjective experiences of bilingualism mediated by their ideologies of language, and by the power relations out of which these emerge (Pavlenko 2001; Schieffelin, Woolard and Kroskrity 1998; Woolard and Schieffelin 1994)? This chapter considers how the study of language socialization in bilingual settings can help to answer such questions. While centrally concerned with issues of linguistic and cultural reproduction, language socialization research also strives to take fully into account the agency of language learners – their capacity for creativity, improvisation, resistance, even subversion – and is thus attentive to the relational, dynamically emergent properties of linguistic and sociocultural systems (Kramsch 2002). In the pages that follow, in keeping with certain basic assumptions of the language socialization research paradigm, the bilingual subject is regarded not only as a locus of bilingual competence, but, equally important, as an agent of bilingual practice. To this end, the focus here will be on the emergence of bilingual subjectivities: their production and reproduction, and in many cases their transformation, through processes of language socialization.

subjectivity in language socialization studies

The notion of subjectivity, often associated with post-structuralist social theory, is largely concerned with the ontogenesis and ontology of consciousness: that is, the ways in which individuals come to know themselves, reflexively, as selves, and to experience the world and their own being-in-the-world accordingly. To be sure, scholarly concerns with such matters pre-date post-structuralism. Writing almost three-quarters of a century ago, George Herbert Mead (1995 [1936]: 86) suggested that increasing scholarly attention to what he variously characterized as 'the experience of the individual', 'the point of view of the individual' and 'that...which is peculiar to the individual, that which is unique in his experience' had grown out of the study of society and social organization by such pioneering nineteenth-century figures as Comte and Spencer. But these and related themes that would later become focal points of inquiry in the social sciences, such as how particular kinds of subject positions take shape within complex social systems, how and why particular individuals come to occupy or inhabit them, and how such processes are socially regulated and regimented, were not fully articulated and elaborated until the mid to late twentieth century, when they were taken up by late structuralist and early post-structuralist thinkers such as Lacan (1968 [1956]), Althusser (2003 [1966–67]), and Foucault (1970 [1966]). As developed by these scholars (particularly Althusser and Foucault), the notion of subjectivity serves to conceptualize the dynamic tension between the individual as social actor or agent and the subject position that she or he occupies within a given social order (which inevitably places certain constraints on agency). Crucially, it takes into account that this tension is itself highly contingent in that it is modulated by a broad array of social and historical factors – particularly those implicated in the constitution and exercise of power, ranging from state apparatuses and religious institutions to what Foucault (1988) characterizes as 'technologies of the self'.

The central role of language in producing and reproducing subjectivities (as acknowledged by all of the aforementioned theorists) suggests provocative questions for the study of bilingualism. What constitutes a bilingual subjectivity? In what ways might bilingual subjectivities differ from monolingual subjectivities? Inevitably, such questions demand attention to issues of socialization, in particular, language socialization. It is not yet clear how the young child first becomes aware of the ways in which, and the extent to which, members of his or her community organize the linguistic resources of that community as two distinct codes. For that matter, in many settings, such as those where a 'creole continuum' or 'dialect chain' can be said to exist, or where language boundaries are a matter of political and ideological contestation (Urciuoli 1995; Irvine and Gal 2000), these tend to be thorny matters for all involved, including the researcher. Whatever the circumstances, doubtless it is largely through language socialization that the child gains understanding of such issues and develops the ability to use the linguistic resources available to him or her in strategic, locally intelligible ways.

The development of locally intelligible subjectivities is a central theme (though it may not be couched in these terms) in virtually all language socialization studies (Kulick and Schieffelin 2004). Studies conducted in bilingual settings demonstrate that the availability of two codes, however they may be distinguished locally and however the relationship between them may be conceptualized, constitutes an important resource that speakers can and do draw upon in socializing culturally preferred subjectivities. One example is Fader's (2001) study conducted in a Hasidic Jewish community in New York City, which examines how literacy practices involving English and Yiddish are used across home, school and other community settings to socialize girls in markedly gender-specific ways which, ultimately, constitute an important means by which symbolic boundaries separating the Hasidim from other groups (including other Jewish groups) are maintained. Another example is Baquedano-López's (2001) study of the ways in which narratives in Spanish and in English serve to socialize children to differing kinds of identities (as members of a transnational Mexican-American ethnic community and as members of a much larger multi-ethnic society) in a Catholic parish in Los Angeles. Taken together, examples such as these suggest that virtually all aspects of subjectivity, including affective stances, morality, gender identity and ethnic identity, are shaped in culturally specific ways, and in accordance with local cultural preferences for the most part, through language socialization. Such studies reveal the extent to which notions of bilingualism are context-specific and ideologically mediated, while demonstrating that they are instantiated in and through ethnographically observable communicative practices.

Recently, Kulick and Schieffelin (2004: 354–6) have urged language socialization researchers also to take into consideration 'bad subjects': those individuals, relatively few in number but found in every community, who persistently display culturally dispreferred traits and/or engage in non-normative, 'deviant' behaviours. (This notion of the 'bad subject' is thus used in Althusser's value-neutral sense to refer to persons 'who do not recognize or respond to calls to behave in particular, socially sanctioned ways' [ibid: 355].) As Kulick and Schieffelin point out, 'the focus on expected and predictable outcomes is a weakness if there is not also an examination of cases in which socialization doesn't occur, or where it occurs in ways that are not expected or desired' (ibid). In a bilingual setting, such an unexpected or undesired outcome might be the apparent failure or refusal of children to acquire both languages. Such outcomes may be blamed on the 'failure' of the children's mothers, or of women in general, to transmit the community's traditional or heritage language to the next generation (Constantinidou 1994; Pavlenko 2001); but as Heller (1994) points out, such judgements may be rooted in a 'discourse of failure' in which women themselves have a certain investment, and may mask (or render ambiguous) what might otherwise be regarded as quite successful outcomes of local socialization processes. In any case, language socialization research in such settings must account for processes of reproduction as well as 'why socializing messages to behave and feel in particular ways may also produce their own inversion' (Kulick and Schieffelin 2004: 356).

Language socialization research has yet to address these matters in depth, but there is evidence from other bodies of research to suggest that this is indeed an important and productive direction for future investigations. Some studies of adult second-language acquisition, for example, indicate that individuals may seek to learn another language as a form of conscious resistance: a means of self-consciously becoming, in effect, 'bad subjects' vis-à-vis their first-language communities of origin. Pavlenko (2001: 139) reports that some Japanese and Polish women 'learn English in order to escape gender relations and gendered linguistic practices typical for their own cultures and perceived by them as hierarchical and demeaning'. Similarly, she notes, McMahill's (1997) study of feminist ESL classes in Japan 'suggests that for many Japanese students the concepts of English and feminism are closely related, which renders their learning and using of English empowering'. Other work cited by Pavlenko suggests that it is possible for a second-language learner to be a 'bad subject' vis-à-vis her host community: Siegal (1996) found that some Western women, while learning Japanese in Japan, 'resisted dominant gender ideologies, encoded, in their opinion, in Japanese "women's language," even though at times their resistance came at a price of not "having an authentic

238 identity practices

voice" in their second language and not being perceived as fully fluent and proficient' (Pavlenko 2001: 140).

studies of language socialization in bilingual/multilingual settings

Most of the pioneering studies of language socialization (Schieffelin and Ochs 1986a, 1986b) focused on interactions between young children and their caregivers in monolingual small-scale societies; others were conducted in larger-scale societies such as the US and Japan, but likewise focused on relatively homogeneous monolingual communities (an important exception being Heath 1983). These studies stressed microethnographic analysis of 'everyday life' (Schieffelin 1990), yielding classic ethnographic descriptions of these communities as well as fine-grained, strongly longitudinal accounts of how individual developmental processes unfold within them. More recent studies carried out in postcolonial societies, dependencies with ties to distant metropoles, and indigenous and diasporic communities situated within the geopolitical boundaries of the US, Canada, Mexico, and other large, ethnically diverse societies have directed attention to the role of language socialization in the emergence of syncretic communicative practices, language shift, language obsolescence, and other contact-induced linguistic and sociocultural phenomena (Garrett and Baquedano-López 2002).

Language socialization research of recent years has thus become increasingly concerned with ideologies of language and political economy of language, and much of the impetus for these developments has come from work done in bilingual and multilingual settings. But in any study that has a socio-historical or longitudinal dimension – as do all language socialization studies, by definition – bilingualism cannot be taken as a stable state or property of either communities or individuals. Rather, it must be regarded as a dynamic, contingent phenomenon that takes quite different forms and trajectories in different sociocultural and sociohistorical settings, and that may be only a relatively fleeting phase in a community's history or in the lifespan of an individual speaker. Kulick's (1992) pioneering study of rapid language shift in the small Papua New Guinean village of Gapun set an important precedent for many recent and currently ongoing studies by demonstrating that language socialization practices, always a prime site of linguistic and sociocultural reproduction, may also be the source of far-reaching changes: in the case that Kulick examines, a community-wide shift from bilingualism to monolingualism.

Particularly relevant to the present discussion is Kulick's analysis of how the two main languages spoken in this community, Taiap and Tok Pisin, have come to be mapped onto the villagers' dualistic notion of the self. Taiap, the traditional local vernacular, is now steeped in associations with the 'backward, pagan' ways of the ancestors, and with *hed*, the wilful, selfish, antisocial side of the self. Meanwhile Tok Pisin, a fairly recently introduced language of wider communication, is strongly associated with Christianity, literacy and the world beyond Gapun; it is thought to express *save*, the sociable, cooperative, enlightened side of the self. In Gapuners' syncretic cosmology, dramatic, instantaneous transformations of persons and things are possible, and indeed are to be expected, provided that conditions conducive to such transformations are in place. Therein lies their dilemma: an overabundance of *hed* in village life, and a regrettable shortage of *save*, are causing Gapun to remain mired in the old, backward ways. This renders the villagers unable to *kamap*, that is, to develop, and to join the rest of the developed world in enjoying a comfortable, modern way of life filled with technological marvels and endlessly abundant consumer goods. The way out of this dilemma, they believe, is to suppress outward manifestations of *hed* while cultivating (and prominently displaying) *save*. 'In using Tok Pisin,' Kulick explains, 'villagers are thus expressing an important and highly valued aspect of self...But in doing this, they are also constituting a situation in which their vernacular is becoming less and less desirable and important' – a situation in which Taiap is literally 'losing its ability to express positive aspects of self' (1992: 21). The ultimate effect, Kulick convincingly demonstrates, is that Gapun children no longer get sufficient exposure to Taiap to become proficient speakers of the language: '[T]here is no demand on children to speak Taiap, nor is there any reward for speaking it' (ibid: 222).

Viewing this situation in terms of subjectivity suggests that the introduction of Tok Pisin and exogenous cultural forms of which it is the primary medium (particularly Christianity) has resulted in a significant reworking of the relationship between language and subjectivity in Gapun. Kulick notes that prior to the introduction of Tok Pisin, multilingualism was highly valued; being able to speak the vernaculars of other groups in the region (with whom there was intermittent contact) was 'the traditional cultural ideal' (1992: 69). To be a Gapuner was to be bi- or multilingual. But this was an era in which the local languages coexisted in a more or less egalitarian, non-hierarchical relationship; no particular language was regarded as intrinsically superior, and no group sought to impose its language on other groups. This changed drastically with the introduction of Tok Pisin, a language spoken by powerful outsiders (such as plantation labour recruiters and missionaries) whose clear intent was to impose both their will and their ways on others, and in effect, to transform them into wholly new kinds of subjects, such as indentured labourers and Christians.

New kinds of subjects, in turn, meant new kinds of subjectivities: new ways of experiencing and understanding the known world and one's place within it. For Gapuners, this entailed, among other things, new ways of being bilingual and of experiencing bilingualism – that is, new forms of bilingual subjectivity. Gapuners' newfound conviction that suppressing *hed* would enable them to *kamap* – a collective aim that would scarcely have been conceivable prior to the introduction of Tok Pisin and the exogenous cultural forms with which it was associated – gave them a new goal to strive for, one that entailed a whole new way of being. To suppress *hed* was to suppress Taiap, which in effect was to suppress one's own bilingualism, one's own bilingual self – all in the interest of radically changing Gapun's place in a heretofore unknown, indeed unimaginable social and cosmological order. Kulick's study thus makes clear that processes of sociocultural reproduction and change, in bilingual settings as in all others, cannot be explained without reference to the complex relationships among political economy, ideology, and everyday communicative practices, particularly language socialization practices.

the socialization of age-appropriate bilingual subjectivities in st lucia

By examining how individual developmental processes unfold within their broader sociocultural and sociohistorical contexts, from micro to macro levels of analysis, language socialization researchers are able to investigate how events and interactions in the everyday lives of individuals shape their perceptions and experiences of their social worlds, and of their own positions within those worlds. Language socialization research is not just a matter of producing detailed ethnographic accounts of individual developmental trajectories and the local settings in which they occur; an important overarching goal is to understand how the experiences and actions of individuals relate to (that is, how they shape and are shaped by) larger sociocultural and sociohistorical processes.

In bilingual communities, shifts in the (re)production of bilingual sub-jectivities tend to become particularly salient at the junctures between generations, as members of one generation are socializing members of the next in ways that may or may not result in the production (or reproduction) of a succeeding cohort of bilingual speakers and subjects. In my own language socialization study, conducted in the Caribbean island of St Lucia, I examine a situation in which members of the first local generation of bilinguals – young adults at the time of my fieldwork, and in most cases parents of young children – were socializing those children in ways that yielded a wide range of outcomes, from near-monolingualism to varying degrees of bilingualism. The two languages involved are Kwéyòl, an Afro-French creole language which is a legacy of the island's French colonial period (1651–1814), and the present-day official language, English, which became established during a subsequent British colonial period (1814–1979).[1] The English spoken by most St Lucians in everyday conversation is actually a distinctive non-standard variety of English that I have described elsewhere as Vernacular English of St Lucia, or VESL (Garrett 2003). For present purposes, however, I apply the label 'English' broadly (as St Lucians generally do) to encompass the full spectrum of local variation.

At present in St Lucia, Kwéyòl–English bilingualism is widespread, and the majority of the population is bilingual to one degree or another. But St Lucian bilingualism at the present historical moment (as in numerous other societies) encompasses a broad span of variation, arrayed between elderly rural Kwéyòl monolinguals and an emerging generation of young urban English monolinguals. In the small rural community where I conducted my fieldwork, Morne Carré, many of the oldest residents are monolingual speakers of Kwéyòl, while most persons middle-aged and younger are bilingual (to varying degrees) in Kwéyòl and English. This generational difference reflects in part an important shift with regard to formal education: many members of the eldest generation never attended school, but their children were able to do so, particularly after a primary school was established in Morne Carré itself in the early 1970s. Most of today's generation of children are also bilingual to one degree or another, their proficiency in Kwéyòl and English broadly reflecting the extent to which each language is (or is not) used with them by their caregivers and other members of their households. This varies considerably: in some households, caregivers are diligent about speaking only English with children, while in others, particularly those where grandparents or other elderly relatives reside, Kwéyòl may be used almost exclusively. Consequently, even within this small community, some children, during their pre-school years, are virtually monolingual Kwéyòl-speakers, while others are virtually monolingual English-speakers.

Most Morne Carré households, however, fall somewhere between these two extremes, with adults speaking mostly Kwéyòl among themselves but showing a strong preference for the use of English with children. The preference for the use of English *by* children is even stronger; children are expected to respond in English even when addressed in Kwéyòl by an angry or impatient caregiver. Most St Lucian adults subscribe to a sort of locally adapted notion of subtractive bilingualism: it is widely and quite firmly believed that the simultaneous acquisition of Kwéyòl has a profoundly detrimental effect on children's acquisition of English. As a result of Kwéyòl's putative potential for interference (contamination would not be too strong a word), adults insist that children must learn to speak English before they are allowed to begin speaking Kwéyòl. While English must be explicitly taught to children, Kwéyòl need not be taught at all; it will come naturally, adults say, and they assume that children will eventually begin speaking Kwéyòl of their own volition.

In Morne Carré, as the preceding suggests, there are strong community norms of age-appropriateness with regard to the use of Kwéyòl and English. Attention to how these norms of age-appropriateness are manifested in everyday interactions yields insight into how age-inflected subjectivities take form (i.e. are socialized) in individuals of various ages. Just as important, it offers insight into how those subjectivities are continually changing over time: both human developmental time (i.e. time as reckoned with regard to the lifespans of individuals) and sociohistorical time (i.e. time as reckoned with regard to the local community and/or the broader society's trajectories over the course of successive generations, and as the life experiences of members of those generations differ due to social and historical factors).

Below I consider some excerpts taken from my recordings of everyday interactions in Morne Carré. My focus is a particular dimension of subjectivity formation that I take to be of universal relevance: the age cohort or generation dimension. While its significance for everyday social life clearly varies across cultures and communities, this dimension tends to be highly salient in language socialization studies that have been conducted in bilingual settings and others characterized by episodes of language contact (e.g. Kulick's study as described above). For present purposes, the central concern is how a child develops a sense of himself or herself as 'belonging to' a particular age group vis-à-vis other age groups, and how socialization to use (or not to use) particular linguistic resources contributes to that process.[2]

rosie's mixed input

In most Morne Carré households, young children are immersed in a richly verbal environment in which both Kwéyòl and English figure prominently. The proportions vary considerably from one household to another, however, depending on such factors as the age, occupations and social networks of the child's elders and caregivers. For example, if grandparents are present in the household, they may be monolingual Kwéyòl-speaking farmers who have never attended school and who rarely leave the village. At the other end of the spectrum are elder siblings and cousins, who are likely to be oriented toward secondary schools, peer groups and wage-earning jobs in the capital city; these adolescents and young adults speak primarily English, and may in fact have quite limited proficiency in Kwéyòl.

However much Kwéyòl is spoken by a child's caregivers, in many households relatively little Kwéyòl is directed to the child herself; or else it is directed to the child and then immediately followed by an English utterance more or less equivalent in meaning (as often happens when a caregiver is distracted, frustrated or impatient), with no real expectation or desire that the child respond to, or even demonstrate understanding of, the Kwéyòl utterance. It *is* expected, however, that the child will attend to, and respond immediately to, English utterances, particularly imperatives, such as those in the following excerpt from a caregiver's speech to a young child. The interaction is between Coletta, a 21-year-old woman, and a 20-month-old toddler named Rosie. Coletta is the daughter of Rosie's mother's sister, and one of Rosie's primary caregivers; Rosie's mother died of an illness shortly after the child was born, whereupon Coletta's mother took her into their household. In this excerpt, Coletta is calling out from the house because it is time for Rosie to have her bath. Rosie is in the yard, where she has been quietly amusing herself by searching for discarded bottle caps.

1 Come and bathe!
2 Wo::y! [*an exclamation of frustration or exasperation*]
3 Ladjé'y. Fè vit.   Drop it.
   Drop it. Do [it] quickly.
4 Tout bagay kaka chyen a, ou ka jwé andan'y.
   Every dog-shit thing, you're playing in it.
5 Pasé ay benyen. Go and bathe.
   Go and bathe.
6 Ou ka wèvé, Rosie? Tjups.
   Are you (day-)dreaming, Rosie? Tjups ['*tooth-suck*' *sound expressing disapproval or exasperation*]

As this small torrent of words issues forth, it is likely that only a few among them, such as *come, bathe* and *drop,* stand out as meaningful for Rosie. Rosie knows that she must respond, and respond immediately; but it is Coletta's posture, the hard fixity of her gaze and the tone of her voice, at least as much as the propositional meaning of her utterances, that make it unmistakably clear to Rosie that she must stop what she is doing (she has been scolded before for picking bottle caps out of the dirt) and 'come' at once. For her part, Coletta knows well that Rosie does not understand everything that she has just said, some of it in Kwéyòl, some in English. But from Coletta's perspective, it could hardly be otherwise, even if she had spoken only in English. Rosie is not even two years old yet, after all; Coletta has been talking as much to herself as to the child.

The above comments are semi-conjectural on my part, but they are not merely speculative; they are based in ethnographic insight into St Lucian ideologies of language and folk understandings of how children's language acquisition unfolds. Despite adults' concern that young children, from the time they first begin to produce recognizable single words, should acquire English and English only, many caregivers do use Kwéyòl in addressing children, particularly when irritated or impatient. But English is the preferred code for use with children, particularly young children, and it is assumed that they understand English better than Kwéyòl; hence the tendency for adults to juxtapose English imperatives with Kwéyòl ones, as Coletta does in lines 3 and 5 in the excerpt above. Notice that she does not provide an English equivalent in line 4, which is an instance of what Goffman (1981) characterizes as 'self-talk'; Coletta neither intends nor desires that Rosie understand this utterance. It seems plausible that the same can be said of line 6, despite the seemingly vocative mention of Rosie's name.[3]

From the perspective of Rosie and other young children in this bilingual community, an implicit but unmistakable message can be inferred from such instances of mixed input: on those occasions when adults use two different codes in their child-directed speech, only the utterances in one of those two codes, English, need be attended to, understood for their propositional content, and responded to. Doubtless the juxtaposition of Kwéyòl utterances with their English equivalents is a means by which young children (quite possibly even preverbal children) begin to develop an understanding that their elders recognize two distinct codes, and that the boundary between the two, quite porous at times, is much more sharply drawn at other times, particularly when children are involved. Such juxtapositions are also a means by which children begin to recognize the systematic correspondences (phonological, semantic and syntactic) between English as spoken locally and Kwéyòl (Garrett 2003), and by which they begin to develop some degree of 'passive' understanding of Kwéyòl, or at the very least, of a subset of commonly used Kwéyòl imperatives, scolds, rhetorical questions and other affect-laden utterances (Garrett 2005). But any inclination that young children might have to produce Kwéyòl utterances of their own is effectively squelched by language socialization practices such as those examined below, which cumulatively and recursively emphasize that English, not Kwéyòl, is the language that children are to use, and that Kwéyòl is an 'adult' code. Thus children become conscious from an early age, perhaps well before they begin to speak, that the only subject position available to them in their bilingual community is that of the monolingual English-speaking child who may (but need not) also have a fair degree of passive understanding of Kwéyòl. As a direct function of their age and corresponding social status (with all of the behavioural constraints that this status entails), to be a speaker of Kwéyòl, or a bilingual speaker, is not an option for them – at least, not yet.

tonia's code-mixing

Morne Carré children sometimes do produce Kwéyòl utterances, however; and like children growing up in bilingual environments everywhere, they sometimes code-mix. Adults consider these to be problems that must be corrected as quickly as possible, lest they become entrenched and impede the child's acquisition of English. Indeed, local language socialization practices are to a great extent oriented toward this particular end – which doubtless has the ancillary effect of reinforcing and reproducing among adults their own ideologically based notions of English and Kwéyòl as two wholly separate, unproblematically discrete codes (cf. Garrett 2000). The following interaction occurred in another Morne Carré household between a child named Tonia (age 2;11) and her mother, Paya, a woman in her early twenties.

1	Paya:	Your hand dirty?
2	Tonia:	Yeah
3	Paya:	With what?
4	Tonia:	Zo
		Bone
5	Paya:	Zo?! Bone!

Tonia's hand is greasy because she has been eating a piece of chicken. In line 4, in response to her mother's question, she produces the Kwéyòl word *zo*, 'bone'. Paya's immediate response – following a repetition of Tonia's utterance that functions here as a rhetorical question – is to model the English equivalent *bone*, in an urgent tone of voice. Although she does not do so here, in many such cases Paya made sure that Tonia repeated the modelled English utterance and pronounced it in a passable manner. At another point during the same recording session, Tonia code-mixed fairly extensively in an utterance directed to me, prompting a more elaborate correction from Paya:

1	Tonia:	Paul, sòti la before me knock ou.
2	Paya:	What you tell Paul?
		Sòti la avan ou knock li?!
		Get away from there before you knock him?!
		Say 'Come out from there before I knock you',
		that's what you have to say.
3	Tonia:	[*Unintelligible*]
4	Paya:	You cannot talk. You can talk?
5	Tonia:	Yeah
6	Paya:	Talk for me to hear you.

Although Tonia's initial utterance is a mix of English and Kwéyòl forms (line 1), when Paya repeats it in the form of a rhetorical question, shifting the two pronominal forms accordingly, the only English form retained is the verb *knock* (line 2); otherwise the utterance is rendered entirely in Kwéyòl, suggesting that Tonia's use of Kwéyòl forms a moment earlier was much more salient to Paya than her use of English forms. Paya follows her rhetorical question with a model utterance in English, prompting Tonia to repeat it verbatim. Tonia's failure to repeat the model utterance clearly (line 3; she may be playfully garbling it) is met with the suggestion that she 'cannot talk', a semi-playful reproach which suggests that Tonia is behaving in a babyish manner, that is, not acting her age (line 4). But another noteworthy aspect of this interaction is that Paya is so intent on correcting the code-mix (or simply Tonia's use of Kwéyòl) that she makes no comment at all about *what* Tonia is saying to me, which under other circumstances would almost surely have prompted a rebuke (or at least a warning) to the effect that Tonia is being 'womanish', that is, being too forward or assertive for her young age by directing an unmitigated imperative and physical threat to an adult. Although verbal teasing between adults and children is sometimes tolerated and occasionally even encouraged (Garrett 2005), adults rarely allow children to initiate a teasing exchange. In general, children's speech, both to adults and to other children, is fairly rigidly constrained by local norms of age-appropriate forms of speech, and adults are quick to correct a child who violates those norms. In these and other ways, children are encouraged to be highly conscious of age-appropriate behaviours, particularly verbal behaviours; and as suggested by the excerpts above, exclusive use of English is one of the most fundamental aspects of age-appropriate speech for young children, so important that it sometimes trumps pragmatic considerations.

The importance of age-appropriate use of language is made further evident by the fact that even primary-school-age children in Morne Carré take it upon themselves to engage their preschool-age siblings in corrective routines like those examined above. In the following excerpt, elder brother Shawn (age 7) corrects younger sister Tonia (age 2;10) in an interaction that I recorded approximately one month earlier than those above. In this excerpt, two other persons are also involved: Tonia's elder sister, Brita (age 5), and once again the children's mother, Paya, who is overhearing their interaction from an adjoining room.

1	Tonia:	Shawn, ga' sa
2	Shawn:	Not 'Ga' sa', 'Look at that'
3	Brita:	'Look at that'
4	Tonia:	Look at that
5	Shawn:	You know the word,
	[exasperated]	when you finish you not saying it.
		Say 'Look at that'
6	Tonia:	Look at that
7	Shawn:	'Look at that', eh
8	Brita:	'Ga'- You saying 'Gadé sa'?
	[to Tonia]	
9	Tonia:	Gadé sa, gadé sa, gadé sa!
	[mischievously]	
10	Paya:	Say 'Look at that'
	[from adjacent room]	
11	Tonia:	Look at that

As this excerpt suggests, by the time children reach the age of Tonia's elder siblings, their notions of Kwéyòl and English as two separate, separable codes, one of them suitable for use by children and the other not, are well established. By their fifth year (the year in which they begin school), most Morne Carré children have become well accustomed to monitoring their own speech as well as that of their peers and (especially) younger children for instances of code-mixing; indeed, they tend to be almost hawkishly vigilant about it. Of course, sometimes the transgressions are wilful ones. The phrase *gadé sa* 'look at that', often reduced to *ga' sa* in casual speech, is well known to most children from their earliest years, and is brief enough that older children can often get away with using it in contexts of loosely supervised play with their peers. In the excerpt above, it is not clear in line 1 whether Tonia is aware that *ga' sa* is a Kwéyòl expression, and hence unacceptable for her to use (that is, likely to draw expressions of disapproval and corrective measures from her siblings and mother); but by line 9, after Shawn has corrected her, provided the English equivalent (with a bit of reinforcement from Brita) and had her repeat it, it is clear enough that Tonia is using *ga(dé) sa* self-consciously and mischievously: now she chants it in a sing-song voice, only to be reproved by Paya and compelled to repeat the English model once again. As might be expected, Paya's intervention settles the matter, at least for the time being.

older children's use of kwéyòl in unsupervised peer contexts

Despite adults' concern that children become proficient speakers of English without interference from Kwéyòl, most Morne Carré children do acquire some knowledge of Kwéyòl, and in most cases some speaking proficiency, particularly during middle to late childhood. As this suggests, many children actively resist, at least occasionally, the age-based restrictions on their use of Kwéyòl that were outlined above. Not surprisingly, this resistance increases as children get older and begin striking out on their own, spending more and more time with peers and beyond the earshot of adults. Corresponding roughly to the early to middle primary school years, this period is marked by a number of important shifts in children's levels of responsibility and self-sufficiency in home and community contexts. Beginning school is itself a socially salient developmental milestone; children of school age begin to be entrusted with other responsibilities such as taking care of younger siblings in their mothers' absence, running errands that involve travelling several minutes' walk from home, and performing tasks that involve some element of potential physical danger to self, other persons or property, such as using a cutlass (machete) to cut weeds or tending to the burning of the household trash pile. Doubtless, being deemed competent to take on responsibilities such as these, and spending increasing amounts of time in the company of peers, can be correlated with important shifts in children's subjectivities.

In the following excerpt, a small group of boys ranging in age from four to seven years are playing together near the community soccer/cricket field. The field lies on the village's periphery, just beyond the last houses where the settled area gives way to a mix of cultivated land and 'bush' (forest). Other than I, there are no adults within earshot. Up to this point the boys have been using mostly English while playing and chatting among themselves. But as they have traipsed toward the playing field and have gotten farther and farther from their homes, they have begun to use Kwéyòl more and more freely. In this unsupervised context, they noticeably begin to act out adult masculine identities; no caregivers are around to make them use English, so they are free to switch to Kwéyòl, speaking like older boys or men rather than like small children.[4] Beyond issues of code selection, note the coarse remark made by Rick, the oldest boy present, in line 1; such an utterance certainly would not have been tolerated if overheard by an adult, and Rick would have been scolded for using language that is *twòp nonm* 'too man[nish]'. The same

can be said of his use of the word *bonnda*, 'ass', in line 5; the more polite
Kwéyòl term is *fès*, and even more preferable for a child Rick's age would be
an 'English' term such as the hypocoristic *bumbum*. In the excerpt below,
the boys engage in a sort of quintessentially masculine bonding experience,
collectively stopping by the side of the road, at the edge of *wajyé-a*, 'the bush',
to urinate. Much to the amusement of the other boys, seven-year-old Zacchie
decides to take this as an opportunity to defecate as well.

1   Rick: Kité mwen ladjé pisa. Bon tibway- !
               Let me take a piss. Hey boy-!
2   Zacchie: Sòt' la, Maklin!
               Get away from there, Maklin!
3   Rick: Paul, mako'y! Aaah, Paul fè – !
               Paul, peer at him! Aaah, Paul went – ! [pretends he has a
               video camera]
4   Maklin: Ba mwen fè an try eh Rick, ba mwen fè an try
               Let me have a try eh Rick, let me have a try
5   Rick: Sa kay djouké bonnda'w
               That's going to poke your ass
6   Zacchie: Mwen vlé tjò- a piece of toilet paper
               I want a piece- [switches to English]
7   Maklin: Paul, ay pwan an tjò toilet paper anba wajyé-a ba'y
               Paul, go get a piece of toilet paper in the woods for him
8   Paul: La ni toilet paper anba wajyé-a?
               There's toilet paper in the woods?
9   Zacchie: Wi. Sa ki toilet paper mwen wi
               Yeah. That's my toilet paper [holding up a leaf]
10 Paul: Ohh?!
11 Zacchie: Um, um, pli lotan, sa- um, moun té ka- um, fè pou-
               Um, um, more long time, that- um, people- um, used for-
12 Rick: Toilet paper yo wi
               Their toilet paper
13 Zacchie: Toilet- toilet paper yo wi
               Toilet- their toilet paper
14 Paul: Oh, ki moun ki di'w sa?
               Oh, who told you that?
15 Zacchie: An moun ki di mwen sa wi, Paul
               A person/Someone told me that, Paul

Zacchie, whose family is particularly strict about his use of English, has been
trying his best to keep up with the Kwéyòl banter of the other boys, one
of whom is younger than he. Maklin, the youngest boy present, lives in a
predominantly Kwéyòl-speaking household where his near-monolingual
grandmother is one of his primary caregivers; consequently, his proficiency

in Kwéyòl far exceeds Zacchie's. (This, along with his lack of proficiency in English, are both fairly unusual for a child of Maklin's age and of this generation.) Noteworthy here is Zacchie's apparent reluctance to use the English borrowing *toilet paper*: in line 6 he hesitates, apparently searching momentarily for a Kwéyòl word before resigning himself to a code-switch (which involves producing an entire English noun phrase, despite the fact that he has already produced the Kwéyòl word *tjò*, 'piece [of]'). His use of the term *toilet paper* is effectively ratified by both Maklin and Paul (lines 7–8; there is in fact no equivalent Kwéyòl term in common usage), whereupon Zacchie uses it again himself, this time without hesitation, in line 9.

Soon thereafter, Zacchie seems to come up against the limits of his Kwéyòl grammatical proficiency in attempting to construct an anterior-tense utterance (line 11); he is apparently trying to say *An tan lotan, moun te ka sèvi sa-a pou* toilet paper *yo*, 'A long time ago, people used to use that [leaves] as their *toilet paper*'. It may also be that he is once again hesitating to use the English term *toilet paper* as part of this ambitious foray into Kwéyòl; in any case, this is what the older boy Rick understands to be happening, as evidenced by his suggestion of the term in line 12. Zacchie quickly accepts the candidate term proffered by the elder, more fluent Rick, who by proffering it has effectively sanctioned its use.

The preceding excerpt suggests that Kwéyòl indexes adulthood for these boys, and that certain kinds of Kwéyòl lexical items and turns of phrase (*ladjé pisa, bonnda*) index adult masculinity. It also underscores the extent to which Kwéyòl and English have become compartmentalized for children of this age – possibly even more so than for some adults. From a developmental pragmatic perspective, Zacchie's apparent hesitation to use the commonplace English borrowing *toilet paper* might be regarded as a kind of overgeneralization or hypercorrection phenomenon. Making his best effort to keep up with the other boys' use of Kwéyòl, he is reluctant to resort to the use of any identifiably English form, notwithstanding the fact that English borrowings and code-switches are quite heavily used among male adolescents and all but the oldest male adults.

intergenerational conflict over older children's use of kwéyòl

As noted previously, and as seen in the above excerpt, the degree to which children in Morne Carré are spoken to in Kwéyòl and allowed to speak Kwéyòl themselves varies considerably from one household to another. Even within the same household, adults' attitudes and practices may vary, giving rise to occasional disagreements. In the excerpt below, such a disagreement between Bettina, a woman in her late thirties, and her daughter Coletta, age 21, flares up in regard to Calton, the nine-year-old nephew of Bettina and cousin of Coletta who lives with them. Coletta is largely responsible for supervising Calton, as her mother works in town and is away for most of the day. Coletta does not allow Calton to speak Kwéyòl in her presence, and chastises him severely if she overhears him speaking it to anyone else (but this very rarely happens). Although she herself often addresses Calton in Kwéyòl and expects him, unlike the much younger Rosie, to understand her when she does so, she permits him to reply only in English. (Note that Coletta uses nothing but Kwéyòl with her mother as well as with Calton in the exchanges below.) Bettina, on the other hand, takes a more balanced view: she thinks that it is important for children to know both Kwéyòl and English, and that while they should be encouraged to use English, they should not actively be prevented from (much less punished for) using Kwéyòl. Most of the time her opinion does Calton little good, however; along with Rosie, he is usually under Coletta's strict supervision, and he sticks to English out of fear of her harsh reprisals.

As this excerpt begins, I have just asked Calton a question in Kwéyòl about what he is doing. Stooped over a large basin of water in the yard, he is washing leaves for his aunt, who is in the kitchen preparing to use them in making a herbal skin remedy. Calton is in an ill humour at having to do this chore, and he has mumbled a short answer to my question in English.[5] But Coletta, sitting about three metres away, has not heard him clearly, and is under the mistaken impression that Calton has responded to my Kwéyòl question in Kwéyòl (or 'Patwa', as it is referred to here and in casual conversation by most St Lucians).

1	Coletta -> Calton:	Sa ou di la, Calton?!
		What did you say there, Calton?!
		Tann mwen waché lanng ou an djòl ou wi!
		Just see if I don't rip your tongue right out of your mouth!
2	Bettina -> Coletta:	Kité timanmay-la bat mizè'y, Coletta. Tjups
		Leave the child alone, Coletta. Tjups
3	Calton -> Coletta: [*complainingly*]	She say- You always there telling somebody something
4	Bettina -> Coletta:	Kanté timanmay ka palé Patwa,
		So many children speak Patwa,
		mi Paul vin' apwann Patwa,
		here's Paul come to learn Patwa,
		ou pa vlé Calton palé Patwa?!
		[and] you don't want Calton speaking Patwa?!
5	Coletta -> Bettina:	Calton pa ka palé pyès Patwa
		Calton doesn't speak any Patwa
6	Calton -> Coletta:	When I get big, what I will say?
7	Bettina -> Coletta:	I bon pou djòl ou,
		It's good [enough] for your mouth,
		i pa bon pou djòl li?!
		[but] it isn't good [enough] for his mouth?!

Coletta's luridly threatening rebuke of Calton for speaking Kwéyòl (line 1), characteristically, is in Kwéyòl. Bettina's response (line 2) is likewise in Kwéyòl, as are virtually all of her everyday exchanges with Coletta. Calton's protest (line 3), however, is in English; he knows well that for him to speak Kwéyòl here would only exacerbate the situation, and he would not dare to speak Kwéyòl to Coletta in any case. Indeed, the fact that he responds at all in this situation is somewhat uncharacteristic; he probably would not have done so if Bettina had not already stepped into the fray and made clear that she does not agree with Coletta. This becomes still more explicit as Bettina elaborates her position by pointing out that many children speak Kwéyòl, and that I have come all the way from the US to learn the language (line 4); she follows this with a rhetorical question implying that Coletta has no business telling Calton not to speak Kwéyòl. Coletta's response (line 5, delivered in a sullen tone – she knows that she will have to defer to her mother) that Calton 'doesn't speak any Patwa' is pointedly disingenuous. Coletta is well aware that Calton *can* speak some Kwéyòl; what she means here is that he does not (and had better not) speak it in her presence. Calton's response to this (line 6), again in English, but posed rather daringly in the form of a rhetorical question (he is only able to run the risk of addressing his elder cousin in this fashion because Bettina is there to shield him from Coletta's response), alludes to the fact that at nine years, he is fast approaching the age at which Coletta will no longer be able to exert the kind of control that she is accustomed to having over his use of language. Bettina finally settles the matter (for the moment, at least) by posing a rhetorical question to Coletta (line 7), pointing out that if Kwéyòl is good enough for Coletta to speak, it is good enough for Calton to speak.

The various excerpts that have been examined here reveal that children in Morne Carré are both implicitly and explicitly socialized to distinguish sharply between two normatively differentiated codes, Kwéyòl and English, and to observe fairly strict norms of age-appropriate use of those two codes. Notions of age-appropriateness prove to be somewhat fluid and contingent, however, permitting some opportunities, particularly as children get older, to experiment with the use of both codes and with the ideologically constructed boundary between them (a boundary which in practice proves to be rather fuzzy). As they do so, children are gradually making their way along a loosely age-graded developmental trajectory that both constrains and enables them in the course of everyday interactions as they position and re-position themselves in relation to others through participation in an increasingly diversified range of activities. Ultimately, the ability to draw on both English and Kwéyòl as communicative resources, and to deploy the forms and features associated with these two codes in socially and pragmatically competent ways, is crucial to the emergence of locally intelligible adult subjectivities – a hallmark of which, at the present sociohistorical moment in Morne Carré and in St Lucia more generally, is bilingualism.

conclusion

Kulick and Schieffelin (2004: 351–2) remark that an important shortcoming of certain influential works of contemporary social theory is that 'the socialization of habitus, or the early reiterations of language that initiate processes of becoming a culturally intelligible subject, are assumed and asserted more than they are actually demonstrated...[W]e know *that* they happen...but we don't know *how.*' The preceding examples of language socialization activities, fleeting moments extracted from the flow of everyday events in the lives of a few children in one St Lucian community, illustrate some typical types of interaction through which these children's emergent bilingual subjectivities are progressively, recursively shaped through mundane interactions with significant others: adult caregivers, siblings, peers, even visiting anthropologists. The language socialization research paradigm offers a powerful and versatile approach for gaining insight into such developmental phenomena. Even the few brief interactions that have been examined here provide insight into important age-graded shifts in children's developmental trajectories as they move from the relatively rigid constraints on language use to which they are subject in early childhood to the relative autonomy that becomes increasingly (if intermittently) available to them during middle childhood.

In bilingual settings where children's acquisition and use of two codes is a value-laden, ideologically charged, discursively elaborated process – as seems to be the case more often than not – a language socialization approach can also yield important insights into the ways in which local, face-to-face contexts and interactions are impinged upon (often orthogonally or indirectly) by extralocal factors. In the St Lucian case, these include recent and still ongoing changes in the relationship between English and Kwéyòl in St Lucian society, the imperatives of nation-building (Garrett 2007), and the ongoing shift from a primarily agricultural to a primarily service-based economy (which in Morne Carré has implications for the relevance of formal education, for household subsistence strategies, for the life chances and personal aspirations of members of the younger generations, etc.). Mapping out these sorts of micro–macro connections for the St Lucian case is beyond the scope of this chapter, but Kulick's (1992) study of Gapun provides an elegant model, as do several other ethnographic studies of language contact phenomena in bilingual/multilingual settings (e.g. Errington 1998; Gal 1979; Hill and Hill 1986; Rampton 1995b; Tsitsipis 1998). All of these cases suggest that transformations of local subjectivities via changes (often quite subtle changes) in everyday communicative practices play a pivotal role in determining the extent and degree of bilingualism among individuals, as well as the relative stability of bilingualism at group and community levels.

The notion of subjectivity taps into the tension between individual agency and the social factors that simultaneously enable and constrain it. Applied in concert with language socialization approaches, it offers excellent possibilities for bridging the gap between socially oriented and psychologically oriented approaches to bilingualism, bilingual acquisition, and related phenomena ranging from code-switching to language shift. Such an approach proceeds from the assumption that bilingualism, in addition to being a socially, culturally and historically diverse phenomenon, is rooted in political economy: in contingent relationships of hierarchy and inequality, dominance and subordination. These contingent relationships, in turn, are ideologically mediated in ways that may not be readily discernible, but are enormously consequential in that as they guide individuals' understandings of the world and their actions in it. Longitudinal, empirically grounded, ethnographically informed investigations of the ontogenesis of bilingual subjectivities can illuminate processes of individual human development, processes of sociocultural reproduction and change, and crucially, the dynamic relationships that link them.

notes

1. Since 1979, St Lucia has been an independent nation-state. English remains the sole official language and language of instruction, but Kwéyòl has gained increasing prestige and official recognition in recent years (Garrett 2000, 2007).
2. For a related analysis and discussion involving members of three distinct age groups (adults, older children, and younger children), see Garrett (2005).
3. These two utterances, particularly line 6, are perhaps not 'pure' instances of self-talk; they may be more akin to what Goffman characterizes as 'afterburn', an affect-laden type of utterance that is intended to be (over)heard, but not attended to or responded to, by a co-present other or others. The fact that I was present as an observer (engaged in videotaping Rosie) when Coletta produced these utterances is yet another factor that must be taken into consideration in these regards. (As is typical among young adults in Morne Carré, Coletta and I used a liberal mix of English and Kwéyòl in our day-to-day interactions.)
4. I was present, of course, but as a sort of tag-along companion rather than as a caregiver; the children knew very well that I was not at all averse to their use of Kwéyòl. (For that matter, they also knew that I, quite unlike most adults, was not averse to taking part in children's play activities from time to time.) As a single non-St Lucian adult male who had no children of his own but spent much of his time with small children and their (mostly female) primary caregivers, and who was making special efforts to become a proficient speaker of Kwéyòl, I occupied a rather unconventional (though warmly accommodated) subject position in village social life.
5. I lived in the same household compound as Calton (in a small freestanding house of my own) and interacted with him on a daily basis. I often spoke to him in Kwéyòl, and virtually without exception, he always replied in English. This informal arrangement was unusual with respect to local norms of adult–child interaction, but it was standard practice for the two of us and was accepted as such by others, including Coletta, out of deference to my need to practise my Kwéyòl as much as possible. Even so, as this excerpt suggests, under no circumstances would she have tolerated Calton using Kwéyòl in replying to me.

references

Althusser, Louis (2003 [1966–67]). *The Humanist Controversy, and Other Writings*. London: Verso.

Baquedano-López, Patricia (2001). Creating social identities through *doctrina* narratives. In Alessandro Duranti (ed.), *Linguistic Anthropology: A Reader*, pp. 343–58. Oxford: Blackwell.

Constantinidou, Evi (1994). The 'death' of East Sutherland Gaelic: Death by women? In Pauline Burton, Ketaki Kushari Dyson and Shirley Ardener (eds), *Bilingual Women: Anthropological Approaches to Second Language Use*, pp. 111–27. Oxford: Berg Publishers.

Döpke, Susanne (ed.) (2000). *Cross-Linguistic Structures in Simultaneous Bilingualism*. Amsterdam: John Benjamins Publishing Company.

Dunn, Cynthia D. (1999). Coming of age in Japan: Language ideology and the acquisition of formal speech registers. In Jef Verschueren (ed.), *Language and Ideology: Selected Papers from the Sixth International Pragmatics Conference*, vol. 1, pp. 89–97. Antwerp: International Pragmatics Association.

Errington, J. Joseph (1998). *Shifting Languages: Interaction and Identity in Javanese Indonesia*. Cambridge: Cambridge University Press.

Fader, Ayala (2001). Literacy, bilingualism, and gender in a Hasidic community. *Linguistics and Education* 12(3): 261–83.

Farris, Catherine (1991). The gender of child discourse: Same-sex peer socialization through language use in a Taiwanese preschool. *Journal of Linguistic Anthropology* 1(2): 198–224.

Foucault, Michel (1970 [1966]). *The Order of Things: An Archaeology of the Human Sciences*. New York: Pantheon.

—— (1988). Technologies of the self. In Luther H. Martin, Huck Gutman and Patrick H. Hutton (eds), *Technologies of the Self: A Seminar with Michel Foucault*, pp. 16–49. Amherst: University of Massachusetts Press.

Gal, Susan (1979). *Language Shift: Social Determinants of Linguistic Change in Bilingual Austria*. New York: Academic Press.

Garrett, Paul B. (2000). 'High' Kwéyòl: The emergence of a formal creole register in St. Lucia. In John H. McWhorter (ed.), *Language Change and Language Contact in Pidgins and Creoles*, pp. 63–101. Amsterdam: John Benjamins Publishing Company.

—— (2003). An 'English Creole' that isn't: On the sociohistorical origins and linguistic classification of the vernacular English of St. Lucia. In Michael Aceto and Jeffrey Williams (eds), *Contact Englishes of the Eastern Caribbean*, pp. 155–210. Amsterdam: John Benjamins Publishing Company.

—— (2004). Language contact and contact languages. In Alessandro Duranti (ed.), *A Companion to Linguistic Anthropology*, pp. 46–72. Oxford: Blackwell.

—— (2005). What a language is good for: Language socialization, language shift, and the persistence of code-specific genres in St. Lucia. *Language in Society* 34(3): 327–61.

—— (2007). 'Say it like you see it': Radio broadcasting and the mass mediation of creole nationhood in St. Lucia. In *Identities: Global Studies in Culture and Power* 14(1): 135–60.

Garrett, Paul B., and Patricia Baquedano-López (2002). Language socialization: Reproduction and continuity, transformation and change. *Annual Review of Anthropology* 31: 339–61.

Goffman, Erving (1981). *Forms of Talk*. Philadelphia: University of Pennsylvania Press.

Heath, Shirley Brice (1983). *Ways with Words: Language, Life, and Work in Communities and Classrooms*. New York: Cambridge University Press.

Heller, Monica (1994). *Crosswords: Language, Education and Ethnicity in French Ontario*. Berlin: Mouton de Gruyter.

Hill, Jane H., and Kenneth C. Hill (1986). *Speaking Mexicano: Dynamics of Syncretic Language in Central Mexico*. Tucson: University of Arizona Press.

Hymes, Dell (1972). On communicative competence. In John B. Pride and Janet Holmes (eds), *Sociolinguistics: Selected Readings*, pp. 269–85. Harmondsworth: Penguin.

Irvine, Judith T., and Susan Gal (2000). Language ideology and linguistic differentiation. In Paul V. Kroskrity (ed.), *Regimes of Language: Ideologies, Polities, and Identities*, pp. 35–83. Santa Fe: School of American Research Press.

Kramsch, Claire (ed.) (2002). *Language Acquisition and Language Socialization: Ecological Perspectives*. New York: Continuum.

Kulick, Don (1992). *Language Shift and Cultural Reproduction: Socialization, Self, and Syncretism in a Papua New Guinean Village*. Cambridge: Cambridge University Press.

Kulick, Don, and Bambi B. Schieffelin (2004). Language socialization. In Alessandro Duranti (ed.), *A Companion to Linguistic Anthropology*, pp. 349–68. Oxford: Blackwell.

Lacan, Jacques (1968 [1956]). *The Language of the Self: The Function of Language in Psychoanalysis*. Baltimore: Johns Hopkins University Press.

Le Page, Robert B., and Andrée Tabouret-Keller (1985). *Acts of Identity: Creole-Based Approaches to Language and Ethnicity*. Cambridge: Cambridge University Press.

McMahill, Cheiron (1997). Communities of resistance: A case study of two feminist English classes in Japan. *TESOL Quarterly* 31(3): 612–22.

Mead, George Herbert (1995 [1936]). The problem of society: How we become selves. In Ben G. Blount (ed.), *Language, Culture, and Society: A Book of Readings*, pp. 85–94. Prospect Heights, IL: Waveland Press.

Ochs, Elinor (1990). Indexicality and socialization. In James W. Stigler, Richard A. Shweder and Gilbert Herdt (eds), *Cultural Psychology: Essays on Comparative Human Development*, pp. 287–308. Cambridge: Cambridge University Press.

—— (1993). Constructing social identity: A language socialization perspective. *Research on Language and Social Interaction* 26(3): 287–306.

Ochs, Elinor, and Bambi B. Schieffelin (1984). Language acquisition and socialization: Three developmental stories and their implications. In Richard A. Shweder and Robert A. LeVine (eds), *Culture Theory: Essays in Mind, Self and Emotion*, pp. 276–320. Cambridge: Cambridge University Press.

—— (1995). The impact of language socialization on grammatical development. In Paul Fletcher and Brian MacWhinney (eds), *The Handbook of Child Language*, pp. 73–94. Cambridge, MA: Basil Blackwell.

Paugh, Amy (2005). Multilingual play: Children's codeswitching, role play, and agency in Dominica, West Indies. *Language in Society* 34(1): 63–86.

Pavlenko, Aneta (2001). Bilingualism, gender, and ideology. *International Journal of Bilingualism* 5(2): 117–51.

Rampton, Ben (1995a). Language crossing and the problematisation of ethnicity and socialisation. *Pragmatics* 5(4): 485–513.

—— (1995b). *Crossing: Language and Ethnicity among Adolescents*. London: Longman.

Schieffelin, Bambi B. (1990). *The Give and Take of Everyday Life: Language Socialization of Kaluli Children*. Cambridge: Cambridge University Press.

—— (1994). Code-switching and language socialization: Some probable relationships. In Judith Felson Duchan, Lynne E. Hewitt and Rae M. Sonnenmeier (eds), *Pragmatics: From Theory to Practice*, pp. 20–42. Englewood Cliffs, NJ: Prentice Hall.

Schieffelin, Bambi B., and Elinor Ochs (1986a). Language socialization. *Annual Review of Anthropology* 15: 163–91.

—— (eds.) (1986b). *Language Socialization Across Cultures*. Cambridge: Cambridge University Press.

—— (1996). The microgenesis of competence: Methodology in language socialization. In Dan I. Slobin, Julie Gerhardt, Amy Kyratzis and Jiansheng Guo (eds), *Social Interaction, Social Context, and Language: Essays in Honor of Susan Ervin-Tripp*, pp. 251–64. Mahwah, NJ: Lawrence Erlbaum Associates.

Schieffelin, Bambi B., Kathryn A. Woolard and Paul V. Kroskrity (eds) (1998). *Language Ideologies: Practice and Theory*. Oxford: Oxford University Press.

Siegal, Meryl (1996). The role of learner subjectivity in second language sociolinguistic competency: Western women learning Japanese. *Applied Linguistics* 17(3): 356–82.

Tsitsipis, Lukas D. (1998). *A Linguistic Anthropology of Praxis and Language Shift: Arvanítika (Albanian) and Greek in Contact*. Oxford: Clarendon Press.

Urciuoli, Bonnie (1995). Language and borders. *Annual Review of Anthropology* 24: 525–46.

—— (1996). *Exposing Prejudice: Puerto Rican Experiences of Language, Race, and Class*. Boulder, CO: Westview Press.

Woolard, Kathryn A., and Bambi B. Schieffelin (1994). Language ideology. *Annual Review of Anthropology* 23: 55–82.

12

heteroglossia and boundaries

benjamin bailey

processes of linguistic and social distinction

Language is the primary semiotic tool for representing and negotiating social reality, and it is thus at the centre of social and political life. Among its myriad social and political functions is to position speakers relative to a wide variety of phenomena including co-present interlocutors, the activities in which speakers are engaged, and various dimensions of the wider world, including social identity categories and their relative value. To speak is thus to position oneself in the social world, i.e. to engage in identity practices (cf. Le Page and Tabouret-Keller 1985).

All language provides linguistic and discursive forms rich in social connotations for the negotiation of identity. Monolingual individuals exploit various registers, accents, sociolects, word choices, etc. for the omnipresent tasks of positioning themselves and others within social categories and the larger social world. Members of bilingual communities typically have an expanded set of linguistic resources for these ongoing social negotiations and often a broader range of relevant social categories to enact or contest. On the linguistic level, they can draw forms from two languages as well as hybrid forms resulting from language contact. On the social and cultural level, many straddle social and cultural boundaries and are familiar with relatively diverse cultural frameworks for interpreting and evaluating the world and positioning themselves and others within it.

In this chapter, I use the notion of heteroglossia (Bakhtin 1981) as a conceptual entrée to social meanings of bilingual speech[1] and related identity negotiations. Heteroglossia addresses (a) the simultaneous use of different kinds of forms or signs, and (b) the tensions and conflicts among those signs, based on the sociohistorical associations they carry with them (cf. Ivanov 2001). The first part of this definition of heteroglossia subsumes formal definitions of bilingualism (as the coexistence of two linguistic systems) or code-switching (as the alternation of codes within a single speech exchange) (Gumperz 1982;

Heller 1988). While heteroglossia denotes the use of different kinds of forms or signs, the term does not refer, particularly, to the 'distinct languages' that are commonly seen as constituting bilingualism. To the contrary, Bakhtin coined the Russian term *raznorechie* to refer to intra-language varieties within Russian, varieties with competing social and political implications, and the term is sometimes translated as 'the social diversity of speech types' rather than 'heteroglossia'. The fact that heteroglossia encompasses both mono- and multilingual forms allows a level of theorizing about the social nature of language that is not possible within the confines of a focus on code-switching.

While code-switching research commonly treats the distinctiveness of codes as a given, from a phenomenological perspective, languages or codes can only be understood as distinct objects to the extent to which they are treated as such by social actors. From the socially-infused perspective of heteroglossia, judgements about what counts as 'different kinds of forms or signs' are based on the way social actors appear to distinguish among forms, rather than analysts' *a priori* claims.

The second part of the definition of heteroglossia captures the inherent political and sociohistorical associations of any linguistic form, i.e. its indexical meanings (Peirce 1955), or social connotations. These indexical meanings, or historical voices, are not explicit or static, but rather must be interpreted on the basis of constellations of forms in particular interactional and sociohistorical contexts. Such meanings are thus shifting, subjective and negotiated.

I approach identity in similarly processual terms. Following Barth's (1969) seminal work on ethnic groups, I approach identity as constituted through the *boundaries* that groups construct between themselves, rather than the characteristics of group members. The term 'identity' comes from Latin, *idem*, meaning 'the same', and identities are constituted by socially counting as 'the same' as others or counting as 'different' from others. This formulation foregrounds the subjective, social reality of individual actors, in that it is their judgements and activities, rather than static characteristics of individuals, that serve to constitute categories. Social identity is a function of two subjective processes: 'self-ascription' – how one defines oneself – and 'ascription by others' – how others define one (Barth 1969: 13). These processes of ascription are not based on the objective sums of differences or similarities among groups: 'some cultural features are used by the actors as signals and emblems of differences, others are ignored, and in some relationships radical differences are played down and denied' (ibid: 14). All individuals have multiple characteristics and allegiances, so it is the situational and selective highlighting of commonalties and differences that is characteristic of identity groupings (Moerman 1965). Analysis of identity thus revolves around the questions of how, when and why individuals count as members of particular groups.

The same semiotics of distinction involved in social boundary work can be applied to ways of speaking (cf. Irvine 2001 on 'style'). Ways of speaking are constituted as distinct through contrast, rather than through any inherent characteristics, just as identities are constituted through boundary marking processes (or lack thereof). As is the case with identity categories, what counts as a socially meaningful opposition among linguistic forms is subjective, shifting, and ideologically infused. To a linguist whose perspective privileges formal categories, for example, any bilingual speech may be highly salient because of the alternation of two codes, thus constituting a distinctive style. To the monolingual majorities in the US and most of Western Europe, mono-lingualism is an emblem of citizenship and belonging, and any language alternation is an exercise in distinctiveness. To a bilingual child of international migrants, however, code-switching in intragroup peer interaction may not commonly be perceived by members as very distinct from speaking to such peers without alternation.

These subjective processes of differentiation are linked to power, and in relatively stable social and linguistic situations, the social and linguistic categories favoured by dominant groups come to be seen as natural through processes of hegemony or symbolic domination (Bourdieu 1991; Heller 1995). In the United States, for example, White, English monolinguals are the dominant group, both economically and politically. This economic and political power is extended, via symbolic domination, to broader standards for social evaluation. Even though the majority of historical immigrants to the US have not been English-speaking, and even though the country is increasingly Latino and non-White, being a monolingual Anglophone, speaking a variety of Standard English, and being White constitute one as an unmarked American. Highly naturalized categories of race, language and national identity thus merge in the popular mind into an essentialized unity.

Social change, through migration, can serve to denaturalize and problematize boundaries and essentialized unities. Bilingual children of international labour migrants, for example, problematize boundaries through straddling linguistic and social worlds in their language and identity practices (Auer 1984; Poplack 1988; Gal 1988; Zentella 1997; Bailey 2002). Similarly, in urban, postcolonial contexts in Africa, migration has blurred traditional social boundaries and associations of particular identities with particular ways of speaking (Myers-Scotton 1993). Code-switching in such contexts is often frequent, intra-sentential, and unmarked in intragroup peer interactions, serving as a form of unmarked, discourse contextualization or serving no identifiable function at all. By failing to treat two or more languages as a meaningful opposition in certain contexts, such social actors effectively erase the boundary that constitutes the two languages as distinct. This calls into question the very foundation of bilingualism as a rubric or perspective for socially-oriented research on language.

Children of immigrants also undermine naturalized language–race–nation unities by (a) asserting or enacting identities that cross-cut received categories in ways that expose and controvert the assumptions on which the categories are based, and (b) bringing with them social classification systems that were dominant in the countries of origin but that contradict host country categories (Bailey 2001). In the United States, for example, the categories Black and White have been a central organizing principle of society for centuries, but many post-1965 immigrants from Latin America and Asia do not fit neatly into these categories. Latinos from the Caribbean, in particular, bridge the categories Black and White in ways that undermine the popular American notion of Black and White as representing unbridgeable distance. Such immigrants not only bridge such categories in terms of phenotype, they also maintain understandings of themselves as essentially Latino or Spanish, thereby countering the primacy of phenotype-symbolized race in US social classification. This problematizing of essentialized boundaries can occur in any situation in which the macro-social categories in countries of origin, the result of specific histories of social relationships, do not match those in destination countries (Mittelberg and Waters 1992).

In this chapter, I first contrast popular and formal linguistic approaches to language with more heteroglossic, social ones to contextualize the historical privileging and constitution of code-switching as a discrete object of study. I then briefly review research on code-switching in order to introduce the type of code-switching – code-switching as a discourse mode (Poplack 1980) – that particularly problematizes assumptions of difference in bilingual talk. A short segment of bilingual speech from Dominican American peer group interaction is presented to highlight the utility of the notion of heteroglossia relative to a narrower focus on code-switching, in analysing identity negotiations in talk. Finally, I argue that code-switching and bilingualism might best be approached as social constructions, as is common with identity categories. The social constructionist perspective affords analytical insights while recognizing the power of the on-the-ground hegemonic social reality that bilingual speakers face in societies with monolingual language ideologies.

popular and linguistic approaches to language

Among the intertwined reasons for the distinctive salience of bilingualism in Western societies are a) the naturalization of monolingualism in the ongoing nation-building projects begun in Europe during the last several centuries, and b) the referentialist nature of modern, Western language ideologies, both popular and academic. As the historical development of language-nation ideologies is explicitly discussed in Part One of this volume, I briefly review contemporary popular language ideologies and epistemology in formal linguistics.

Language is popularly understood as denotation, in which words stand for, or represent, things or ideas. The function of language is seen as the communication of propositional information, as in a conduit metaphor (Reddy 1979), and the maximally efficient transfer of such information is seen as 'good communication'. This folk theory of language, communication and efficiency is intertwined with living in capitalist, industrialized, bureaucratized, widely literate societies, which privilege certain types of productivity and efficiency. Social functioning of language is seen as epiphenomenal in this folk model, except when social variation is perceived as impairing the efficient transmission of propositional information.

This folk understanding is layered with hegemonic ideologies that privilege language varieties that are associated with powerful and privileged groups in society. These varieties are seen as being 'accentless' and 'correct', and ideal for 'good', i.e. propositionally efficient, communication. Divergences from this ideal standard – whether associated with class, ethnicity/race, or region – are considered marked and less desirable. In the United States, for example, varieties of English that are associated with written language and the speech of educated, middle- and upper-class White Americans in the Midwest (Lippi-Green 1997; Silverstein 1996) are identified as normal and desirable, even by speakers whose speech does not approach these varieties.

Formal linguistics also treats the social and political functioning of language as marginal, approaching language as a semiotic system in and of itself. The primary interest is in relationships among elements of this system, abstracted from any actual uses or instances of language. The boundaries of the system are implicitly taken to be the boundaries of the language, an idealization that is not necessarily compared to actual speech, which may or may not be bilingual (see Auer, this volume). Linguists generally focus on meanings that remain stable across time, speakers and contexts – i.e. denotational meanings – and pay relatively little attention to actual use of language, i.e. social action. In taking a formal, synchronic approach to language, formal linguists thus neglect relationships between linguistic forms and the social and political worlds that are described and negotiated through those forms.

Both folk and formal linguistic models of language may reflect more general cognitive predispositions. Silverstein (2001), for example, has shown that awareness of pragmatic function of language is closely tied to the degree to which forms are referential, segmentable and context-reflecting. Thus, people can articulate form-meaning relationships relatively well when the relationship is referential; when the forms are segmentable (as are morphemes) rather than scalar (as is pitch); and when the forms refer to some pre-existing phenomenon or situation rather than establishing it through the act of speaking. The popular notion of language as a system of discrete (segmentable) symbols for describing (referentially and context-reflecting) a pre-existing world, as well as the linguistic emphasis on form, may be partly a result of the fact that some dimensions of language are simply more accessible to conscious awareness than others.

From both a popular perspective of language-as-denotation and a linguistic perspective of language-as-synchronic-system, code-switching represents an aberration. From the linguistic point of view, it involves the overlapping of two systems that are *a priori* conceptualized as distinct and discrete. From a popular view, it appears redundant and irrational. If language is an instrumental vehicle of propositional information, then why use more than one language, unless a linguistic deficiency prevents one from making utterances entirely in one language (Woolard 2004: 75; Meeuwis and Blommaert 1998: 78)?[2] Code-switched speech also diverges radically from the ideological ideal way of speaking, which is monolingual and shows no effects of language contact such as phonological effects of other languages (i.e. 'foreign accent').

The popular and linguistic perspectives that monolingual speech is normal and natural subtly inform code-switching research even in more socially and politically oriented disciplines such as anthropology. Researchers in linguistic anthropology and related disciplines regularly attend to bilingual speech in ways that they do not necessarily attend to monolingual speech. The driving question of much anthropological code-switching research, 'Why do they do that?' is not put with equal force to the myriad other things speakers do in talk that are not bilingual. By casting bilingual speech as a marked form that calls for explanation of a type that monolingual speech does not, such research implicitly reproduces the folk and linguistic beliefs of monolingual speech as the natural form (Woolard 2004: 75).

heteroglossic and anthropological approaches to language

In contrast to formal and folk-models of language, heteroglossia takes as its starting point the social and pragmatic functioning of language: '...verbal discourse is a social phenomenon – social through its entire range and in each and every of its factors, from the sound image to the furthest reaches of abstract meaning' (Bakhtin 1981: 259). The notion of heteroglossia is thus congruous with traditions in anthropology of approaching language as essentially social, e.g. 'the main function of language is not to express thought, not to duplicate mental processes, but rather to play an active pragmatic part in human behaviour' (Malinowski 1965: v2: 7). This orientation does not deny the referential, or denotational, function of language, but conceptualizes reference as merely one pragmatic function among many in a system that is intrinsically pragmatic (Silverstein 1976: 20).

The Bakhtinian notion of heteroglossia overlaps in significant ways with the semiotic and linguistic anthropological notion of non-referential indexicality as developed by Peirce (1955) and Silverstein (1976). Both are types of inter-textuality, in which meanings of forms depend on past usages and associations of those forms rather than the arbitrary referential meaning carried by the form. From these perspectives, language is never a neutral instrument of pure reference, as actual speech always occurs in a social context, which is never neutral or ahistorical. Talk and texts thus need to be understood in terms of past and ongoing social and political negotiations of which they are a part, not as forms in isolation:

> The living utterances...cannot fail to brush up against thousands of living dialogic threats, woven by socio-ideological consciousness around the given object of an utterance; it cannot fail to become an active participant in social dialogue. After all, the utterances arises out of this dialogue as a continuation of it and as a rejoinder to it – it does not approach the object from the sidelines. (Bakhtin 1981: 276–7)

Non-referential indexical meanings are linked to history just as Bakhtinian voices are. Such indexical form–meaning relationships arise from historical usages by speakers in particular social positions. It is through recurrent connections between a social phenomenon or context and a linguistic form that non-referential indexical meanings are constituted to begin with (Peirce 1955). Particular phonetic patterns index a speaker's regional origins, for example, only through associations with actual speakers and their talk.

The emphasis on the inherent political dimension of all talk separates the Bakhtinian notion of heteroglossia from many sociolinguistic approaches to language variation, in which correlations between forms and categories of speakers is the focus, rather than the sociohistorical connotations or voices of the forms. In US correlational sociolinguistics (cf., e.g. Rickford and Eckert 2001), social categories have been treated as given, i.e. pre-existing any interaction, and the agency of individuals and the role of ideology in language use has been downplayed, or even denied (cf., e.g. Labov 1979: 328). Emphasizing the political and historical dimensions of language also stands in stark contrast to formal linguistics, of course, which takes a synchronic approach to language and meaning.

While indexicality and Bakhtinian heteroglossia encourage social and political readings of language and interaction, they are very difficult to operationalize. Indexicality, for example, has been described in relatively concise theoretical terms, but it encompasses a very large range of phenomena. Non-referential indexical forms are highly varied, ranging from phonetic features, to word choice, to visual features, to other stylistic dimensions of talk. The nature of indexical objects and the spatial and temporal distance between the indexical form and its object can also vary greatly (Silverstein 1992). While the scope of this semiotic dimension of talk makes it an attractive area for theorizing, it is difficult to make such theory operational because of the social, contextual and individual specificity of form–meaning relationships in the indexical mode (Hanks 2001: 120).

code-switching research: from degeneracy, to metaphorical strategy, to local discourse contextualization, to no identifiable function

Research on social functions and meanings of code-switching since the 1950s has repeatedly shifted in emphasis. Many language analysts through the 1960s, including those focusing on bilingualism (e.g. Weinreich 1953: 73) treated (intra-sentential) code-switching as linguistic interference, with connotations of linguistic, social or cognitive deficit. This orientation simply mirrors the dominant Western language ideology of monolingual speech as normal and code-switching as a mixed-up jumble that reflects speakers' inability to speak properly.

Starting in the early 1970s, John Gumperz (Blom and Gumperz 1972; Gumperz 1982) led research that countered this orientation, presenting code-switching as a form of skilled performance through which individual social actors could communicate various social and pragmatic meanings. Rather than representing a linguistic deficit or degeneration, code-switching was presented as complex, systematic and socially strategic behaviour.

Gumperz's (Blom and Gumperz 1972) early formulation focused on two functions of switches. *Situational* switches were made in response to changing situations, e.g. the need to accommodate to co-present speakers in one language or another. *Metaphorical* switches were more socially indexical. By partially violating an expected situation-code correlation, some aspect of meaning (parallel to a Bakhtinian voice) associated with the switched-into language is brought into the conversation. In such metaphorical switching, then, changes in language *effect* changes in context and social roles, without apparent prior changes in the physical or outward context.

At one level this formulation tends toward an essentialized linking of language, identity and sociocultural worlds. It is only when there are relatively conventionalized associations between language and social meanings that switches generate metaphorical meanings. Empirical research has shown that such metaphorical meanings are most often generated in situations where codes are relatively compartmentalized (e.g. Kroskrity 1993) or politically charged (e.g. Heller 1992) and have strong 'we' vs. 'they' associations (see also Maehlum 1996 for a critique of Blom and Gumperz's original work). More generally, empirical work shows that analysts' ideologies of languages as discrete systems are only sometimes consonant with the ideologies to which speakers appear to orient when talking. The empirical variation in ideologies to which speakers demonstrably orient illustrates the shortcomings of privileging the formal category of code-switching. A more socially oriented perspective, such as heteroglossia, can better account for this variation across social and historical contexts.

Beginning in the early 1980s, many researchers began documenting code-switching that was not done in response to changes in situation and did not generate metaphorical meanings. Auer (1984, 1988, 1995, 1998) pioneered an influential and ongoing tradition of work that linked such socially unmarked code-switching to the omnipresent local exigencies of coordinating interaction. In this conversational management, or discourse contextualizing, mode, switches do not necessarily co-occur with external changes in the context (situational switches) or effect significant shifts in sociocultural framework (metaphorical switches). Individual switches instead serve local contextualization functions. In such unmarked discourse contextualization switching, conventionalized associations between particular codes and social worlds are at least partially suspended by participants (although not necessarily by co-present overhearers). Shifts in codes function as signals that there is a concurrent shift in speech activity – e.g. to a repair sequence or to a rhetorical question – but not necessarily in sociocultural framework. The act of alternation itself, rather than the direction of the shift, is the important dimension for discourse contextualization. This use of code-switching as a tool for local discourse management has been documented by numerous researchers, often with disparate labels. Zentella (1997) refers to such switching in terms of 'conversational strategies', 'in the head communicational factors', and, following Goffman (1979), 'footing'. Myers-Scotton (1993) calls this 'code switching as the unmarked choice', and Gumperz (1982) subsumes it under a larger category of 'conversational code switching'.

In these contexts of unmarked code-switching among peers, it is not always possible to ascribe *any* function to a particular switch. In a corpus of 1,685 switches among young New York Puerto Rican girls, for example, Zentella (1997: 101) assigns fewer than half of the switches to specific conversational strategies, or functions, because most of the individual switches do not have a clear, analytically defensible function and do not co-occur with particular interactional patterns. Similarly, Meeuwis and Blommaert (1998: 76) find that multilingual talk among Zairians in Belgium can represent 'one code in its own right', and that the insistence on two distinct languages as the frame of reference for this form of speech is not helpful in terms of interpreting it. Such work fundamentally challenges the taken-for-granted distinctiveness of the languages used in code-switching and the taken-for-granted distinctiveness of code-switching as a communicative phenomenon.

Key to such research have been methods and epistemologies associated with conversation analysis and with anthropology. Conversation analysis, which shaped Auer's seminal work, insists on empirical, electronically recorded data. This insistence, in conjunction with the availability of portable electronic recording devices by the late 1970s, is one reason for the increased documentation of unmarked, frequent and intrasentential code-switching. This type of code-switching is most common in informal, intragroup peer interaction, and portable recording devices allowed taping in the natural settings where this type of talk spontaneously occurs. Recordings – and resultant transcripts – made such switching patterns impossible to ignore.

Conversation analysis methods also limit the effects of individual subjectivity and assumptions by prescribing very narrow bases for explanation and argumentation: the analyst can invoke only those social constellations that interlocutors themselves demonstrably treat as meaningful in the interaction. While this can lead to austere analyses that are limited in scope to formal structures of conversation, the rigour of the method has encouraged more defensible claims about social meanings within code-switching research.

Interlocutors publicly display, and continuously update for each other, their ongoing understandings of talk. Implied in each turn is an understanding, or uptake, of the prior turn. Thus, the turn 'Fine' in response to the turn, 'How are you?' displays a particular understanding of that prior turn. Because interlocutors must make these negotiations visible to each other to achieve a degree of intersubjectivity, analysts can 'look over their shoulders' to gain a window onto the understandings that interlocutors themselves display of these processes (cf. Heritage and Atkinson 1984: 11). If individuals do not treat code switches in their interlocutors' prior turns as socially loaded, metaphorical actions, the analyst has no empirical basis for arguing that such switches encode significant metaphorical meanings, even though the analyst may *a priori* assume that they do.

A parallel methodological orientation in anthropology also contributes to efforts to see past popular and formal linguistic ideologies. The fieldworker consciously works to bracket cultural assumptions and understand subjects' worlds through members' categories, i.e., from an emic or native's point of view. The active suspension of commonsense assumptions helps one to partially overcome the omnipresent social science problem of subjectivity, e.g., to see meanings of code-switching as a code-switching subject might see them.

heteroglossia and identity in a bilingual segment of talk

To illustrate heteroglossia and its application to issues of identity, I present a segment of transcript below that documents a few moments of bilingual talk between two Dominican American high school students in an everyday interaction during a break at school. The two students, Janelle and Isabella, define themselves, and are defined by others, in multiple ways. Janelle was US-born and raised, and therefore a citizen, and had been to the Dominican Republic only once, as a baby. She identified herself as Spanish or Dominican, but outsiders frequently took her to be Black American until they heard her speaking Spanish. Isabella, who came to the United States at age 7, identified herself as Dominican or Spanish, and was occasionally seen by outsiders as Black American or Cape Verdean American.

The socially based construct of heteroglossia has several advantages over the narrower and formally defined construct of code-switching as a means to understanding social identity negotiations in this talk. Specifically, (a) heteroglossia can encompass socially meaningful forms in both bilingual and monolingual talk; (b) it can account for the multiple meanings and readings of forms that are possible, depending on one's subject position; and (c) it can connect historical power hierarchies to the meanings and valences of particular forms in the here-and-now.

[JS #2 12:26:40] Isabella (came to the US around age 7) and Janelle (US-born) are sitting on steps outside of the main school building at the end of their lunch period. Isabella has returned from eating lunch at a diner near the school, and she has been describing the turkey club sandwich and cheeseburger she had just eaten.]

Janelle:	Only with that turkey thingee //*ya yo estoy llena.* ['I'm already full']
Isabella:	//Two dollars and fifty cent.
Janelle:	That's good. That's like a meal at //Burger King.
Isabella	//That's better than going to Burger King, you know what I'm saying? And you got a Whopper, french fries, and a drink. And the french fries cost a dollar over there.
Janelle:	For real?
Isabella:	*Sí, sí cómo no?* ['Yes, really.']
Janelle:	*Mírale el ombligo. Míralo. Se le ve, ya se lo tapó.* ((looking at a passerby)) ['Look at her belly button. Look. You can see it, she already covered it.']
	(.5)
Isabella:	*Seguro porque se lo enseñó.* ['She must have showed it.'] ((laughing))
	(1.5)
Isabella:	But it's slamming, though, oh my God, mad ['a lot of'] turkey she puts in there.
Janelle:	That's one thing I l-, I love the way *como l-* ['how th-'] the American be doing sandwich, they be rocking ['are excellent'], them things, yo, they put everything up in there, yo.
Isabella:	De pla:ne, de pla:ne. ((an airplane passes overhead))

The notion of code-switching is less useful in analysing this interaction than the broader and socially-infused concept of heteroglossia. Janelle and Isabella code switch into Spanish several times in this segment, but none of the switches generates any obvious metaphorical meanings. One switch into Spanish – *Mírale el ombligo...* – functions to hide the meanings of their talk from a non-Spanish-speaker passerby about whom they are talking, but it is not obvious what social functions, if any, are served by the other switches.

While such switches are locally unmarked, the concept of heteroglossia affords attention to meanings in a larger sociopolitical field. Janelle and Isabella's switches are *locally* unmarked in terms of identity negotiations, but frequent switching as a discourse mode is always socially marked in a wider US society in which being a monolingual English speaker is an ideological default against which difference or distinctiveness is constructed (Urciuoli 1996). The perspective of heteroglossia allows one to distinguish between *local* functions of particular code switches and the functions in the larger socio-political field of identity formation in ways that a more formal perspective of code-switching does not (cf. Myers-Scotton 1993: 149; Zentella 1997: 101).

Meanings of code-switching are contested in this larger sociopolitical field. Various nativist English-only groups, for example, have sponsored legislation to criminalize the use of languages other than English in many contexts, including school, government and workplace. They portray such language alternation as undermining American unity, citizenship and decency. Many academics of the last 25 years, in contrast, have treated such code-switching as a discourse mode which can be seen as a form of resistance to dominant discourses of unquestioning assimilation (Gal 1988: 259), or as a means of constructing a positive self in a political and economic context that disparages immigrant phenotypes, language, class status and ethnic origins (Zentella 1997: 13). The ways in which these meanings vary depending on one's subject position – speaker, nativist American, or socially oriented language analyst – illustrate the subjective and social construction of heteroglossic meanings that is characteristic of talk more generally.

The focus in code-switching research on constellations of linguistic features that are officially authorized as codes or languages, e.g. 'English' or 'Spanish', can contribute to neglect of the diversity of socially indexical linguistic resources within codes. The English that Isabella and Janelle use in the exchange above, for example, includes prescriptivist standard American English forms, non-standard vernacular forms, lexical forms associated with African American English, and grammatical forms that occur only in African American English. Their talk also includes an explicitly intertextual reference to popular culture: Isabella's *De pla:ne, de pla:ne* as she observes a plane passing overhead. This utterance represents an example of Bakhtinian double-voicing, in which words are spoken as if they are to be understood as being in quotation marks. Her utterance is an intertextual reference to the words spoken by actor Herve Villechaize at the opening of each episode of the television show *Fantasy Island*, which premiered on US television in 1977. Villechaize spoke these words with strong second-language phonology as *de plane, de plane*, and the phrase entered the popular culture vocabulary of many Americans, who still use it to verbally mark the passing of airplanes overhead.

Their Spanish similarly indexes particular linguistic histories. Their pronunciation of word-initial *y* as an affricate /dʒ/ (e.g. in *ya yo*), and their elision of syllable final /s/ (e.g. in *e(s)toy*), for example, are characteristic of Caribbean Spanish, particularly Dominican and lower class varieties (Lipski 1994). Word order used by Isabella – *mad turkey she puts in there* – suggests the influence of Spanish discourse patterns on her English. She preposes the direct object of the verb in this segment in what has been called fronting, focal object construction (Silva-Corvalán 1983: 135), or focus-movement (Prince 1981). These heteroglossic forms in both English and Spanish – whether at the phonological, lexical, grammatical or discourse level – index social histories, circumstances and identities in ways that a binary perspective of code-switching commonly neglects.

A further strength of heteroglossia as a perspective is that it directs the analyst to historical social relations, rather than just details of surface form, to interpret language meanings. Each of the locally unmarked linguistic features enumerated above, for example, draws its meaning from contrast with an implicit field of alternate forms, the relative valences of which are a function of historical power relations. Code-switching and other language contact features are meaningful only in contrast to monolingual speech. Caribbean Spanish phonology is meaningful in contrast to Mexican, South American and peninsular varieties, particularly Castilian. African American English is meaningful in contrast to varieties associated with White Americans, and the youth vocabulary contrasts with the vocabulary of adult speakers.

In each case, the meaningful opposition is between an unmarked form associated with groups historically or currently in power (monolingual Americans; speakers of Castilian varieties of Spanish; White Americans; and adults) and marked forms that index lower positions in social hierarchies. Meaningful oppositions arise in this instance not on the basis of formal distance among forms, but on the basis of historical power differentials with which particular forms are associated. The perspective of heteroglossia explicitly bridges the linguistic and the sociohistorical, enriching analysis of human interaction.

The variety and juxtaposition of linguistic resources by Janelle and Isabella in the above exchange reflect their negotiations of social boundaries and meanings. Their alternation of English and Spanish and contact forms diminish a linguistic boundary that others have created. Their ongoing use of forms (e.g. code-switching, African American English, and Dominican phonology) that are disparaged by dominant groups suggests resistance to hegemonic belief systems regarding language. Maintenance of non-prestige forms can serve as a vehicle of resistance to disparaging discourses on language, race and identity from dominant groups in society and reproduce local solidarity. Their use of forms associated with urban African American youth, particularly Janelle's use of African American English syntax, suggests both longer-term contact with African Americans and identification with African American experiences. Janelle's use of the term 'American' to refer to a group that is implicitly distinct from her suggests (although she is US-born and a US citizen) that she identifies herself with reference to another nation-state or in terms of racial/ethnic categories in which she doesn't count as 'American'.[3] The juxtaposition of diverse linguistic elements in single utterances, e.g. *I love the way como I- the American be doing sandwich* reflects social negotiations and a social reality in which neither linguistic practices nor social identities fit into static, unitary categories of language and identity.

It is tempting to label Isabella and Janelle's identities and ways of speaking as 'hybrid', 'mixed' or 'syncretic', but I argue against the *analytical* use of such terms here because they so easily express and reproduce dominant ideologies of essentialism. The term 'hybridity' is only meaningful against a backdrop of essentialism that analysts generally claim to have rejected. While many postcolonial theorists use the term to refer to novel cultural forms with roots in seemingly disparate experiences, others struggle with the terms. Critics argue that 'hybridity', like popular folk-terms such as 'diversity', 'multicultural', 'heterogeneous' and 'pluralism', can all pay lip service to certain types of social difference, while implicitly reinforcing the political and economic boundaries that constitute those groups as different and unequal (Hutnyk 2005; Young 1995; Chow 1998).

In labelling a system as syncretic, an analyst highlights the discrete heritage of individual components of a system and suggests some incommensurability of those parts. Since all social systems are a function of multiple influences and histories, what counts as a relevant opposition within a system is a contested, subjective and shifting question. As with the term 'hybridity', 'syncretism' carries with it connotations of pure and coherent anterior systems. Beliefs or practices are most often termed syncretic when they violate Western analysts' implicit assumptions of purity and inherent discreteness.

In anthropology, for example, the term 'syncretic' has often been used to describe the religious practices of the Afro-Caribbean, as if European Catholicism and African religious beliefs and practices were each pure and fundamentally different. When Christianity includes pagan practices such as celebration of evergreen trees around the time of the Winter solstice, however, it is not seen as syncretic. Linguistically, English is not commonly seen as a hybrid, or creole language, despite the readily apparent effects of Norman French on the language(s) of Britain from the period following the Norman Conquest in 1066. Languages, or language change, that develop from European colonization of other parts of the world, in contrast, are typically seen as hybrid or creole, e.g. Jamaican creole or Haitian creole. Whether one counts two aspects of a system as discrete and not-entirely-compatible, and therefore syncretic, depends on one's subject position and historical power relations rather than the nature of the forms or systems in and of themselves. While analysts can use these terms as parts of projects that are not essentializing (e.g. Hill and Hill 1986), these words are intertextual, carrying with them connotations of usage in essentializing projects.

code-switching as a social construction

While the notion that identity categories such as race or ethnicity are socially constructed is now an academic commonplace, bilingualism, as both a popular and analytical category, is not generally seen as a social construction. There are fundamental parallels, however, in the social and political processes through which difference is constructed among social identity categories and among the linguistic forms that count as bilingual talk. Both, for example, are popularly seen as having self-evident, empirical bases, and both form parts of the highly naturalized assumption of a language–race–nation unity. In both cases, however, the conceptualizations, salience and social significance of the categories are a function of social and political processes rather than inherent, or essential characteristics of members of the categories. The fact that bilingual speech draws both popular and academic attention may tell us relatively little about the nature of code-switching, and relatively more about popular and academic language ideologies of Western nation-states.

Conceptualizing bilingual speech as a social construction does not minimize its on-the-ground social implications. An example from social identity categories can help make this clear: the fact that Black–White race in the United States is a social construction, for example, does not make race an illusion or socially insignificant (Omi and Winant 1994). Race has been, and remains, a central organizing principle in the United States and a way of representing, rationalizing and reproducing tremendous social inequality. Approaching race as a social construction, however, allows one to see that race is not about essential biological difference (which is how race is popularly construed) but about social history. What is socially significant about race is a distinctively violent history of coercion and inequality, not details of hair texture, skin shade or other morphological features. The social constructionist perspective directs attention to the political and historical processes through which race has been constituted and given such significance in the US.

Similarly, approaching monolingualism and bilingualism as socially constructed does not change their social force at the level of lived experience, but it does show that this social force is not a function of formal, or inherent linguistic differences among what count as languages. If bilingual talk is an especially meaningful mode of speaking, it is not the nature of the forms that make it so but rather particular social and political histories.

Studying bilingual talk can be a route to understanding social boundary work not because of the formal nature of bilingual talk, but because all talk is social and political. In contexts such as Western societies where code-switching has been made to count as particularly socially meaningful, insights into identity negotiations can come from attention to the social and political processes that have made monolingual-versus-bilingual speech a meaningful opposition. Analytical constructs that are based on form, such as code-switching, or that imply anterior, pure essences, such as hybridity, divert attention from the social and political nature of language, behaviour and meaning. More processual and socially-infused constructs such as heteroglossia and indexicality better direct attention to the irreducibly sociohistorical and ideological bases of language meanings and identity construction. Heteroglossia and indexicality are fundamentally about intertextuality, the ways that talk in the here-and-now draws meanings from past instances of talk. Such terms encourage us to interpret the meanings of talk in terms of the social worlds, past and present, of which words are part-and-parcel, rather than in terms of formal systems, such as codes, that can veil actual speakers, uses and contexts.

notes

1. In this chapter I use the terms 'bilingualism', 'bilingual speech' and 'code-switching' interchangeably. My interest in bilingualism here is only in its instantiation in speech, not as a state or capability.
2. This language ideology is also reflected in commonly expressed folk explanations for code-switching: 'they/we switch because they/we don't know the word in the other language'; 'they/we switch so that person X can understand better'; and 'they switched to hide what they were saying from person Y'.
3. In everyday Dominican American usage, the term 'American' (or *americano*) refers to 'White American' (cf. Urciuoli 1996 among New York Puerto Ricans). United States-born Dominican Americans such as Janelle identify themselves as 'American' in some contexts, e.g. in referring to citizenship or the passport they have, but they identify 'what they are' as Dominican/Spanish/Hispanic. These categories are mutually exclusive from the category White/American in local terms.

references

Auer, P. (1984). *Bilingual Conversation*. Philadelphia and Amsterdam: John Benjamins.
—— (1988). A conversation analytic approach to codeswitching and transfer. In M. Heller (ed.), *Codeswitching: Anthropological and Sociolinguistic Perspectives*, pp. 187–213. New York: Mouton de Gruyter.
—— (1995). The pragmatics of code-switching: A sequential approach. In L. Milroy and P. Muysken (ed.), *One Speaker, Two Languages: Cross-disciplinary Perspectives on Code-Switching*, pp. 115–35. Cambridge: Cambridge University Press.
—— (ed.) (1998). *Code-Switching in Conversation: Language, Interaction and Identity*. London and New York: Routledge.
Bailey, B. (2001). Dominican-American ethnic/racial identities and United States social categories. *International Migration Review* 35(3): 677–708.
—— (2002). *Language, Race, and Negotiation of Identity: A Study of Dominican Americans*. New York: LFB Scholarly Pub.
Bakhtin, M.M. (1981). *The Dialogic Imagination: Four Essays* (M. Holquist, trans.). Austin: University of Texas Press.
Barth, F. (1969). Introduction. In F. Barth (ed.), *Ethnic Groups and Boundaries: The Social Organization of Culture Difference*, pp. 9–38. Boston: Little Brown and Co.
Blom, J.P., and J.J. Gumperz (1972). Code-switching in Norway. In J. Gumperz and D. Hymes (ed.), *Directions in Sociolinguistics*, pp. 407–34. New York: Holt, Rinehart and Winston.

Bourdieu, P. (1991). *Language and Symbolic Power* (G. Raymond and M. Adamson, trans.). Cambridge, MA: Harvard University Press.

Chow, R. (1998). *Ethics After Idealism: Theory-Culture-Ethnicity-Reading*. Bloomington, IN: University of Indiana Press.

Gal, S. (1988). The political economy of code choice. In M. Heller (ed.), *Codeswitching: Anthropological and Sociolinguistic Perspectives*, pp. 245–64. Berlin, New York and Amsterdam: Mouton de Gruyter.

Goffman, E. (1979). Footing. *Semiotica* 25: 1–29.

Gumperz, J.J. (1982). *Discourse Strategies*. Cambridge and New York: Cambridge University Press.

Hanks, W. (2001). Indexicality. In A. Duranti (ed.), *Key Terms in Language and Culture*, pp. 119–21. Malden, MA and Oxford: Blackwell Publishers.

Heller, M. (1988). Introduction. In M. Heller (ed.), *Codeswitching: Anthropological and Sociolinguistic Perspectives*, pp. 1–24. New York: Mouton de Gruyter.

—— (1992). The politics of code-switching and language choice. In C. Eastman (ed.), *Codeswitching*, pp. 123–42. Cleveland and Avon: Multilingual Matters.

—— (1995). Language choice, social institutions, and symbolic domination. *Language in Society* 24(3): 373–406.

Heritage, J., and J.M. Atkinson (1984). Introduction. In J.M. Atkinson and J. Heritage (eds), *Structures of Social Action: Studies in Conversation Analysis*, pp. 1–15. Cambridge: University of Cambridge Press.

Hill, J.H., and K. Hill (1986). *Speaking Mexicano: Dynamics of Syncretic Language in Central Mexico*. Tucson: University of Arizona Press.

Hutnyk, J. (2005). Hybridity. *Ethnic and Racial Studies* 28(1): 79–102.

Irvine, J.T. (2001). 'Style' as distinctiveness: The culture and ideology of linguistic differentiation. In P. Eckert and J.R. Rickford (eds), *Style and Sociolinguistic Variation*, pp. 21–43. Cambridge and New York: Cambridge University Press.

Ivanov, V. (2001). Heteroglossia. In A. Duranti (ed.), *Key Terms in Language and Culture*, pp. 95–7. Oxford and Malden, MA: Blackwell Publishers.

Kroskrity, P.V. (1993). *Language, History, and Identity: Ethnolinguistic Studies of the Arizona Tewa*. Tucson: University of Arizona Press.

Labov, W. (1979). Locating the frontier between social and psychological factors in linguistic variation. In Wong (ed.), *Individual Differences in Language Ability and Language Behavior*, pp. 327–40. New York: Academic Press.

Le Page, R.B., and A. Tabouret-Keller (1985). *Acts of Identity: Creole-based Approaches to Language and Ethnicity*. Cambridge and New York: Cambridge University Press.

Lippi-Green, R. (1997). *English with an Accent: Language, Ideology, and Discrimination in the United States*. London and New York: Routledge.

Lipski, J.M. (1994). *Latin American Spanish*. London and New York: Longman.

Maehlum, B. (1996). Codeswitching in Hemnesberget – Myth or reality? *Journal of Pragmatics* 25(6): 749–61.

Malinowski, B. (1965). *Coral Gardens and their Magic*. Bloomington: Indiana University Press.

Meeuwis, M., and J. Blommaert (1998). A monolectal view of code-switching: Layered code-switching among Zairians in Belgium. In P. Auer (ed.), *Code-Switching in Conversation: Language, Interaction and Identity*, pp. 76–98. London and New York: Routledge.

Mittelberg, D., and M.C. Waters (1992). The process of ethnogenesis among Haitian and Israeli immigrants in the United States. *Ethnic and Racial Studies* 15(3): 412–35.

Moerman, M. (1965). Ethnic identification in a complex civilization. *American Anthropologist* 67: 1215–30.

Myers-Scotton, C. (1993). *Social Motivations for Codeswitching: Evidence from Africa.* Oxford: Clarendon Press.

Omi, M., and H. Winant (1994). *Racial Formation in the United States: From the 1960s to the 1990s* (2nd edn). New York: Routledge.

Peirce, C.S. (1955). Logic as semiotic: The theory of signs. In J. Buchler (ed.), *Philosophical Writings of Peirce*, pp. 98–119. New York: Dover Publications.

Poplack, S. (1980). Sometimes I'll start a sentence in Spanish y termino en Espanol – toward a typology of code-switching. *Linguistics* 18(7–8): 581–618.

—— (1988). Contrasting patterns of codeswitching in two communities. In M. Heller (ed.), *Codeswitching: Anthropological and Sociolinguistic Perspectives*, vol. 48, pp. 215–44. Berlin, New York and Amsterdam: Mouton de Gruyter.

Prince, E. (1981). Topicalization, focus-movement and Yiddish-movement: A pragmatic differentiation. *Proceedings of the Seventh Annual Meeting of the Berkeley Linguistics Society*, 249–64.

Reddy, M. (1979). The conduit metaphor: A case of frame conflict in our language about language. In A. Ortony (ed.), *Metaphor and Thought*, pp. 284–384. Cambridge: Cambridge University Press.

Rickford, J.R., and P. Eckert (2001). Introduction. In P. Eckert and J.R. Rickford (eds), *Style and Sociolinguistic Variation*, pp. 1–18. New York and Cambridge: Cambridge University Press.

Silva-Corvalán, C. (1983). On the interaction of word order and intonation: Some OV constructions in Spanish. In F. Klein-Andreu (ed.), *Discourse Perspectives on Syntax*, pp. 117–40. New York: Academic Press, Inc.

Silverstein, M. (1976). Shifters, linguistic categories, and cultural description. In K.H. Basso and H.A. Selby (eds), *Meaning in Anthropology*, pp. 11–56. Albuquerque: University of New Mexico Press.

—— (1992). The indeterminacy of contextualization: When is enough enough? In P. Auer and A. DiLuzio (eds), *The Contexualization of Language*, pp. 55–76. Amsterdam: John Benjamins.

—— (1996). Monoglot 'standard' in America. In D.L. Brenneis and R.K.S. Macaulay (eds), *The Matrix of Language: Contemporary Linguistic Anthropology*, pp. 284–306. Boulder, CO: Westview Press.

—— (2001). The limits of awareness. In A. Duranti (ed.), *Linguistic Anthropology: A Reader*, pp. 382–401. Malden, MA and Oxford: Blackwell Publishers.

Urciuoli, B. (1996). *Exposing Prejudice: Puerto Rican Experiences of Language, Race, and Class.* Boulder, CO: Westview Press.

Weinreich, U. (1953). *Language in Contact: Findings and Problems.* New York: The Linguistics Circle of New York.

Woolard, K.A. (2004). Codeswitching. In A. Duranti (ed.), *A Companion to Linguistic Anthropology*, pp. 73–94. Malden, MA: Blackwell.

Young, R. (1995). *Colonial Desire: Hybridity in Theory, Culture and Race.* London: Routledge.

Zentella, A.C. (1997). *Growing up Bilingual: Puerto Rican Children in New York.* Malden, MA: Blackwell.

part four
linguistic form and linguistic practice

13

bilingualism, praxis and linguistic description

lukas d. tsitsipis

All attitudes to language and linguistic change are fundamentally ideological, and the relationship between popular and expert ideologies, though it is complex and conflictual, is closer than one might think.

(Deborah Cameron, Verbal Hygiene, 1995:4)

introduction

I define bilingualism as a sociopolitical semiotic nexus of praxis cum ideology.[1] In this nexus a certain lexico-grammatical space is perceived as divided into two different coded varieties. By this definition, monolingualism is a sociopolitical semiotic nexus of praxis cum ideology that perceives no such division. In linguistic theory this basic definition has been transformed in such a manner as to allow research to erase the praxis cum ideology component. Thus, bilingual phenomena are targeted as a juxtaposition of coded varieties warranting a certain kind of description. I base my analysis on the assumption that a great deal of what enters into the study of linguistic problems is actually a kind of ideology supported by various institutional or community structures. In handling bilingual phenomena we face two broad lines of linguistic ideology: that of the structuralist tradition which traces its theoretical principles from Descartes through Saussure to modern rationalism-positivism, and the alternative (and actually oppositional) trend of praxis-focused research. Even though this scheme may strike the reader as too simplified, I argue that it grasps the principal points of relevance to an ongoing discourse on bilingualism. One main goal of this chapter is to explore various approaches to praxis in sociological theory, in order to see how linguistic description is portrayed in such theoretical schemes, and what such approaches buy us for comprehending bilingualism.

For some sociological models it can be argued that they do not address either linguistic or sociolinguistic issues directly. But they do so indirectly, and it would be wrong not to profit from the light they shed on linguistic praxis. Furthermore, I will avoid here very rigid definitions of praxis, emphasizing instead how the notion emerges in sociological and sociolinguistic theory. No single definition of praxis appears to have all the required advantages over other, competing definitions. It is therefore more prudent to discuss theories rather than definitions and see how they handle bilingual empirical data. However, as a basic and minimalist definition of praxis I would offer the following: praxis includes the active involvement of social agents in the production and reproduction of social structure as mediated by ideologies. And social structure so formed, in its turn, affects social agents. According to this view, agency and structure are in a constant dialectic. An adequate study therefore of social phenomena (among which language looms large) should focus on all such components.

An important thing to notice is that we are not dealing here with entirely new phenomena. Bilingual (and multilingual) communities have been immersed in praxis throughout their history. Speakers of various speech communities have constantly been faced with their own role as speaking-social agents, the fate of the languages of their repertoires, and the role of broader powers, be they a state or any other kind of a wider, enveloping social formation. And this has happened and is still happening in various degrees of awareness. The erasure from view of such a praxis approach to issues of bilingualism and its reasons will be one of the main topics of discussion in the next, theoretical part of this chapter.

All members of society are socially and historically located agents; as a result, at any given time, in any given place, the position of different kinds of speakers varies. The categories that concern us specifically here are, first, the category of 'linguistic expert', and second, its distinction with regard to the 'average speaker', constructed as some kind of lay person. Members of these categories are expected to partly converge and partly diverge in their understanding and handling of bilingual problems. If nothing else, they may share similar traditions, and these traditions often crosscut each other. For one thing, members of various bilingual communities quite frequently find themselves under the hegemonic grip of power structures influencing their way of looking at their own sociolinguistic condition. Linguistic experts, on the other hand, may not serve the same goals as other locally situated speakers. Nevertheless, members of bilingual communities constantly address themselves to both their own locally inherited (and transformed) experiences and those of the more canonically authoritative linguistic and public discourse.

For the analysis presented here it should be borne in mind that both a theoretical and a more empirical part that examines specific examples are necessary. I first analyse various sociological views that focus on praxis and provide useful concepts for the development of my argument; and second, I apply these concepts and notions to data from the bilingual Greek–Albanian speech communities of modern Greece. In all these, an explicit comparison is made between a more traditional linguistic (and sociolinguistic) descriptive framework, on the one hand, and a praxis-derived one, on the other.

some views and genealogies of praxis-oriented theory

Linguistics grew in the nineteenth century in a climate highly charged with the teachings of positivism. This trend took an even more radical turn in the first decades of the twentieth century. Positivism as a philosophical (and scientific) tradition attempts to study social phenomena on the basis of models derived from the so-called positive sciences. In its history, the concept of positivism has been associated with what is viewed as scientific understanding based on observable facts and the laws discoverable from their observation, even though the concept has often acquired other meanings as well (Williams 1976: 238–9). Thus, language is studied as a rule-governed entity divorced from the contingencies affecting the communities of its speakers and from their agency. Even though other paradigms, such as phenomenology, emerged, positivism dominated the scene of linguistic science. Phenomenological approaches, on the contrary, focus on interpretative schemes rather than neglecting the study of social phenomena as rooted in human agency. And this is done in such a manner as to make speakers' understandings of their own linguistic production more visible (for a discussion of such phenomeno-logical theories in relation to communicative practices, see Hanks 1996; for an analysis of dominant linguistic paradigms and dissenting voices, see Hymes 1974a). A basic outcome of the positivistic emphasis has been the treatment of language and language-related phenomena as facts outside the control of human agency. But positivism has had a strong appeal to thinkers who wished to see in their work the justification and legitimation of 'scientific' principles. One consequence of that was for positivism to marginalize phenomenology. A detailed history of such clashes and transitions is of course beyond the scope of this chapter. But in the spirit of this work it will suffice to say that the more a trend is associated with positivistic views the more it buys its acceptance in the dominant academic discourse. In the light of this observation it is interesting to see how praxis-oriented approaches have come to be in more demand recently than they used to be in the past. It is therefore useful to turn to some sociological views relevant to my discussion.

Giddens (1993 [1976]: 131–2) focuses attention on what he calls the '*reified mode*' (emphasis in the original). This mode he attributes to lay actors when they confront social phenomena and collectivities as entities. These 'entities' are understood as produced not by agents but as alien objects in nature. They are thus perceived as dislocated from their basic essence as human products. It must be added here that not only lay actors, but also much of linguistics and social science, have followed this reified mode (see Gal and Irvine 1995, for a discussion of reification in the construction of languages).

We can define reification as the tendency to make things more concrete than they actually are, and attribute to them thing-like properties alienating them from human agents. In his early treatment of the rules of sociological method, Giddens (1993 [1976]: 132) highlights a basic aspect of praxis that transcends the reified mode of thinking: actors can dissolve reification by realizing that structures are their own products, and, as a consequence, recover control over them. Both the dominance of reification and attempts at its dissolution will be glimpsed later in my discussion of the examples. At the root of all this lies the process of structuration. Structuration is the structuring of social relations across time and space in virtue of the duality of structure; and the duality of structure refers to structure as the medium and outcome of the conduct it recursively organizes. That is, structure cannot be imagined outside of action (Giddens 1984: 374–6; also my definition of praxis above).

If these broad lines of analysis hold for various categories of social agents, they should also hold for the collectivity of linguists. In sociolinguistics and linguistic anthropology quite a few attempts in the direction of praxis have been very successful recently. Such scholarly efforts have bracketed our inherited, common-sense understanding of language as an object uncontrollable by human agents (see for example Hanks 1990, 1996; also Fabian 1982: 14–50, on what he calls 'processual bilingualism'; Hill 1993: 69–93, on the dialectic between structure and practice, and Urciuoli 1998).

One may argue that the critique advanced in the previous lines holds also for the study of monolingualism. And this is largely true. In the light of this analysis though, bilingualism is highly charged politically, since it incorporates an inherent component of power relations. It is not therefore to be viewed as just an extension of the former. Linguistic codes, because of their endowment with properties of the reified mode, come into contact with speakers' understanding. As such they are loaded with differential symbolic values, thereby permitting the symbolic domination of one code over the other (Bourdieu 1991). Such symbolic domination enables speakers to view one language as being inherently endowed with properties not shared by other languages or dialects. And this happens even when speakers are not competent in the code to which they attribute a certain kind of superiority. A contingent relationship between agents and their spoken (and written) languages is thus frequently transformed into an iconic relation in which languages appear to mirror inherent (naturalized) features of social groups and vice versa (for iconicity and iconization see Gal and Irvine 1995 and Irvine 2001).

In the light of this analysis one can observe that the reifying dominant ideology can serve the interests of the nation-state, for example, in reproducing standardized monolingualism (see also Pujolar and Jaffe, this volume). This state-promoted monolingualism struggles to inscribe in speakers' consciousness one particular code as a pure, functionally adequate and most natural linguistic variety. This ideology dictates that we read in this code some features that make it 'essentially' different from other dialects or languages. Linguistics as an academic discipline inevitably gets caught in the regulatory activities of the state or other powerful infrastructures in their efforts to marginalize those linguistic varieties that are threatening to the norm of monolingualism. It provides a helpful hand in isolating and reifying linguistic structure by purifying it from whatever 'deviant' features show up in it or in the context of its use (including also other linguistic varieties, or meanings that cannot be controlled by central powers; Marcuse 1991). It thus finds itself unwittingly in the service of those powerful structures. Linguistic science is thus implicated in state or infrastructural regulatory efforts, regardless of the success or failure of the social reproduction of various formations and institutions (state, academia, bureaucracy, etc.). This note of caution is necessary since social reproduction is not always a predictable outcome of the struggles for its achievement (Woolard 1985: 738–48).

It is here that some of the advantages of praxis-oriented approaches start emerging. In some versions of sociological thinking, it has been argued that the question of which model does a more adequate job should be based on the criterion of which theory addresses theoretical concerns as well as practical, political and moral ones (see Gilroy 1992 [1987]). To give an example, a theory that does not treat the notion of *race* as a separate category, either to accept or to negate it, but examines it along with other social and economic parameters is to be preferred over other, more isolationist approaches. A praxis approach to problems of bilingualism is, on the one hand, richer theoretically since it targets not just linguistic codes but also agents, ideologies and their inter-relationships; and on the other, it is directly relevant to the social protagonists whose interests are at stake. Members of local communities do not just speak their languages mechanically. They have views about the fate of the one or the other code of their bilingual repertoires. They are concerned about the ways their languages are involved in getting a living, in their children's education and their acceptance by other sectors of the society, in providing symbolic means for the expression of social and political stances, and much more. It therefore makes a difference if one of the codes is being devalued and the other is becoming dominant, or if, because of their bilingualism, speakers form targets of exclusion or discrimination. It should be kept in mind that bilingual behaviour, like any other human activity is not a neutral and value-free condition but one that is being constantly self- and other-monitored and evaluated.

This explains why praxis approaches are more widespread today than they used to be in earlier decades. But there is an even deeper reason for preferring a praxis-oriented approach. In late modernity we can no longer take for granted a strict separation between those who hold knowledge and those who do not (see discussion of expert systems below). In the so-called post-traditional society (Giddens 1991), the Self is undergoing complex transformations, resulting in a tension between expert and lay knowledge. A new space is being opened up, and local actors lay a claim on controlling a large portion of it. Any approach that would focus primarily on linguistic structures and a bit of their surrounding context and neglect agency and ideology would be ill-equipped to come to terms with the novel social conditions characterizing post-traditional society.

From the analysis so far it becomes obvious that there are things in relation to bilingualism that we need to explain. More traditional or, if you prefer, modernist sociolinguistics has not been indifferent to issues related to praxis aspects; and we owe a great deal to earlier works as far as our understanding of some crucial problems is concerned (see Gumperz 1972: 219–31 for a classical treatment, and, of course, the whole ethnography of communication paradigm as developed by Gumperz and Hymes 1972; also Hymes 1974b). But, as mentioned above, a richer perspective is to be preferred over a more restricted one. This need is imposed on us with even greater force now that the conditions of late modernity have enhanced the networks of communication and contact among various social groups and sectors of society found at spatial distance from each other. As stated in the introduction, bilingual praxis is not a new phenomenon. However, now members of various communities turn upon their own condition more reflexively than in earlier historical periods. This kind of reflexivity, consisting in looking at one's own Self as well as at Otherness (local experiences vs. linguistic expertise), cannot be handled effectively by restricting research on bilingualism to the traditional structuralist paradigm.

Nevertheless, radical forms of power do not always allow the praxis aspects of the problem to emerge in speakers' consciousness, since they actively efface them (Lukes 1974). Radical forms of power are those processes that block, to a significant extent, the possibility of the dissolution of reification discussed above. But, even though the dissolution of reification at the level of common-sense understanding is not easily attainable in our Western linguistic tradition, speakers in their daily interactions are always engaged in bilingualism as praxis (cf. Gumperz 1982; Rampton 1995).

Bilingual practices as forms of social interaction are constantly reproduced (exactly as other forms of structure are reproduced) and this reproduction entails their change. Projecting this on Giddens's theory of social dynamics, bilingual structures of the communities are the outcome as well as the medium of the linguistic activities carried out by human agency. This condition brings in a component of contingency in the relations of various categories of human agents with their linguistic codes in use: for example, Rampton's (1995) study of 'crossing' offers a detailed examination of the ways adolescents in a British educational and community context creatively switch into stylized forms of linguistic varieties (Asian English, Creole and Panjabi) not their own. But, while such language crossings afford their speakers means for the emergence of various subjectivities, they are not all the same in terms of their innocence or power, and therefore they are not equally distributed, due to important social differences in positions with respect to relations of power.

On the basis of the preceding discussion one can ask: where exactly do various social agents converge and where do they diverge vis-à-vis bilingualism?

This question can be asked with regard to many positions, but here I wish to focus on local communities on the one hand, and linguistic academic traditions, nation-states and global structures on the other (the latter being closer to what one may call social formations and/or institutions). Linguistics as a legitimate mode of scientific knowledge carries within it features of the reified mode. It treats its subject matter in a way that facilitates its study in the frame of normal science. However, linguistics is also tied to another historical condition highlighted above: the state bureaucracy and ideology. Both these strands provide linguistics with enabling resources and justification to treat bilingualism as a juxtaposition of two lexico-grammatical systems of perceived unequal status in terms of their potential for referential clarity and rational achievement (Silverstein 2001). It is hard therefore for differing local interpretative schemes to take momentum, if the inherited emphasis falls primarily on the comparison of referential entities (Errington 1998). Of course, this is true also of academic interpretative schemes which differ from the dominant discourse. Thus, while it is always hard to challenge the doxa, that is, the generally unquestioned mainstream view, it is all the more difficult for social agents positioned out of the range of institutionalized resources and legitimacies. Nonetheless, speakers and more institutionally structured agencies tend to converge variably and by degrees. Where do they diverge? I want to suggest that divergence is more obvious in their degree of empowerment: who has the power to control a certain capital of expertise and to what extent.

In late modernity, expert systems of knowledge (rooted in early modernity) exercise a degree of authority over lay agents by deskilling them, that is, by disembedding themselves from their own roots in local knowledge (Geertz 1983; Giddens 1991: 137–9). Linguistics is such an expert system, stemming from the institutions of academia and regulatory state apparatuses. Its ideologically formulated principles are enshrined as a legitimated body of expert knowledge. They are consequently disseminated down to local communities through schooling and the media, and exercise a strong hold over their conceptions of language. In terms of power differential this process entails a divergence. Nevertheless, deskilling is in constant tension with reskilling, which effects, in Giddens's analysis, a 'dialectic of control'. No matter how strong and endowed with trust expert knowledge is, there are always open spaces which can be filled in with local linguistic ideologies. Nowhere does this appear to be more obvious than in bilingualism, where speakers constantly address themselves to two differently structured semiotic, grammatical systems. Due to the dialectic of control and since the expert–lay actor divide is more or less a fluid condition, heavily dependent on historical contingencies, one cannot predict with a fair amount of certainty whether it can be easily overcome or not.

If we grant Giddens's (1993 [1976]) critique of Marx as offering only broad lines of a theory of praxis (obsessed as he was with the political economy of capitalism), we should acknowledge Gramsci as a more culturally minded Marxist. He has more to say about a linguistics of praxis. We can trace here one important thread of the genealogy of praxis-oriented approaches. Gramsci was not specifically interested in bilingualism per se. He was, however, interested in tracing the historical conditions of Italian multidialectalism, influenced as he was by his early work in the tradition of 'neolinguistics'. This helped him understand the relations between a hegemonic and a subaltern culture in ways parallel to the ones that neolinguistics used to understand relations between areas as relations of direction in linguistic prestige (Forgacs and Nowell-Smith 1985: 164).

Gramsci offers analyses strongly reminiscent of more recent praxis theories. When he discusses what he calls 'normative grammar' (1985: 180–4), he talks about a reciprocal monitoring among speakers who come together to produce a grammatical conformism or norm. This closely resembles the way Giddens understands the reproduction of structure. And when he describes country people as trying to imitate urban speech in a chase by subaltern classes of the ways of speaking of the dominant classes and intellectuals, he frames his analysis in a spirit that was later developed by Bourdieu (1984, 1991) in terms of symbolic domination and distinction. But a very important line of Gramsci's thinking is the one that gives priority to a comparative perspective in the analysis of historical grammar. The national language cannot be imagined outside the horizon of other languages that exert an influence on it (linguistic innovations introduced by returning emigrants, translators, readers of foreign documents, travellers, etc.). This is strongly reminiscent of Bakhtin's (1981) notion regarding the heteroglossic awareness of speakers, that is, awareness of the tension between languages and sociolects when the one is seen through the eyes of the other. Also we should include here versions of Critical Discourse Analysis which give priority to discursive and cultural praxis (Fairclough 1995). Critical Discourse Analysis aims to reveal the ideological presuppositions that shape any kind of discourse, particularly those discursive forms that are endowed with power. It thus deconstructs the supposed innocence or neutrality of the various discursive events, texts and genres. All these are praxis-oriented comparative perspectives in stark opposition to whatever comparisons are recruited by the positivist neogrammarians, with their focus on exceptionless sound laws, or the various grammatical theories searching for Platonic essences underlying speech variation.

problems of bilingualism in greece and the structure of domination

In the Greek nation-state bi- (multi-)lingualism in its praxis aspects has had a complex history that cannot be traced here in its totality; indeed, my focus is on particular enclaves of Albanian (Arvanitika)–Greek bilingual communities. I intend to cite these as cases in which some of the analytical concepts presented above can be applied. It will suffice to say in this context that historical conjuncture has produced circumstances that have blocked a full recognition of minority languages in Greek modernity (with the exception of the Turkish language as spoken in Thrace, northeastern Greece), although these conditions are now changing in various contradictory ways through the influence exerted and the directives issued by the European Union, which requires its members to recognize minority or lesser spoken languages.

The conditions for the emergence of the Greek nation-state were ripe since early modernity, that is, since well before the nineteenth century. Arvanitika-speaking communities have therefore long had to face the heteroglossic situation of addressing themselves to the dominant language, Greek (Bakhtin 1981). As the process of subordination intensified, and the conditions of late modernity settled in through institutional networks linking local enclaves with the national infrastructures, the linguistic shift that turned Arvanitika, a variety of the southern major dialect division of Albanian known as Tosk, into a threatened language also intensified. Indeed, Arvanitika has been undergoing complex and tense relations with Greek since the appearance of Albanian speakers in the thirteenth and fourteenth centuries in what is now Greece (Tsitsipis 1998).

The data to be analysed here consist primarily of extracts from a popular conference that took place in Athens in 1998, and in which bilingual Albanian (Arvanitika)–Greek speakers acted as participants in their dual capacity as community members and as intellectuals debating issues related to the languages of their repertoire (Greek and Arvanitika).[2] However, a praxis approach is well equipped to handle various kinds of data not limited to this body of conference discourse. I also cite and analyse an extract from a published source, and a narrative fragment illustrating spontaneously produced implicit views on bilingualism from one of the Arvanitika–Greek speech communities. The main methodological tool used to arrive at my analysis is an interpretative approach to ethnographically collected data (albeit data that have been collected at various time intervals, and given the circumstances, have some qualitative differences among them). For example, the conference materials have involved me in a more intensively reflexive engagement with other participants. As was the case for other participants, I too had to negotiate a double identity. I was both a linguistic anthropologist and a citizen concerned about sensitive matters touching on issues of tolerance, acceptance of otherness, and democracy. Such an event therefore does not closely resemble what we have historically understood as a typical fieldwork situation (although this is changing). But an interpretative approach is also required of a researcher when s/he analyses written texts like my first example below. Such texts obtain their full meaning and become transparent if they are juxtaposed or compared to other kinds of evidence. For example, it is possible to discover continuities (or discontinuities) between the text written by a philologically and historically trained observer and the narrative as offered by a consultant in so-called typical fieldwork conditions. These (dis)continuities can tell us something about degrees of deskilling, or how bilingualism is locally understood and enacted, or the extent to which various social agents have been empowered by the discourse of monolingualism. A combination of interpretative approaches to ethnographic materials with a critical discourse and sociolinguistic focus on the data has helped me arrive at some demystification of speakers' and authorities' ideologies of bilingualism and monolingualism.

In the light of the above observations it is useful to briefly discuss some of the consequences of the official national linguistic ideology. In a series of brilliant analyses of this ideology as underlying the expert system of linguistic knowledge the late A. Christidis (1999) talks about *linguistic mythologies*. This ideological system emanates from both the Greek state apparatuses and many linguistic scholars. By adopting the reified mode and endorsing the process of empowering infrastructures and linguists, linguistic mythologies construct an ideal image of Greek monolingualism. In its turn, this mythological construction (one that views Greek as an essence endowed with purity, clarity, complexity and overall superiority vis-à-vis other languages) is invested with trust by various categories of thinkers and lay actors.

This becomes better understood if we briefly discuss a condition prevailing over the last ten or fifteen years in Greece (and quite likely elsewhere) that resembles 'moral panic' (see Cameron 1995: 82–5). A moral panic is a condition channelling various anxieties and hostilities that show up temporarily in a society towards a selected target. Public reaction in such cases goes overboard and becomes disproportionate to whatever is the real problem. And the apparent problem need not be the same as the real one; indeed, it usually is not.

The directives of the EU concerning the treatment of minority languages and the declared equal status of all European languages as well as the massive appearance in Greece of economic immigrants (primarily Albanians) have caused a feeling of insecurity about the fate of the Greek language. An orchestrated ideological discourse, equally constructed and shared by the mass media, print journalism, popular and expert opinion, has exercised a grip over national consciousness such that there is a strong feeling that the Greek language is seriously threatened. This concern is being enhanced by earlier and current versions of nationalist ideology preaching that the Greek language (and Greekness as a whole), which has been persecuted by various enemies (primarily Jewry), should be guarded against its predators. This has recently reached a degree of hysteria.

But as with all ideological pronouncements this one too is fraught with contradictions. Why would a language believed by its speakers to be 'the mother of all languages' because of its allegedly inherent properties of resilience and superiority, all of a sudden, become such a fragile 'entity' susceptible to deterioration? A further contradiction has to do with the double standards characterizing official language ideology. Greece is arguing (and very justifiably so) for the right of the Greek language to enjoy the same status as other, more powerful European languages. But what is demanded of the Brussels headquarters for the Greek language abroad is not also a rule followed in the domestic treatment of minority languages (Albanian, Vlach, Romani, etc.) back home. Moral panic constructed and fed by linguistic ideologies comes to the rescue, justification, and perpetuation of official monolingualism. A characteristic example comes from a speaker on a TV programme who suggested that we should receive foreign tourists visiting Greece with a banner saying: 'Barbarians, welcome to Greece'. This pronouncement, the outcome of ideologically enshrined views, promotes a very special kind of monolingualism. Its racializing and exclusionist discourse deems Greek as superior compared to other languages, and, recursively, ancient Greek as more pure than modern Greek (for recursiveness see Gal and Irvine 1995).

A striking token, not of moral panic but of a supposedly sober genre (that of historical observation), comes from a philologist of Arvanitika origin, Biris (1960), who has this to say about the retreat of Arvanitika and the advancing encroachment of Greek on the communities' repertoires in the early 1960s:

> In the Arvanitika villages, at least in those ones which had the privilege of transportation, recent decades have been characterized by the evolution of civilization, the decrease in the usage of Arvanitika and the advancement of Greek. Today it is only in some isolated villages that one can hear Arvanitika mixed with distorted Greek spoken by old people. However, in areas where the ease of transportation has brought about an intensive contact of old Arvanitika villages with the city the life of these peasants has nothing to remind us of the earlier characteristic peculiarities. (my translation from Greek; for references and a more extensive analysis see Tsitsipis 1998: 11–12; more on Biris below; for a Bakhtinian theorizing of such examples see Tsitsipis 2004)

The example suggests that a highly evaluative statement stands as a witness to the local (even though sophisticated) agent's deskilling in accepting the official linguistic ideology. This linguistic mythology constructs Greek as an essence iconically related to progress and cultural advancement, and construes it as distant from anything perceived as a peculiarity. The expert reifying linguistic knowledge normalizes the image of the Greek language and hegemonically spreads this normalization in various directions. Greek has also perceivable peculiarities but no one talks about them, unless one has to choose between the standard language and other dialects.

The study of popular conference events has not been adequately theorized. That is, what happens in matters linguistic and ideological when consultants become theoreticians by enacting multiple identities has not been targeted in the sociolinguistic literature on bilingualism as a crucial component of deskilling and reskilling. This by no means constitutes a purely micro-sociological phenomenon since deskilling, reskilling and empowerment link the local with institutional infrastructures. Furthermore, Gramsci's and Bourdieu's insights on the chasing of the prestige linguistic model by subaltern classes (as a hegemonically produced form of symbolic domination) attest to a crucial dialectic. This is the dialectic between dominant forms of linguistic ideologies and their local imitations and refractions. In addition to that, a focus on such popular events reveals various kinds of contradictions that descriptions of local understandings of bilingual phenomena often oversimplify.

The following extracts come from various amateur philologists and linguists who, at various times during the event, make frequent references to linguistic concepts which have been appropriated from a particular field of expert knowledge, in an attempt to turn their own discourse into a discourse of authority (see Tsitsipis 2004).[3] Such an expert discourse, by returning to the local communities, is being endowed with both trust and a distancing suspicion. Local ideologies therefore frequently show a contradictory nature (Tsitsipis 1998). As a consequence, a constant deskilling and reskilling of consultants–participants is taking place vis-à-vis this body of expert knowledge. And this expertise is moulded in a framework of praxis as locally understood and as deriving its power and legitimation from the experiences of local communities. Here is therefore what the examples are telling us in terms of the phenomena under investigation: beyond simple structural descriptions of bilingualism and a mere focus on interactional routines (as understood in interactional sociolinguistics) long-term praxis looms large. Speakers of the examples, as socially positioned agents, afford us a glimpse of how they experience their bilingual condition in a heteroglossic struggle between their voice and the voice of institutional authority. The extracts are given in my translation from Greek.

(1) EZ: In Greece, there is still in circulation the logic of old linguistics on the basis of which we take language, a perfect language, to be foundational and the dialects to reflect local deteriorations. But things are not like that. We should rather start from local codifications, that is what people actually speak in their localities. From this point on there is a synthesis growing around a common activity and thus a common language is emerging.

(2) GK: We started out discussing Arvanitika as a language or a dialect, and we can use other terms too, primarily [derived] from linguistics. But then we make a transposition [of the subject] and start talking about Arvanites [the people]. And I have the feeling that we use, on the occasion of a linguistic phenomenon, terms that refer to ethnological characteristics.

(3) AK: When we are dealing with a people that has been identified with a regenerated Greece, a dilemma, or, rather a pseudo-dilemma, is posed. What is going on? Are we Greeks or not? We have built Greece. If we are Greeks we have to leave the language [Arvanitika] behind. There is a kind of logical and emotional trap here that has been set up for Arvanites people who have become the victims. At this moment it is quite hard to convince people that being Greek does not negate being Arvanitis and using Arvanitika.

(4) AK: I was so unlucky in my life to have to witness this language, with such deep roots on Greek soil to lose its blossom. When I was a small child I used to speak half Greek half Arvanitika. If we want to form a picture of contemporary conditions, in my village there are coffee-houses and there are also cafeterias. In the coffee-houses they speak Arvanitika. [I]n the cafeterias the young people speak Greek.

(5) PT: I believe that the language is one. This is Arvanitika or, as we call it, Shkiptariki.[4] Albania should be considered the matrix for all of us wherever we happen to be: in Egypt, in Turkey, in Bulgaria and wherever else a diaspora has taken place, and, of course, the language has developed some local features of its own.

The speaker of extract (1) appropriates the word of linguistic authority, a discourse that is endowed with the monopoly of control supported by both linguistic rationalism and state ideology. But the speaker reframes it in various directions. He almost negates the official linguistic classifications even though his turn at talk – and this is quite significant – addresses these classifications. Both a deskilling and a reskilling are taking place here. We witness a momentary empowerment of a representative of the local communities to place the official discourse under a shadow of doubt. Given the fact that this speaker is enacting the identity of a conference participant, rather than that of an interview informant, he goes even further and introduces the interesting idea that a language solidifies around a set of practical activities.

The speaker of (2) feels uneasy about the course the discussion has been taking in the direction of disconnecting two 'entities': Arvanitika and the ethnic group that speaks the language. The point is not trivial. He is enacting a widely spread ideology characterizing the local communities: language and the people along with their activities should be viewed in one stroke as indissolubly related. Since he is not a sociolinguist he is not concerned about methodological issues. He is treating the matter here in the reified (or essentializing) mode. Community members hold to the view that the language partakes of the essence of the people and vice versa. The source of his uneasiness and confusion, therefore, is the shattering of this iconic relationship by other participants. This is a feature of Arvanitika ideological practice that

I have called elsewhere (Tsitsipis 2003) 'indexical / iconic totality': a mutual mirroring of the one 'entity' into the other. And such an ideology forms a ground on which 'lay' actors' ideas converge quite frequently with official discourses (i.e. educational and linguistic) stemming from institutional infrastructures and the media. Such discourses promote an essentialist ideology according to which linguistic and ethnic features are consubstantial and have a life outside human agency and historical contingencies.

The speaker of (3) is striving to endow Arvanitika with legitimacy through the recruitment of the genealogy of the Greek nation. This is also a widely shared feature of Arvanitika ideology, and is a site par excellence of the domination of the national imagining through its reproduction at the local level. There is abundant factual evidence suggesting that the uprising against the Ottoman rule in the nineteenth century, and even earlier, was the complex outcome of the efforts of various multilingual Balkan communities at the stage of the initial formation of their national consciousness. There is nothing remarkable therefore about such a process. But this is not what the speaker of the extract is pointing to here. This participant, through erasure (Gal and Irvine 1995), promotes Arvanitika intervention up to the role of the main or sole protagonist. But he simultaneously subordinates it to the dominant aspirations. No one would expect, for instance, French Canadians to try to achieve legitimacy for the French language by arguing that they have contributed to the building of an English (-speaking) nation, unless, of course, they want to show pacifist intentions by concession. But Arvanitika has never been a co-official language with Greek, not even a recognized minority language. Neither has any other minority language for that matter. An apparent contradiction thus shows up in this speaker's words: Arvanitika language (and ethnic identity) can only obtain legitimacy through the genealogy of the nation-state that engineered its subordination. Early enough, professional historians and philologists (for one example, see Biris 1960 and discussion above) have made efforts to trace Arvanitika origins back to ancient Greek tribal groups. Through the use of a partly historical,[5] partly metaphorical, discourse Arvanitika identity is endowed by Biris and others with virtues such as bravery, pride, love of freedom etc., all perceived to characterize Greekness. Thus in this example, as in (2) above, lay views converge with more official ones, as against extract (1). The speaker of (1) manages to partly diverge from the official views due to a (however short-lived) empowerment. But extract (3) is also shrouded in a quasi-academic discourse (part of the speaker's locally emergent identity), as becomes obvious from the terms 'dilemma' and 'pseudo-dilemma', a mixture of political, sociological and journalistic jargon.

Extract (4) enacts another well attested ideological-linguistic praxis, that of reducing language to an essence that functions beyond and above its referential and indexical role. In this view, language takes on a life of its own. It is a species unto itself, an ideology that I have called 'sublimation'

(Tsitsipis 2003), and which also exemplifies the reified mode. In this extract, the explicit referent is Arvanitika, but the same ideology is used by a variety of scholars and activists to characterize Greek too. Adherents to this ideology also include professional linguists.

Two interrelated points are relevant to my discussion here: a continuity between local Arvanitika views and more institutionally enshrined ideologies, on the one hand, and the subordination of the first to the second, on the other. Arvanitika may be the explicit referent of the speaker of (4), but it is anchored in a wider ideology that dictates its own terms as to how linguistic processes should be viewed. Notice that sublimation contributes to the emergence of a Darwinian rationality, since floral and faunal species can be endowed with naturalized resilience or resistance powers. And so are languages if viewed not as going through human agency, but as leading a life divorced from such agency. This is the meaning of expressions such as the ones in (4) where the speaker foregrounds the metaphorical description of Arvanitika as 'having deep roots on Greek soil' and as 'losing its blossom'. In extract (5), the speaker reproduces the main tenet of the Greek national imagining, the Herderian idea that the language is one, and that it carries a primordial relationship with the people speaking it. It is simultaneously the means through which monolingualism is preserved in the face of threatening bilingual practices and diversity, and the outcome of enshrined understandings of linguistic phenomena. Here too, as in the previous example, the explicit referent is Arvanitika, but the logic informing the speaker's utterance is that of the official national view. In fact, a large part of speakers' thinking over the last several decades is the product of their constant exposure to a combination of journalistic, educational and nationalist pronouncements. Arvanitika speakers are quite prompt to mention perceived differences between their locally used variety of the language and other varieties as spoken elsewhere; but the concluding statement of extract (5) stems most directly from linguistic descriptions and circulating discourses on dialectology.

As stated above, our approach should be able to handle other kinds of data too. With reference to the five brief extracts cited, one may object that there is something spurious about their selection: they are all ideologically loaded metalinguistic statements spontaneously offered by linguistically unsophisti- cated but aware speakers. Let me turn therefore to another example from an old man (in his eighties back in the early 1980s) from an Arvanitika-speaking village of mountainous Greece. I cite the example in a simplified orthography with regard to some of its phonological features, with interlinear glosses and the use of bold characters for the Greek parts of the switches without marking Greek loans in Arvanitika:

(6) 1   Dale, dale **kache kache** o thom nji istori
           wait, wait **sit sit** I'll tell a story
     2   ne nji milj e nen kjint e dimbet

in one thousand nine hundred twelve (date 1912)
3   ish nje taghmatarch e kei
    there was a major and had
4   zerikiotet, kirjakatet, edhe kukurjotet
    people from (the villages) of Zeriki, Kiriaki, and Kukura
5   e kei nje dhimiri dhjaleksur Arvanitet burrat
    and had chosen a team (consisting) of Arvanites men
6   **itan palikarja dhiladhi**
    they were, that is, brave men
7   **aftus tus ihe dhjaleksi protopalikaradhes** ishen ter
    he had chosen them (to be) ultra-brave men all they were
8   otan ish kindino brema kindineps na Turko
    when there was a danger at night to be threatened by a Turk
9   tergonjemi embiston berdha
    we sent a person to be trusted inside
10 andehjin ne bor, ne te ftohet, ne ter kjeronjet
    (they) could take the snow, the cold, and all kinds of weather

The speaker of (6) does not explicitly address any language or bilingual issues. But significant implicit ideological nuclei emerge in his narrative (see Tsitsipis 2003). The narrated events are historically located in the context of the so-called Balkan wars in the early 1900s. The drafting of soldiers that is reported here takes place among Arvanitika speakers (as Greek citizens), who are depicted as having all the properties characterizing Greek imagery. They are brave and can endure weather hardships. In fact at lines 6 and 7 we witness two major switches to Greek which foreground the draftees' bravery. The national imagining, even though not stated, serves as a backdrop against which we can understand the whole story. The Arvanitika identity is legitimated through the genealogy of the nation-state as having the monopoly of violence and being the measure of everything else. The way the speaker perceives and constructs the narrated events suggests his deskilling vis-à-vis those powerful structures. Such structures manage to absorb and appropriate local identities with enormous consequences for Arvanitika speakers' bilingual consciousness.

As the theoretical discussion and the analysis of the extracts suggest, schemes of linguistic description form a kind of capital or an expert knowledge system.[6] This expert system is generated by the community of professional linguists, educators, the media and infrastructural institutions. Such bodies are constantly striving to legitimize and keep control over it. But any kind of ideologies or knowledge about the use, structure and value of linguistic materials does not originate solely from within the official discourses; local communities do have their own views. However, in the historical process, local communities are frequently deskilled in the sense that they allow legitimacy of such knowledge to be transferred to central systems of control, endowing them with their trust. One additional reason for the successful imposition of expert knowledge is that some of the aforementioned bodies of power (community of linguists, educators) often function as *communities of practice* (Holmes and Meyerhoff 1999: 173–83). That is, their members are in a constant mutual engagement developing certain characteristic kinds of shared discursive repertoires with a well-defined focus, managing thus to enhance their authority. This becomes a particularly sensitive and vexed issue when it comes to bilingual conditions. For these, par excellence, cause academia and state authorities to be on the alert as they perceive a potential threat to the standardist and purist ideal of monolingualism. Nevertheless, local voices are occasionally reskilled by reappropriating this knowledge and by combining it with their own original views as stemming from their experiential worlds. Thus, they can go through various kinds and degrees of empowerment, from temporary and ephemeral to long-term and structuring.

concluding remarks

Social theories about praxis are not absent from considerations of bilingual phenomena. Some concepts, though, derived from such theories, were not initially designed to cover specific sociolinguistic questions, and have not always had much currency in the literature. In this chapter I have treated bilingualism as a social praxis with a focus on a receding language of modern Greece, Arvanitika. Notions such as deskilling, reskilling, empowerment, reified mode, symbolic domination, hegemony etc. were found useful in handling the data and in putting in relief the mutually interlocked processes of linguistic ideological practices among local communities, on the one hand, and the official state and professional linguistic discourses, on the other. It must be noted here that, even though much recent research has focused on power and symbolic domination, more work needs to be done in this direction. We need to make explicit how conceptualizations of bilingualism are locally formed through the structuring power of deskilling, reskilling and empowerment; and how and to what extent a reified mode of understanding circulates, is adopted, and occasionally contradicted among and by local communities and 'expert' communities that have appropriated the legitimacy of providing the 'correct' and 'scientific' version of linguistic phenomena. Such an approach, in line with other similar work, contributes to the shattering of the view that official linguistic descriptions of bilingual processes are insulated from their consequences; and furthermore that local linguistic 'folk theories' do not constantly address the enshrined versions of bilingualism.

acknowledgements

I would like to thank Monica Heller, the volume's editor, for valuable comments, suggestions and insights that helped me improve the initial draft.

Thanks should also be extended to Palgrave's external readers, and to my colleague Panos Arvanitis for technological support in formatting the final product. I remain the only one responsible for whatever weaknesses or errors have crept into this piece.

notes

1. I call the process 'semiotic' since language is after all a system of signs. I call it 'sociopolitical' to emphasize the obvious sociological character of bilingualism, and I use the term 'nexus' to indicate the close dialectic between use and ideology.
2. The 1998 conference proceedings were edited posthumously by the organizers (Empirikos et al. 2001), and include events concerning other minority languages too. I was also a participant, but only in the Arvanitika event, and was invited to contribute the Foreword to the relevant section of the volume.
3. Participants covered a wide range of specialties and identities: journalists, activists, political theorists, folklorists, various municipal authorities, etc. Most of the participants had something to contribute to the discussions, but some remained silent. The examples extracted here for analysis are all from male participants. This skewing in favour of the representation of the male voice is due entirely to the fact that the three active female participants were all specialists: one a professional historian, the second a sociolinguist of Arvanitika origin working on her dissertation at that time, and the third an anthropologist whose participation was limited due to health problems. The participants whose words are extracted here are educated Arvanitika speakers who are not specialists in sociolinguistics, anthropology or sociology; they practise other professions such as law, and some are elected representatives to municipal posts.
4. Shqip and Shqiptar, spelled with [q], are terms used in Albania to refer to the language and its speakers (nationals) respectively but are known in various morphological shapes to Greek-Albanians too.
5. I call it 'partly historical' since authors of this tradition should be credited for a fair treatment of the historical details to some extent. Biris, for example, has a very good grasp of urbanization and the conditions leading to language shift, but his exposition is heavily loaded with ideological and evaluative statements. In the title of his work, Arvanitika speakers are called 'The Dorians of Modern Hellenism'; here the ethnic-linguistic label of an ancient Greek tribe is used to construct Arvanitika communities as agents and building blocks in the narrative of the perceived national continuity.
6. Many sociological theories do not explicitly include linguistic knowledge among the various kinds of abstract or expert knowledge systems, even though in many other junctures in the development of the theory of structuration, for example, linguistic theory provides a helping hand. I suspect that expert systems are viewed by many sociologists as having immediately visible practical consequences (medical expertise, technological science, etc.) which does not seem to be the case with regard to language. The latter, according to Western language ideologies, is taken to be outside the realm of practical consequentiality. If my reading is correct, this attitude constitutes yet another form of misrecognition or mystification since it makes the consequences of linguistic praxis invisible.

references

Bakhtin, Mikhail M. (1981). *The Dialogic Imagination: Four Essays by M. M. Bakhtin* (Michael Holquist ed., trans. by Caryl Emerson and Michael Holquist). Austin, TX: University of Texas Press.

Biris, Kostas. Μπίρης, Κώστας (1960). *Αρβανίτες: Οι Δωριείς του Νεοτέρου Ελληνισμού.* Αθήνα. [*Arvanites: The Dorians of Modern Hellenism*]. Athens [no publisher provided].

Bourdieu, Pierre (1984). *Distinction: A Social Critique of the Judgement of Taste* (trans. by Richard Nice). London: Routledge.

—— (1991). *Language and Symbolic Power* (trans. by Gino Raymond and Matthew Adamson). Cambridge, MA: Harvard University Press.

Cameron, Deborah (1995). *Verbal Hygiene*. London and New York: Routledge.

Christidis, A.-F., Χριστίδης, Α. - Φ (1999). *Γλώσσα, Πολιτική, Πολιτισμός.* Αθήνα: Εκδόσεις Πόλις [*Language, Politics, Culture*]. Athens: Polis Publications.

Empirikos, L. et al. (eds), Εμπειρίκος Λ. κ.α (2001). *Γλωσσική Ετερότητα στην Ελλάδα.* Κέντρο Ερευνών Μειονοτικών Ομάδων. Αθήνα: Εκδόσεις Αλεξάνδρεια. [*Linguistic Alterity in Greece*]. Centre for the Research of Minority Groups. Athens: Alexandria Press.

Errington, Joseph J. (1998). *Shifting Languages: Interaction and Identity in Javanese Indonesia*. Cambridge: Cambridge University Press.

Fabian, Johannes (1982). Scratching the surface: Observations on the poetics of borrowing in Shaba Swahili. *Anthropological Linguistics* 24: 14–50.

Fairclough, Norman (1995). *Critical Discourse Analysis: The Critical Study of Language*. London and New York: Longman.

Forgacs, David, and Geoffrey Nowell-Smith (1985). General introduction to Antonio Gramsci. In *Selections from Cultural Writings*, pp. 1–15. London: Lawrence and Wishart.

Gal, Susan, and Judith T. Irvine (1995). The boundaries of languages and disciplines: How ideologies construct difference. *Social Research* 62: 967–1001.

Geertz, Clifford (1983). *Local Knowledge: Further Essays in Interpretive Anthropology*. US: Basic Books.

Giddens, Anthony (1984). *The Constitution of Society: Outline of the Theory of Structuration*. Berkeley and Los Angeles: University of California Press.

—— (1991). *Modernity and Self-Identity: Self and Society in the Late Modern Age*. Cambridge, UK: Polity Press.

—— (1993 [1976]). *New Rules of Sociological Method* (first published by Hutchinson 1976). Cambridge, UK: Polity Press.

Gilroy, Paul (1992 [1987]). *There Ain't No Black in the Union Jack* (first published by Unwin Hyman Ltd 1987). London and New York: Routledge.

Gramsci, Antonio (1985). *Selections from Cultural Writings* (ed. by David Forgacs and Geoffrey Nowell-Smith, trans. by William Boelhower). London: Lawrence and Wishart.

Gumperz, John (1972). The speech community. In Pier Paolo Giglioli (ed.), *Language and Social Context*, pp. 219–231. Middlesex: Penguin.

—— (1982). *Discourse Strategies*. New York: Cambridge University Press.

Gumperz, John J., and Dell Hymes (eds) (1972). *Directions in Sociolinguistics: The Ethnography of Communication*. New York, Chicago and London: Holt, Rinehart and Winston, Inc.

Hanks, William F. (1990). *Referential Practice: Language and Lived Space among the Maya*. Chicago and London: University of Chicago Press.

—— (1996). *Language and Communicative Practices*. Boulder, CO: Westview Press.

Hill, Jane H. (1993). Structure and practice in language shift. In Kenneth Hyltenstam and Ake Viberg (eds), *Progression and Regression in Language: Sociocultural, Neuropsychological, and Linguistics Perspectives*, pp. 69–93. Cambridge: Cambridge University Press.

Holmes, Janet, and Miriam Meyerhoff (1999). The community of practice: Theories and methodologies in language and gender research. *Language in Society* 28: 173–83.

Hymes, Dell (1974a). Introduction: Traditions and paradigms. In Dell Hymes (ed.), *Studies in the History of Linguistics: Traditions and Paradigms*, pp. 1–38. Bloomington and London: Indiana University Press.

—— (1974b). *Foundations in Sociolinguistics: An Ethnographic Approach*. Philadelphia: University of Pennsylvania Press.

Irvine, Judith T. (2001). Style as distinctiveness: The culture and ideology of linguistic differentiation. In Penelope Eckert and John R. Rickford (eds), *Style and Sociolinguistic Variation*, pp. 21–43. Cambridge: Cambridge University Press.

Lukes, Steven (1974). *Power: A Radical View*. London: Macmillan Press.

Marcuse, Herbert (1991). *One-Dimensional Man: Studies in the Ideology of Advanced Industrial Society*. London: Routledge.

Rampton, Ben (1995). *Crossing: Language and Ethnicity among Adolescents*. London and New York: Longman.

Silverstein, Michael (2001). From the meaning of meaning to the empires of the mind: Ogden's ortholological English. In Susan Gal and Kathryn Woolard (eds), *Languages and Publics: The Making of Authority*, pp. 69–82. Manchester, UK and Northampton, MA: St Jerome Publishing.

Tsitsipis, Lukas D. (1998). *A Linguistic Anthropology of Praxis and Language Shift: Arvanitika (Albanian) and Greek in Contact*. Oxford: Clarendon Press.

—— (2003). Implicit linguistic ideology and the erasure of Arvanitika (Greek-Albanian) discourse. *Journal of Pragmatics* 35: 539–58.

—— (2004). A sociolinguistic application of Bakhtin's authoritative and internally persuasive discourse. *Journal of Sociolinguistics* 8: 569–94.

Urciuoli, Bonnie (1998). *Exposing Prejudice: Puerto Rican Experiences of Language, Race, and Class*. Boulder, CO: Westview Press.

Williams, Raymond (1976). *Keywords*. London: Fontana Press.

Woolard, Kathryn A. (1985). Language variation and cultural hegemony: Toward an integration of sociolinguistic and social theory. *American Ethnologist* 12: 738–48.

14

bilingualism and the analysis of talk at work: code-switching as a resource for the organization of action and interaction

lorenza mondada

introduction

One major characteristic of bilingualism is the way that speakers deploy resources from what may be recognized as two different languages. The meanings of such code-switching, or the motivations of language alternation in bilingual talk, have been discussed within a variety of theoretical paradigms. Whereas the 'allocational' paradigm represented by Fishman's domain analysis sees social structure as determining language choices, the 'interactional' paradigm introduced by Gumperz sees these choices as a way of locally achieving a specific interactional order (Wei 2005: 376). Within the latter paradigm, conversation analysis (CA) takes a specific stance, stressing the importance of the situated moment-by-moment organization of interaction, of the intelligibility it has for the participants, and of the membership categories that are achieved and made relevant within the interaction itself. Within this framework, the sense of the plurilingual resources used by speakers can neither be mechanistically related to a set of predetermined factors, such as identities or social structures, nor associated with imputed intentions, strategies or goals of the participants. Instead, the questions asked (and answered through analyses of empirical data) are: how do participants orient to bilingual resources? Which problems are solved by participants' procedures of exploiting bilingual resources? What intelligibility is given to these resources through the specific and local ways in which they are mobilized? What kind of 'procedural consequentiality' does the orientation have for the construction of identities, social categories or language diversity, i.e. what are the demonstrable consequences of this orientation and its manifestation in the specific sequential unfolding and organization of the interaction?

In this context, the sense of the difference produced by the use of plurilingual resources is dealt with as flexible and dynamic, depending on the interactional activities participants are engaged in. As Auer (2005: 405–6) suggests, this local perception and interpretation of code-switching can be either *discourse-related* (i.e. related to a functional differentiation and structuration of activities), or *participant-related* (i.e. oriented to the specific membership and competence of the co-participants and thus to issues such as identities and social relations; cf. Auer 1984 for the original formulation of this distinction). Even if it is difficult to disentangle these two aspects, code-switching need not be associated *a priori* with identity, ethnicity or social categories; it can achieve and display them in various ways under different circumstances and within different activities, but this has to be demonstrated by the analysis of the very way in which interaction gets organized. In this sense, what the conversational approach to bilingual talk produces is the embodied and situated sense of bilingual resources and practices produced by the participants (and not imposed by the researchers).

In what follows, we will adopt this analytic stance on bilingual talk-in-interaction in professional settings. We will show that bilingual resources can contribute to the specific shaping of an activity; this, in turn, can be seen as claiming/displaying particular ways of doing, and therefore as achieving or ascribing membership to locally relevant categories.

code-switching in professional talk-in-interaction

Code-switching in interaction has been widely studied in informal contexts, in ordinary conversations within families, peer groups or friends (see Auer 1998; Wei 2005). Although it has been studied in work contexts where minorities and immigrants were concerned (Day 1994; Heller et al. 1999), it has been much less considered in talk-in-interaction in institutional and professional contexts, for example where international experts are collaborating together. One reason seems to be that code-switching, and even more so, code-mixing, are thought to principally characterize informal contexts; on the contrary, formal contexts would tend to adopt, if any, more controlled forms of bilingualism (involving, for instance, mediators such as bilingual chairmen, or (un)official interpreters). One consequence is that there is a very thin literature about the detailed analysis of bilingual interactional practices within expert work (with the exceptions of Firth 1990; Wagner 1998; Rasmussen and Wagner 2002; Skårup 2004; Mondada 2004a; Müller in prep.). The interest of studying the workplace in this perspective is that the issues involved in these interactions can be professional, institutional and organizational as well as ethnic or social: the relevance of each is a matter that is decided and displayed by the participants, thus showing us, as analysts, the range of issues code-switching can deal with.

At the same time, research on interaction in the workplace has emphasized the importance of multimodal resources for professional practice (see Luff, Hindmarsh and Heath 2000), looking at the way in which teams are coordinated, decisions are collectively taken, artefacts are jointly looked at, etc. But it has not studied the plurilingual resources which are involved as these workplaces become more and more decentralized, distributed among distant places, and involve the mobility of international professionals. In this context, the study of plurilingual practices at the workplace can reveal crucial resources related to the efficient management of professional activities. Thus, this chapter aims at observing the mobilization of bilingual resources in the workplace, viewing code-switching as a resource among others by which participants make accountable, recognizable and interpretable what they are doing in a complex work situation. A particular empirical case will be used as the base for our analysis: code-switching practices in talk at work during a surgical operation where the chief surgeon is simultaneously addressing his team, an international audience connected through videoconference from an amphitheatre, and a small group of experts providing advice and comments.

In this kind of complex interactional setting, code-switching is a resource *endogenously* defined and oriented to by the participants (versus its *exogenous* definition by the researchers), used by them to organize multiple activities and their participation frameworks in distinct, albeit embedded, and orderly ways. More generally, the observation of such a specific setting can shed some light on the contribution of code-switching practices to the organization and accomplishment of both interactional and institutional order. One issue addressed here will be the mutual embeddedness of these two orders, the interactional and the institutional: how does the former contribute to achieve the latter? How is the latter consequential for the organization of the former? How are they reflexively elaborated in the shape given to plurilingual interaction by the participants?

The perspective adopted here is an ethnomethodologically inspired conversation analytic stance (cf. Sacks 1984; Schegloff 1972, 1999) on code-switching (cf. Auer 1984; Cromdal 2001; Wei 2002): it articulates *sequential analysis* (see Drew 2003 and Heritage 1995 for brief introductions), which deals with the turn-by-turn organization of code-switching (Auer 1995), with *membership categorization analysis* (Sacks 1972; see Watson 1994 and Silverman 1998 for presentations), which deals with the categories made recognizably relevant by the speakers in their use of plurilingual resources and in the course of their actions. Key issues in conversation analysis to which this chapter will return include the local accomplishment of the orderliness of talk, of action and of social relations, and the participants' orientations to the detailed organization accomplishing that orderliness. This focus on the locally emergent order of interactions is based on the following insights:

- Talk, as action, is *temporally* organized. Taking time into account means taking into account the step-by-step way in which turns and actions progressively *emerge* within talk-in-interaction, as well as the contingencies that can appear at any moment of the unfolding of talk. Talk is shaped in an indexical, i.e. context-related way, progressively incorporating contextual elements made locally relevant by the participants.
- Talk as it unfolds in real time is organized through finely tuned pluri-linguistic and multimodal details (such as verbal cues, but also gestures, facial expressions, glances, body movements...) which cannot be *imagined* but only *observed* in naturally occurring social interactions.
- This detailed sequential order is constituted through the coordination of participants' practices and embodied interpretations, and therefore has to be considered from within the members' perspectives (and not by projecting on them an omniscient exogenous analyst's vision, external to the observed action).

The data we will analyse here show that participants orient toward the temporal and contingent character of their practices and toward the embeddedness of talk and embodied performance, and that this orientation is materialized in the very way in which they produce the order of these practices.

This conception of how interaction works entails a particular perspective on code-switching, showing how it works as a resource for the organization of bilingual talk-in-interaction:

- Code-switching is understood as an endogenous resource, i.e. a resource defined and shaped by the participants, that produces a specific order of interaction.
- This resource is mobilized by participants in temporally and sequentially relevant ways: the appropriateness of code-switching is adjusted to the contingent and emergent construction of the turn and of the sequence.
- Choosing code-switching instead of another possible resource for organizing a given practice confers a specific accountability or intelligibility to the activity and to its actors, and produces specific interactional and social positionings of the participants.
- Participants orient to this specific intelligiblity of bilingual interaction produced by code-switching and reflexively adjust to it in the production of their next turns.

a specific context for the study of systematic practices

The data on which we will base our analysis were videotaped in the surgical department of a major French hospital. They document a complex activity going on in the operating room: the chief surgeon and a team are operating on a patient, using a minimally intrusive technique consisting in inserting into the body, without opening it, an endoscopic camera and the necessary instruments. The endoscopic image is displayed on the monitors in the operating room and looked at by the surgeons while they operate; it is transmitted by a videoconferencing device to an amphitheatre where an audience of advanced trainees is witnessing the operation projected on a big screen. In the same amphitheatre, a group of experts is also following the operation, both advising the surgeon about possible alternatives to the procedure and making comments for the audience. Thus, the event analysed here is a complex one, articulating various types of activities (such as operating, demonstrating the operation, advising, teaching) and involving interactions among members of the team, including interactions between the surgeon and the trainees (who can ask questions through a microphone set on each of their tables), and between the surgeon and the experts (see Mondada 2003, 2004a, 2004b).

In such a situation, participants face a practical problem: how to distinguish and to articulate various juxtaposed courses of action and the participation frameworks related to them? While this problem could be solved by mobilizing different linguistic (prosodic, syntactic, lexical) resources, code-switching is one which sets up a recognizable contrast between segments of action, situating and categorizing them in various ways. As we will see, this resource organizes not only action, but also participation, and thus also the distinction among different participant statuses as well as among categories, membership and social relations.

The code-switching practices studied here involve two sets of linguistic resources, oriented to and identified by the participants as 'French' and 'English'; the latter is characterized by some speakers as an 'English lingua franca spoken with a French accent', as this excerpt shows:

(1) (tc27028V/K1/15'22)

```
1    MAU    donc: je vais essayer de: d'abord (      )
            so: I will try to: first (      )
2           (.) d'abord merci à charles
            (.) first thanks to charles
3    LEL    maurac, maurac, maurac,
4    MAU    oui,
            yes,
5    LEL    it's better if you sp[ea:k euh (1.0) your
6    MAU                          [yes
7    LEL    international english [please,
8    aud                          [((laugh[ter))
9    MAU                                  [okay
10   LEL    very goo::d english [(.) <okay, ((laughing))>
11   MAU                        [((laughs))
12   MAU    thank you vo- for your invitation charles
13   LEL    hh hhh
```

```
14   MAU    and euh: (.) i performed this morning (.) euh extraperitoneal
15          approach (.) of (.) adrenalectomy, ((continues))
```

Lines 1–2 constitute Maurac's first videotransmitted turn at the beginning of his operation. His opening turn, in French, thanks the coordinator of the event, Charles Lelac, and projects more to come. However, Lelac, in a rush-through (Schegloff 1982: 76), produces a summons (3) (cf. Schegloff 1972), answered to by the recipient (4), and introduces a request repairing the linguistic choice Maurac has just made (5, 7). French is not nominated as such, but English is categorized in an expanded sequence, first formulated as 'your international english' (5–7) where 'English' is modified by the adjective 'international', itself prefaced by a possessive pronoun, indicating the particularity of that variety. This first formulation is received with some laughter; Lelac joins them in his turn's continuation, done with an ironic assessment ('very goo::d english' 10). Thus, participants orient to the fact that the event is going on in this kind of non-native English (and to which I will refer henceforth with the simplified gloss 'English'). French is not presented in a symmetric way as an available resource; this asymmetry shows an orientation of the participants to an 'official' stream of action, defined by English. As we will see, this does not exclude other streams of action and does not predefine the way in which activities in English will empirically and indexically be accomplished as such. As a result of this sequence, Maurac repairs his first turn, thanking Charles Lelac again and continuing in English.

However, English is not the only resource used, as the following excerpt shows, taken from another operation:

(2) (tc28038/k1d1/9')

```
1    BER    .h what is surprising, (0.5) is that (0.4) this part (0.5)
2           was not infiltrated, (1.0) by local anaesthetics.
3           (10.0)
4    BER    prends, lache ça. ça sert à rien. .h prends ça.
            take, let this. this is not helping for anything. .h take this.
5           (0.7)
6    BER    ouais.
            yeah.
7           (1.8)
8    WIL    are there any questions from budapest?
9           (1.3)
10   AUD    eh ya we have eh one questions. (.) .h how can you
11          deci:de (.) eh: (0.6) that you perform that laparoscopically,
12          or this technique,
13          (1.4)
14   BER    tsk .h (0.6) yes (1.0) yes. .hhh i no longer use
15          laparoscopy for hernia. (1.0) because i prefer local
16          anaesthesia in (.) all the cases. (0.9) °une kellie, ( )°
                                              °a retractor ( )°
17   pat    °( )°
18   BER    ça va, vous n'avez pas mal?
            is that okay, aren't you feeling bad?
```

```
19   pat    non (   )
            no
20   BER    qu'est-ce qu'i dit?
            what is he saying?
21   ass    qu'est-ce que vous dites monsieur marouani?
            what are you saying mister marouani?
22   pat    (   )
23   ass    ah mais ça c'est le tensiomètre là, on vous prend la [tension
            oh but that's the tensiometer there, we are taking your [pressure
24   BER                                                          [ah oui.
                                                                  [oh yes.
25          (0.5)
26   BER    °okay°. .hh eh i use eh local anaesthesia in all the cases,
27          (0.7) and, according to the type of hernia, (0.5) i choose a
28          technique. (0.8) in about (.) eh e:ighty percent cases (0.7)
29          it's a plug, (0.9) and in other cases, c'est pas bien là.
                                                    it's not good there.
30          (1.6)
31          it's eh: . Lichtenstein procedure,
```

The participation and activity frameworks of the broadcasted explanation and of the team's work are observably distinguished in the recorded event; they are *made hearable* in their differences. This distinction can be changed in the course of the action and is not just signalled or indexed, but indeed *accomplished* by the organization of participants' talk, in which code-switching, among other resources, is mobilized. Thus, it achieves a constant re-elaboration of the context by the participants themselves, in what Peter Auer calls 'discourse-related' code-switching, defined as a contextualization cue indicating a shift in any feature of the context such as footing, activity type, or topic, and indicating the way in which complex turns are structured (see Auer 1984, 1995). In our data, code-switching is used to contextualize different streams of action addressed to different recipients.

In excerpt (2), above, multiple participants and activities are intertwined: the chief surgeon, Dr Bertin, is both dissecting and explaining what he is doing in English (1–2), but he is also giving instructions to his assistant in French and in a lower voice (4–6). The expert, Dr Wilson, works as a chairman offering a distant audience from Budapest the chance to ask questions (8), an opening which is indeed taken up by a trainee (10–12). The question gets an answer (14–16), which ends with a request for an instrument to the assistant (16), followed by a side sequence with the patient (17–24) in French. The answer to the question is continued with a partial repetition in line 26, and the explanations goes on, with other possible insertions of instructions and evaluations (29) to the team.

Thus, this situation is characterized by:

- Multiple streams of action ('multi-activity'), either successive or simultaneous. These courses of action have to be organized by participants in a recognizable way; they also have to be organized in an adequately timed way, so that the temporality of the operation is correctly embedded in the temporality of the talk-in-interaction.

- A complex sequential organization, where multiple inserted sequences are often intertwined. Code-switching contributes to the recognizable delimitation of sequences (such as first and second parts of adjacency pairs, side sequences and other insertions) and to the recognizability of specific units or chunks within the turn (such as the instructions to the team, which are often embedded in it without being separated by any pause, although they can be prosodically marked by lower and faster voices). Turn constructional units (TCUs, cf. Selting 2000), which compose the turn, are dealt with both retrospectively and prospectively, within a constant orientation toward the accountability of what has been done, and the projection of the next action, which can either be a step in the surgical procedure or a next turn or unit in talk-in-interaction.
- Multiple linguistic resources, which are relevantly placed within the sequential unfolding of turns-at-talk, in a methodical and systematic way. Code-switching is managed by participants in order to constantly answer (members') questions: 'Why that now?' and 'What's next?' (Schegloff and Sacks 1973).
- Multimodal and visual resources, such as the organization of the operating field, the organization of the video perspective on it, the use of the instruments, constituting, through participants' actions, changing 'contextual configurations' (Goodwin 2000: 1490), i.e. a range of semiotic fields shaped by the participants' mobilization, through gestures, of various medias, artefacts, material objects.

the surgeon's delimitation of participation framework

If we look a little more in detail at the systematic ways in which French code-switched elements are inserted in English explanations, we see three different possibilities: we will present a short *set* of examples for each of them, that is a set of occurrences characterized by the same sequential environment. They show that the discontinuity represented by the insertion of a code-switched element can be dealt with either as not affecting the ongoing talk or as more or less seriously perturbing it. This in turn reveals the ways in which bilingual resources can be used in order to structure activity.

A **first set of cases** shows a minimization of the discontinuity expressed by the code-switching:

(3) (TC27028K1d1/36'30/montreAgauche/e1OTO)

```
1   LEL    we cut here (0.8) the: (.) superior pellicule,
2   WIL    °beautiful°
3   LEL    here too (0.6) and euh (.) when that
```

```
4              is done, (0.4) after that we kno:w that
5              montre à gau:che (.) on the: ri*ght side,*
               show to the right
  ass                                       *CAMERA MOVES TO LEFT*
6  LEL         we have no problem, and the dissection
7              will be very very easy,
```

(4) (TC27028K1d1/35'26/mDiaphr/e9TO)

```
1  LEL         and we have dissected (0.5)
2              montre-moi *mieux. non, plus *là-bas,
               show me *better. no, more there,
  ass                  *CAM IS ADJUSTED------*ZOOM-->
3              *the (0.6) superior* artery,
  ass                  --->*
```

Here, code-switching signals transitions in the activity and in the participation framework. These changes are organized not by an *a priori* association between activities and codes, but by the constraints and projections of each stretch of talk and element of action.

More particularly, in all these cases:

- the explanation is going on in English; it is suspended, often *not* at a turn constructional unit (TCU) boundary;
- a segment in French is inserted by the same speaker;
- after the insertion, the previous ongoing talk is continued from the point at which it was suspended.

In some cases, there is a pause before and/or after the insertion, but in others no gap is observable. We can notice that the temporal unfolding of the explanation is shaped by the activity of operating (as it is observable in excerpt 3, lines 1–4; after this first stretch, there are fewer pauses, since the operation is suspended and the explanation is the only activity going on). In all the cases, the insertion is done at a point of the ongoing turn where more is projected to come, either syntactically or prosodically. This next projected element is provided after the insertion, as a continuation of the previous segment, without any hitches, hesitations or repetitions. Thus, a minimization of the discontinuity represented by the insertion is displayed.

Although the insertion is done in a way that allows it to recognizably initiate another action and to be addressed to a participant other than the one in the previous talk, what it accomplishes is an action that makes possible the very next step of the ongoing explanation. The insertion is an instruction given to the team in order to accomplish a necessary condition for the next action. It is answered as such by an action of the assistant (who for example adjusts the endoscopic camera to make an anatomical detail visible; this movement can even be repaired, as in excerpt 4): the insertion represents a sequence of paired actions (instruction / instructed action). In this sense,

French insertions are not part of an independent stream of action, but of an action necessary for the explanation to go on. They shape the timing of the turn's unfolding in a way that depends on the surgical procedure: the way in which French is inserted into English is less related to the organization of the syntax of the English commentary than to the organization of the action of demonstrating or of operating, with its specific sequentiality.

A second set of sequences is more frequently observable in the data; in these cases, a distinct turn format is used:

(5) (TC27028V,STR,K1-d1/16'07intro/e1TO)

```
1 LEL  and now (0.9) we a- (0.6) oké allez tampon (0.9)
                            okay come on tampon
2      we are going to CUt the main adrenal vein,
3      (1.5) after that i just going to explain,
4      (0.8) *what we (1) want to do,
   ass      *INTRODUCES THE TAMPON--->
```

(6) (TC27028K1D1/38'30mlavcave/e11TO)

```
1 LEL  i think that if the patient is in a supine position,
2      .h it's VEry difficult, (.) and we imagine also that
3      here montre la veine cave .h we imagine that *he:re the:the
            show the vena cava
   ass                                       *MOVES CAMERA-->
4      main adrenal* vein, eh eh she looks like if it was antErior,
            ---->*
```

(7) (K1d1/24'22biplong)

```
1 CAD  okay so: as you see euh (.) °°hooh tu bouges hein michelle,°°
                            °°hooh you move around don't you michelle°°
2      (2.7)
3 CAD  euh as you see i try to: (0.5) s:- (.) squeletize and
4      control, (0.9) the vessels.
```

(8) (TC11068V/K2/d1/28'/p44/e1vals)

```
1 CAD  so it's (.) important to stay as (.) sans trop bouger oui merci
                            without moving too much yes thanks
2      (1.0)
3 CAD  it's important to stay as close as possible, (.) to
4      the gastric wall.
```

As in the previous cases, we have an insertion done by the current speaker. But, unlike the previous ones, after the insertion in French, the suspended talk is restarted by repeating the segment initiated just before the insertion. Usually this segment is the beginning of the syntactic constituent (as in excerpt 8, 'it's (.) important to stay as' line 1, repeated line 3). It is repeated without the conjunctions that tie back the initial utterance to the previous turn (as 'so' at the beginning of line 1, excerpt 8), which is no longer relevant. By this repetition, the speaker displays an orientation to the insertion as a discontinuity possibly making problematic the retrospective relation with the beginning of the segment.

We can note that the insertion is not always limited to a request, as in the previous cases, but can concern longer sequences, as in excerpt (2) above: in that case, the insertion initially concerns a request submitted to the team. But immediately after, another insertion is accomplished, with a question to the patient, whose answer is not heard by the surgeon: thus he initiates a repair of his understanding in the next turn. This produces another adjacency pair – another question/answer (lines 21–22) – between the assistant repeating the question and the patient answering with another question, answered in turn by the assistant. The surgeon displays an understanding of the exchange, and the second insertion is therefore closed by a return to the initial suspended segment.

Insertions are therefore dealt with as possibly perturbing (or not) the sequential continuity of the ongoing action. Their perturbing potential is displayed by the turn format adopted by the speaker, namely by the way in which the turn is continued after the French code-switch.

In a third set of cases, the most extreme one, the insertion is followed by its own topical development, in which a retrospective account describing what just happened is provided, and *not* by the continuation of the previous suspended talk, which is abandoned.

(9) (k2d1/28'10/prblFat/e14TO)

```
1    aud   do you use euh (.) coagulation or section, or
2          aren't you afraid ehm to use monopolar coagulation.
3    REV   °°(non c'est pas ça)°°
4    ass   °°t'as entendu,°°
5    REV   no we have the habit to: .h to use euh .hh a monopolar
6          coagulation, (0.4) for this kind of dissection, (0.6)
7          but in f- in fact i thin- <attend(ez) attends
                                     <wait wait
8          y a tout bouge, ((faster))> y a tout qui bouge,
           there is all moving, ((faster)) there is all moving,
9    ass   °c'est la graisse qui revient°
           °that's the fat which comes back°
10   REV   ouais. (.) c'est la graisse qui revient. .h so you see the
           yeah, (.) °that's the fat which comes back.
11         problem, euh:: sometimes we have to: (.) to (er)begin, (.)
12         the dispo(d)ition (.) in order to have a good vision, hh (.)
13         and so it's not very easy. (0.4) SO:, (0.3) .h no problem,
```

In this case, a question from the audience receives an answer after a brief insertion (3), the placement of which, just after a first pair part (the question), is noticed by the assistant orienting to the relevance of a second pair part (the answer) in this position (4). This answer is progressively abandoned, first perturbed and delayed, and then replaced by a switch to French dealing with an unexpected sudden event, the drastic modification of the anatomical space by the incursion of fat (which had been kept aside by a plier) into the surgical theatre, which renders the operation impossible.

In this case, the unexpected event is first dealt with by an insertion in French by Daccard. Second, this insertion is expanded by an adjacency pair initiated by the assistant and responded to by the surgeon (lines 9–10). Third, a retrospective comment in English describes and theorizes what just happened, and in a way normalizes it (going from 'you see the problem' to 'no problem'). Here, the segment in English does not continue the previous explanatory talk but is tied to what has been managed in French: the communication internal to the team is dealt with as publicly displayed, as manifesting a possible problematic moment, which has to be renormalized for the audience. In this sense, what happens in French and in English are two activities which reflexively configure each other's intelligibility. The explanation in English retrospectively elaborates and reshapes not only what has been said in French, but also what happened in the body.

In the three sets discussed so far, the surgeon deals with the situation by separating two types of activities (explaining or describing his action and instructing or requesting something), as well as two types of recipients (the audience and his team). By code-switching, he organizes his engagement in different streams of action, differentiating them in a clear and parsimonious way. However, these courses of action are permeable in various respects: the team's actions accomplish prospectively the condition for the next surgical or explicative step, and are therefore sequentially related; in addition, their actions are available for public scrutiny thanks to the video transmission, and in certain cases are further re-elaborated by a retrospective account.

the expert's reconfiguration of the operating space

The differentiation of the team and the audience is not only a matter of participation framework; it is also a matter of geographical space, strengthening the spatial division between the operating room and the amphitheatre. It is a way of making intelligible the articulation between two social and material spaces, one dedicated to the operation and the other one dedicated to teaching. For instance, audience members' questions are never asked in French. This distinction, however, is relativized by two considerations: first, it is constantly locally (re)accomplished, mantained by subsequent code-switches in specific sequential positions; second, it is contingent upon the way in which participants organize their action, and not determined by the geography of the setting.

It is interesting to look at the way in which the expert enters in this configuration: the very category of 'expert' is itself a phenomenon constituted through the organization of the activity that has to be reconstructed on the basis of the participants' orientations. In fact, the expert is himself a 'surgeon', and therefore a potential 'colleague' of the operating surgeon; he is also often someone who has done an operation just before and who has subsequently joined the expert's panel in the amphitheatre. These multiple possible categories show that, although separated geographically from the operating room, the colleague could be considered as part of it. Therefore, from the perspective of a Membership Categorization Analysis (as introduced by Sacks 1972), the question concerns the methods by which one of these categories is made relevant, as well as the way in which the expert makes his action understandable and recognizable as the action of an 'expert', a 'surgeon', a 'colleague' or even a 'member of the surgical team'.

If we consider self-selections by the expert and actions initiated by him, we see that they mobilize very different turn formats. Due to space constraints, we will mention only a few of them, relevant for the code-switching issues which concern us here.

A first format is shown by the following cases:

(10) (k2d1/30'30/liverRetractor)

```
1   REV    °zoom avant°
           °zoom forth°
2   SED    yves,
3   REV    yes,
4   SED    don't you think the liver retractor could be (.)
5          a little more to the left, so that it can help you,
6   REV    yes, yes, yes (.) [maybe
```

(11) (k2d1/34'25/space)

```
1          (1)
2   SED    yves,
3   REV    yes
4   SED    you open the spain- euh the space between spleen and
5          left cro[ss right,
6   REV    [yes, i have not so lot of choice,
```

(12) (30'27balloon)

```
1          (14)
2   SED    euh pierre-alexan:d[re,
3   DAC                       [yes,
4   SED    is the balloon deflated now,
5   DAC    yes
6   SED    okay.
7          (15)
```

This set of brief excerpts shows a method used by the expert to re-engage within the course of action: a summons–answer adjacency pair (Schegloff 1972) followed by a first pair part initiated by the expert, generally a question.

The summons–answer pair was first described by Schegloff (1972) as taking place at the very beginning of telephone conversations (corresponding the former to the ring and the latter to the 'hello?') in order to check the mutual availability of participants. Here the summons–answer occurs in the middle of the operation, securing the re-engagement of a distant participant after a lapse during which he was not the primary addressee of the surgeon (cf. Mondada in press). In this case, both the summons–answer sequence and the question are in English. In asking his question, the expert is both 'doing being the expert' and engaging in didactic questions for the audience.

A very different format can be adopted by the expert, as in the following case. The surgeon, Daccard, has just agreed, after some discussion, to change his instrument and to adopt a bipolar hook he generally does not use. The excerpt begins as Daccard indicates, both visually and with the initial announcement (1), that he is going to use it.

(13) (TC11068/K1D1/40'11bip)

```
1    DAC   okay (.) euh: i- i use the bipolar,
2          (3.2)
3    SED   i think it is the first time i see
4          you using this instrument,
5    DER   (([laughs]))
6    DAC     [yes,
7          (2.7)
8    DAC   °( ) (quand même) ( )°
             (nevertheless)
9          (1.9)
10   LEL   ah i faut serrer très peu avec la nôtre là
             oh you have to clasp very little with our one there
11         pierre-alain hein,
             pierre-alain haven't you
12         (0.4)
13   LEL   ouais. il faut un petit espace,
             yeah. you need a small space,
14         (1.1)
15   DAC   j'ai un petit espace
             i have a small space
16   LEL   parfait.
             perfect.
17         (1.2)
18   DAC   mais euh j'ai rien quand même
             but ehm i don't get anything anyway
19   LEL   ah mais i faut l'courant aussi,
             oh but you need some juice too,
20   SED   he he he[ he he °he° (.) .hhh
21   LEL          [.hh
22         (4.0)
23   DAC   vous êtes d'accord avec ce que j'fais là?
             do you agree with what I'm doing here?
24   SED   c'est beau,
             it's great,
25   LEL?  .hh hh h
```

```
26        (12.1)
27  DAC   i i i think it is interesting to:
28        (2.1)
29  DAC   °( ) (de plus en plus ça) (.) doucement°
          °( ) (more and more this) (.) slowly°
30        (1.8)
31  SED   you see pierre-alain. it WORks,
32  DAC   yes it works.
33        (0.8)
34  DAC   no no i think it's it's very interesting
35        because euh (.) in fact you can see here what you
36        have to euh do euh, (.) euh when you have a local
37        haemorrhage, and ((continues))
```

After Daccard's announcement (1), the first expert, Sedaine, makes an assessment (3–4) dealing with his manipulation of the instrument as exceptional. This assessment is received with some laughter by Daccard's assistant, and with a 'yes' by himself (6). But, after a pause, a unintelligible comment in French follows: the switch and the lower voice signal the emergence of a problem to be addressed in the team's space of action. After a short pause, the other expert, Lelac, gives a first suggestion (10–11) stating a condition which is positively embodied in Daccard's modified action during the short pause (12); this is further expanded by Lelac in the next turn (13), and confirmed again by Daccard (15) and his adjusted action. Again an assessment is produced closing the sequence (16). Nevertheless, the problem persists (18) provoking another suggestion (19), which is accompanied by laughter from both experts (20–21). This time the instrument is successfully used by Daccard who closes the sequence by checking the agreement of both experts. This is responded to by Sedaine's assessment (24) and Lelac's laughter. The sequence being closed in French, Daccard switches into English to initiate an evaluation of the procedure (27). This is suspended, by a type of inserted instruction in French we analysed above (29), and by an inserted sequence in English (31–32), but it is then restarted.

Various observations can be made here:

- Both experts self-select in order to give suggestions to the surgeon at a difficult moment: they do that in French and by engaging immediately in the (inter)action without any summons–answer sequence.
- Lelac's instructions to the operating surgeon are followed by him in a visible way, step by step, and evaluated as such.
- In this context, Lelac displays not only his expertise but also a familiarity with the instrument used (referred to with the possessive pronoun 'la nôtre' / 'ours' 10). In this way, he situates himself as a 'co-member of the team', even as the 'authority of the team', more than as an 'external expert'.

- Laughter and hyperbolic assessments (24) display an ironic responsiveness to Daccard's invitation to agree with him, and contributes to the familiarity and informality of this insert in French.

This expanded insertion in French is closed by the participants returning to English and by Daccard continuing his demonstration and providing a retrospective summary (this refers back to a problem preceding the inserted sequence, which is not commented upon and, in this way, ignored from the perspective of the official course of action in English). Code-switching is used here as a resource contributing to structuring the various activities and their hierarchical embeddedness, in which the experts are engaging as team members more than as audience members.

In other cases, as in the last excerpt, this order can be blurred by an emergency or a persistent difficulty disrupting the course of the demonstration, which is abandoned (cf. above, excerpt 9). In this case, the expert can differentiate his interventions, which can recognizably be produced as a 'colleague's' suggestion aligning with the emerging difficulty or as an 'expert's' didactic question (at the end):

(14) (TC11068k3/20′02difficulty/e18TO)

```
1    DAC   °j'crois qu'y a un problème là.°
           °i think there's a problem here.°
2          (5.1)
3    DAC   attends y a quelqu'chose qui va pas. (0.4) pousse-la,
           wait there's something wrong. (0.4) push it,
4          (0.6)
5    DAC   .hhh euh re- re repoussez un petit peu le: l:- l'anneau,
           .hhh euh push the th- the ring a little bit ag- again
6          (0.6)
7    DAC   push: push the nasogastric tube please.
8          (1.2)
9          slowly,
10         (2.4)
11         okay, (.) push,
12         (2.5)
13   DAC   ça va pas? (1.3) vous n'y arrivez pas?
           doesn't it work? (1.3) don't you succeed?
14         (5.3)
15   SED   euh pierre-alain,
16   DAC   yes,
17   SED   could you comment on the difficulty you have now?
18   DAC   YES eh (.) <oké oké, c'est bon, c'est bon, ((faster))> (0.4)
                       <oké oké, it's right, it's righ, ((faster))>
19         .h main- maintenant vous commencez à tirer s-
           .h no- now begin to pull on-
20         (1.2)
21   DAC   ouih (.) doucement
           yeahh (.) slowly
22         (0.6)
```

```
23  DAC  voilà, oké. you see here the bulge, (0.8) i can't see
          here it is, okay.
24        the bulge until now.
25        (1.3)
26  DAC  continuez,
          go on,
27        (2.2)
28        continuez, tirez encore, (0.5) tirez encore,
          go on, pull again, (0.5) pull again,
29        (6.3)
30  DAC  ouais mais vous n'passez pas l'anneau. (0.4) my problem is that-
          yeah but you don't pass the ring. (0.4)
31        (1.4)
32  SED  tu dois ouvrir l'anneau complètement hein
          you have to open the ring completely don't you
33        (2.0)
34  DAC  non i passe pas. (2.1) on passe pas, il est trop-
          no it doesn't go through. (2.1) it doesn't go through, it is too-
35        (1.7)
36        voilà (.) tirez bien, (0.5) tirez, (0.3) o:ké. (.) ça y est.
          here we are (.) pull well, (0.5) pull, (0.3) o:kay. (.) that's it.
37  SED  you see how he is obliged to stretch (0.3) the stomach
38        to: to put the banding.
39        (13)
```

This fragment is extracted from a decisive phase of the operation, in which a ring has to be put around the stomach in order to reduce its volume. The operating surgeon, Daccard, notices a problem (1) and solves it (36). The way in which this is interactionally managed constitutes its accountability as a 'difficulty': (a) this category is *explicitly named* (Daccard speaks of 'problème' 1, and the expert, Sedaine, of 'difficulty' 17), and (b) these categories are *displayed* by the disrupted coordination of the multi-activities at hand. Although the problem is initially noticed and dealt with in French with the team, instructions in English are given just afterwards (7, 9, 11), dissolving the distinction between doing the operation and demonstrating it. Moreover, explanations are initiated in English but not continued or suspended (as in lines 18 or 30).

In this sequence, the expert self-selects for accomplishing very different actions:

- The first time (15), he re-engages in English with a summons–answer pair, followed by a request for an explanation. This request is acknowledged by Daccard, but not realized, the temporality and organization of the operation taking precedence over the demonstration.
- The second time (32), Sedaine self-selects in French, without any pre-sequence, and gives a suggestion to Daccard, who has just abandoned a fragment of explanation.

- At the end of the excerpt (37), Sedaine self-selects again in English and addresses the audience: he doesn't speak *to* Daccard anymore, but speaks *about* him (with a third person pronoun).

In this way, Sedaine methodically adopts different positions within the activity, oriented to different recipients. In a very local way, he switches from one participation space to another, performing different kinds of actions: as chairman securing the continuity of the demonstration, as colleague and co-member of the team, and as teacher providing comments on what happens in the absence of the surgeon's explanation.

shaping the flexible interactional and institutional orders

The empirical data examined here show a specific *and* systematic use of code-switching as an organizational resource in a complex work setting. Even though English as a lingua franca is presented and dealt with as the official language of the event being broadcasted, French is another resource contributing to the intelligibility of the organization of talk and action in a context of multi-activity. We tried to show that the distribution of these plurilingual resources is not mechanical (not determined by fixed *a priori* factors) but methodical (in the sense of Garfinkel 1967: accomplished by systematic members' procedures). Participants orient to the relevant use of code-switching and reflexively constitute its relevance by choosing specific sequential positions and by shaping specific regimes of accountability of what is going on. This opens up the possibility of reconfigurations of participation frameworks, category-bounded activities and delimitations of recognizable groups. In this sense, local and contingent uses of code-switching accomplish a flexible geography of action and of social relations.

More specifically, code-switching has configuring effects on various levels:

- It contributes to the recognizability of the organization of turns and sequences, especially in environments where frequent insertions and expansions are observable. In this sense, code-switching makes observable the way in which participants orient to the questions 'why that now?' and 'what's next?' in the production and interpretation of their ongoing practice, thereby contributing to fundamental features of turn and sequence construction.
- It contributes to the recognizability of multi-activities, distinguishing between various streams of action: more particularly, activities such as operating have an order which does not necessarily converge with the order of talk-in-interaction. The latter is nevertheless intertwined with the organization of the former, incorporating its contingencies and constraints as configuring dimensions producing the intelligibility of the ongoing talk.

- It contributes to multiple recognizable orientations to recipients and to participation frameworks. It achieves the way in which participants themselves shape, distribute and reconfigure relevant categorization devices, by orienting to the speakers in terms of paired categories, such as 'evaluating expert' / 'operating surgeon' or 'colleague' / 'colleague', 'chief surgeon' / 'assistant', 'expert' / 'trainee'). Moreover, these orientations build groups, alliances, hierarchical positions and (a)symmetries through the ways in which either they align, assemble and unify the participants so categorized or oppose, distance and rank them. Being dynamic, these orientations, embedded into the organization of talk, of action and of interaction, provide resources for drawing or displacing boundaries, for reinforcing straightforward categorizations or for reconfiguring them.
- It contributes to making visible and intelligible the institutional order in which the action is going on, by defining its public dimension, by categorizing events as 'officially broadcast', 'submitted to public scrutiny' or 'concerning restricted areas and persons'.

In this sense, code-switching contributes to our understanding of the active and creative use of local resources for the organization of action. The interactional approach of code-switching and bilingual talk emphasizes the embodied and situated sense of plurilingual resources and practices as they are dynamically shaped by the participants themselves in the course of their interactions.

In this chapter, we emphasized a perspective dealing with code-switching as an endogenous flexible resource for constituting the interactional order. This perpective shows that code-switching is not the manifestation of bilingual identities either in an *a priori*, generic or a mechanical way: code-switching exhibits efficient situated and contingent capabilities of simultaneously organizing action, configuring context, and doing categorial positionings of participants. In the workplace, this shows that code-switching can be a powerful resource for building the order of work activities; this order is achieved by specific ways of doing, that are locally anchored in the participants' identities and at the same time elaborate them.

transcript conventions

Data were transcribed according to conventions developed by Gail Jefferson and commonly used in Conversation Analysis.

[	overlapping talk
=	latching
(.)	micro pause
(0.6)	timed pause
:	extention of the sound or the syllable it follows

.	stopping fall in tone
,	continuing intonation
?	rising inflection
mine	emphasis
°uh°	quieter fragment than its surrounding talk
.h	aspiration
h	out breath
((sniff))	described phenomena
< >	delimitation of described phenomena
( )	string of talk for which no hearing could be achieved

An indicative translation is provided line per line (in italics), in order to help reading the original.

Descriptions of gestures and actions are transcribed according to the following conventions (cf. Mondada 2003):

* *	a gesture is delimited between two symbols and synchronized with corresponding stretches of talk
cam	the participant making the movement is identified in the margin if (s)he is not the same person as the actual speaker
ZOOM	gestures and movements are described in small capitals
-----	the gesture is held until the next closing boundary symbol
---->	the gesture is held until the next symbol, situated on the following line
....	gesture preparation
,,,,,	gesture retraction

references

Auer, P. (1984). *Bilingual Conversation*. Amsterdam: Benjamins.
—— (1995). The pragmatics of code-switching: A sequential approach. In L. Milroy and P. Muysken (eds), *One Speaker, Two Languages: Cross-Disciplinary Perspectives on Codeswitching*, pp. 115–35. Cambridge: Cambridge University Press.
—— (ed.) (1998). *Code-Switching in Conversation: Language, Interaction and Identity*. London: Routledge.
—— (2005). A post-script: Code-switching and social identity. *Journal of Pragmatics* 37: 403–10.
Cromdal, J. (2001). Overlap in bilingual play: Some implications of code-switching for overlap resolution. *Research on Language and Social Interaction* 34: 421–51.
Day, D. (1994). Tang's dilemma and other problems: Ethnification processes at some multicultural workplaces. *Pragmatics* 4(3): 315–36.
Drew, P. (2003). Conversation analysis. In J. Smith (ed.), *Qualitative Psychology: A Practical Guide to Research Methods*, pp. 132–58. London: Sage.
Firth, A. (1990). 'Lingua franca' negotiations: Toward an interactional approach. *World Englishes* 9(3): 269–80.
Garfinkel, H. (1967). *Studies in Ethnomethodology*. Englewood Cliffs, NJ: Prentice Hall.

Goodwin, C. (2000). Action and embodiment within situated human interaction. *Journal of Pragmatics* 32: 1489–522.

Heller, M., M. Campbell, P. Dalley and D. Patrick (1999). *Linguistic Minorities and Modernity: A Sociolinguistic Ethnography*. London: Longman.

Heritage, J. (1995). Conversation analysis: Methodological aspects. In U. Quasthoff (ed.), *Aspects of Oral Communication*, pp. 391–418. Berlin: De Gruyter.

Luff, P., J. Hindmarsh and C. Heath (eds) (2000). *Workplace Studies*. Cambridge: Cambridge University Press.

Mondada, L. (2003). Working with video: How surgeons produce video records of their actions. *Visual Studies* 18(1): 58–72.

—— (2004a). Ways of 'doing being plurilingual' in international work meetings. In R. Gardner and J. Wagner (eds), *Second Language Conversations: Studies of Communication in Everyday Settings*, pp. 27–60. London: Continuum.

—— (2004b). Téléchirurgie et nouvelles pratiques professionnelles: les enjeux interactionnels d'opérations chirurgicales réalisées par visioconférence. *Sciences Sociales et Santé* 22(1): 95–126.

—— (in press). Turn Taking in multimodalen und multiaktionalen Kontexten. In H. Hausendorf (ed.), *Gespräch als Prozess*.

Müller, A. (in prep). *Sprache und Arbeit. Ein Beitrag zur Ethnographie der innerbetrieblichen Kommunikation anhand von Fallstudien in Frankreich, Spanien und Deutschland.*

Rasmussen, G., and J. Wagner (2002). Language choice in international telephone conversations. In K.K. Luke and T.S. Pavlidou (eds), *Telephone Calls: Unity and Diversity in Conversational Structure across Languages and Cultures*, pp. 111–31. Amsterdam: John Benjamins.

Sacks, H. (1972). An initial investigation of the usability of conversational materials for doing sociology. In D. Sudnow (ed.), *Studies in Social Interaction*, pp. 31–74. New York: Free Press.

—— (1984). Notes on methodology. In J.M. Atkinson and J. Heritage (eds), *Structures of Social Action*, pp. 21–7. Cambridge: Cambridge University Press.

—— (1992). *Lectures on Conversation*. London: Blackwell, 2 vols.

Schegloff, E.A. (1972). Sequencing in conversational openings. In J.J. Gumperz and D. Hymes (eds), *Directions in Sociolinguistics: The Ethnography of Communication*, pp. 346–80. New York: Holt, Rinehart and Winston.

—— (1982). Discourse as an interactional achievement: Some uses of 'uh huh' and other things that come between sentences. In D. Tannen (ed.), *Analyzing Discourse: Text and Talk*, pp. 71–93. Washington: Georgetown University Press.

—— (1999). Discourse, pragmatics, conversation analysis. *Discourse Studies* 1(4): 405–35.

Schegloff, E.A., and H. Sacks (1973). Opening up closings. *Semiotica* 8: 289–327.

Selting, M. (2000). The construction of units in conversational talk. *Language in Society* 29: 477–517.

Silverman, D. (1998). *Harvey Sacks and Conversation Analysis*. Cambridge: Polity Press.

Skårup, T. (2004). Brokering and membership in a multilingual community of practice. In R. Gardner and J. Wagner (eds), *Second Language Conversations: Studies of Communication in Everyday Settings*, pp. 40–57. London: Continuum.

Wagner, J. (1998). Silences in international communication. In D. Albrechtsen et al. (eds), *Perspectives on Foreign and Second Language Pedagogy*, pp. 79–91. Odense: Odense University Press.

Watson, R. (1994). Harvey Sacks' sociology of mind in action. *Theory, Culture and Society*, 11: 169–86.

Wei, L. (2002). 'What do you want me to say?' On the Conversation Analysis approach
    to bilingual interaction. *Language in Society* 31(2): 159–80.
—— (ed.) (2005). Special Issue: Conversational Code-Switching. *Journal of Pragmatics*
    37: 275–410.

15

the monolingual bias in bilingualism research, or: why bilingual talk is (still) a challenge for linguistics

peter auer

introduction

For a long time, linguists found it difficult to account for the use of two or more 'languages' within one utterance by the same speaker. It was acknowledged of course (from the nineteenth century onwards, at the latest) that languages can 'borrow' structures from other languages without ever returning them to the 'owners' (to stick to this somewhat problematic metaphorical field). No doubt languages such as German or, even more so, English had massively copied lexical and – to a lesser extent – grammatical elements (above all derivational affixes) from other languages, such as Latin or French. However, these borrowings were exclusively analysed post factum, i.e. after they had become fully incorporated into the borrowing language. Few linguists were interested in languages whose status was unstable and ambiguous; among them was the Austrian Hugo Schuchardt who investigated 'mixed' languages such as creoles and Romani varieties as early as 1884 and came to the conclusion 'dass eine Sprache A ganz allmählich, durch fortgesetzte Mischung, in eine von ihr sehr verschiedene B übergehen kann' ['that a language A can transform slowly but steadily, by constant mixture, into a language B which is very different from it']. He continued on a somewhat fatalistic note: 'Für die Beantwortung der Frage aber ob sie an einem bestimmten Entwickelungspunkt noch A oder schon B zu nennen sind, fehlte es uns gänzlich an Kriterien' ['However, we would lack all criteria to answer the question whether they can still be called still A or already B at a certain point of development'] (1884: 10).

On the level of the individual, the coexistence of two languages only started to become a topic some time later, when linguists became interested in speakers with a foreign 'accent', or in those who 'wrongly' used the grammar of their second language because their 'mother tongue' had a different structure and the acquisition of the second language had not been fully successful. In contradistinction to borrowing, processes of such 'interference' (as this seemingly mechanistic overlay of one language over the other was aptly called; cf. Weinreich 1953) were considered to be entirely derivative of the two language systems (or their cognitive representations) which interfere with each other in the individual. What was observed in the (imperfect) bilingual was analysed as either a transient or a non-successful case of second language acquisition which left the interfering languages unaffected. Both phenomena (borrowing on the level of the linguistic system and interference on the level of the individual learner) were thereby treated in such a way that they did not question the existence and autonomy of the two languages in contact. Both could be handled within an approach to language which started from the seemingly trivial assumption that there *were* languages such as German, Latin or French which could be neatly and unambiguously separated from one another.

In this chapter I argue that the most profound way in which bilingual talk (code-switching, mixing, and the rest) has challenged linguistics is the fact that its analysis leads to the inevitable conclusion that this assumption cannot be taken for granted. Bilingual talk blurs the line between language A and language B, but also between 'langue' and 'parole', between linguistic systems and their usage, between knowledge and practice. It questions the starting point of linguistics as a whole: in code-switching studies, it turns out that a 'language' cannot be a prime of linguistic analysis (cf. Le Page 1989).

The idea that linguistics has as its object self-contained linguistic entities (systems) called languages, and that bilingualism is a derivative of the combination of two of these languages, is of course part and parcel of the nation-state language ideology which dominated European thinking at the time when linguistics established itself as a discipline. The nation-state ideology views a language as a 'natural' reflex of nationhood (and inversely, a common language as a justification for nation-building); each nation has one (and only one) national language. It led to the compartmentalization of linguistic research into the European national philologies which left little room for research on those cases which the model obviously did not fit. More important than disciplinary divisions, however, was the reification of the national languages which this language ideology implied; they were treated as 'natural' facts, despite the enormous purificational efforts most European nations had to invest in their very creation. For the burgeoning new discipline of (structural) linguistics, these languages appeared to be (the only) solid objects. It was forgotten that they showed a high degree of structural regularity and homogeneity precisely as a consequence of the standardization processes which had led to their emergence, and the language ideology which accompanied it. In this framework, bilingualism, if it was considered at all, could only be treated as a form of individual deviance, from which an individual 'suffered' unless s/he was a 'perfect' bilingual (i.e. double monolingual), and sometimes even then: obviously, if belonging to a nation was identified with speaking its (one) language, then speaking two languages implied belonging to two nations, having two national identities; and how could somebody be both 'German' and 'French', or both 'Japanese' and 'Chinese'?

This benign neglect of bilingual talk lasted until the middle of the last century. The attraction it has developed since then for linguists of all backgrounds neatly mirrors the transformation linguistics underwent as a discipline at that time. First, the neglect of situated language use (*parole*) was challenged by the inclusion of pragmatics and discourse or conversation analysis into linguistics. Spontaneous data began to be analysed in their own right, not just in terms of a deficient application of a rule apparatus. The beginnings of this pragmatic turn in linguistics were quite independent from research on bilingualism; they started in different branches of linguistics, heavily relied on other disciplines such as philosophy and sociology, and remained within a monolingual framework. However, they laid the grounds for viewing code-switching (a) as a performance phenomenon which nonetheless showed a good deal of regularity (Poplack 1980) and (b) as a discourse strategy which had its own discourse-functional meaning (Gumperz 1982). Second, socio-linguistics established itself as a new paradigm. Bilingualism became a social issue together with large-scale immigration movements into countries which so far had considered themselves to be monolingual, and with language rights movements insisting on the maintenance or even revitalization of 'old' minorities in the European nation-states. Third, generative linguists moved away from analysing idealized speaker/hearers and turned to the direct investigation of the principles of Universal Grammar; and since bilingual speakers doing code-switching/-mixing could be presumed to use such principles, bilingual talk provided access to UG (as do, for instance, creoles). The search for universal constraints of code-switching found its origin and theoretical justification in this line of thought.

All these changes, and the truly impressive amount of research they have triggered, have greatly increased our knowledge of bilingualism as a social and individual phenomenon. Nevertheless, I believe that there are at least three issues which continue to challenge linguistic thinking, all tied to the central question: can bilingual talk be reduced to two-sided monolingual talk? These issues, which are the topic of this chapter, are:

(1) where does one language stop and the other start in bilingual talk?
(2) where does code-switching/-mixing belong – to grammar or performance? and
(3) are the languages used in bilingual talk the same languages that are used in monolingual talk?

Orthodox linguistic thinking as established over the history of linguistics presupposes a clear answer to the first and second questions, and a positive one to the third. It is only in this way that the assumptions about languages as bounded systems which have been foundational in the discipline can be upheld.

where does talk in one language ('code', variety) stop and talk in the other start?

Many investigations from the 1980s onwards (including Auer 1984; Li 1994) have shown that in certain speech communities, languages tend to be opposed to each other in systematically meaningful (i.e. discourse-functional) ways, and in such a way that neither the speakers nor the analysts have great doubts about assigning a given stretch of talk to one language or the other. Even in these communities though, there are certain stretches of talk which are of ambiguous or ambivalent status regarding their categorization as language A or language B. Studies on other bilingual communities, particularly those in which the two varieties in contact are structurally closely related, and those in which the use of the two languages is not discourse-functional (i.e. on code-mixing), have been added in recent years (cf., among many others, the contributions in Auer (ed.) 1998), and it has become more and more obvious that the clear-cut alternation between one language/variety and the other (code-switching in the strict sense of the term as used in Auer 1999) is but one case of bilingual talk.

Utterances may belong to both 'codes' in play and therefore be ambivalent. More precisely, the 'codes' may converge to such a degree that for the speakers and recipients of bilingual talk, no clear delimitation is possible.[1] Among the clear cases of ambivalence are so-called homophonous diamorphs or their approximations, but also discourse markers such as hesitation particles (*uhm*) or agreement markers (*mm*), and proper names.[2] Since Michael Clyne's 1967 book, we know ambivalent stretches of talk may facilitate or even trigger switching from one language into the other. Examples (1) and (2), below, show two cases of such a triggering (or, in a less deterministic way of speaking, facilitating) of code-switching by near-homophonous diamorphs.

(1) Clyne (1980: 400): German descent immigrant in Australia

wir nehmen unsre biecher **fär vier** (-) *for four periods*
we   take   our   books   for four
'we take our books for four – for four periods'

Here, the near-homophonous diamorphs are dialectal German /fɛr/ and Australian English /for/ as well as German /fiːr/ and Australian English /for/.[3] The closeness of German and English facilitates switching into English, the dominant language of this speaker, which in itself is likely to be due to the non-availability of the German equivalent of English *periods*. In the transcription, italics indicate what would count as English according to the linguist's judgement. This follows common usage in bilingualism research which enforces a dichotomic opposition between the two languages. But triggering shows that the perceived distance between the two languages is not always the same (as it should be the case between two language systems), but rather a matter of degree.

(2) Bierbach and Birken-Silverman (personal communication, 2003): male Italian guestworker in Germany, old-age pensioner in Germany

was essena, was trinken, **alles chemie (-) alles *chimica* (-) *non c'è niente naturale***
what eat   what drink   all chemistry   all chemistry   NEG there-is nothing natural
'what we eat, what we drink, it's all chemical, all chemical, there is nothing natural'

Here, the near-homophonous diamorphs are German /kemi:/ and Italian /kimika/. The dominant language of this speaker is Italian (his German exemplifies what has been called a 'guestworkers' pidgin'), and he uses the closeness of Italian and German in order to switch into the latter. The transition is smoothened by the repetition of *alles chemie* in a mixed version (German quantifier, Italian head in the noun phrase *alles chimica*).

While these examples seem simple enough (and abound in the literature: cf. Clyne 1987; Muysken 2000), they already indicate an important problem: it is not the linguists who decide on how convergent two structures need to be in order to facilitate a bilingual speaker's switch from one language into the other, but rather that the decision is up to the bilinguals themselves. It thereby turns out to be a matter not only of structural distance but also of the perception of this distance between the 'codes' which in turn may be subject to attitudinal matters, including language ideologies.

There is an additional issue. In the two examples cited above, the near-homophonous diamorphs do not differ from the respective words in monolingual talk. However, bilinguals do not usually speak like two-fold monolinguals. Rather, the 'codes' they oppose in 'code-switching' are THEIR variants of the respective monolingual codes. In the discussion of the two examples, we assumed that the convergence is purely linear, or syntagmatic (*in praesentia*), and that it is this on-the-spot convergence which creates fuzziness in the transitions from one language/'code'/variety into the other (and maybe even triggers it). This, however, is not necessarily the case, since the systems themselves can converge (paradigmatically, or *in absentia*). The simplest case is lexical convergence: bilinguals copy lexical items from language B into language A. Consider the following example:

(3) Bierbach and Birken-Silverman (personal communication, 2003): female middle-aged Italian guestworker born in Sicily, living in Germany

basta   ca   c'è   frau diener
enough that there-is Ms Diener

si   rump tutt- u **scist**.
REFL breaks whole the shift

die macht die ganz atmoschphäre da   drin
she makes   the whole atmosphere   there in-there

'if there wasn't Frau Diener the whole shift would break down. She makes the whole atmosphere in there'

While the third turn component of this utterance is clearly dialectalized German, and *Diener* a German family name (and as such outside of what can be translated), the middle turn component contains an element which could be classified either as an integrated loan or as an ad hoc lexical insertion from German into Italian (dialect): *scist* 'shift'. Accordingly, using italics for German and normal font for Italian, the utterance might just as well be transcribed as:

si   rump tutt-u *scist*.
REFL breaks whole the shift

Scist derives from the German word *Schicht* /ʃiçt/ in its local dialectal form with a coronalized fricative instead of the standard palatal one: /ʃiʃt/. Syllable-final /ʃt/ is not well-formed in Sicilian and the palatal fricative therefore turns into an alveolar. This phonological adaptation ('integration') might be taken as an argument for *scist* having been copied into the variety of Sicilian/Italian spoken in Germany by immigrants/guest workers. As part of this variety, it may 'trigger' the switch into German, since it is a homophonous diamorph of German *Schicht*. However it is well known that phonological integration also occurs ad hoc and is not restricted to established loan-words, and that established loans may surface in their quasi-original shape (see example 6 below and the subsequent discussion). If we consider *scist* to be an ad hoc borrowing, then we are dealing not with convergence between two distinct language systems, but with an example of insertional mixing preparing alternational code-switching (cf. Auer 1999 for this terminology).

Here is another example:

(4) bilingual Italian adolescents in Germany; data from 1980s: Auer (1983: 337)

quandə sono   sceso   de quella scuola da   a **hauptschule**;
when   to-be-1.Sg. descend-PART from this   school from the 'secondary modern' (= the lowest level in the German school system)
'when I left this school the "secondary modern"'

sənə   venutə   in   quella quella scolə
to-be-1.Sg. come-PARTICPLE in   this   this   school
'I came into this other school' (= the more prestigious, middle level in the German school system)

u **deutsch** a mi (-) era uguale com=enda a **hauptschule**;
the German for me – was same   as   in   the 'secondary modern'
German (as a subject) was the same for me as in 'secondary modern'

gar   keine (prob) (–)
PARTICLE no (problem)
'no problem at all'

wir schreiben   keine diktate   nix;
we write-1.Pl.Präs. no   dictations nothing
'we write no dictations, nothing'

Again, there is a code-switch from Italian (dialect) into German. Two words in the Italian passage preceding the switch may have facilitated this transition: the word *hauptschule* (a particular German school type), and the word *deutsch* as a school subject. In both cases, the fact that there are no equivalents in Italian supports their classification as part of these Italian adolescents' variety of Italian. On the other hand, they may also be analysed as ad hoc borrowings, i.e. as a case of code-switching (or -mixing) themselves. Under one interpretation, the convergence is paradigmatic, under the other, it is syntagmatic.

Issues of indeterminacy of this kind are a notorious problem for studies on code-switching/-mixing, rendering the idea that bilingual talk can (as the term 'bilingual' suggests) be studied by separating stretches of talk in one language from those in the other problematic. I will argue in the next section that there is no way of drawing a clear boundary between integrated borrowings on the one hand (which could then function as diamorphs for their 'monolingual' counterparts in the source language, and hence serve as facilitators of language alternation), and language switching of a single lexical item (which of course cannot be its own facilitator) on the other. In the section after that I will show that grammar is also affected. Here, the point is that there is no monolingual 'area of security' to which we linguists can turn in order to describe and make sense of the bilingual data: the monolingual speakers and their grammars which we tend to refer to are of no help.

Various researchers on bilingualism have shown that ambiguous stretches of talk between language A and language B not only 'happen' but are *made* to happen by the speakers. Speakers may, for interactional reasons, wish to produce a conversational contribution which cannot be classified as language A or language B. The most straightforward way of doing so is the intra-turn translation of an utterance into the other language, with the effect of performing (more or less) the (same) action twice, but in two languages. Monica Heller (1988) has described code-switching as a way to achieve 'strategic ambiguity' (and neutrality) in certain contexts in such a way. For structural linguistics, these cases are unproblematic since despite the fact that the speaker wants to keep language choice open, the turn-internal stretches of talk in language A and language B are easy to identify. More difficult are grammatical units in which elements from two different languages are conjoined by ambivalent elements which can be part of both. Kathryn Woolard (1987, again in 1999: 7) gives an example of an intentionally hybrid utterance of this kind. It is the standard opening phrase of a Catalan comedian (Eugenio):

(5) Woolard (1999: 7)

el **saben**　aquel...
he know-3.Pl. this-one...
'do you know this one...'

It draws its humour exactly from this hybridity: the verb *saben* is either Catalan or Castilian, while the third person pronoun *el* is Catalan and the object pronoun *aquel* is Castilian. Between these elements the neutral *saben* functions as a pivot, making the utterance as a whole impossible to classify as either Castilian or Catalan, and the transition from Catalan into Castilian impossible to locate exactly.

In the examples discussed so far, the ambiguous stretches of talk were short. However, the same ambivalence may be found over larger units as well. Celso Alvarez-Cáccamo (1990) reports on Galician/Castilian bilinguals in Galicia who use Galician prosody with Castilian lexical items and syntax in certain situations. Since the two varieties are very close in structural terms, prosody is enough to make Castilian grammar and words sound Galician. The speaker thereby camouflages their use of Castilian without wholeheartedly speaking Galician. The structural hybridity of talk is mirrored by its social-interactional neutrality.

borrowings: grammar or discourse?

I have started out with a very simple observation, i.e. the fact that the exhaustive, non-residual segmentation of bilingual talk into utterances in one language and utterances in the other is not always possible, or at least more problematic and more presupposing than is often thought. I have used the structuralist terms 'paradigmatic' and 'syntagmatic' to refer to two kinds of convergence which stand in the way of such a segmentation. It is tempting to conclude that paradigmatic convergence is tantamount to convergence of two systems, while syntagmatic convergence is a discourse phenomenon. This, however, is not true. There is a continuum of insertions with ad hoc (nonce) borrowing at one extreme, and sedimented borrowings (words which are habitually used by a certain speaker or even in a bilingual community) at the other extreme. Only in the second case is the borrowing part of the 'system' of the receiving variety (i.e. shared knowledge in the speech community).

While the extreme points of the continuum are relatively easy to describe, there are many intermediate positions on this scale which are less obvious. Many researchers on bilingualism therefore argue that a clear boundary between discourse (nonce borrowing) and the language system (lexical loans) cannot be defined (cf. Treffers-Daller 1994; Gardner-Chloros and Edwards 2004; Backus 1996; Angermeyer 2005: 325). The most obvious criterion, i.e. phonological and morpho-syntactic integration into the receiving language, is not only gradual in nature itself, it also does not yield satisfactory results: as mentioned before, ad hoc insertions can be integrated just like established loans. Take the following example of a French verbal stem (*cueill-*) inserted into an Alsatian (dialectal) sentence:

(6) Gardner-Chloros and Edwards (2004): French-Alsatian code-switching in Strasbourg

ah voilà, nitt dass se   do *cueill*ier, un gehen dann uf d'ander Sit
PART   not that they there pick-INF, and go   then to the other side
'yes there you are, they shouldn't pick, and then go to the other side'

There is no established loan word *cueillier(e)* in Alsatian. The word is made up from a French verbal stem (cf. French *cueill+ir*) and a dialectal infinitive ending (*-ier* = /iːr/) and inserted into an Alsatian sentence frame. In this frame, a non-integrated French verb would sound awkward. In order to make the insertion well-formed, the speaker uses a German (and Alsatian) strategy which dates back hundreds of years as a way of integrating Latin and French stems, i.e. the suffix *-iere(n)*.[4] This strategy itself is a French borrowing, but established in German and integrated into its morphology since the Early New High German period. The result is the ad hoc production of a compromise form in which there is a mixture between the two languages: a verb with a French stem and a Germanic suffix.

It may be objected that morphological integration was facilitated by the strong morphological similarity of the two languages in this particular case (the infinitives *-ir* and *-ier,* both /iːr/). This surely cannot be said of the following example of an English ad hoc insertion into a Russian frame:

(7) Angermeyer (2005:329)

čto vy duma-ete nepravil'no s   ètim   *estimate*-om?
what you think-2.Pl. wrong   with this-INSTR estimate-INSTR
'what do you think is wrong with this estimate?'

Again, *estimate* is not an established loan in Russian. However, the speaker makes the noun fit into the Russian sentence frame by adding the instrumental case to it, as it ought to be with a Russian noun.

The matter of integration has been discussed here in a very simplistic way, referring to surface integration by morphological means only. Of course there are more subtle methods of integration, both in phonology and phonetics and in grammar. With regards to the latter, Poplack and colleagues (e.g. Poplack and Meechan 1995) have shown that insertions which are not surface-marked for integration into the matrix language can nonetheless be syntactically integrated by obeying the structural requirements of word order of the surrounding language. In all these cases of integration of an ad hoc item, the item is used according to the system of the surrounding language without actually becoming a part of it (in this case, a part of the vocabulary).

But what does it mean to say that an insertion is or is not part of the linguistic system of the language into which it is inserted? If structural adaptation does not provide a feasible method to establish the loan status of an insertion, what we are left with is frequency of use. However, it is obvious that frequency of usage is nothing but a very superficial generalization over individual usage patterns. While some speakers may use the inserted items regularly, others may not even know it. While some speakers may use the inserted item to replace an item in the receiving language, others may give it a specific meaning, etc. It certainly does not provide an explanation of how items are copied from one language and integrated into the other. To find such an explanation, the underlying steps (practices) which lead to social diffusion have to be investigated.

I want to suggest that at least in the beginning of the structural sedimentation of a lexical insertion from language B into the system (lexicon) of language A, discursive strategies can be identified. Regularly, there is a difference between the first use of an (ad hoc) borrowing within a conversation, and the subsequent uses of the same word. That is, the first insertion is marked as an unexpected language choice, and thus metapragmatically framed as a deviation from the 'proper' (i.e. cooperatively established) language choice at that moment. Later the same word is used without such marking. For instance, in the following extract from a group discussion with Italian adolescents in Germany, one of the boys uses for the first time in this interactional episode the German word *Lehre* in an Italian (dialectal) context. (The Italian equivalent for 'apprenticeship' would be *apprendistato*. We do not know whether it was known to the speaker – chances are it was not. However, the

word was known in the community and used by (some) adult Italians. This
is reflected in the way the German insertion is treated in a conversation in
which an adult Italian was present.)

(8) Italian/German/Italian dialect

Al.: ho=   pensatə= cha=mo: forse fazzə   primo=**una:** (-) **na**   *Lehre*,
    have-1.Sg. think-PART that now perhaps make-1.Sg. first   a[std.] (-) an[dial] apprenticeship

    (-) che c'ho a   practica roppə è più megliə
        that I-have the practice   then   is more better
    'I thought that perhaps first I'll go on a (-) an apprenticeship, so that I have more practice,
    this is better'

The speaker hesitates before he uses the German word, marking his word
search by the repetition of the indefinite article, the elongation of the vowel
in the second syllable of the first variant of the article, and by the pause
between the two. The word is articulated carefully in standard German. In
the subsequent conversation, the same word is used again several times by
the same speaker, but each time without such a marking, and partly in a
colloquially reduced version (without the final schwa):

(9) subsequent uses of *Lehre* by the same speaker, in chronological order

(a) voglə   fa   prima na *lehr;*
    want-1Sg make first   a   apprenticeship
    'I first want to do an apprenticeship'

(b) dopp che=   hai   fatt=   a *lehr* (.)   continua a scuolə
    after   that-CONJ have-2Sg made-PART the apprenticeship continues the school
    'after you've finished your apprenticeship, school continues'

(c) prima=a *lehre*   andá   u *tege*
    first   an apprenticeship go-INF   the T.G.[5]
    'first an apprenticeship – then grammar school'

(d) fare prima na *lehre;* (-)   qu=   è più megliə e que   prendə a *praxis;*
    do   first   an apprenticeship that-CONJ it-is more better   and that-CONJ take-2.Sg. the practice
    'do an apprenticeship first; so that it is better and so that you have practice'

(e) più meglə a fa prima na *lehre*   che ro   cioé veramend=a *praxis*
    more better to do first   an apprenticeship so-that then PART really   the practice
    'it is better to do an apprenticeship first so that then (you've) really (got) practice'

Here, we can observe sedimentation *in statu nascendi*. All uses of *Lehre* are
insertions into an Italian dialectal matrix, of course; but the more the speaker

repeats the word, the less it is treated as an 'intruder' into Italian, and the less its usage becomes problematic from the point of view of language choice. It goes without saying that a fully established loan word would not be framed in such a way.

In a recent dissertation on bilingual talk in New York small claim courts involving translators, Angermeyer (2005; also cf. Angermeyer 2002) has shown that other-language insertions of this kind can be used in order to create cohesion. He observed that the vast majority of lexical insertions used by the interpreters are words that had been used by one of the participants before, usually in the source text to be translated. Sometimes it also was the litigant or claimant who inserted items used by the translator in his or her subsequent turns, as in the following example:

(10a) Angermeyer (2005: 28), simplified; claimant wants be compensated by landlord for having had to hire an exterminator for her apartment

Claimant:	Eso es de ((shows a receipt))
	'that's for...'
Interpr.:	es de
	'it's for...'
Claimant:	eso es del del **fumigador** [que fue
	'that's for, for the exterminator who came'
Interpr.:	[*that's for the **exterminator***

who [*went to the apartment*

Claimant:	[***exterminator***
Arbitrator:	*ah, sorry*
Claimant:	[***exterminator***
Interpr.:	[desculpe
	'sorry'

There is no reason to believe that *exterminator* is an established loan in Spanish as spoken in NYC (in fact, the claimant uses the word *fumigador*). However, once the translator has introduced the English term (in 10a), the claimant uses this term herself as an insertion in her Spanish utterances; see the following extract from the same proceedings, which occurred after (10a):

(10b) Angermeyer (2005: 28), same participants as (10a)

Arbitrator:	*what else are you* [s
Interpr.:	[que yo tuve que
	'that I had to'
Arbitrator:	*suing* [*for besides this and this?*
Claimant:	[eh que que
	'uhm to to'

Interpr.:	y que? [y
	'and what?' and'
Claimant:	[eh ah solicitar un ex un *exterminator* de verdad
	'I had to solicit a real exterminator'
Interpr.:	*so I had to f ah find a real exterminator.*
Arbitrator:	*okay.*

As in the Italian example, the first occurrence is marked (here in a dialogical fashion: the Spanish-speaking claimant takes up the interpreter's translation of his *fumigador* into English by repeating it twice, as if she was eager to memorize it), while in the subsequent uses the newly acquired or remembered word is used as if it had always been part of the speaker's repertoire. Examples such as these mark the beginning of 'integration' – a discursive strategy. Individual use is the starting point, and a loan is nothing more than the consequence of the repeated use of an item.

I have argued for a continuum of lexical insertions from ad hoc (nonce) borrowings to established loans. But if this is true, the question must be asked: where does switching/mixing belong – to the language system or to discourse? The question links up with the old dilemma about the nature of grammatical constraints on bilingual talk. Many researchers have pointed out that code-mixing is subject to certain (language specific) structural constraints, and have described structured ways of making the two grammars compatible. These clearly reflect some kind of linguistic knowledge (competence) on the part of the speakers. On the other hand, only rarely have linguists written 'grammars' of code-mixing (in a non-metaphorical sense of the word), since (apart from extreme cases such as fused languages like Michif or Copper Island Aleut; cf. Bakker 1994) mixing, although constrained, is not obligatory and predictable, and therefore outside the reach of grammar (in the sense of the *ars obligatoria*). The problem is not all that unfamiliar to linguists who work on grammaticalization, or in some version of exemplar theory in phonology, both of which question the clear division between grammar and discourse. So here we have a second area of indeterminacy.

the two codes of code-switching/-mixing

The examples of paradigmatic convergence discussed above concerned lexical insertion. Most researchers on bilingualism agree that insertion requires, by its very nature and definition, a grammatical frame of the receiving language into which the borrowed item is inserted. It is generally concluded that although a high number of insertions of language B elements may occur in a grammatical unit (such as a sentence, clause or complementizer phrase), they cannot change its belonging to language A. There remains a neat imbalance between what Myers-Scotton (e.g. 2002) calls the 'matrix language' which provides the grammar of the unit as a whole, and the inserted elements which find their place in this matrix. Grammar (morphology and syntax) tells us which language a grammatical unit 'really' belongs to, the lexicon is superficial. This is a conviction which is as old as linguistic research on language contact. As early as 1898 Hermann Paul expressed it as follows:

> Er [der Einzelne] wird vielleicht, wenn er beide [Sprachen] gleich gut beherrscht, sehr leicht aus der einen in die andere übergehen, aber innerhalb eines Satzgefüges wird doch immer die eine die eigentliche Grundlage bilden, die andere wird, wenn sie auch mehr oder weniger modifizierend einwirkt, nur eine sekundäre Rolle spielen. (1898: 366)
> ('He [the individual] who masters the two [languages] equally well, will perhaps very easily go from one into other, but within a sentence construction, there will always be one [language] which forms the real basis, the other will play a secondary role, even though it may be more or less a modifier.')

More than a hundred years later, Myers-Scotton echoes this conviction when she writes:

> One of the languages involved in C[ode]S[witching] plays a dominant role. This language is labelled the Matrix Language (ML), and its grammar sets the morphosyntactic frame [...]. (1993: 229)

Let us therefore look at grammar, and pursue Myers-Scotton's argument somewhat further here.

The matrix language in this model provides (most of) the grammatical morphemes and the word/morpheme order of the clause as a whole. Myers-Scotton's theory acknowledges that some morphological elements from the embedded language may nonetheless appear in a sentence (so called early system and bridge system morphemes). What must be provided by the matrix language, however, are system morphemes which have grammatical relations external to their head constituent (e.g. those which assign or receive thematic roles) such as morphemes taking part in subject/predicate congruence, case, tense and aspect morphology (cf. Myers-Scotton 2002: ch. 3).

There are, however, clear counter-examples to this claim. In this case, a constellation of morphemes (including late system morphemes) is taken over as a whole and inserted into the matrix languages. Myers-Scotton calls these complex insertions 'embedded language islands' and postulates that their internal make-up follows the grammar of the embedded language. Embedded language islands occur, among other things, when the grammar of the matrix language and that of the embedded language are non-congruent. She gives the following example:

(11) Myers-Scotton (2002: 99): English/Swahili, data from 1988

a-na-i-tumi-a   *for personal purposes*
3sg-nonpast-obj-'use'-FV
'he uses it for personal purposes' (refers to his car mentioned in previous discourse)

Here, the set prepositional phrase *for personal purposes* is an island within a Swahili sentence. The island occupies the position of an adverbial phrase in Swahili, but its internal syntax is well-formed according to English syntax, not according to Swahili syntax.

The model is attractive because it predicts a neat separation of the domains of the two grammars in contact. One is responsible for the matrix, the other for the insertions, even when they are internally complex. However, Raihan Muhamedova (2006) has described code-mixing between Kazakh and Russian and between Uighur and Russian in Almaty which systematically contradicts this pattern. Among the systematic structures she identified which have a direct bearing on the question of embedded language islands we find nominal Russian islands (NPs) in Kazakh (or Uighur) complementizer phrases. Cf. the following extract:

(12) Muhamedova (2005: 83–4): Kazakh/Russian[6]

Men me (.) menıñ bala-m   bar, žetpıs alpïs-nšï žïl-ǧï.
I   I   my   child-POS1P EXIST seventy six-ORD   year-ADJ
I   I (.) have a child, born in seventy six

высш-ий   школ-dï bïtïr-d osïnda
high   ??   school-AKK finish-3Ps here
He finished high school here

(.) *транспорт-н-ый*   milicija[7]-da iste-dı.
      traffic-SUFF-NOM.Sg.MASK   police-LOK   work-3Ps.
and then he worked here with the traffic police

The speaker inserts the complex Russian noun phrase высш-ий школ into a Kazakh matrix frame, which receives the Kazakh accusative suffix *-dï*. However, in contradiction to the prediction by Myers-Scotton's model, this embedded language island is not well-formed in the donor language, Russian: in monolingual Russian the noun phrase would be высш-ая школа. Two differences between monolingual and 'bilingual' Russian are noteworthy. First, in the insertion the Russian head of the NP, школа, has lost the final vowel (truncation). This is remarkable since the suffix carries the most important morphological information in Russian (such as case, gender and number in the noun). Thus, while the Russian suffix /-a/ marks the word as a feminine noun, its truncated equivalent as used in code-mixing cannot be assigned gender any longer (or, if the rules of monolingual Russian are applied, its gender is now masculine). Second: the adjective modifying the head carries a suffix, but from the point of view of monolingual Russian, it is the masculine suffix (/ij/) instead of the feminine one (/aja/) which is required to achieve congruence with the (monolingual Russian) feminine noun школа. What has happened? Saying that the noun's gender has changed from feminine to masculine would be monolingually biased. More plausibly, the Russian feminine noun has lost its gender entirely, and the /ij/-suffix in высш-ий has become the unmarked form of adjectival ending. At this point it is important to know that Kazakh has no gender. This means that, as the matrix language, Kazakh not only governs the external syntax of the insertion (i.e. its position within the sentence and its case, cf. the suffix), but it also influences its internal structure: the Russian used in the embedded language island has converged with Kazakh. It is therefore substantially different both from monolingual Russian as spoken in Russia, and also from Russian spoken by the same informants in Almaty who only rarely speak simplified Russian (without gender) in monolingual talk.[8]

This is not a singular case. Take the following, somewhat more complex example from the same data set:

(13) Muhamedova (2005: 85): Kazakh/Russian

Sosïn ne (–) o orïs   *заведующ-ий*-lar   ke-p
then   uhm (–) r Russian director-NOM.Sg.MASK-Pl   come-CONV
then uhm (–) when the directors (of the library) come

žaňaǧï *книж-н-ый*   *выставк-а*-lar   tema-lar-ï-n   ne-ler-i-n
this/uhm book-ADJ-NOM.Sg.MASK exposition-?Sg.FEM-Pl theme-Pl-POS3P-AKK thing-Pl-
POSS3P-AKK

sura-ǧan-da, ...
ask-PART-LOK
and uhm ask for the themes and things of the book expositions ...

Again, the matrix language of this CP is Kazakh. The complex insertion we are interested in is the noun phrase made up of a modifying adjective and a head noun: книж-н-ый выставк-а. Once more, the Russian island (or rather: its head noun?) additionally receives a Kazakh suffix (the plural -*lar*). In monolingual Russian, 'book expositions' is книж-н-ые выставк-и, with the plural obligatorily marked on both the head and the modifier (the singular is книж-н-ая выставк-а, feminine marked both on the head and the modifier). However, the island produced by the bilingual speaker has the structure shown in Figure 15.1; or alternatively, in Figure 15.2. (The thick bracket marks non-congruence from the monolingual Russian point of view.)

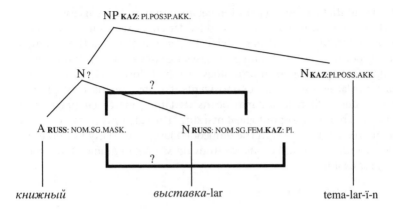

Figure 15.1

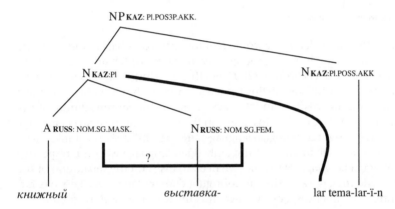

Figure 15.2

Under both analyses, the NP книж-н-ый выставк-а fails to satisfy the requirement that islands be well-formed in the embedded language. As in the first example, the adjective receives a suffix which, according to Russian grammar, is masculine, while the head noun has a feminine ending. Again, there are good arguments that the latter is not analysed as a gender suffix any longer, and that the former is a gender-neutral adjectival suffix. In addition, example (13) shows a change in the number-marking system of Russian. While monolingual Russian requires number to be marked both on the head and on the adjectival modifier, Kazakh marks plural on the head only. книжный выставка-*lar* is a plural NP, which is marked according to the Kazakh system on the head noun (using the Kazakh suffix).[9] The modifier is unmarked for number. In sum, all the morphology of this island is Russian, yet the way in which this morphology used is not Russian, but Kazakh. Is the embedded NP then Russian or Kazakh?

It turns out that the neat separation between the two languages which the distinction between matrix and embedded language seems to guarantee is not achieved in Myers-Scotton's model. The author gives another example for this by pointing out that numerous cases are attested in which the matrix language fails to provide the morphology of a single inserted lexical item, i.e. in which the latter is strong enough to 'ward off' matrix language integration. As a consequence, 'bare forms' may be inserted into a matrix language frame which would require morphological marking. They are ungrammatical both in the matrix language and in the embedded language. Many examples for this can be found in Louis Boumans's study on Moroccan Arabic/Dutch code-mixing, for example:

(14) Boumans (1998: 218)

> mša *discothek*
> go   disco
> 'we went to the disco'

Arabic as the matrix language would require a preposition (/l-/) and a definite prefix on the noun; however, the speaker integrates Dutch *discothek* without such a marking. Myers-Scotton (2002: 66) therefore insists on not equating the matrix language with any existing language, let alone the monolingual contact language (ibid) – it is just an 'abstract frame for the morphosyntax of the bilingual CP'. While bare forms question the identity of the matrix language with the respective monolingual language, the Kazakh/Russian examples given above question the identity of the embedded language with the respective monolingual language. Here, too, we need to insist on the separation of the embedded language and the monolingual contact language. This has far-reaching consequences. For instance, it is unclear how notions such as the Myers-Scotton's 'congruence' between the matrix and the embedded language (the lack of which is made responsible for the occurrence of islands) should be defined. It is even unclear how morpheme order and late system morphology can be established without reference to the corresponding monolingual variety; this is crucial, since of the identification of the matrix language relies on it: if the latter cannot be equated with the monolingual code, we have no means of identifying it. The conclusion, however, is inevitable: bilingual talk cannot be analysed as a mixture of two monolingual codes. An alternative has been formulated in a 1998 paper by Mark Sebba in which he shows that congruence is indeed a condition for mixing, but that this congruence is not defined by the linguist looking at monolingual codes, but by the bilinguals themselves, who achieve it by strategies such as 'harmonization', 'neutralization', 'compromising' and 'blocking': 'Bilinguals "create" congruent categories by finding common ground between the languages concerned' (Sebba 1998: 8). Sebba argues that a bilingual community establishes the congruence of the categories of the languages involved the longer it exists; or, in other words, paradigmatic convergence in grammar will take place under conditions of long-standing bilingualism.

conclusion

In this chapter I have argued that the traditional approach to bilingual talk as the combination of two pre-existing language systems is hard to reconcile with syntagmatic and paradigmatic cases of 'code convergence' and therefore leads to a number of difficulties. In the second section, syntagmatic and paradigmatic 'code convergence' were shown to result in factual and/or perceived stretches of ambivalent talk between language A and language B. In the next section, I have argued that paradigmatic convergence in the lexicon (borrowing) is best analysed as an ongoing process of sedimentation based on ad hoc insertions the beginnings of which can be observed as interactional strategies within an interactional episode. The section after that showed that the distinction between matrix language and embedded language is useful but that the two must not be equated with the respective monolingual varieties since structural convergence may take place between them which does not occur in monolingual speech (even by bilingual speakers). As a consequence, I suggest that the starting point of bilingual analyses can no longer be two languages, but rather a collection of discursive and linguistic practices used by bilingual speakers in a community, and based on certain grammatical/lexical/ phonological feature constellations. These constellations may be opposed to each other for functional reasons (as in discourse-functional code-switching), or they may stand side by side and constitute one speaking style (and therefore one 'code'), or they may become amalgamated into a new system such as in the so-called 'mixed' (or fused) languages (cf. Auer 1999). Seen from this perspective, the separation of two 'codes' in terms of historical languages becomes a secondary issue.

The answers to the questions that I raised at the beginning of this chapter – i.e. (1) where does one language stop and the other start in bilingual talk? (2) where does code-swiching/mixing belong, to grammar or performance? and (3) are the languages used in bilingual talk the same languages that are used in monolingual talk? – are therefore hard to give in the first two cases, and negative in the third. With respect to (1), it seems that the bilingual speakers can choose to make the issue relevant or irrelevant, and that in both cases, ambiguous stretches of talk may result. With respect to (2), there is evidence that sedimented patterns of mixing (including what is known as borrowing) have their origin in discursive practices which may or may not make their way into the language 'system' (in terms of the shared linguistic knowledge in a community). Together with the negative answer to the third question, these results suggest that the assumption of bound linguistic systems as the object of linguistic research is questioned by bilingual practices. This is the challenge which bilingualism continues to represent for linguistics.

notes

1. Hill and Hill (1986) use the structuralist term of syncretism (irrelevance of an opposition) to refer to such linguistic objects.
2. With the exception of royalty and popes, a name designating a certain person does not translate into its equivalent (if there is one) in the other language; an Englishman by the name of *Charles* cannot be called in German by the equivalent of this name in this language, *Karl*; the translation would destroy the referential force of the proper name, and the speaker would not be heard as referring to 'Charles' any longer.
3. Depending on the phonetic realization of the words, particularly the final /r/, the objective contrast between the languages may be more or less pronounced.
4. The dialectal form has deleted the standard German final -*n* (as in all unstressed -*en#*-sequences) and in the present case, presumably due to an allegro rule, the -*e*- preceding this -*n* as well. Note that the word is thereby made to sound very much like the French equivalent (from which it is only distinguished by the quality of the /r/).
5. 'Technical Gymnasium', a form of secondary school.
6. While Kazakh is usually written in Cyrillic, it is transliterated here, partly to highlight the difference between the two languages, and partly because Cyrillic is not well-suited for Kazakh phonology.
7. *Milicija* is an established Russian loan word in Kazakh.
8. As Muhamedova shows, the restructuring of Russian as a genderless language is quantitatively the dominant pattern in Kazakh/Russian code-mixing, although it rarely occurs in monolingual Russian spoken by the same informants (also see Auer and Muhamedova 2005).
9. Note that the Kazakh number suffix is not attached to the Russian stem, but to the Russian word form in the feminine singular. The stem is reanalysed from выставк-а as выставка.

references

Alvarez Cáccamo, Celso (1990). Rethinking conversational code-switching: Codes, speech varieties, and contextualization. In *Proceeding of 6th Annual Meeting Berkeley Linguistic Society. General Session and Parasession on the Legacy of Grice*. Berkeley: Berkeley Linguistic Society, 3–16.

Angermayer, Philipp (2002). Lexical cohesion in multilingual conversation. *International Journal of Bilingualism* 6: 361–93.

—— (2005), *'Speak English or what?' – Codeswitching and interpreter use in New York Small Claims Courts*. Unpublished PhD thesis, New York University, Dept. of Linguistics.

Auer, Peter (1983). *Zweisprachige Konversationen*. Unpublished PhD thesis, University of Constance.

—— (1984). *Bilingual Conversation*. Amsterdam: Benjamins.

—— (ed.) (1998). *Code-Switching in Interaction*. London: Routledge.

—— (1999). From codeswitching via language mixing to fused lects: Toward a dynamic typology of biligual speech. *International Journal of Bilingualism* 3: 309–32.

Auer, Peter, and Raihan Muhamedova (2005). 'Embedded language' and 'matrix language' in insertional language mixing: Some problematic cases. *Italian Journal of Linguistics* 17(1): 35–54.

Backus, Ad (1996). *Two in One: Bilingual Speech of Turkish Immigrants in the Netherlands*. Tilburg: University Press.

Bakker, Peter (ed.) (1994). *Mixed Languages: 15 Case Studies in Language Intertwining*. Amsterdam: IFOTT (Instituut voor functioneel onderzoek van taal en taalgebruik) at the University of Amsterdam.

Boumans, Louis (1998). *The Syntax of Codeswitching: Analysing Moroccan Arabic/Dutch conversation*. Unpublished PhD thesis, University of Nijmegen.

Clyne, Michael (1967). *Transference and Triggering*. The Hague: Mouton.

—— (1980). Triggering and language processing. *Canadian Journal of Psychology* 34: 400–6.

—— (1987). Constraints on code-switching: How universal are they? *Linguistics* 25: 739–64

Gardner-Chloros, Penelope, and Malcolm Edwards (2004). Assumptions behind grammatical approaches to code-switching: When the blueprint is a red herring. *Transactions of the Philological Society* 102(1): 103–29.

Gumperz, John (1982). *Discourse Strategies*. Cambridge: Cambridge University Press.

Heller, Monica (1988). Strategic ambiguity: Codeswiching in the management of conflict. In M. Heller (ed.), *Codeswitching: Anthropological and Sociolinguistic Perspectives*, pp. 77–97. Berlin: Mouton.

Hill, Jane, and Kenneth Hill (1986). *Speaking Mexicano*. Tucson: University of Arizona Press.

Le Page, Robert (1989). What is a language? *York Papers in Linguistics* 13: 9–24.

Li, Wei (1994). *Three Generations, Two Languages, One Family*. Clevedon: Multilingual Matters.

Muhamedowa, Raihan (2006). *Untersuchung zum Kasachisch-Russischen Code-Mixing (mit Ausblicken auf den uigurisch-russischen Sprachkontakt)*. Munich: Lincom

Muysken, Pieter (2000). *Bilingual Speech: A Typology of Code-Mixing*. Cambridge: Cambridge University Press.

Myers-Scotton, Carol (1993). *Duelling Languages*. Oxford: Clarendon.

—— (2002). *Contact Linguistics*. Oxford: Oxford University Press.

Paul, Hermann (1898). *Principien der Sprachgeschichte*. 3rd printing. Halle: Niemeyer.

Poplack, Shana (1980). Sometimes I'll start a sentence in Spanish y termino en espanñol: Toward a typology of code-switching. *Linguistics* 18: 581–618.

Poplack, Shana, and Marjorie Meechan (1995). Patterns of language mixture: Nominal structure in Wolof–French and Fongbe–French bilingual discourse. In L. Milroy and P. Muysken (eds), *One Speaker, Two Languages*, pp. 199–232. Cambridge: Cambridge University Press.

Schuchardt, Hugo (1884). *Slawo-deutsches und Slawo-italienisches*. Graz: Leuschner & Lubensky.

Sebba, Mark (1998). A congruence approach to the syntax of code-switching. *International Journal of Bilingualism* 2: 1–20.

Treffers-Daller, Janine (1994). *Mixing Two Languages: French–Dutch Contact in a Comparative Perspective*. Berlin: Mouton.

Weinreich, U. (1953). *Languages in Contact*. The Hague: Mouton.

Woolard, Kathryn (1987). Codeswitching and comedy in Catalonia. *Pragmatics* 1: 106–22.

—— (1999). Simultaneity and bivalency as strategies in bilingualism. *Journal of Linguistic Anthropology* 8(1): 3–29.

16
the future of 'bilingualism'

monica heller

In the winter of 2006, I received a phone call from a journalist for the local outlet of the State-run French-language radio. She was working on a report on 'the quality of the French spoken by francophone youth in Toronto'. She was concerned because, as a *Québécoise* who had been in Toronto for six years, she noticed that she had a hard time understanding local youth; that they used a lot of English; that they didn't seem 'proud' to be francophone, the way she and her classmates in Quebec had been at their age. For her, a language is 'like a muscle; if you don't use it, it atrophies'. That is, each person starts out with one language; bilingualism can only take away from it. You end up 'speaking neither language properly', and this puts you at a disadvantage in job interviews, or when you want to talk to people from other places.

I arranged for her to interview six high school students (including, I have to reveal, my son and his best friend, both of whom were happy to go into ideological battle against the dominant discourse). She asked them if they did not find it difficult to keep up their French; they all looked at her blankly and said no, they didn't find it difficult. She asked if they had a hard time communicating with Francophones from other parts of the world, say France, or Quebec. Oh, yes! they said. Those people speak very strange French, ours is much clearer. She asked how they felt about being bilingual (actually, several of them are multilingual, with family ties to places like Italy and Algeria). They said it's a big advantage; although you can't really count on having a secret language, it turns out too many people share their French–English bilingualism with them.

The show that was eventually aired took no account of these responses. It was a show about the difficulties of trying to maintain French in an English world, about the struggle to attain the quality of French you would expect in a monolingual environment, about the importance of fighting for the minority language cause. It was a programme about an idea of bilingualism in which the state, state agencies and large numbers of actors have a major stake.

This volume has made a case that what we have been studying all these years is perhaps less bilingualism than 'bilingualism', that is, our work has oriented to a concept which makes sense only within the discursive regime of the nation-state, with its homogenization and equation of language, culture, nation, territory and state. Now that we are asking questions about that regime, now that we are imagining other, more complicated and fluid ways of organizing ourselves, we are questioning the concept, and therefore also how best to understand the phenomena we associate with it.

In many ways, the questions asked here are quintessentially late modern. We are reluctant (as Tabouret-Keller points out in her Afterword) to give up entirely any notion of system and boundary, any notion of constraint (whether physical or social). At the same time, we can no longer see these as fixed, natural, essentialized or objective; rather, we want to understand them as ongoing processes of social construction occurring under specific (and discoverable) conditions (many of them of our making, all of them made sense out of in some social way).

In addition, we understand that the very concept of 'bilingualism' is a doorway; what has been hitherto an anomaly to be explained, becomes instead central to our understanding of current social change. The very phenomena that the term captured (hybridity, movement, polyphony, multivalency, ambiguity) are the ones most characteristic of our times. And so, while the term still harks back to the idea of a fixed system which we are trying to move away from, the ideas it indexes begin to show us in what directions we can move. 'Bilingualism', as a result, splits into two related phenomena.

The first is the idea of bilingualism, and what it tells us about ideologies of language, society, culture and cognition. That is, we need to know what ideas about bilingualism people have, if any; who remains wedded to formerly dominant ideas about bounded systems, and who is trying to dislodge them? In favour of what? Why? This is of course a fundamentally and overtly political question: it asks in whose interest it is to construct language(s) and their relationships in certain ways, and in whose interest it is to attribute what value to various ways of managing ideologically organized linguistic forms and practices – or rather, of managing the variability that has always been at the heart of questions about bilingualism.

The second is, then, those variable forms and practices themselves, that is, the observable ways in which people draw on linguistic resources in situ, and how this connects up to the circulation of resources over time and space, as well as to the circulation of people through activities where resources and discourses are produced and distributed. How to capture what exactly it is that people are doing with language? How to explain what it means? How does it fit in with other social practices?

The chapters in this volume have proposed a number of ways in which to address this question. Or perhaps, put differently, they have recognized, and begun to work through, the methodological implications of seeing bilingualism as ideology and practice. The authors in this collection have argued that we have to pay attention to a number of things at once. We need to pay attention to the political economy of linguistic resources, that is, to who produces them, who controls their circulation, and who controls their value. In the globalized new economy, this works differently from the ways it used to, and so our ideas about territory (which really assume a society in which the most important forms of communication are face-to-face, or at any rate extremely circumscribed in time and space) are now complicated by mobility and by multiple forms of far-ranging communications. Similarly, as national markets come into new tensions with international markets, and as the market itself becomes more oriented to communication-related forms of production and consumption, and to language-related products, the meaning and value of linguistic variability is shifting. Finally, it seems very clear that both language and identity are being commodified, often separately. What are the consequences of this for our ideas about what constitutes language? or for our ideas about what constitutes appropriate ways of managing linguistic diversity? or of what counts as legitimate language?

The question also remains of how all this works out on the ground. We therefore need to pay attention to situated practice. Even when conditions are relatively stable, there are always local contingencies. In times of change, we can see how social construction of categories, value and relations of power work only by identifying sites that are revealing and examining how actors draw on available resources to conduct their daily lives.

At the same time, we need ways of connecting the two. We can follow the trajectories of spaces, of discourses, of goods and of actors, rethinking socio-linguistic ethnography in ways more oriented to process and practice than to community or identity. Nonetheless, the idea of 'bilingualism' does allow us a purchase on what counts as relevant categories; already we are oriented to discovering how speakers organize their linguistic resources (perhaps as 'languages', perhaps not), and how that categorization helps organize social categories and the positioning of individuals with respect to them. It points us to a focus on how boundaries happen: how people and practices get included and excluded, and what happens to them and to the categories as a result.

Bilingualism is thus a kind of fault line, a space particularly sensitive to and revealing of social change, both in terms of how we understand it and in terms of the phenomena we see when we orient our gaze in the ways we have learned to, and which we need to find new ways of describing and explaining, since the older frame no longer holds so well. We need to explain the various little things that no longer add up.

Some of these things can be captured by some of the following vignettes (all from my own experience or fieldwork). They all point to ways in which canonical associations of language, culture and individual identity break down, sometimes in ways which stop social life from unfolding altogether, sometimes in ways which are neutralizable or erasable.

- A Chinese couple on a downtown Toronto thoroughfare stop a Chinese girl and ask for directions. But they ask in Chinese, and she doesn't speak the language of the ancestors who once came to Canada from China.
- In the late 1980s, I go to visit a Serbo-Croatian (sic) heritage language class in Zurich. Many of the students are Albanian speakers from Kosovo. In Toronto, third generation speakers of southern Italian dialects are sent to learn standard Italian as their 'heritage language'.

In both these cases, someone is assuming the wrong thing about other people and their linguistic competence or associated ethnolinguistic identity. Someone who looks Chinese doesn't speak Chinese, someone whose family originally comes from Italy doesn't speak standard Italian (or maybe doesn't speak Italian at all), children from the state of Yugoslavia turn out not only to not speak the same language but to come from groups at war with each other.

In other cases, languages turn out to be floating around in unexpected places.

- In Ottawa, someone receives an email from Portugal, in Portuguese, asking about a product. She sends out an email to all employees: can anyone speak Portuguese? Someone in IT can, it turns out. Problem solved.
- A colleague in France receives a phone call from the police. They need help interpreting tapes of a wire-tapped suspected drug smuggler speaking to contacts in Canada. The suspect is from Senegal, and lives in France. It turns out he learned Canadian French in Central America, on the drug route from South to North America.

All these cases are destabilizing from the perspective of dominant ideologies. They challenge existing modes of regulation and surveillance (in the case of the French police, quite literally) in which expectations about the distribution of linguistic resources figure directly or indirectly. They make it difficult to categorize, and therefore to judge.

Thus in some ways, we can say that the idea of bilingualism held the seeds of its own transformation. Once we accept that things are not actually uniform, we have to see the things that will not fit in any fixed frames. As soon as we start looking closely at real people in real places, we see movement. We see languages turning up in unexpected places, and not turning up where we expect them to be. We also see them taking unexpected forms. Just moving to an idea of bilingualism is not enough containment for this movement and multiplicity, probably not under any circumstances, but certainly not under current ones.

Close inspection of bilingualism also holds the seeds of a reanalysis of the relationship of sociolinguistics to social theory. In order to account for this multiplicity and this movement, it becomes necessary to move away from separation of linguistic from social forms and processes. The explanation for the things that don't add up, or don't fit, requires linking the two.

In linking social practice to social structuration, sociolinguistics can also directly address some of the major questions of contemporary social theory, questions about how social organization happens; about the relationship between the experience of everyday life and social structuration; about agency and structure. It can also help address current concerns about social change, allowing us to trace the trajectories of social actors and their construction of meaning, and hence to grasp the sense-making activities which orient social action.

Finally, it speaks to the manifold activities involving action about language. Who gets access to what linguistic resources, what counts as valuable resources, these have long been important questions, and the globalized new economy only accentuates their importance. Currently, these questions tend to emerge most clearly in the areas of language education and immigration. We worry about our own competitivity on the international market, a competitivity which, we believe, will be enhanced by multilingualism. At the same time, we worry about losing the privileges mastery of our own language in a national (or in the case of languages like English, French and Spanish, international) market provides. We worry about challenges to that privileged position from immigration, while actively recruiting immigrants; or we worry about losing human resources while depending on global circulation of those resources for national development.

To provide one illustration from the First World: the province of Ontario runs a television advertisement in 2006. It follows a young woman in casual business dress as she walks through an office talking in Hindi on a cell phone. She opens a door to a conference room, and sits down at a table at which are already seated several people (men and women, apparently of a variety of origins). She says in English that she has spoken to her contacts in Mumbai and that the material is on its way. Then text appears on the screen, representing the English language training programmes the government provides to immigrants.

This ad can be read in different ways. It certainly speaks to the central trope of Canadian public immigration debate: the government says we need highly-skilled immigrants to ensure economic growth (and not coincidentally to provide the basis for support of an aging population). Those immigrants arrive, and fail to get jobs in their field. The mainstream diagnosis is that the problem is mainly language, and possibly employer reluctance to hire people whose backgrounds are unfamiliar. The ad kills two birds with one stone: it shows that the language skills of immigrants are actually of value to a company (that material would never have gotten out of Mumbai if the

Hindi-speaking employee had not been able to mobilize her personal contacts through their shared, possibly native, language), and that language training in English allows them to make the bridge to the dominant language of work, thus not requiring Canadians to have to learn Hindi themselves (never mind that a highly-skilled Indian probably already speaks English).

At the same time, of course, language training is also read the other way around; third language programmes in Canada, once thought of as heritage language programmes aimed at facilitating immigrant children's school success, are now recast as international language programmes open to all, with the idea of concentrating on languages of immigration which also happen to have value on the international market (such as Japanese, Mandarin, Cantonese, Hindi, Urdu or Spanish). Indeed, the Canadian province of Alberta recently broke with the Canadian tradition of focusing on French–English language education, and adopted a policy requiring all schools to teach a second language, the choice of which would be up to them.

Traditionally, we have approached these questions by asking which techniques of language training produce results that most closely approximate either a standard version of a language or some idea of what a 'native speaker' might sound like, assuming that indeed the 'problem' is language, and that language education can fix it. Here we are arguing that things are probably more complicated than that. That the 'problem' may not be language at all, but that language instead may be serving as a terrain for the construction of boundaries and relations of power in ways that are legitimate within dominant discursive regimes. That constructing language as the problem may serve to mask the construction and reproduction of relations of difference and inequality (since, ostensibly, language can be learned and is therefore not inherently exclusionary). That learning (and abandoning) languages may be a matter of social positioning, with all the risks and dangers (and thrills and opportunities) that entails. That operating with the idea of language as bounded in the first place may be primarily a matter of reproducing specific discursive regimes.

This all situates the study of bilingualism in the realm of the political, insofar as the central questions it asks are about how meaning relates to difference, to boundaries, to inequality. Perhaps more fundamentally, it situates the study of language within the realm of the social, and insists that the study of the social is incomplete without an apprehension of language as social practice.

postface
politique et idéologie: le cas du bilinguisme
andree tabouret-keller

« Les idéologies ne supportent pas le pluralisme »
Aharon Appelfeld, *Histoire d'une vie*, 2004, p. 125[1]

introduction

L'ouvrage dirigée par Monica Heller rompt avec une longue tradition de dénégation du caractère politique des situations linguistiques, qu'elles soient unilingues, bilingues ou plurilingues, et des investissements idéologiques dont elles font l'objet: « Le concept même de bilinguisme est un produit idéologique », affirme Monica Heller. Le bilinguisme est ainsi considéré comme un révélateur des enjeux politiques et de leurs justifications idéologiques dans les sociétés contemporaines. Sous le titre *Bilingualism: A Social Approach*, les études réunies, quoique visant en principe des situations bilingues, traitent en réalité de situations linguistiques complexes à propos desquelles l'affirmation de M. Heller se vérifie.

Les difficultés sociolinguistiques que la politique exploite, en les idéologisant pour les mettre en lumière ou bien pour les cacher, sont connues. Elles se manifestent dans divers malaises: malaises des minorités sans langue reconnue, des langues sans écriture et sans place dans les grands médias, malaises des nationalismes, des colonisations linguistiques, des politiques de globalisation linguistique, malaises enfin de la souffrance subjective de ne pas être entendu, même quand la langue dans laquelle cette souffrance s'exprime est parfaitement audible.

L'expression *politique*, de même que celle d'*idéologie*, est polysémique. Dans les lignes qui suivent – et sauf précision additionnelle – elles seront entendues, pour la première en référence à l'art et la pratique du gouvernement des sociétés humaines, impliquant hiérarchies et pouvoirs, pour la seconde en référence aux cadres de pensée de nos univers d'existence, impliquant, par delà religions et philosophies, des représentations foisonnantes, souvent intuitives pour le grand public. Qu'une langue idéalisée soit un objet pour les passions subjectives, objet sans contre-partie dans la réalité, redouble en quelque sorte ses potentialités imaginaires.

Dans la première partie de ce texte, et pour nouer le débat engagé autour de la nature idéologique du concept de bilinguisme, j'évoquerai deux exemples déjà anciens qui illustrent deux thèses extrêmes et contradictoires: le bilinguisme est un pur problème pédagogique, le bilinguisme est un pur problème politique. La seconde partie abordera le grand thème du livre, les transformations du bilinguisme entraînées par les options du libéralisme économique et politique. L'examen des nouveaux agencements linguistiques révèle quelques uns des défis de société actuels, tant politiques qu'idéologiques: globalisations face à régionalisations, colonialismes classiques face à colonisations économiques actuelles, nationalismes et pouvoirs d'Etat face à institutions internationales, impératifs idéologiques face à tensions épistémologiques, défis intriqués les uns aux autres. En conclusion, j'interrogerai la pertinence de la notion d'hétérogénéité qui pourrait subsumer les processus analysés, toujours complexes, et permettre de recentrer l'interrogation sur une question fondamentale, le rapport entre les contraintes systémiques des langues et l'apparente absence de limites des transformations tant sociales que linguistiques.

Mon propos n'est pas d'offrir au lecteur un résumé, ni même un survol de l'ouvrage – qui ne saurait rendre justice à l'entreprise de Monica Heller – mais plutôt de marquer l'intérêt que je lui trouve en retenant les questions que sa lecture me suggère. Je n'ai pas pris le parti de l'érudition qui aurait abouti à une bibliographie massive mais celui du témoignage qui mobilise l'expérience que j'ai de la dimension sociale du bilinguisme.

deux exemples anciens

le bilinguisme, un pur problème pédagogique?

L'Empire britannique dans son extension sur les autres continents, s'emploie à justifier la propagation de l'usage de la grande langue internationale qu'est déjà l'anglais dès la seconde moitié du 19ème siècle et recommande de tolérer, voire de promouvoir le bilinguisme dont l'un des termes doit être l'anglais: le bilinguisme, est-il affirmé, est uniquement un problème pédagogique, toute mention des répercussions de ce qu'il faut bien appeler une politique linguistique à grande échelle, est écartée. C'est ce qui ressort du compte-rendu d'une *Conference on bi-lingualism*[2] d'une demie-journée – une demie journée pour un Empire dans lequel sont parlées des centaines de langues différentes –, invitée à l'occasion de la Conférence impériale sur l'éducation de 1911 à Londres. Les obligations du pouvoir colonial sont claires: il convient d'introduire les populations des colonies à l'écriture et à la lecture dans une langue de valeur internationale, l'anglais.

Les travaux de la Conférence sont présidés par *The Right Honorable W. Runciman* qui ouvre la séance par ces mots:

Now, I am delighted to say, the topic (bi-lingualism) has ceased to be one of political interest [...]. I propose that such discussion we have this afternoon should be purely on the educational aspects of the subject and not at all on the political aspects of the subject. As educationists we here this afternoon have nothing whatever to do with politics. (245–6)

L'allocution d'ouverture de Runciman est un chef d'œuvre d'habileté. Aucune interdiction n'y est formulée, mais quand il s'agit de l'épineuse question de l'éducation publique en Inde et, plus généralement de la reconnaissance et de l'usage des langues non-européennes, la discussion est circonscrite par avance: le bilinguisme ne concernera ici que l'anglais et une autre langue européenne, comme le hollandais (*the Dutch language*) en Afrique du Sud, le français au Québec ou bien le gallois au Pays de Galles. Un tel pouvoir de dénégation du caractère politique des situations linguistiques pourrait laisser pantois si ce n'est que chacun peut citer des exemples actuels de cette subtile stratégie qui allie deux dénégations: 1. le bilinguisme n'est pas un problème politique, 2. s'en tenir à la seule pédagogie n'est pas une mesure politique.

le bilinguisme, un problème politique par excellence?

A la veille de la première guerre mondiale, les vastes territoires des Empires allemand et austro-hongrois abritent de multiples minorités linguistiques de langue allemande; la transmission de la langue allemande y est une préoccupation majeure car elle constitue le lien principal de l'appartenance au peuple allemand. En 1910, paraît en langue allemande, *Der moderne Utraquismus oder die Zweisprachige Volksschule* (L'utraquisme moderne ou l'école primaire bilingue[3]); cet ouvrage dont l'optique est ouvertement politique a connu un large écho, en particulier dans les milieux de l'enseignement. Son auteur, Onisifor Ghibu, citoyen hongrois de langue allemande, définit de manière générale le bilinguisme scolaire comme corrélat politique de l'existence de langues d'État qui ne concernent généralement qu'une partie de la population et sont, dans des régions plus ou moins étendues, différentes de celles parlées par les enfants. Il vilipende les écoles primaires bilingues, tout particulièrement celles qui reçoivent les enfants allemands en dehors de l'Allemagne et aliènent leur appartenance au peuple allemand.

Ghibu condamne le bilinguisme et exprime non sans violence le souci de sauvegarder l'appartenance allemande. Bien qu'il évoque les problèmes didactiques, il affirme sans ambages que le bilinguisme est un problème politique. La position de Ghibu est claire: l'intention des États d'éduquer les peuples dans le bilinguisme est une utopie hors de portée. Pourrait-elle être réalisée, qu'elle serait absolument à rejeter, pour des raisons d'ordre supérieur qui dépassent l'intérêt politique immédiat (1910: 26). Ghibu s'oppose en effet à toute entreprise d'assimilation linguistique, qui est aussi – dit-il – une assimilation à la mentalité et à la race au pouvoir (1910: 8). Fléau des temps modernes, l'utraquisme ne peut que conduire à des désastres, le danger d'abê-tissement, le ramollissement des peuples, la perte du moral, la dépravation des temps modernes. L'utraquisme en tant que risque d'assimilation (*Assimilation*) des races entre elles doit donc être rejeté sans hésitation: en plus des dangers qu'il comporte, il constitue un viol politique (*politische Vergewaltigung*).

Ces deux exemples, opposés dans leurs conclusions et leurs préceptes, issus d'une histoire aujourd'hui dépassée, formulés dans une terminologie obsolète, contiennent en germe les difficultés et les potentialités actuelles des situations de bilinguisme.

de quelques défis actuels

globalisations et régionalisations

Les deux cas précédents illustrent des globalisations linguistiques à leurs débuts, au tournant des 19ème et 20ème siècles: l'une, aujourd'hui réussie, est la généralisation du recours à l'anglais comme *lingua franca* d'extension mondiale, l'autre, qui a échoué, est la généralisation du recours à l'allemand, dans la zone restreinte de l'Europe, de l'Ouest, Centrale et Orientale. La première fut étayée par des mesures concrètes telles l'occupation militaire et civile, le commerce des marchandises, le remaniement, voire l'instaura-tion des institutions législatives, l'extension de la scolarisation avec le souci d'éradiquer l'analphabétisme; elle s'appuie actuellement sur la domination des Etats Unis, puissance anglophone. La seconde, qui n'ignorait pas les mesures concrètes, dans l'Empire d'Autriche – Hongrie, en Afrique Equatoriale et de l'Ouest, dans l'Empire allemand aussi, a vu disparaître ses colonies avec la guerre de 1914–18, et ses racines idéologiques – une langue, un peuple (*Volk*) – se sont avérées insuffisantes pour garantir le maintien, voire l'extension d'un emploi conséquent de l'allemand en dehors des territoires traditionnellement de langue allemande, Autriche et Allemagne.

La globalisation visée dans l'ouvrage concerne avant tout le domaine complexe de l'économie, la question posée étant de savoir dans quelle mesure les options de l'économie actuelle ont une incidence sur les pratiques sociales de bilinguisme. En tant que mise en contact de l'anglais avec de plus en plus de langues et de plus en plus de leurs locuteurs, le bilinguisme s'étend tout en se diversifiant. Les pratiques de l'anglais résultant d'une scolarité primaire en anglais sont pour un temps plus homogènes que quand la langue est apprise sur le tas. Si, comme nous avons de bonnes raisons de le supposer, cet anglais normalisé, de type scolaire, est par la suite utilisé pour une communication étendue tant par ses objets que par les conditions où elle a lieu, il va se diversifier. Les formes d'anglais véhiculaires parlées en Inde ou dans les pays anglophones équatoriaux peuvent être distantes les unes des autres, d'autant qu'elles sont soumises à de plus ou moins intenses pressions de *code-switching*. Le domaine où la globalisation de l'emploi d'un anglais relativement unifié est le plus cohérent, est celui de l'échange d'informations spécialisées: plus cet échange est pointu (informations boursières du *stock market*, par exemple), plus la langue est codée.

Deux types de processus se développent ainsi de manière concurrente. L'un aboutit à l'augmentation à grande échelle des différenciations au sein de ce qui fut une même langue d'exportation normalisée, leur étude a de beaux jours devant elle. L'autre tend à la restriction de la différenciation dès lors que l'emploi de cette langue est déterminé par un secteur sur-spécialisé de la communication; qu'un tel secteur soit globalisé ne fait pas de doute, il est d'autant plus apte à une extension mondiale qu'il requiert des ressources linguistiques d'un ordre strictement technique. Le trafic aérien qui se fait en anglais, représente un cas de globalisation spécialisée, à la fois commerciale et technique, ou encore le suivi informatisé du marché mondial du café par une même agence centrale (lieux et quantités des stocks au départ, à l'arrivée, marchandises vendues, en cours de transport, moyens de transport, cours des prix, etc.), mais ce ne sont pas là les seuls exemples.

Ainsi faut-il parler d'une pluralité de processus de globalisation en cours et sans doute d'une hiérarchies entre eux: ils n'ont pas tous la même étendue ni le même impact, ils peuvent s'ignorer les uns les autres, leurs histoires diffèrent, les entreprises globalisantes traitent d'objets éminemment divers, des logiciels américains aux tee-shirt chinois. Néanmoins, un commun dénominateur les unit désormais, leur outil de gestion, la médiation informatique, qui par un biais ou par un autre implique des emplois de l'anglais.

Ce « monde » globalisé mais hétérogène n'est de loin pas *le* monde. Les réseaux de communication qui surplombent ce dernier peuvent avoir de très larges mailles qui laissent passer d'autres dynamiques linguistiques et recouvrent d'autres réalités sociales de bilinguisme. A de plus petites échelles, les régions englobées dans des ensembles de type étatique, tentent de promouvoir la consistance de leur identité par des politiques linguistiques dites régionales. Celles-ci sont particulièrement actives en Europe de l'Ouest, de l'Est et du Centre mais ne manquent sur aucun continent. Elles se caractérisent par la mise en place de diverses mesures de protection et de promotion des langues locales, à la fois comme instrument et comme symbole des communautés qui les parlent. Le bilinguisme qui en résulte est inégal et différencié. En Europe de l'Ouest, la langue régionale est la parente pauvre; dans les régions à faible taux de scolarisation, à l'inverse, cela peut être la langue d'État qui soit encore peu diffusée et la langue parlée localement qui reste vigoureuse. C'est sans doute dans de telles circonstances, que, face à la langue d'État, les langues locales offrent le plus de résistance à la disparition. Mais une fois qu'un parler est devenu largement minoritaire, la pression de la modernité – dépeuplement des zones rurales, urbanisation, colonisation par les médias qui sont loin de tous nécessiter la maîtrise de la lecture – leur laisse peu de chance.

Réalités et conséquences sociales de ces bilinguismes si divers mobilisent les idéologies traditionnelles d'un creuset national lié au territoire et à la langue, d'une identité unifiée, si possible homogène, d'une langue pure de tout métissage. Les arguments de la globalisation économique sont tout autres: une version du progrès en termes de croissance obligée, alliant la liberté des échanges – et combien ce terme de liberté charrie avec lui non pas une idéologie mais une sorte de magma idéologique! – avec celle de la réalisation maximale de profits (on ne peut compter l'amour de l'argent comme une idéologie).

colonialismes classiques et colonisations économiques actuelles

Les colonialismes classiques, dont le 19ème siècle est la grande période, ont instauré des bilinguismes spécifiques à chaque puissance coloniale. Par exemple, l'exigence de l'administration coloniale française d'avoir des interlocuteurs parlant non seulement français mais un français correct était sans commune mesure avec le souci affiché de l'administration anglaise de parler les langues locales et sa tolérance vis à vis de formes d'anglais locales, pourvu que les pratiques de l'anglais gagnent du terrain. Les implantations des langues des grandes puissances coloniales: anglais, français, allemand, néerlandais, portugais, espagnol, russe, principalement, aboutirent à des pratiques sociales diverses, inégalement réparties selon le mode de vie des populations, dans le monde rural ou dans les villes, et selon leur condition économique. La carte actuelle de la co-existence des langues de la colonisation avec l'une ou l'autre des très nombreuses langues africaines dessine encore, malgré le mouvement des indépendances, les traits majeurs de la vieille carte coloniale du continent. Dès avant les colonialismes, de nombreuses régions de l'Afrique – gardons cet exemple – étaient bi- voire plurilingues, par exemple, avec le swahili ou le dioula comme langue véhiculaire. Les immenses urbanisations actuelles bouleversent la donne traditionnelle par la formation de poches linguistiques et culturelles hautement hétérogènes. Par delà la présence de nombreux parlers différents qui serait le propre de situations complexes, l'hétérogénéité colore les échanges langagiers quotidiens. Elle déborde les mécanismes restreints du *code-switching* dans la mesure où elle est inséparable de conduites culturellement marquées, cette hétérogénéité est anthropo-linguistique. C'est-à-dire que la production de sens est au moins aussi importante, sinon souvent plus, que la stricte production d'informations.

La globalisation des cours des produits et des marchés financiers donne lieu à des pratiques de concurrence dont la langue n'est pas l'enjeu. Est-ce que les colonisations marchandes, par le pétrole et ses dérivés, l'habillement, les produits alimentaires, entre autres, sont néanmoins des creusets pour le bilinguisme, sans doute, mais pas de manière étendue. Les milliers d'ouvrières chinoises qui cousent les *sweet-shirt*, dont l'Europe se dit inondée, ne savent pas un mot d'anglais. Si certaines d'entre elles suivaient des cours d'anglais – cela n'est pas impossible – ce n'est pas à cause de la globalisation mais comme une des conséquences de sa représentation selon laquelle la connaissance de l'anglais est favorable à une mobilité professionnelle ascendante. Par ailleurs, le bilinguisme généralisé n'est pas le garant d'une croissance économique, comme l'a illustré l'exemple du Japon où la connaissance de l'anglais est un objectif scolaire.

pouvoirs d'état et institutions internationales

Les pouvoirs des Etats s'exercent au profit de la langue, ou des langues qui sont utiles à la mise en œuvre des principes de leurs constitutions et de leurs gouvernements successifs, au premier chef par le biais des systèmes éducatif et administratif, de l'appareil judiciaire, dans une moindre mesure de l'armée et de la politique extérieure. S'il ne reste sans doute plus de gouvernement qui soit opposé au bilinguisme, aucun n'est indemne d'éléments de politique linguistique favorisant une langue, parfois deux, dite langue d'Etat ou langue officielle, voire langue nationale, au détriment d'une ou de plusieurs langues institutionnellement non reconnue, ou bien reconnues de manière ambiguë. Obtenir une communication généralisée dans la langue d'Etat a pu être le modèle de nombre d'Etats de l'Europe de l'ouest; entre les deux guerres mondiales il fut atteint dans de larges couches sociales – en France, le *monolingualism* fut largement réalisé, en particulier dans le corps des instituteurs et, plus généralement, des fonctionnaires. Dans nombre de régions des pays de l'Europe du Sud et Orientale, large zone émaillée d'un grand nombre de territoires linguistiques, un tel *monolingualism* d'Etat est resté une exception. Des *monolingualism* régionaux ou locaux lui résistaient dans des régions transfrontalières – les frontières étatiques ne coïncident pas avec les limites des aires linguistiques, le pays basque ou la Catalogne en sont de bons exemples – ou bien dans des poches linguistiques plus ou moins importantes, résultant de colonisations antérieures (par exemple, les minorités de langue allemande évoquées par Ghibu cité ci-dessus), ou encore les aires des langues régionales originales comme le breton; bien que le nombre des locuteurs monolingues se raréfient leurs langues restent investies par la passion identitaire, voire le nationalisme, alliés ou non à des allégeances religieuses. On peut penser aux tensions actuelles issues de la guerre en Yougoslavie ou bien des politiques de russification dans l'ex-URSS, entre autres. Les identités linguistiques et culturelles peuvent dans de tels cas faire l'objet de dangereuses crispations, d'autant plus qu'elles offrent un terrain de choix aux manipulations politiques qui orchestrent sans vergogne les idéologies de l'autochtonie, de la communauté idéalisée des origines ou de la pureté de la langue.

Les enjeux de la globalisation sont relativement indifférents aux revendications identitaires aussi longtemps que les exigences des marchés n'en sont pas contrecarrés. Pour l'homme de la rue, les pouvoirs multinationaux ou supra nationaux, sont difficiles à localiser, voire à identifier car leurs sigles sont mystérieux, voire mystificateurs. Des formes de pouvoir, institutionnalisées à des niveaux supra-étatiques, tentent de se faire entendre – par exemple, l'ONU, l'UNESCO, les Institutions européennes, leur existence et leurs noms sont devenus familiers par les mesures adoptées et les rencontres dont la grande presse se fait l'écho, mais il n'est pas certain que leurs objectifs soient connus des grandes masses autrement que de manière intuitive.

Le pouvoir en matière de langues de telles institutions d'une part se limite à leur fonctionnement interne et d'autre part à l'adoption de dispositions diverses que chaque Etat peut par la suite ratifier, voire mettre en œuvre. On sait que la France qui n'a ratifié la Charte européenne des langues régionales et minoritaires qu'en 2005, ne s'est pas donné les moyens de l'appliquer au prétexte que cela nécessiterait une révision de la Constitution. Cela n'enlève rien aux bénéfices de l'existence d'une telle Charte car son énoncé est à soi seul une référence qui peut faire autorité pour les revendications régionales ou minoritaires. Il n'en reste pas moins que là où la Charte a pu être implémentée, les langues revigorées par les mesures en leur faveur restent fragiles et n'ont généralement pas pu dépasser un usage dont l'augmentation est plus liée à la connaissance scolaire qu'à des pratiques sociales. Le cas de l'Irlande est classique à cet égard: des mesures prises en faveur de l'irlandais dès le début des années vingt, ont certes abouti à une courbe croissante des locuteurs déclarant connaître la langue alors que la courbe des locuteurs déclarant la parler n'a pas cessé de décroître.

La situation linguistique actuelle, en Europe de l'Ouest particulièrement, se complique par l'installation de plus ou moins larges ensembles de populations issues de l'immigration – l'Allemagne à elle seule compte environ un million d'immigrants venus de Turquie et, par ailleurs, environ un million d'arabophones. Dans les agglomérations urbaines la présence de ces populations à langues autres ajoute à la complexité déjà existante. Les métropoles sont plurilingues comme n'importe quel déplacement dans un moyen de transport urbain collectif peut l'illustrer. Par ailleurs, aucun de ces ensembles linguistiques n'est homogène en son sein, car le bilinguisme des différentes générations n'a pas la même composition: les toutes jeunes générations, nées dans le pays d'immigration sont moins bilingues que ne l'étaient leurs parents, génération bilingue intermédiaire, entre leurs propres parents souvent encore unilingues dans la langue du pays d'origine et leurs propres enfants tendant à devenir unilingues dans la langue du pays d'accueil.

permanences idéologiques et tensions épistémologiques

Des permanences idéologiques peuvent être esquissées. La différenciation d'avec les parlers des étrangers – l'expression *Barbare* « Barbares, ceulz qui sont de estrange langue » (Erasme, 14ème siècle) désignait pour les Anciens ceux qui ne parlaient ni le latin, ni le grec, de manière plus générale les étrangers – est indissociable de la conviction que ces étrangers sont eux aussi différents. On se rappelle que dans les années vingt du 20ème siècle, le mot d'ordre populaire et efficace présidant à l'accueil des immigrés aux Etats Unis (entre 1900 et 1914, près de 15 millions de personnes prirent pied aux Etats-Unis, en 1930, 5 millions de plus y étaient arrivés) était celui d'*americanization*, concept dont le volet principal était l'assimilation linguistique. De larges populations bilingues en ont résulté qui n'ont aujourd'hui encore pas entièrement disparu et se renouvellent à la faveur de nouvelles immigrations; l'idéologie dominante était alors celle d'un modèle unique de citoyen et d'une société homogène, elle fait place aujourd'hui à des modèles de pluralisme culturel, voire linguistique, la pratique de l'anglais américain restant incontournable.

Dans les réticences qui s'expriment à l'égard de la globalisation, la question des langues joue sa part en sourdine. En Europe, la métaphore de la parenté des langues a dominé tout le 19ème, sa productivité n'a pas disparu aujourd'hui car elle est à la racine de la représentation du lien serré entre l'exercice du pouvoir et l'unification des Etats-nations autour de leur langue nationale. De telles idéologies en condamnant le bilinguisme en font un objet politique dont le ciment est la représentation de la langue comme unité à cohérence interne fortement focalisée: l'unité de langue justifie l'unité de territoire et inversement, langue et territoire justifient ensemble l'unité de la communauté qui à son tour va être invoquée pour justifier unité de langue et de territoire. Une circularité complète fonctionne qui explique la durée persistante de l'association étroite entre identité territoriale et usage d'un idiome, association le plus souvent cimentée dans une dénomination unique, désignant à la fois un territoire, ses habitants et leur langue (Bretagne, Bretons, breton, parmi de très nombreux exemples possibles). Pour le commun des locuteurs l'expérience d'un espace propre et d'un temps propre à la vie courante est familière. Sa langue lui semble un attribut naturel qui justifie l'attachement identitaire qui le lie à elle. Pour autant, le concept abstrait de la langue comme objet naturel, élaboré par la philosophie des Lumières et dominant au 19ème siècle, lui reste lointain. Que les hommes politiques fassent usage de l'idéologie de la naturalité de la langue est tout à leur intérêt, un tel discours non seulement oblitère le caractère politique de la langue mais flatte le locuteur en l'assurant du respect de sa langue, sa plus intime propriété.

A première vue, les tensions épistémologiques se situent sur un autre plan. La représentation des langues en tant que systèmes stricts, la notion d'une relative autonomie de ces systèmes elle-même font débat. A l'opposé du naturalisme, le structuralisme met en avant non les objets en tant que tels mais les relations entre les « objets », des phonèmes aux mythèmes. Le discours politique et à travers lui, celui sur la globalisation, ou encore sur le libéralisme, joue de l'opposition aujourd'hui courante entre le *structurel* et le *conjoncturel*. Dans le cas du bilinguisme, structure et conjoncture sont mobilisées l'une et l'autre, voire toutes les deux, comme arguments idéologiques dès lors qu'il s'agit de dénoncer la malfaisance des mélanges et des métissages, de la mixité et de l'hybridation, voire de la dépravation des mœurs. Le vocabulaire est confus, les écarts entre le discours des spécialistes – celui tenu dans un ouvrage comme celui-ci – et celui des médias se creuse. Ce qui réellement est en cause, tant au plan théorique qu'empirique, c'est l'alternative entre un ensemble de représentations dont le commun dénominateur est la clôture – du système entier, homogène et étanche d'une langue à la nation bornée qui parle cette langue – et un ensemble différent qui met l'insistance sur l'imprévisibilité des transformations, la tension entre le souci d'universaux et celui d'une créativité ouverte. En politique, idéologie et épistémologie s'interpénètrent.

quelques questions en guise de conclusions

Il est difficile d'échapper à la tentation méthodologique. Le genre humain est assurément complexe tout en étant homogène dans le sens où tout humain est en mesure d'assurer sa reproduction et la transmission de l'humanité. Ce n'est qu'à partir du moment où l'on définirait en son sein des différences indépassables – les races – qu'il serait alors question d'hétérogénéité. De même, nos langues sont toutes linguistiques – bien qu'il y ait de nombreux modes de communication autres, il n'y a pas de parlers humains qui soient a-linguistiques – quelques que soient par ailleurs leurs diverses modalités de complexité.

C'est dans la mesure où l'on tente, comme c'est le cas dans cet ouvrage, de rendre compte et d'étudier des évènements langagiers empiriquement donnés comme des pratiques sociales indissociables de leur support de parole, que l'on se trouve confronté à des objets hétérogènes, c'est-à-dire mobilisant deux ou plusieurs types de rationalité que l'on tente alors de subsumer dans de nouvelles théories avec des concepts nouveaux; cela s'observe dans les courants de l'anthropologie du langage qui prennent de plus en plus d'ampleur.

La question fondamentale qui parcourt les textes réunis dans ce volume – absence de limites des transformations tant sociales que linguistiques par contraste avec les limites résultant des contraintes systémiques – reste ouverte. Sans doute faut-il distinguer des niveaux de contraintes, et, parmi celles-ci, contrainte indépassable, le fait que la parole est arrimée au corps: le souffle de la voix qui porte la parole passe par les orifices de la respiration et de la déglutition. Par ailleurs, la part des déterminations génétiques de l'accès au langage est de nos jours une question vive qui n'est pas tranchée bien qu'elle mobilise d'importantes investigations. Enfin, un vaste chantier est en cours, qui concerne l'articulation entre les dimensions sociales du bilinguisme et sa portée culturelle.

notes

1. Aharon Appelfeld, *Histoire d'une vie*, Paris, Le Seuil, 2004. Traduit de l'hébreu (Israël), par Valérie Zenatti. Edition originale, *Sippur hayim*, Jérusalem, Keter, 1999.

2. *Conference on Bi-lingualism, House of Commons Papers*, vol. XVIII, 244–66 (sans date mais correspond à 1911).

3. Onisifor Ghibu, *Der moderne Utraquismus oder die Zweisprachige Volksschule*, Langensalza, Hermann Beyer u. Söhne, 1910. L'expression « utraquiste » désignait les établissements dans lesquels grec et latin étaient intégrés au cursus ordinaire; par extension et non sans dérision, elle en vient à désigner les établissements « qui s'adressant à de larges couches de population de langue étrangère à la langue de l'Etat, au petit peuple auquel il s'agit d'inculquer, à côté de sa langue maternelle, une seconde langue, l'enseignement de l'allemand comme matière dans un cursus donné dans une autre langue, soi disant langue d'Etat » (Ghibu 1910 : 1). Son emploi est courant dans de tels contextes.

english summary of tabouret-keller's postface

afterword
politics and ideology: the case of bilingualism

Tabouret-Keller situates our current debates about the political and ideological nature of thinking about bilingualism in a long history. She shows how, at the beginning of the twentieth century, we can already see public debates which alternately argue that bilingualism must be completely abstracted away from politics (the example she gives is an argument that bilingualism can be understood as a purely pedagogical question) or, on the contrary, that it must centrally be treated politically (in her example, bilingual education in central Europe is critiqued as assimilatory). That is, as long as we have talked about it, our own positions have led us either to mask or, on the contrary, to aim to reveal how bilingualism is caught up in relations of power. How that happens, and why, is a matter of conditions on the ground, that is, of the particular ways in which individuals and groups are situated with respect to the construction of nation-states and of their colonies.

Current conditions only heighten the importance of understanding this aspect of the social construction of the idea of bilingualism, and of the terms on which bilingualism is discussed (as identity, as natural attribute, as enrichment, as problem, as contamination, as technical skill; as cognitive, social, economic, or political; and so on). This includes an apprehension of spaces where language(s) are not explicitly problematized, as opposed to those where they are. The particular forms that globalization takes today allow for the development of regional forms of global languages as well as for variation in forms of multilingualism, that is, for a multiplication of forms and practices with varied reaches, and varied value. The spaces where these emerge are tied to the concrete manifestations of globalized markets, that is, to what forms exactly are taken by increased mobility of goods and people, increased facility of communication, and restructuring of arrangements and relations of production and consumption.

In the end, we are possibly simply living with a current twist on long-standing concerns about boundaries between Us and Them. It is also possible, however, that we are facing a particular epistemological tension between the *structural* and the *contingent*, both of which are mobilized in the service of particular ideologically-informed discourses, but both of which also serve fundamentally as tools of analysis and explanation. This leaves us with the open question of the relationship between constraint and transformation, and therefore of the nature of the relationship between linguistic and social processes.

index